Clinical Case Management with Persons Having Mental Illness

A Relationship-Based Perspective

JOSEPH WALSH

Brooks/Cole
Thomson Learning

Australia • Canada • Denmark • Japan • Mexico • New Zealand • Philippines • Puerto Rico •
Singapore • South Africa • Spain • United Kingdom • United States

Social Work Editor: Lisa Gebo
Editorial Assistants: Susan Wilson,
  Joanne von Zastrow
Marketing Manager: Jenny Burger
Publisher/Executive Editor: Craig Barth
Project Editor: Tanya Nigh
Print Buyer: Stacey Weinberger

Permissions Editor: Bob Kauser
Production Service: Robin Gold/Forbes Mill Press
Copy Editor: Ardella Crawford
Cover Designer: Roger Knox
Cover Printer: Webcom Ltd.
Compositor: Wolf Creek Press
Printer/Binder: Webcom Ltd.

Printed in Canada

1 2 3 4 5 6 03 02 01 00 99

For permission to use material from this
text, contact us by
    web: www.thomsonrights.com
    fax: 1-800-730-2215
    phone: 1-800-730-2214

Library of Congress
Cataloging-in-Publication Data

ISBN 0-534-34852-1

For more information, contact:
Wadsworth/Thomson Learning
10 Davis Drive
Belmont, CA 94002-3098
USA
www.wadsworth.com

International Headquarters
Thomson Learning
290 Harbor Drive, 2nd Floor
Stamford, CT 06902-7477
USA

UK/Europe/Middle East
Thomson Learning
Berkshire House
168-173 High Holborn
London WC1V 7AA
United Kingdom

Asia
Thomson Learning
60 Albert Street #15-01
Albert Complex
Singapore 189969

Canada
Nelson/Thomson Learning
1120 Birchmount Road
Scarborough, Ontario M1K 5G4
Canada

  This book is printed on
acid-free recycled paper.

About the Author

Joseph Walsh, Ph. D., L. C. S. W. is an associate professor of social work at Virginia Commonwealth University. He received his academic degrees from the Ohio State University. Joe has been a direct services practitioner in the field of mental health since 1974, first in a psychiatric hospital and later in community mental health center settings. He has provided services to older adult and general out-patient populations, but has specialized in services to persons with serious mental illness and their families. Since 1993 Joe has been at VCU, teaching courses in generalist practice, clinical practice, and research. He continues to provide direct services to clients at the university counseling center and also at area shelters, clubhouses, and group homes. Joe was the 1998 recipient of the National Mental Health Association's George Goodman Brudney and Ruth P. Brudney Social Work Award, given annually to recognize significant contributions to the care and treatment of persons with mental illness. Joe is also co-author with Kia J. Bentley of *The Social Worker and Psychotropic Medication: Toward Effective Collaboration with Mental Health Clients, Families, and Providers.*

I dedicate this book to my parents, Rosella and the late John Walsh, who encouraged and supported the careers of all five of their children.

Contents

Preface

Case management literature is curiously devoid of material emphasizing the primacy of establishing productive relationships with highly impaired clients as a prerequisite to other interventions. My motivation to write this book is a desire to share what I have learned in my 25 years of experience (19 of them full-time) working with clients who have mental illness and their families. But the most important lesson I have learned is that there is no substitute for a positive relationship with a client as a condition for facilitating change. I have been concerned that many practice texts on this topic have been written by academics (admittedly, I am one) with little relevant practice experience. These texts, though somewhat useful, are limited by a lack of appreciation for the immense complexity of the work. I hope this book will fill a gap in the literature regarding the clinical skills necessary to provide good case management service.

I have conceived this book as a useful and theoretically substantive resource for graduate students and direct practitioners in the human services as they carry out their practice roles with clients in a variety of settings. I hope that the book will make a contribution, through its symbolic interactionist theoretical orientation, to the way case managers conceptualize the development of relationships with their clients. Ideally, this book will fill a gap between the current emphasis on case management practice as a programmatic response in the treatment of mental illness and what I think is a lack of attention to the case managers' methods for organizing their practices. I hope readers will feel more competent to work with clients and will be able to sustain clinical relationships over many months or years. This book provides case managers with intervention techniques for use with many types of clients with mental illness and also with their families, who are so important as natural support providers.

With the current emphasis on consumer advocacy, self-help, and case management interventions of assessment, planning, service linkage, monitoring, and advocacy (rather than psychotherapy), writers in the human service professions are reluctant to emphasize verbally-based counseling strategies. The attitude seems to be that doing so may perpetuate out-of-date assumptions that persons with schizophrenia, for example, can be cured with psychotherapy. This book attempts to counter this bias with a focus on the case manager's use of self, in addition to other resources, to help clients cope with stress more effectively and experience personal growth. I assume that the major mental illnesses are primarily, though not exclusively, disorders of brain functioning. Still, in any clinical relationship, the practitioner must have the ability to form an attachment, to earn the client's trust, and to provide crisis and supportive counseling as part of a comprehensive intervention plan. I promote this perspective in this book, though I also support the range of other interventions noted above.

AN OUTLINE OF THIS BOOK

The book is organized into five sections. The *introduction* describes the evolution of case management practice and its application to various types of problems in human functioning. I provide an overview of the book's theoretical framework and then introduce the clinical case management model, which incorporates mental health counseling roles into the more traditional case management activities of brokerage and advocacy. A chapter on the policy context of practice explores "macro" influences on case management that contribute to the modality's potential and limitations. An awareness of social policy should assist the case manager in actively developing service resources to meet each client's unique needs, rather than reacting to more impersonal, administratively-generated program goals. It should also sensitize the worker to the ethics of professional relationships; that is, to their appropriate scope and boundaries. This chapter includes a discussion of managed care and its influences on service delivery.

Part Two of the book includes the *theoretical base* of case management practice, which focuses the remainder of the material. A chapter on the theories of symbolic interactionism, ego psychology, and cognition/behavior presents an organizing framework for developing relationships with clients and for better understanding their unique views of the world. A chapter on the community context of practice considers the relevance of community and social support theories to clinical case management. The worker needs to understand these to know how best to develop functional social supports for clients, a major skill component of clinical practice. In this chapter I present the results of a research project in which I attempted to ascertain clients' own perceptions of their significant support experiences. An instrument for assessing and monitoring informal supports is included in the chapter.

Part Three includes seven chapters on *working with individuals* from five distinct diagnostic categories. The first chapter in this section considers the case manager's role in psychotropic medication management. Most clients described in the following six chapters take medications as part of their treatment, and the case manager may assume much practical (if not legal) responsibility for insuring that this process is carefully implemented and monitored. Next, clients with schizophrenia and schizoaffective disorder, bipolar disorder, major depression, schizotypal personality disorder, and paranoia are discussed in separate chapters, along with strategies for assessment, relationship building, and intervention. Empirical tools for monitoring symptoms and progress are also provided, and each chapter includes case examples. I discuss the impact of mental illness on the client's existential and religious beliefs, with implications for family cohesion, using results from another study I conducted.

Part Four includes four chapters on *working with families.* The variety of issues here includes the development of the case manager's ability to function as a family educator about mental illness and to engage families in partnership, rather than adversarial, relationships; strategies for the development of family education and support groups; and the special role of the group facilitator for reaching out to ambivalent family members to encourage their participation in a support group.

Part Five includes two chapters about *working with persons having mental illness in groups.* Material is presented to help case managers become better able to facilitate an effective leadership process in treatment groups (including skills-training, support, and psychoeducational groups), and how to function as effective consultants with peer-run, self-help groups.

In summary, I believe this book is unique in comparison with other volumes published on similar topics in the past five years. This is the first book in some time that attempts to focus on the elements of the clinical counseling relationship to other intervention perspectives in client care. I hope that the book's emphasis on the worker's use of self as the primary resource will be attractive to members of all helping professions.

ACKNOWLEDGEMENTS

My first thanks goes to my editor, Lisa Gebo, who supported my desire to write this book and provided me with gentle guidance throughout its composition, even during the rainy months when her home was at risk of sliding into the Pacific ocean. I have appreciated the wide discretion she provided me as I organized the book's content.

I want to thank various of my colleagues for their generous time and feedback in reviewing early versions of the chapters in this book. First, my friend and colleague, Kia Bentley reviewed several chapters and co-authored earlier versions of the material on psychotropic medications that became chapter six. Next, Heather Hewitt, case manager extraordinaire, co-authored early versions of chapters 16 and 17 and reviewed several other chapters. She was particularly helpful in her observations about how my academic presentations matched the realities of practice. Sharon MacDonald performed an extensive literature review for me on which much of chapters two and three was based. Finally I am indebted to the members of the School of Social Work Writer's Group, especially Rosemary Farmer (who shares my interest in mental illness) but also Ann Nichols-Casebolt, Liz Cramer, Humberto Fabelo, Pam Kovacs, Stephen Gilson, and Susan Ainsley McCarter, who graciously took time from their own writing projects to review portions of my work.

I don't know if I will ever write another book, so I want to acknowledge here the mental health professionals with whom I have worked over the years whose influence on my development has been most profound. Some of these fine people were case managers, but I have had the good fortune of working with and learning from persons representing many disciplines. They include Larry Ackerman, Nancy Adkins, Richard Baumgardner, Karen Berry, Amy Baker Dennis, Marie Froelich, Libby Gomia, Heather Hewitt (again), Jack Johnson, Chuck Komp, Roger Lansman, Jan Lantz, Ruth Ann Linabary, Val Marsh, David Merkle, John Morcos, Virgie Noe, Frank Orosz, Kathy Orosz, Janet Pakov, Bob Quinn, Laura Rappaport, Elaine Rentel, Mary Riegel, Vicki Swingle, Margaret Walsh, Jean Weisenbaugh, and Ken Weiss.

Regarding this book, I offer special thanks to the reviewers, whose comments resulted in a much improved final product. They include

John Belcher, University of Maryland, Baltimore
Bruce Friedman
Bob Jackson, Colorado State University
Jim Lantz, Ohio State University
Mary Fran Libassi, University of Connecticut
Thomas McGovern, Texas Tech Medical Center
Barbara Shank, University of St. Thomas

At the Brooks/Cole–Wadsworth Publishing Company, I would like to acknowledge the efforts of Jennie Burger (marketing manager), Ardella Crawford (copyeditor), Tanya Nigh (senior production editor), Robin Gold (production editor), Joy Westburg (advertising), Susan Wilson and Julie Martinez (assistant editors), and, once again, Lisa.

Finally, much love to Margaret, Brian, Nate, and Robyn.

PART I

Introduction

I

An Introduction to Clinical Case Management

This chapter introduces the concept of case management, the approach to mental health service delivery that will serve as the organizing framework for interventions throughout this book. In the first section I share a story to provide an example of the rewards one can experience in working with persons who have mental illness. Following a brief overview of the book's theoretical orientation (which is described more fully in Chapter 3), I define case management, its associated roles and activities, and present several models of case management practice for working with clients. Next I discuss the modality of *clinical* case management, emphasizing the importance of a positive worker-client relationship. Finally, I discuss the therapeutic components of the worker-client relationship in case management and the positive implications for clients and professionals in promoting the clinical aspects of the practice approach.

THINKING ABOUT CASE MANAGEMENT

The Joys of Working with Persons Having Mental Illness: A Story

Twenty-five years ago, a young psychiatric hospital attendant in his first week on the job sat nervously in a "unit meeting" with patients and staff. The meeting, held in the large dining area, was part of the therapeutic milieu in this 19-bed unit that was part of a 120-patient, 50-acre, 6-unit private psychiatric hospital. This unit was reserved for clients with long-term mental illnesses such as schizophrenia, manic depression (as it was then called), major depression, and dual diagnoses of mental illness and substance abuse. The patients were typically in the hospital for three to six months, sometimes for more than a year. In this weekly meeting, headed by the unit's medical director, patients requested privileges and planned for social activities. The patients and staff, about 30 total, voted on each request, with the majority vote carrying. It was an important part of patient self-government.

The new attendant, having graduated from college with a sociology degree and no firm career plans, was scared to death. He didn't know much about mental illness other than what he had absorbed from the media and a few psychology courses. The patients frightened as well as fascinated him.

One patient at the meeting was legendary in the hospital. Adam was *severely* psychotic despite high doses of chlorpromazine. He could barely tolerate *any* social interaction and would often accost and scream at any persons (other patients, staff, family members, and visitors) who looked at him in what he perceived as the "wrong" way. Patients and staff from the other five hospital units avoided him. He routinely requested to be placed in the isolation room to keep calm. Knowing all this, the new attendant could not help looking at Adam.

Adam soon spoke up. "I have an issue. What are we going to do about all these people who are out to make me crazy by following me around and staring at me?" He was obviously referring to the new staff member. "This hospital is supposed to help people, but I keep getting persecuted by these new intruders. They stare at me and try to make me fail."

The attendant was startled, first by Adam and then by his own quick response. "Are you talking about me, Adam? I thought you might be, since I'm the only new person around here today."

Adam didn't look up but responded with a quivering voice, fighting to keep control. "Yes."

"I'm sorry if I've bothered you," the new attendant continued, in the most soothing tone he could muster. "I don't want to make your life difficult. I'd like to help, if I can. I'm going to be working here awhile, I hope, and I want to help you and everyone else, too. But it will take me awhile to become comfortable, and learn how to be helpful. I hope I can come to be your friend. Can we give it a try?"

Adam was quiet and still did not look up, but eventually responded, "Okay."

The meeting moved on to other matters, but afterward, many staff and even several patients privately congratulated the new attendant on his positive exchange with Adam. They felt that the attendant had diffused a potentially volatile scene and set the stage for a decent relationship with Adam and the other patients who witnessed his reaching out.

It was a *great moment* for the new attendant. He felt on top of the world for days afterward, believing that perhaps he *could* succeed in this line of work after all.

The attendant in this story, of course, was I. And it *was* the first great moment I experienced in working with clients who have mental illness. It was the first of many (I have loved my work, and have found my rewards in many good relationships with clients), but it has rarely been matched for the exuberance I felt. Twenty-five years later, part of the story is special to me for its irony. What I said to Adam—"I'd like to help, if I can. I'm going to be working here awhile ... but it will take me awhile to become comfortable, and learn how to be helpful"—still characterizes my attitude toward my clients. That is, I *have* been working in this field for awhile, and I'm *still learning* how to be helpful.

The practice of clinical case management in the field of mental illness is enormously complicated. We are sometimes led to believe that science is on the verge of discovering a limited set of causes for mental illness and that some new type of treatment (including medications and some case management models) will finally result in clients' being able to function "normally." But each clinical situation is different, and no single means of intervention works well for every client. In fact, work over time with a *single* client is a series of successes and failures. All serious professionals I have met admit to learning from every client they have worked with, and all are modest about their level of expertise. There are rarely easy solutions to clients' problems. There are only challenges, many of which bring great rewards (for case managers and clients alike) but also great disappointments. As Helen Harris Perlman (1979, p. 208) has written, "If a helper's expectations are realistic, that is, if they are commensurate with the possibilities and limitations present in the persons/circumstances being worked with, there will be rewards to support one's sense of usefulness to another."

I cannot imagine a human services career with any other clients than those with mental illness. Having been a ward attendant for five years, I was later a clinical social worker and case management program supervisor in several community mental health centers. I am frequently asked how I can tolerate this frustrating work or why it suits me so well. Any personal psychodynamic themes about the issue I keep to myself, preferring to dwell instead on the joys I have experienced in my work. I think of the interesting, amusing, stimulating, touching, and inspiring clients I have worked with and how they have enriched my life. I have never received a high salary, but I have envied the careers of very few other people. Through the years, I have been able to maintain that sense of exuberance I felt after my first interaction with Adam back at the psychiatric hospital.

I cannot deny my frequent frustrations, ongoing stresses, failures to intervene effectively, occasional feelings of professional incompetence, and witnessing of sad and even tragic outcomes for many clients and their families. I would not want to give any aspiring professional the impression that a case manager's career is uniformly upbeat. For example, we must tolerate ambiguity in many decisions about client intervention and must tolerate often skimpy administrative and supervisory support. We must confront managed care objectives that restrict services to save money, financial incentives that drive agencies, our own self-care needs that sometimes conflict with those of the client, role and status differences between ourselves and our clients, rude and obnoxious client behaviors, policies promoting only a pseudo-empowerment of clients, and our bureaucratic (vs. professional) socialization within agencies. But the career offers an exciting challenge, and any case manager who does his or her best should always feel proud in spite of mixed client outcomes.

A Theoretical Framework

A basic premise in clinical case management is that effective intervention depends on the engagement of the client in a working relationship. This book explores relationship development from the theoretical perspective of *symbolic interactionism.* This theory is rooted in sociology and provides an internally consistent framework from which to understand how *all* people form their sense of self from relationships with others. Persons with mental illness lose at least some of their capacity for relationships because of their cognitive or mood impairment. They may experience social disconnections, such as hallucinations or delusions, and may have reduced ability to generate the shared social meanings required to process everyday social situations. From a symbolic interactionist perspective, when one's capacity to utilize symbols, or shared social meanings, is restricted, the capacity for human relationship is diminished.

Persons are no longer able to assume appropriate social roles when they do not understand what others expect of them (see Chapter 4).

This theory is consistent with strengths-based and empowerment perspectives of clinical case management and offers much to guide the worker in connecting with inarticulate, ambivalent, paranoid, or otherwise socially detached clients. As a theory of human behavior, symbolic interactionism is applicable across practice settings, and because it is a sociological theory, it can accommodate a variety of more specific direct practice approaches. Thus, the reader can conceptualize relationship development within this broad theoretical context while using other practice theories in specific contexts. The other theories emphasized here for helping clients change include *ego psychology* (for conceptualizing levels of ego functioning, defensive behavior, strengths, and the processes of coping and adaptation) and *cognitive/behavioral theory* (for organizing more task-focused intervention strategies). Again, the unique focus of the book is its emphasis on the case manager's use of self in formulating interventions with clients and families. Included in almost every chapter are case examples from my own practice.

One apparent paradox in the book's theoretical orientation needs clarification. I rely on the *Diagnostic and Statistical Manual of Mental Disorders* (DSM) (American Psychiatric Association, 1994) as a primary source in describing types of clients. The DSM is based on a medical model of mental illness, which is at odds with symbolic interactionism's focus on social rather than internal processes and on the unique meanings all people bring to their perceptions. I use the DSM because it is the standard reference text case managers and other professionals use to communicate about types of clients and effective interventions. I classify clients according to similarity of symptoms without intending to imply that they are alike as people. I believe that many clients have brain disorders that, while not yet understood, restrict their cognitive and affective processes in significant ways. Still it should be clear in this book that I see all persons with mental illness as unique and strive to help them make adjustments, not by focusing on illness but on their capacities to grow in their relationships.

DEFINING CASE MANAGEMENT

Case management is an approach to social service delivery that attempts to ensure that clients with multiple, complex problems and disabilities receive the services they need in a timely, appropriate fashion (Rubin, 1992a). It is practiced in such fields as mental health (adults with mental illness and emotionally disturbed children and adolescents), child welfare, aging and long-term care, alcohol and drug treatment, health care, and the public welfare system. Case managers may work independently or as members of coordinated teams. The case manager is responsible for service coordination and for helping the client hold elements of the service system accountable for adequate service delivery. Service objectives in case management include continuity of care, accessibility, accountability, and efficiency. Two driving principles of case management practice are that clients tend to get lost or frustrated and to drop out of treatment without a central point of integration, and that the community contains many resources that can meet the needs of clients.

CASE MANAGEMENT
AND MENTAL ILLNESS

Since the 1980s, case management has been a major intervention modality for direct practice with persons having mental illness. The major mental illnesses clients experience include schizophrenia, bipolar disorder, major depression, anxiety disorders, and personality disorders. Clients may also have coexisting substance-use disorders. Their problems with functioning mentally and socially result in at least occasional psychiatric hospitalizations or crisis intervention episodes. Case managers generally provide their care in mental health agencies, and the clients' range of needs may include housing, income support, medical care, job training, recreation, living skills development, counseling, and medication. Case management is considered essential for these clients because the resources and personnel needed for service delivery are spread across agency systems. Intervention goals tend to focus on social adaptation, coping skills development, and empowerment rather than cure of the mental disorder. With a community-based approach to intervention, the client's potential for adjustment to his or her disorder and the environment is increased.

The concept of case management emerged in mental health literature during the 1970s, but the practice can be understood as the modern application of social casework techniques that have a century-old tradition in social work and nursing. Between 1890 and 1920, social casework was the hallmark of social work, and its mediating and linkage functions included all activities designed to influence behavior and improve client welfare (Lubove, 1965). With the influence of Freud's writings during the 1920s the treatment of mental illness in social work became more psychoanalytic and less social (Ehrenreich, 1985). The nursing profession, with its interest in community health practice, further developed the casework approach to intervention after this time.

Despite the development of community mental health centers in the 1960s and 1970s, community casework modalities were not emphasized among the helping professions as agencies promoted office-based, therapeutic counseling for persons with mental illness, to the extent that they were treated at all. Mental illness was still conceived of as a reaction to stressful situations faced by persons who did not have adequate psychological coping abilities (Bloom, 1984). The most seriously impaired clients still spent much time in state hospital facilities, which were not well coordinated with the community centers and did not promote continuity of care (Fellin, 1996).

The re-emergence of community-based case management was spurred in part by National Institute of Mental Health policies introduced in 1978 to make support services available for clients who were not being adequately served through traditional agency systems (Turner & TenHoor, 1978). The Community Support Program concept, a national initiative, promoted case management. Community care problems at the time included inadequate definitions of mental health service system goals, fragmentation of responsibility for client interventions, the lack of a systematic approach to financing, inadequate agency commitments to clients, and a need for government leadership in planning for mental health service delivery. Case management was identified as a means of enhancing assistance to clients with mental illness, including applications for entitlements, crisis stabilization services, psychosocial rehabilitation and other support services, medical care, support to families and friends, and protection of clients' rights.

Case Management Activities

While basic case management practice activities may differ somewhat depending on the setting, the following functions are inherent to the modality (Intagliata, 1992):

1. Assessment of client needs, strengths, and limitations
2. Planning for appropriate service acquisition
3. Linkage with service providers from various systems
4. Advocacy on behalf of clients with other service providers, in order to insure that those services are made available
5. Monitoring of service quality across providers
6. Evaluation of the overall process

The following example will illustrate these aspects of case management.

Case Illustration

Bethany, age 45, was discharged after a ten-day stay from a crisis housing facility and was referred to a mental health center. Her severe depression and anxiety, bordering on panic, reflected her hopelessness about coping with a recently failed marriage, estrangement from her two daughters, and a related job loss. Although Bethany's need for crisis care was related to current stress, she had a history of depression and anxiety that occasionally impaired her capacity to function outside her home. She had not received professional care beyond her use of antidepressant medications because her family had always taken care of her. She moved into the apartment of a cousin and was, at least temporarily, on her own for the first time.

The case manager *assessed* Bethany's needs, with her collaborative input, to include housing, psychiatric care, and job placement assistance. Her strengths included a successful work history and good social skills. Among her limitations were a severe lack of confidence, dysthymic (moderately but chronically depressed) mood, and an absence of social supports, or persons she could depend on for material and emotional assistance. *Planning* included decisions by the worker and client for Bethany to visit the agency psychiatrist, begin attending church groups again on a regular basis (as a social support), complete a job assessment with the local vocational training agency, and begin to investigate housing options. The worker's *linkage* activities included arranging the first appointment with the physician, contacting the minister to request that he visit Bethany, contacting the job training agency to arrange for an assessment, and gathering information from the local housing authority for her to review. *Advocacy* was necessary with the vocational training agency, whose director was uncertain about Bethany's suitability for their services given her relatively successful work history. The worker needed to solicit and submit letters from the agency physician and previous crisis intervention worker that attested to Bethany's current disability. The *monitoring* of the case management process was carried out through weekly meetings with Bethany, to assure that she was being assisted by all service providers as arranged and to determine her reactions to the process, given her mood disorder. The case manager also monitored the effects of the medication, both positive and negative, on her mental status and physical functioning. *Evaluation* by the worker was ongoing and consisted of reviewing the physician's reports, Bethany's self-reports on her mood and anxiety levels, and reports from the vocational agency about her participation there.

Additional Case Management Activities

While the activities described above are common to all types of case management, the modality can be organized in a variety of ways. Moxley (1996) differentiates system-driven from consumer-driven case management, based on the relative priority given by the workers to a partnership in activity planning, the client's responsibility for self-care, and the extent of activities of other professionals. Fiorentine and Grusky (1990) outline four functions of case management including therapy, linkage, intervention, and services integration. They propose a role-contingency approach, stating that the priorities case managers give to their respective roles should vary depending on service system and organizational policies. When case managers perceive community services to be useful to clients, they primarily perform linkage activities. But more intensive worker intervention is required when case managers perceive that services are not useful or are overly selective. Roberts-DeGennaro (1987) argues that the case manager must possess casework, group work, and community organization skills, as any of these may take priority in community systems.

Limitations of Case Management

The case management approach is potentially limited. Case managers possess only a modest level of authority in some community service systems (Rubin, 1992). If the case manager is responsible for linking clients with a variety of service providers, it follows that he or she should have some authority over how those services are delivered, including decision-making about which are adequate. But though case managers generally have college degrees in a variety of human service professions, most notably social work or psychology, only one-third have graduate degrees (Rothman, 1992). This tends to limit their recognized authority in interdisciplinary work. For example, a case manager might decide that a psychotherapist's treatment for a given client is for some reason inappropriate. Should the case manager approach the therapist about changing the treatment modality? Many therapists would question if a professional with lesser credentials should make judgments about the quality of the therapist's work, but the case manager's monitoring and evaluation of services are considered to be essential roles.

Other limitations of the approach include unclear expectations for job performance and problems with attrition (McClelland, Austin, & Schneck, 1996). Furthermore, when a case manager's job performance is evaluated relative to client outcomes, it is difficult to separate one worker's activities from those of other service providers. Aviram (1990) lists role ambiguity, inadequate resources, a lack of administrative authority, and low salaries as reasons why the case management modality risks failure. Case managers function best when their roles are clearly delineated, and opportunities for professional growth and advancement within their positions might enhance retention and job satisfaction.

Caseload size is often cited as a determining factor of the nature of case manager activity. Caseloads generally range from 15 to 50 clients per worker (Rothman & Sager, 1998). In a literature review, Intagliata and Baker (1983) found that as caseloads increased from 20 to 35 or more clients, workers became more reactive than proactive, and case managers began to do things *for* clients rather than to facilitate their independence and empowerment. When caseloads are high, only the most demanding clients receive service. Harris and Bergman (1987) concluded that when staff-client ratios exceed 1:20, positive client outcomes become significantly less likely. Rose and Moore (1995) point to the irony that as the complexity of client needs increases, caseload size also tends to increase, and educational standards for employment are lowered.

Models of Case Management in Mental Health

Beyond general definitions and role prescriptions, the details of professional case management models have been difficult to articulate. The possible range of activities is usually so broad that it may be impossible to distinguish specific program types. Still, Rapp and Kirsthardt (1996) and Solomon (1992), in separate research reviews, identified four major models of case management, as follows:

1. The *Program of Assertive Community Treatment* (PACT), or *Full Support*
   model, is a problem-oriented approach. The case manager is most attentive
   to the client's limitations, and interventions are focused on preventing
   symptom relapse and extending community tenure by compensating for
   deficits with whatever assistance is necessary. The teaching of coping skills
   is combined with support provision. The case manager must be a creative
   service provider as well as a focal point for the services provided by others.

2. The *Rehabilitation* model places more emphasis on proactive skill building exercises than on remedial interventions. Still, case managers refer clients elsewhere for assistance rather than providing services themselves. The emphasis is on helping clients become successful and satisfied in the social environment of their choice with a minimal amount of professional assistance. The case manager promotes a climate of normalization by de-emphasizing the roles of professional helpers.

3. The *Strengths* model focuses on identifying and building on client strengths for independent living by accessing resources not generally located within the professional service system. It differs from the rehabilitation model in that planning is more client-driven, and there is no predetermined focus on skill building as the intervention of choice. The case manager creates personal and environmental situations where client success can be achieved. This model also demands creative thinking on the part of case managers in developing informal supports.

4. The *Expanded Broker* or *Generalist* model relies on linkages to formal and informal caregiving systems to prevent the hospitalization of clients. These programs tend to be characterized by high caseloads and relatively nonspecific qualifications for case managers. Case managers do not provide interventions on their own and may not have close relationships with many of their clients.

Rapp and Kirsthardt (1996) identified a fifth model, *Clinical Case Management,* which emphasizes the relationship between the client and worker as the essential prerequisite for the client's personal growth. This model, which focuses attention on interpersonal therapeutic technique as well as resource linkage and development, will be discussed in greater detail later in this chapter.

Case management may also be classified according to the characteristics of the host agency. From this perspective the organizational structure of the agency determines the activities of the case manager more than does the philosophy of the program itself. Austin (1996) differentiates between the following:

- The *Broker* model, a generic system of client referral and follow-up
- The *Service Management* model, in which the case manager is fiscally responsible for service care plans
- The *Managed Care* approach, where prospective payments are made to service providers who must then keep service costs within predetermined levels

Intagliata (1982) also offers three models:

- The *Minimum* model, limited to assessment, planning, and referral
- The *Coordination* model, which adds the functions of advocacy, casework, and natural support system development
- The *Comprehensive* model, which further incorporates the activities of crisis intervention, resource development, service quality monitoring, and public education

Schwartz, Goldman, and Churgin (1982) state that the roles and functions of the case manager in a given agency depend on three factors:

- The worker's permitted degree of involvement in direct services
- The nature and size of the caseload
- The extent of worker control over internal and external services and resources

In summary, case management is complex, as it incorporates the influences of agency philosophies, community service system dynamics, community resource availability, and worker skills.

CLINICAL CASE MANAGEMENT

I believe that none of the above descriptions of case management, or the models proposed, adequately take into account the role of the case manager as a service provider, based on his or her relationship with the client and perhaps with the client's significant others. The case manager's interactions with the client are so significant that, if they are not conducted therapeutically, the intervention may fail.

The extent to which case managers act as therapists with their clients has been debated for almost 20 years. Lamb (1982) asserts that case management should be carried out by a professional with therapeutic skills, because only that person can have the necessary knowledge of the client to perform a thorough assessment. The crucial assessment function is never a routine process of ascertaining needs; rather, it involves a full clinical understanding of the client's strengths and limitations in articulating realistic goals. Harris and Bergman (1987) support the clinical model of case management, arguing that by nature the worker's integrative, rational, proactive, and individualized interventions directly counteract the client's maladaptive behavior patterns characterized by globalism, irrationality, reactivity, and perhaps fragmentation of the sense of self. Surber (1994) states that therapeutic interventions within the case manager-client relationship include efforts to alleviate symptoms and suffering, reduce pathology and disability, and enhance functional capacity, relationships, and the sense of well-being. Balancio (1994) emphasizes that the case manager's ability to improve the client's capacity to bond is a prerequisite for interventions by other professionals.

Kanter (1989) sees the need for the case manager to possess a high level of knowledge and professional skill, as well as a commitment to the challenges of long-term intervention. In the context of almost any stressful event affecting a client, the case manager must make a series of quick decisions for appropriate intervention. The case manager must be able to develop a longitudinal view of the client's strengths, limitations, and symptoms, decide the right amount of environmental support, and know how to facilitate client resourcefulness, perhaps at times by withholding support. Components of clinical case management, according to Kanter (1995a) include intermittent psychotherapy, consultation with families and other caregivers, and crisis intervention. He emphasizes an important point often overlooked by program developers—that the engagement phase of the relationship may take many months. This is not to say that no other interventions can take place in the meantime, but it does suggest that developing a stable working partnership with some clients is extremely difficult.

The comprehensive literature review by Sexton and Whiston (1994) supports an emphasis on the worker-client relationship as providing a context for positive outcomes in all clinical situations. The working alliance consists of a positive emotional bond between the parties, mutual comfort in the interactions, and an agreement on goals and tasks, ideally beginning within the first three meetings. This alliance develops over time and, at its best, becomes collaborative. It develops in unpredictable ways from the expectations, beliefs, and knowledge that each person brings to the relationship. Shared meanings of the clinical intervention emerge as the relationship develops. Horvath's (1994) literature review found that the quality of the working alliance, represented by a mutual sense of collaboration, was more predictive of positive final outcomes in therapy than any other variable.

Rapp (1998) states that the case manager-client relationship must be purposeful, reciprocal, friendly, trusting, and empowering. It helps if the worker meets the client in natural settings of the client's choice, maintains a conversational focus, jointly attends to concrete tasks, and overtly delineates the roles that each member will play in the relationship. The case manager should celebrate the client's accomplishments perhaps more enthusiastically than might be appropriate in other intervention modalities.

Because of inherent problems with role confusion and authority in case management, the client might best be served if the worker develops his or her role as a therapeutic resource. It is unlikely that a case manager can carry out the six core activities outlined earlier without providing a therapeutic climate, even if counseling is not an explicit component of those activities. Therapeutic skill is necessary for service monitoring as well as for assessment and planning. Rubin (1992) notes that case managers are not necessarily expected to function as therapists, but they routinely provide personal support. They often, for example, accompany the client to counseling appointments with other professionals and, in the process, spend more time in purposeful conversation with the clients than the counselor does. At those times, they also use therapeutic intervention to deal with the client's problems or symptoms.

Some program developers are reluctant to support the clinical case management approach to service delivery because of concerns that staff may focus on psychotherapy interventions in lieu of the full range of case management activities. It may well be true that many professional staff are effective in some, but not all, case management roles. Neugeboren's (1996) literature review suggests that helping clients to change requires different knowledge than changing policies and programs. Environmentally-focused practice (advocacy and monitoring) requires "sociopolitical" skills, in contrast to "socioemotional" skills (relationship development, assessment, and planning). While this perspective might support a system of care in which a client has a separate clinician and case manager, or perhaps does not include clinical counseling activities, it also underscores the need for ongoing staff development in all areas of case management practice. In fact, Neugeboren asserts that common skills are involved in all case management roles, including decision making, leadership, client representation, and negotiation. No literature suggests that case managers cannot be helped to develop all of these skills.

I do not intend to prescribe a particular practice theory for clinical case management, but two commonly used theories are ego psychology and cognition/behavior (Swenson, 1994). These theories can be used in conjunction with each other throughout the clinical case management process, and they both provide the worker with guidance in relationship development (see Chapter 4).

Therapeutic Aspects of Clinical Case Management

Does good clinical case management always include components of psychotherapy? A survey of definitions of psychotherapy helps us answer this question. Frank and Frank (1993) define psychotherapy as a form of help-giving in which a trained, socially sanctioned healer tries to relieve a sufferer's distress by facilitating changes in his or her feelings, attitudes, and behaviors through the performance of certain activities. Campbell (1996) defines the activity as any form of treatment for mental illness, behavioral maladaption, or other problems assumed to be of an emotional nature, in which a trained person establishes a professional relationship with a client for the purpose of removing or modifying symptoms, reversing disturbed patterns of behavior, or promoting positive personality development. Corsini and Wedding (1995) define the concept as a process of interaction between a worker and client for the purpose of ameliorating the client's disability or malfunction regarding cognitive, affective, or behavioral functions. The worker always utilizes a theory of personality and change along with a treatment modality logically related to that theory.

I have argued thus far that in order to provide quality case management services the social worker must establish a relationship of trust with the client. But does this relationship and the activities stemming from it constitute elements of therapy as defined above? My answer is *yes,* and other writers agree. Johnson and Rubin (1983) describe four therapeutic functions of case management. These include recognizing early signs of the client's decompensation and unmanageable stress, understanding the likely effects of environmental circumstances on the client's functioning, enhancing the client's motivation to participate in treatment, and providing a stable relationship for the client as he or she moves across system boundaries.

Kanter (1985a) believes that effective case management is more difficult than generally acknowledged. He states that in addition to requiring considerable familiarity with psychopathology and its biological and psychological treatment, it requires a thorough knowledge of community resources, skill in assisting families in coping with their troubled relatives, an appreciation of the sociological factors affecting clients, and an understanding of how clients both shape and internalize their environments. The relationship between client and case manager is crucial, as planning requires an appreciation of the client's conscious and unconscious motives for behavior.

Thus, the clinical case management relationship does seem to incorporate elements of psychotherapy. Returning to Frank and Frank's (1993) definition clinical case management can be understood as a form of help-giving in which a socially sanctioned healer (the case manager) tries to relieve a sufferer's distress (the client with mental illness) by facilitating changes in his feelings (e. g., anxiety), attitudes (e. g., paranoia), and behavior (levels of independent living skills) through the performance of certain activities with him or her (relationship-building, assessment, planning, linking, etc.), often with the participation of a group (other service providers in the case management network).

One reason case management practice has been kept separate from therapeutic practice is that clients are said not to benefit from psychotherapy. In reality, only certain types of psychotherapy are inappropriate for this population. Torrey (1988a) writes that insight-oriented psychotherapy, in which the therapist tries to make the client aware of underlying unconscious processes, is useless and probably detrimental in treating persons with schizophrenia. He does maintain, however, that a long-term supportive relationship between the clinician and client can be helpful. He refers to this as supportive psychotherapy, consisting of friendship, advice, practical assistance in securing financial and support services, and caring. Wolberg (as cited in Campbell, 1996) identifies three types of psychotherapy: reconstructive, re-educative, and supportive. The supportive type focuses on promoting development of the client's strengths, with objectives to strengthen existing defenses, elaborate better mechanisms to maintain control, and restore an adaptive equilibrium.

Johnson and Rubin (1983) describe "adaptive psychotherapy" as appropriate for work with persons who have mental illness and define it as a process focused on reality to improve the client's adaptation to the environment, create a milieu of trust, and develop appropriate social relationships. Simpson and May (1982) distinguish between "formal psychotherapy" and "psychotherapeutic management." They define the latter term as the application of psychological understanding to the management and rehabilitation of clients, which often includes establishing a therapeutic relationship, helping the client deal with life problems, and working with his family and significant others. Rapp and Chamberlain (1985) conclude from their research that case managers do not act as therapists for their clients, yet they engage in therapeutic activities, and their role in the amelioration of social problems has a therapeutic effect on symptoms.

In summary, the extent of interaction between case managers and their clients carries great potential for therapeutic impact, and it should be promoted by program administrators.

CASE ILLUSTRATION

Nate was a 25-year-old, unemployed male with schizophrenia. He lived with his mother, who held a full-time job, in a suburban neighborhood of a large Midwestern city. His parents were divorced, and his father lived a few hundred miles away. Nate was referred to the mental health agency from a psychiatric hospital where he had spent several days following a suicide attempt. He had been treated there once previously during his first episode of schizophrenia. Following that discharge he intentionally overdosed on prescription antipsychotic medications. Nate reported afterward that he was extremely upset about his symptoms. The rehospitalization lasted only five days, and Nate had refused to take medications upon his release.

Nate had been extremely withdrawn throughout his adolescence and early adulthood, gradually retreating from family and peers. He attended school and adequately managed daily life but otherwise stayed at home, in his bedroom. He and his mother agreed that during high school, he had read "about a thousand books" of science fiction, played video games, and watched movies. Nate was bright but kept to himself and seemed satisfied to do so. In late adolescence he began to experience hallucinations, including two voices (one soothing, the other threatening), and tactile sensations (a sense of being stroked on the leg, and of being suffocated while trying to sleep). Nate remained withdrawn through this period, but eventually become so depressed and fearful that he was hospitalized. He retained insight into his former self, unlike some persons with schizophrenia, and knew that he was changing in ways that terrified him.

The Worker-Client Relationship

A major problem confronting the case manager from the beginning was Nate's difficulty with relationships. He had a passive-aggressive personality style, at first acting cooperative with goals and objectives but then sabotaging them. He and his mother were continuously critical of each other because of their mutual frustrations, and she could not seem to motivate him to pursue any independent living skills. Nate had rarely felt good about any of his relationships, tending to accuse others of being nonsupportive. He did have a few old friends with whom he liked to visit, but he smoked marijuana and drank with them, which made his symptoms worse. Nate presented himself over time to the case manager as sullen, suspicious, and withholding. The worker sensed that Nate did not enjoy their work together or put himself into it; Nate also had doubts that any professionals could help him.

The case manager's uncertain relationship with Nate remained problematic for months. He did maintain regular contact with Nate for counseling and for a central point of intervention. The worker knew that Nate was depressed, in addition to dealing with schizophrenia, and that he had a sense of fatalism about his future. Nate knew that he had a psychosis and could feel the difference it was making in his life. He was grieving the loss of his former self and was afraid that he might never be functional again. Nate's few long-term relationships eventually ended. He met new peers in his psychosocial rehabilitation programs but resisted involving himself with them because they reminded him of his own limitations. The case manager wondered if Nate could tolerate social interactions sufficiently to persist in his rehabilitation program. He tried to engage Nate in a partnership, which is always necessary for optimal treatment planning. Additionally he hoped to model social skills for Nate to use when interacting with other professionals and peers in his treatment milieu.

Intervention Activities

Nate identified three goals that seemed to motivate him: getting a good paying job, finding his own apartment, and meeting enough people that he could find a few male friends and a girlfriend. These goals were ambitious, but realistic, if Nate pursued them patiently. Nate and the case manager participated in much planning, referral, linkage, advocacy, and monitoring activity over several years. Nate was first linked with a psychiatrist, who developed an effective medication regimen after months of trial and error. The medications controlled, but did not eliminate, his anxiety and hallucinations, and Nate was erratic in his adherence to the drugs. Nate was sensitive to the side effects of all medications, and they did nothing to alter his symptoms of anhedonia and ambivalence. Next, a local service agency assessed Nate's vocational potential. He enrolled in a computer training program that lasted for one year and ended with his referral to a job placement agency. Nate's other activities included participation in a clubhouse program where he could address his interpersonal needs, his acceptance of a volunteer position where he could test his work readiness, and his participation with material resource providers such as the social security administration. A half-dozen professionals worked with Nate on separate tasks. Although his progress was slow, Nate achieved enough competence after two years to look for a private sector job. Job coaching would be provided by a placement service agency.

The Changing Relationship

The issue of timing in the case manager's linkage and advocacy activities with Nate was delicate. The worker needed to determine when Nate was ready for another step in the process of rehabilitation, when he needed to be restrained from moving ahead, when he needed to be pushed, and when services should be withheld to encourage Nate to take initiatives and thus enhance his sense of mastery. The case manager also needed to routinely assess the stability of Nate's thought processes to determine whether cognitive interventions might be effective in supplementing the behavioral milieu. Nate could be demanding and hostile; he would drop out of treatment for weeks at a time as a means of expressing negative feelings to the worker about the intervention plan or his own inadequacies, and at each of these junctures the worker needed to respond appropriately with support or confrontation.

The case manager remained concerned about his relationship with Nate, and about Nate's other relationships. They met every one to two weeks during a two-year period to collaborate on problem-solving strategies regarding his family and peer relationships, and to deal with his anger about the psychotic impairment. The worker, who generally connected well with clients, was frustrated by his apparent inability to encourage Nate to talk openly about his thoughts and emotions. The worker was concerned about Nate's suicide potential; he also wanted to work with Nate's mother on repairing the tensions in their relationship but was not able because of the strong reluctance of both. Nate often expressed frustration with the worker, sometimes directly but most often passively by missing appointments or waiting until he was out of medication before notifying the case manager that he needed a refill. Nate seemed to resent that the worker could not do more for him, and he was envious of the worker's apparently easier life. The case manager, in turn, sought supervisory help in dealing with his own frustration that Nate did not seem to appreciate his efforts or demonstrate consistent motivation to work on his goals. The worker confronted Nate on these points at times and hoped that his directness would model appropriate behavior.

The worker's concerns about Nate's interpersonal limitations and the breadth and pace of the case management plan proved to be wise when the client attempted suicide a second time, three years into his treatment. At that time, Nate was despairing over problems handling the responsibilities of a new job, the first one that really represented independence. Success on this job might have led to his acquisition of an apartment and responsibility for his own budget. Nate was not functioning well on the job and, lacking adequate social supports, feared that there was no hope for his success. Fortunately the suicide attempt was not successful. Nate recovered quickly but decided to move from the area to live with a relative in a rural environment.

Was this intervention a success or a failure? As with many case management interventions, a clear answer is not possible. Nate had achieved a number of gains and demonstrated that he could handle the rigors of an intensive rehabilitation program. He had tolerated being out with the public, professional and otherwise, for three years. On the other hand, his interpersonal limitations and anxieties had continually interfered with his accepting the support that he paradoxically sought. Nate was also an angry person who tended to displace his anger passively on those close to him. The worker's attention to his interpersonal patterns helped Nate improve in this regard, but the slow pace of the working alliance reflected his ongoing detachment. Clearly, Nate had needs for counseling to cope with interpersonal and other stresses as part of his case management plan. He had been a fragile client from the beginning who denied or minimized his illness and tended to resist depending on others. A more impersonal approach to case management might have ended in an earlier breakdown of the intervention process. Perhaps Nate would be able to build on some of his strengths to make an even better adaptation to his new environment.

SUMMARY

The case management approach to service delivery represents an exciting development within the human service professions. Case management has been a particularly innovative modality in the field of mental health, as severely impaired clients with multiple support, growth, and rehabilitation needs have been shown to benefit from it. Full evaluation of the concept can occur, however, only if the arbitrary division of professionals in some settings into "therapist" and "case manager" categories is eliminated. If skilled mental health professionals are supported in their case management activities by thorough professional and administrative sanctioning, clients will be better served. Issues to consider in developing the therapeutic aspects of clinical case management are worker roles, authority, status, training, caseload, and supervision (Rubin, 1992). These factors may be enhanced in the following ways:

1. *Roles* Program developers must acknowledge that case managers provide therapeutic interventions by virtue of their close and long-term associations with clients. While the term "therapist" has some negative connotations with regard to the client population of persons with mental illness, case managers do provide counseling that requires clinical skill, and they should be recruited and trained accordingly.

2. *Authority* For their work to be evaluated adequately, case managers must have the authority to assume overall case responsibility. Rubin (1992) concludes that authority is the most crucial factor influencing the effectiveness of case management, but worker empowerment is not always implemented as prescribed in early conceptual writings on the modality. As long as case managers are thought to possess minimal qualifications compared to other professionals, those with more experience will maintain authority in service provision, contributing to a fragmentation in service delivery.

3. *Status* Administrators must develop career paths for case managers, including the possibility of eventually moving out of their positions, so that turnover is not prevalent. At present, case managers tend to become locked into their roles, and a self-fulfilling prophecy develops as the modality is perceived as the domain of less experienced professionals. Case managers have a high likelihood of burnout, as working exclusively with severely disturbed clients is draining over time regardless of the worker's level of commitment.

4. *Training* All mental health professionals should have ongoing and frequent training, provided through their agencies as well as professional organizations. Case managers should be included as both the recipients and providers of professional development opportunities, as a means of improving skills and maintaining interest and motivation in their work.

5. *Caseloads* Caseload size should be controlled so that case managers can realistically attend to the needs of their clients without feeling

overwhelmed and becoming primarily reactive in their work. As a rule, caseloads of approximately 20–30 clients per worker appear to promote effective intervention.

Administrative support of clinical case management will provide another positive consequence for clients—that of reduced stigmatization. In the past twenty years, mental health professionals have become sensitive to the overt and subtle ways they have blamed clients and their families for either causing mental disorders or contributing to its persistence. Professional attitudes have been changing for the better, but ironically case management has presented clients with a new stigma. That is, clients deemed appropriate for case management are sometimes thought to have little or no potential for psychological growth. Certain types of therapy are unsuitable for clients with mental illness, but it seems premature to deny the usefulness of all counseling modalities, other than crisis intervention. Lin and Kleinman (1988), in observing that the outcome of schizophrenia is better in third-world societies than industrial nations, note that many persons in Western society believe mental illness to be an incurable affliction, and they tend to treat clients as lifelong deviants. The expectation of improvement and the presence of more informal social supports account in part for the better prognosis in rural countries. Among the potential benefits of promoting strong and more therapeutic case manager–client relationships is the fostering of hope that all persons are capable of growth and of finding satisfaction in life. It is imperative that all case managers be aware of the power of their relationships to help clients achieve their potential.

2

♋

The Policy Context of Case Management

Case managers concentrate most of their efforts on developing effective intervention methods with clients. Still, like all practice modalities, case management is driven not only by the pursuit of client-centered outcomes, but also by policies developed by agency administrators and elected officials in local, state, and federal governments. These policies reflect competing values regarding social priorities, acceptable service costs, service goals, and desired practice outcomes. This chapter discusses our society's perspectives on mental illness as a problem requiring publicly-sponsored interventions, including how attitudes have changed over time and how policies influence the organization of case management services. With an understanding of policy trends in mental health care, case managers can function more effectively as client advocates, be more proactive in treatment planning, and better inform clients and their families about relevant policy debates. Further, linkage, advocacy, and mediation routinely require that case managers be familiar with the policies of agencies with which they interact.

MENTAL ILLNESS AS A SOCIAL PROBLEM

One definition of social welfare policy is all collective courses of action in a society which are intended to impact on personal relationships and quality of life toward the goal of mutual support (Gilbert & Specht, 1986). Government provides mutual support functions when citizens experience adverse conditions that prevent their meeting basic needs through family, religious, and economic institutions. An adverse condition becomes legitimized as a social problem when it meets most or all of the following conditions (Meenaghan & Washington, 1980; Rochefort, 1989):

1. It is shared by a considerable number of people within society.

2. It is present over a long period of time.

3. It is recognized as a problem by more persons than those who directly experience it.

4. It is perceived by members of the larger society as not caused by those who experience it.

5. It generates consequences for the society judged serious enough to merit a public response.

The prevalence of mental illnesses such as schizophrenia, bipolar disorder, major depression, schizoaffective disorder, and others among members of our society represents a social problem which is legitimated at all levels of government. Though a standard social definition of mental illness does not exist, it can be understood as a severe and persistent biologically-based mental disorder that interferes with social functioning in such primary aspects of daily life as self-care, interpersonal relationships, and work or schooling, and that may necessitate occasional hospital or crisis care (Goldman & Manderscheid, 1987).

Mental illness is manifest as a social problem in the United States by the numbers of people who experience it and who endure its associated costs. The precise prevalence of mental illness is unknown, but the National Institute of Mental Health (NIMH) offers estimates as reliable as any (Manderscheid & Sonnenschein, 1994). Forty million Americans have a diagnosable mental disorder (excluding substance abuse disorders), and 13 million people experience severe mental illnesses such as those noted above. One in 14 jail inmates has a mental illness (Torrey et al., 1992). Statistics on mental illness among children and adolescents are more difficult to collect, because their care may be provided not only in the mental health system but also in the substance abuse, general health, education, child welfare, and juvenile justice service sectors. Still, it is estimated that 7.5 million (12%) children have a clinical maladjustment, and half of them are severely handicapped in efforts to manage school, family, and community life (Fellin, 1996).

Surprisingly few persons with mental disorders receive professional intervention. Only 20% of those with *any* type of mental health problem receive professional care each year (Fellin, 1996), although *most* persons with serious mental illnesses do (Manderscheid & Sonnenschein, 1994). Sixty-four percent (64.3%) of persons with schizophrenia were treated in 1993, as were 61% of persons with bipolar disorder and 54% of those with major depression. Of those with schizophrenia, 60% were treated as outpatients and 17% as inpatients. In the category of affective disorders, 57.2% of persons with bipolar disorder were treated as outpatients and 7.6% as inpatients. Fifty two percent (52.3%) of persons with major depression were treated as outpatients, and 5% as inpatients.

The direct and indirect social costs associated with the problem of mental illness are great. The total cost of mental illness in the United States in 1985 was $103.7 billion, or 10% of all health care costs (Rice, Kelman, & Miller, 1992). This figure includes the direct costs of in-patient care, nursing homes, providers, prescription drugs, community support, and the indirect costs of social welfare administration, as well as lost economic productivity by clients and family members. A later study updated this cost estimate to $136 billion in 1991 dollars (Wasylenki, 1994). Direct costs have been rising dramatically in comparison with indirect costs.

The costs of community-based case management for persons with mental illness in one urban Midwest location were determined in 1994 dollars to be $29,965 per person per year (Wolff, Helminiak, & Diamond, 1995). Maintenance costs (government payments, subsidies, and in-kind services) were largest, followed by mental health treatment, law enforcement, and family financial burden. The indirect impact of mental illness, also factored into the study, included loss of productivity, family dissolution, and community disorganization in the form of homelessness and other problems. Another indirect impact was the poor quality of life experienced by persons with mental illness, broadly defined as satisfaction with basic living conditions. Significant to the practice of case management, some believe that all of these costs could be reduced by the prevention of client relapse and the more consistent provision of community care and medications (Wasylenki, 1994).

In summary, a significant number of people throughout the country and from all social classes experience mental illness. Many endure a high level of emotional suffering, depend at least partly on others for material support, and might not recover enough to be economically self-sufficient. They experience a low quality of life and are high users of public monies. It is not yet clear which interventions help them attain a maximum level of social functioning and quality of life. Mental illness is thus recognized as a social problem, but there is a lack of consensus on how to address it. Deciding what to do about the problem is controversial among public policy makers, including legislators, government and agency administrators, and even service providers. The causes, course, and outcomes of mental illness are not fully understood. Much professional effort and public money has been spent on the community rehabilitation of clients but with mixed results. Some professionals feel that government has never been strongly committed to supporting community-based care, because of competing health care priorities (Belcher, 1994).

AMERICA'S RESPONSE TO THE PROBLEM OF MENTAL ILLNESS

Mental illness has been recognized as a social problem in the United States since the early 1800s (Grob, 1983). During the colonial era, "insanity" was believed to be the result of personal or spiritual conflicts, and families cared for their disturbed members. With the passing of the colonial era, Americans became more mobile, so the "feeble minded" could not always be cared for by families and tolerant small communities. Asylums developed as a state and community response to the loosening of social structure and predictability. These were initially progressive institutions offering moral treatment: individualized regimens of work and recreation with religious and educational services and much staff attention. Evidence shows that many persons were helped by moral treatment (Caplan, 1969), which in my view supports the importance of the worker/client relationship in the treatment of mental illness.

During the second half of the 1800s, the social developments of immigration and urbanization led to an overcrowding of mental hospitals. The distress and destitution experienced by immigrants often produced behaviors that led to their hospitalization. Further, members of the urban lower class who demonstrated antisocial behavioral patterns were sometimes assessed as being insane. The 1880 census, the only one to count this population, tallied 91,959 persons with mental illness in this country; 41,083 of them lived at home, with the rest in hospitals or asylums (Clark, 1993). It was not until 1955 that public mental hospitals reached their peak population, with 558,000 daily residents and 178,000 admissions occurring each year.

Mental illness finally became a topic for federal policy-making during World War II. It was a personnel issue, as 20% of draftees rejected for duty, and 40% of those given premature discharges, were diagnosed with emotional problems. Also, reform-minded journalists and conscientious objectors employed at state hospitals uncovered atrocious conditions in them (Grob, 1991). With a sense of national optimism that mental illness, and other illnesses, could be effectively combated, the National Institute of Mental Health (NIMH) was founded in 1946. It dispersed funds for research, professional training, and community service programs, and signified an important shift in responsibility for the care of persons with mental illness from the state to the federal level.

Since World War II, social welfare policy has been characterized by a gradual shift from the hospital to the community as the preferred locus of care. The social values of community care and freedom from incarceration became dominant. Federal initiatives culminated in the 1963 Community Mental Health Centers Act, realized through President Kennedy's leadership. Reformers anticipated that these centers would make effective mental health intervention accessible to all who needed it, with far less reliance on state hospitals. Preventive measures would reduce the incidence of mental illness by eradicating both its (vaguely understood) environmental and biological causes. The appeal to economy, however, was equally strong in the evolution of community care. State hospitals were viewed as anachronistic institutions and drains on the public purse. There was hope that the mental health centers, where clients could be cured and mental illness prevented, would result in public savings.

THE EMERGENCE OF CASE MANAGEMENT
AS A POLICY RESPONSE

Until the mid-1970s there was federal support for community mental health center development through matching grants with local communities. However, states and communities did not participate to the extent planned, and eventually the federal formula policy was terminated. Just under half the projected 1500 centers were established. The mental health centers were successful in many ways, but they came under attack from some professionals and family advocacy groups for serving clients with relatively minor emotional problems rather than persons with serious mental illnesses (Hatfield, 1981; Vine, 1982). As late as 1975, only 20% of mental health center clients had ever been hospitalized, and from 1970–78 the percentage of persons with schizophrenia served by agencies actually dropped from 19% to 10% (Mechanic, 1989). These figures do not indicate that prevention was working, because psychiatric hospital admission rates were still high.

The community and state hospital systems coexisted, but a mandate never existed for a unified system of care. This resulted in a lack of central planning, organizational barriers, service duplications, and service gaps. The deinstitutionalization which did occur was, in part, the result of community center availability, the introduction of psychotropic medications, and increased attention to patients' rights, but was also a result of new federal money for persons with disabilities. Hospitals could discharge clients with eligibility for Medicaid, Medicare, and Social Security Disability funds whether or not they were effectively linked with outpatient care providers. By 1989, the average daily state hospital population was 130,000, but the rate of admissions had declined by only 10% since 1970, indicating a "revolving door" phenomenon (Reamer, 1989).

Policy makers who valued the idea of community care became disillusioned with the ongoing difficulties clients faced in trying to become established in community life. By 1980, enthusiasm about the centers, and the idea of mental illness prevention, was waning. Some of this was related to President Reagan's desire to reduce the scope of the federal government and institute discretionary state block grants for social services. Community mental health centers became a lower priority among legislators, as they were costly and voters demanded lower taxes.

But federal policy continued to be influential in addressing the perceived inadequacies of community mental health centers. The NIMH Community Support Program (CSP) emphasized the need to make community services available to clients who were not adequately served through traditional agency systems (Turner & TenHoor, 1978). The assumption that community care was more effective and less expensive than hospital care persisted. In 1963, 96% of public funding for persons with mental illness came from the states, but by 1985 only 53% was state provided, with 38% coming from federal programs (Torrey, 1988b). Still, 70% of public mental health resources remained in hospitals, despite emerging research on the comparable effectiveness of community-based treatment alternatives (Sherman & Dahlquist, 1996).

Innovative program developers, such as Test and Stein (1985) in Wisconsin, demonstrated that community-based programs characterized by assertive case management could reduce psychiatric hospitalizations and improve the social functioning of persons with mental illness, allegedly at a lower cost. Their interventions acknowledged the chronic nature of mental illness and focused on rehabilitation rather than cure. Service goals focused on normalizing the lives of clients by providing them with case management support in securing jobs, housing, socialization opportunities, and access to medical care. This approach was implemented in other sites across the country.

Many state departments, impressed by the efforts of community support programmers and faced with the need to reduce hospital costs, turned over considerable budgeting and planning responsibility to community agencies. The State Comprehensive Mental Health Services Plan Act of 1986 was another federal initiative requiring states to develop and implement plans for achieving an organized system of community-based care for persons with mental illness. A 1990 amendment required the same coordination of children's services. Improvements in the status of children's mental health services are evident (Davis, Yelton, Katz-Leavy, & Lourie, 1995). There has been a marked growth in state children's mental health departments and the coordination of a system of care including early identification and intervention, interagency activities, and the establishment of review boards for placing children in non-hospital settings. Residential and day treatment programs have increased in number.

With the CSP policy shift to community care, case management gained momentum as a favored treatment modality, with its potential to help clients develop productive lifestyles. Further, through case management clients could be linked with informal supports (friends, neighbors, recreation centers, etc.) as well as with formal systems. Two policy goals, not always compatible, were service cost effectiveness and quality of care. The social value of community care was one rationale for shifting money from the state to the community mental health centers; also such care is ostensibly less expensive. Early experiments in community care tended to confirm this, but later the issue of reduced cost was challenged (Mechanic, 1989). In some cases, fewer services are necessary to keep clients out of hospitals than to significantly improve their quality of life. Case managers came under pressure from administrators to keep out of the hospital even those clients who might benefit from a short in-patient experience. In geographic areas with few alternative funding sources, agencies had difficulty providing supportive services to clients even when hospital stays were reduced.

The most frequent criticisms of the public mental health system since 1980 have been the ongoing use of expensive hospital care and a neglect of those with severe mental disorders. Other criticisms include service fragmentation (often related to professional "turf" issues regarding who is most qualified to provide a service) and the reluctance to adopt innovative treatment strategies (Frank & Gaynor, 1994). The community mental health centers act had bypassed state governments, but by 1981 most control of programs was returned to the states in the form of block grants. The Omnibus Budget Reconciliation Act, a product of President Reagan's anti–federalist inclinations, expanded the state's power to make choices about how certain federal funds would be allocated (Rochefort & Logan, 1989). Community centers became more dependent on state funding policies. By 1991, 64% of center funds were coming from the states in the form of revenues, block grants, Medicaid, and user fees. These developments made the enhancement of services for persons with mental illness, with the hope of cost reductions, the top priority of state mental health directors (Ahr & Holcomb, 1985). Financial incentives were expected to reduce state mental hospital use, resulting in innovative case management programs at the local level.

MANAGED CARE AND CASE MANAGEMENT

Presently, health care costs are straining the budgets of both public and private payers. Between 1980 and 1996, total health care expenditures in the United States more than tripled, due to such factors as new technology, a sharp increase in the size of our aging population, and inflation (Davis, 1996). The costs of mental health services rose even more sharply. The causes for this include service utilization increases related to the reduced stigma of mental illness, a continued high use of hospital beds in the 1980s, and the legitimation of substance abuse as a mental disorder.

The concept of managed care, while not new, has advanced in response to this problem. Managed care can be defined as organizational arrangements that alter treatment decisions that would otherwise be made by clients or providers (Mechanic, Schlesinger, & McAlpine, 1995). Its goals are to contain costs, efficiently allocate resources, monitor care, and improve the quality of care. Managed care may take the following forms:

1. Health maintenance organizations (HMOs), which rely on capitation (fixed amounts to cover the health care of individuals) and other incentives to providers

2. Utilization review organizations, which review and monitor provider treatment plans against criteria defining appropriate care

3. Case management systems, in which a provider acts as a service broker and can authorize services

4. Preferred provider organizations (PPOs), networks of providers organized by third-party payers which offer consumers financial incentives for using members of those groups

Managed care organizations offering mental health services are known as behavioral health organizations.

All models of managed care seek to control *who* shall receive *what services* with *what frequency* over *what duration* from *what providers* (regarding discipline and experience) in pursuit of *what outcomes* (Sherman & Dahlquist, 1996). In an ideal situation, the client receives the best care for the fewest dollars. The most common method of allocating resources is the benefits plan. These generally include stricter limits on annual or lifetime expenditures on mental health care than would be enforced in traditional fee-for-service approaches. Mental health and substance abuse benefits are often specified and managed separately from general health benefits in employer-sponsored insurance. In these "carve-out" arrangements, firms contract with provider groups to administer services and manage costs.

The primary reason for the public mental health system's shift toward forms of managed care is Medicaid program cost increases. Since 1970, the Medicaid program has experienced tension between containing costs and promoting access to quality care. Although 16% of Medicaid recipients have physical or mental disabilities, they account for 32% of Medicaid costs. Elders and disabled people make up 30% of recipients and 70% of costs, with the largest proportion of funds going to nursing homes (Edgar, 1996). Certain underinsured groups might also benefit from managed care strategies. For example, persons with mental illness living in rural areas face difficulties in receiving adequate mental health care, as they have limited access to service providers. Health care reform may benefit these clients, as consolidating services within a benefits package might encourage their use of treatment alternatives to crisis care (Shelton & Frank, 1995).

Case management interventions with persons having mental illness can streamline service delivery in keeping with managed care objectives. That is, the modality can ration service while efficiently using formal and informal resources. Kanter (1996a) has argued that the case manager's involvement of significant others (friends and family) in a client's treatment is one way of reducing the amount of professional service that must be provided. He further demonstrates that the process of carefully coordinating intervention plans with clients and other professionals is attractive to managed care administrators, often reducing the projected costs of treatment (Kanter, 1996b). Managed care providers do *not* want long-term hospitalization, vague treatment plans, failure to use community support or recovery groups when warranted, and professionals who generate client complaints (Davis, 1996). All are major areas of case management activity.

Several studies have demonstrated that managed care or "capitated" case management programs can control health care costs for persons with mental illness. Being primarily interested in financial costs, these studies did not focus on quality of life issues. In a New York study, clients in one program used the psychiatric hospital less than a control group of clients receiving fee-for-service case management, with no observed differences in symptoms or functional status (Cole, Reed, Babigan, Brown, & Fray, 1994). Differences in case manager behavior in the two groups appeared to result from the flexibility in client care made possible by the capitation system. That system inspired case managers to develop new services, and case managers became more adept at crisis intervention. Program costs were reduced by 13.8% in year one and 14.5% in year two of the capitated program (Reed, Hennessy, Mitchell, & Babigian, 1994). In a New Hampshire study, fee-for-service case management was compared with an approach that combined capitation with fee-for-service schemes to evaluate the impact of flexibility on community-based treatment (Clark, Drake, McHugo, & Ackerson, 1995). Results indicated a shift from office to community-based practice in the capitation group, although total case management time provided by the groups did not differ. It was not apparent whether these changes had an impact on client outcomes. McCrone, Beecham, and Knapp (1994) compared case management costs with those in a more traditional community psychiatric nursing service in Britain. They identified short-term savings (on hospital care, community health and mental health services, education, law enforcement, social care services, employment services, and housing) with the innovative program, but these did not persist beyond 6 months, implying that the institution of new community services is not inexpensive.

Cost control is not synonymous with low-quality care, but the ability to provide high-quality service in a managed care context is another argument for skilled case management. Costs should not override the value of helping clients achieve a decent overall **quality of life,** which may be defined as one's life satisfaction, living situation, daily activities, family and social relations, financial status, occupation, safety, and physical and mental health status (Lehman, 1988). As noted earlier, in some managed care plans the case manager is not a qualified human services professional but is rather a service broker. This arrangement is quite different from case management practice as defined in this book, and it represents a potential danger to clients of health care that focuses primarily on cost containment. Incentives to contain costs might promote strategies focused on a "status quo" maintenance of clients rather than on their personal growth. Clinical case managers may be able to implement managed care plans that attend to a range of administrative *and* client goals so that chronically impaired clients judged to be "expensive" do not lose eligibility for some rehabilitation programs.

A federal policy goal states that Medicaid cost increases must be reduced without sacrificing access to care and quality services. Still, no one has provided a clear definition of what constitutes quality for managed care. Mental health advocacy groups are concerned that the design of public mental health services is driven by dollar costs rather than by indications of success. Because managed care is relatively new to this country, many questions remain unanswered about its impact on costs and quality of care. Research priorities in managed care for persons with mental illness must include the consequences for quality of care when external management limits overall service availability. Social workers, psychologists, and nurses should have input into the process, given their major roles as case management providers. Their level of input varies across firms.

Tentative solutions have been offered concerning the problems of providing care for persons with mental illness in a reformed health care system. Policy makers have consistently called for case management as a required service for certain populations, including persons with mental illness who receive public health insurance (Taube, Goldman, & Salkever, 1990). Others assert that there should be special managed care corporations for persons with mental illness that use a case management model of intervention (Scheffler, Grogan, Cuffel, & Penner, 1993). Eligibility for such an HMO would be determined by criteria including diagnosis, level of disability, and duration of illness. Case management, delivered individually or in teams, might successfully integrate services and provide effective continuity of care for the most disabled clients.

RESEARCH ON CASE MANAGEMENT RELATED TO POLICY OBJECTIVES

Given the enthusiasm for case management programs among policy makers, it is not surprising that much research for its evaluation has been sponsored by government and academic organizations. The focus of these evaluations is on the *process* of implementation and client *outcomes*. Appropriate research questions include the following (Drake & Burns, 1995):

1. What clients can be best served with case management?
2. How can its implementation be assessed?
3. Which of its many components are crucial?
4. How should it be modified for special populations?
5. Is it more effective than other models of service?
6. Can clients eventually move from more to less intensive forms of care?

This brief research review attempts to determine how well the goals of cost containment and service quality have been achieved.

Case managers must be aware that any of six value frames may drive the evaluation process (Kirkhart & Ruffolo, 1993). Researchers can give priority to the assessed *needs* of consumers, the expressed *wants* of consumers, *professional standards* of care as delineated by those associations, worker adherence to agency *program goals and objectives,* adherence to a *specified theoretical model* of practice, and practice *standards* of key individuals and organizations. The case manager must be clear about his or her own practice values in order to be guided by evaluation criteria that are most relevant to him or her.

Rosenblatt and Attkisson (1993) argue for a refinement of all outcome indicators in case management. Such concepts as safety, welfare, quality of life, and social functioning can be more systematically operationalized, even though some progress has been made in these areas. Measures of clinical status are comparatively well-developed. As outcome measures become standardized, the impact of case management can be understood more holistically.

Research on Implementation

Process evaluation is important because administrators need to understand that the case management service provided matches the prescription. Case managers do not always function the way program developers intend because of the unpredictable effects of the service environment on practice. Brekke and Test (1992) developed a model for measuring community support program implementation that includes seven sets of variables including client characteristics, service content, service amount, locus of treatment, characteristics of the service milieu, staffing patterns, and continuity of care. Teague, Drake, and Ackerson (1995) have used 13 criteria to evaluate community treatment team implementation within the two categories of treatment (continuity of staffing and responsibility, engagement, service, multidisciplinary orientation, and dual disorders treatment capacity) and teamwork mandate (caseload size, service intensity, team intervention approach, and work with support systems, among others). They use activity logs, agency and clinical records, interviews, and observations as data sources. Ford et al. (1995) performed a study of case management implementation in London, measuring the client's maintenance of contact with providers in health care, psychiatric care, residential care, out-patient counseling, and home assistance. All of these studies represent important advances in clarifying what components of a case management program should be evaluated.

Perhaps the most intensive evaluation of a community support system program to date was made through the Robert Wood Johnson Foundation Program on Chronic Mental Illness, done in nine major cities across the United States in the late 1980s (I was a case manager in one of these sites). The program's five goals were to ensure continuity of care, create a flexible financing system, develop a range of housing options, provide a range of psychosocial and vocational rehabilitation supports, and improve client outcomes (Morrissey et al., 1994). This was primarily a service system intervention, focused on the development of local mental health authority.

The research team concluded that a local authority can be created, but it is more difficult to reorganize a service system. The provision and continuity of case management improved in all sites, but it was more difficult to document improvements in client outcomes (Lehman, Postrado, Roth, McNary, & Goldman, 1994). Those outcomes included general life satisfaction, satisfaction with living situation, hospitalization days, symptoms of mental illness, and reported levels of functioning. The researchers concluded that structural change reforming mental health services for persons with serious mental illness is not sufficient to produce improvements in quality of life (Goldman, Morrissey, & Ridgely, 1994). That is, no direct correlation exists between case management program implementation and improved quality of life outcomes. Devising strategies for helping clients achieve their goals requires ongoing financial investments from administrators and policy makers, as well as the creative ideas of skilled case managers.

Research on Client Outcomes

Research on the effects of case management on client outcomes dates back to the early 1980s. Initially, case management services were compared with "traditional," or office-bound, interventions. By 1990, the comparative impact of types of case management programs became a focus of study. In all instances, results have been mixed for a variety of outcome indicators such as costs, use of hospitals, client vocational status, and life satisfaction. These results do not necessarily reflect on the value of case management; rather, researchers need to refine methodologies and distinguish between the activities of case managers in different sites.

Scott and Dixon (1995) reviewed 13 major studies conducted between 1981 and 1994 and concluded that assertive community treatment clearly reduces the rates and duration of hospitalization, and may be less costly over the short-term than other service approaches. These findings support some important goals of case management practice. Still, client improvements in community functioning and resource access were not achieved in all studies, and program costs seem to increase in the long run. The authors note that research findings across sites may differ because programs are modified when transferred from one setting to another. One theme across studies is that, with new programs, the amount of time required to make significant differences in the lives of clients may be two years or more. The authors recommend that family well-being be adopted as an additional outcome indicator, and that researchers include the perspectives of the client, family, and case manager as data sources.

Rubin (1992b) reviewed eight major studies on case management effectiveness performed between 1987 and 1991. He concluded that there is not yet evidence that *particular* case management models are effective in comparison with each other. He summarized mixed results regarding quality of life, social functioning, and cost-effectiveness issues that acknowledged the difficulty of implementing controlled research designs and sorting out the impact of intervening variables. He suggested that methodologies should use blind ratings and establish clearer distinctions between case management practice and the programs containing it. These strategies are costly, but they are beginning to appear.

Draine (1997) reviewed eight experimental case management studies conducted between 1981 and 1993. He points out that while early studies of case management focused on broad models of community care, research over time has focused on narrower applications of the modality, including those for special populations. This suggests that case management has advanced from a generic approach to a range of different applications to special client circumstances. The author also makes the important point that the primary service mechanism should be evaluated (specific goals of the intervention), rather than global client outcomes.

Several case management models have been used effectively in interventions for persons who have mental illness and who are without a home. In the NIMH McKinney Project, 894 homeless mentally ill adults in four cities were exposed to rehabilitation, assertive community treatment, or intensive case management services, depending on which model was offered in each city. Though the specific intervention models differed, all of them used teams of case managers and assertive outreach. The project report noted a 47.5% increase in individuals living in community housing among those who received the intervention. Additionally, 78% of clients had been housed in permanent sites by the end of the program (Shern et al., 1997). While the focus of this study was on housing outcomes for those who were homeless, the multi-site project did use a randomized experimental design in concluding that the services were effective. As with other studies of case management, residential stability, independence, and daily life functions seemed to improve with service provision.

Mature programs have only recently become available for evaluation (Taube, Morlock, Burns, and Santos,1990). Jerrell and Ridgely (1995) compared the effectiveness of a twelve-step, behavioral skills management program with a case management program for persons with the dual disorders of mental illness and substance abuse. While clients in the behavioral skills intervention functioned best overall, both programs offered useful interventions and could be effectively combined. Sands and Cnaan (1994) compared the effectiveness of community treatment and intensive case management teams with clients in urban Pennsylvania. They found few significant differences in outcomes, but noted that community tenure for clients can be maintained with differential levels of service intensity. Marcias, Kinney, Farley, Jackson, and Vos (1994) studied the combined effects of case management and psychosocial rehabilitation services (including scheduled daily activities, staff assistance with social activities, and counseling) to case management alone, and found that the experimental group demonstrated better mental and physical health, fewer mood or thought problems, a higher sense of well-being, and less family burden. The two types of service were mutually supportive. Walsh (1994a) compared two variations of a single case management program (in one clients received group interventions, and in the other they received individual interventions) with regard to natural social support outcomes. I found that the clients receiving group interventions developed more extensive friendship networks.

One gap in research is that case manager effects, rather than program effects, on client outcomes have rarely been studied. Because case management was initially conceptualized rather generically, and is often delivered in teams, it is not often considered that differences in outcomes may be due to individual case manager skills. The work of Ryan, Sherman, and Judd (1994) is one exception to this trend. They studied the implementation of three community support programs and found that, while all were effective, case managers themselves significantly influenced client outcomes when the type of service was controlled. This book is an effort to promote individual case manager skill development as a priority in mental health services provision. I hope that research in this area becomes more common.

Several conclusions can be drawn from the above studies. First, quality of life must be emphasized in research as service providers gear their programs toward reducing service costs in accordance with public policy mandates. This topic merits further inquiry to test the philosophy of managed care and determine the types of community programming that will enhance client well-being. Second, the independent variable of case management is difficult to define clearly enough to make comparisons across studies. Given the reliance on links with other service providers, the case managers, the programs, or the adjunctive community services might be evaluated. Finally, researchers have thus far overlooked the impact of individual case manager skill on service outcomes. Much can be learned about the specific skills which case managers need to perform their jobs well. Of course, this is true of most direct practice modalities.

SUMMARY

Public policy in health care is always driven by the two concerns of providing quality care and keeping costs manageable. In all areas of health care, social policy in the 1960s and 1970s focused on client access to services through such federal programs as the Community Mental Health Centers Act, Medicaid, and Medicare. In the 1980s and 1990s, public policy became more intent on controlling the costs of care. Case management as an intervention is supported by agency and government policy makers because of its potential to control the spiraling costs of mental health care while helping clients make satisfactory adjustments to community life.

Many health care professionals are antagonistic toward the managed care philosophy of cost containment (McClelland, 1996), and there are certainly serious risks to clients when this emphasis overrides quality of life concerns. Still, it seems that managed care in one form or another is here to stay. Clinical case managers must work proactively within this environment, as represented by agency demands for effective and efficient service, to demonstrate that their modality is indeed effective. There is always policy disagreement about what constitutes good quality care, and compromises will always be necessary regarding the public financial support of community care.

A key to attracting administrative support from behavioral health organizations is for case managers to construct clear clinical treatment plans with clients that include focused, realistic, and measurable goals, and interventions that demonstrate attention to efficiency even in a context of long-term service provision. One example of such planning is included in Chapter 6. But always, in their roles as advocates, case managers need to focus on client *wants* and *needs* in evaluating the adequacy of case management services and programs, as these reflect the primary values of human service providers.

PART II

A Theoretical Base
for Clinical
Case Management

3

Symbolic Interactionism and Relationship Development

"How can you spend a whole hour talking to psychotic clients? Nothing they say makes sense." — A clinical psychologist to her case manager colleague during group supervision at a mental health agency.

"I told my psychiatrist that I hear the voice of God at night, and that it soothes me. But she said it wasn't God. She said it was my epiphenomenon." — A woman with schizophrenia to her case manager.

I emphasized in Chapter 1 that effective intervention depends on the engagement of the client in a working relationship. In this chapter I place relationship development into a theoretical context of symbolic interactionism. This theory is highly compatible with the person-in-environment perspective of this book, and it offers much to guide the case manager in connecting with inarticulate or verbally inaccessible clients. I pay particular attention to the concepts of the **definition of the situation, symbolization,** and the **sense of self.** As a theory of human behavior, symbolic interactionism is applicable across practice settings, but it has particular relevance for work with clients who have mental illness. This theory undergirds all the intervention strategies described in Parts Three through Five of this book. I close this chapter with an overview of the ego psychology and cognitive/behavioral practice theories, which can provide case managers with a basis for developing those intervention strategies.

AN OVERVIEW OF SYMBOLIC INTERACTIONISM

Symbolic interactionism seeks a resolution to the dualism of personality and environment by viewing them as mutually developing and interacting (Blumer, 1969; Gergen, 1985; Mead, 1934). Through social interaction, our interpretations of **symbols** (abstract objects and ideas shared by members of a culture), and our selective attention to environmental stimuli, we acquire a sense of meaning about ourselves and the world. The "mind" represents our capacity to respond subjectively to environmental input through conceptualizing, defining, symbolizing, valuing, and reflecting. These activities represent a creative and selective process of construction. Our sense of self develops from our perceptions of how others perceive us. That is, we define ourselves through the attitudes and behaviors of others toward us, and ultimately from the standards of the society. We may experience changes in our sense of self from the changing expectations of others about how we should behave, think, or feel. This role-taking process is somewhat at odds with the psychological perspective of internally-based motivation.

The medium through which we interact is language. Words are symbols, and language is a product of the shared understandings of people within a culture. Social interaction involves an ongoing negotiation of the meanings of terms among persons. As communicators we must share an understanding of the cultural norms and rules governing personal conduct in order for our interactions to proceed coherently. Our consciousness becomes possible through language as we learn to talk to ourselves, or think, using language symbols (Wood & Wardell, 1983).

In summary, symbolic interactionism suggests that socialization is a highly dynamic process throughout our lives, which consists of our creating meanings, understandings, and definitions of situations through social interaction (Mortimer & Simmons, 1978). We cope, adapt, and change as we bring structure to ambiguous social situations in order to solve problems and meet challenges. To summarize the key points of the theory (Charon, 1992):

1. The basic unit of analysis in human behavior is not the individual, but the social act, which requires at least two individuals.

2. Our capacity for *thought* is shaped by social interaction.

3. In social interaction, we learn the meanings of *gestures* and social *symbols* that allow us to develop the capacity for thought. Symbolization is a process of naming social objects and, through agreement with others, having them stand for something else.

4. Language is the primary means by which symbols are conveyed. Language use is not merely the exchange of concrete terms, but a form of constructive human activity.

5. We are capable of changing the meanings of social acts and symbols through our changing *definitions* (understandings) *of situations.* A **situation** is any assembly of people incorporating role expectations and joint activities. Definitions do not arise from any objective criteria, but from each participant's past experiences in similar situations.

6. We can modify our understandings of situations and ourselves because of the ability to think, which is defined as talking to oneself. This allows us to examine possible courses of action, assess relative advantages and disadvantages, and make choices.

7. The ***sense of self*** arises out of social interaction, based on our internalizations of how others perceive us.

SYMBOLIC INTERACTIONISM AND MENTAL ILLNESS

Serious mental illnesses such as schizophrenia and bipolar disorder are at least in part biologically based (Goodwin & Jamison, 1990; Gottesman, 1991), and persons whose disorders feature psychotic symptoms lose some of their capacity for communication due to cognitive impairment or mood *lability.* They may experience hallucinations or delusions, or become socially withdrawn as a result of high levels of anxiety or a loss of motivation to maintain personal attachments. Disorders of thought can reduce one's ability to generate the focused thought processes required to manage social situations. From a symbolic interactionist perspective, the capacity to utilize symbols, or shared social meanings, is restricted. References to cultural symbols are distorted; the meanings given to them by a majority of others is lost, and the person's capacity for human relationship is thus diminished. Impairments in thought or mood result in *new* definitions of social situations, but many of these are idiosyncratic. Persons are no longer consistently guided by a capacity to understand what is expected of them by others.

This process of disengagement by the person with mental illness occurs in stages (Lantz & Belcher, 1988). First, with the onset of symptoms, the person becomes disassociated from others involuntarily, as he or she can no longer symbolize the external world as before. The person defends against these feelings of detachment by creating new, idiosyncratic symbols based on his or her private perceptions. These symbols are not shared, however, and the person experiences rejection because of other's inability to relate to him or her. By definition, "symbolic interaction" without reference to shared symbols is not possible. The person enters a state of isolation, using private symbols to resist complete disconnection from the social environment and entering a symbolic world not shared by the larger society, without stable reference points as a basis for a sense of self. This loss of symbolic ability is never total, however, as it ebbs and flows with the symptoms of the illness. Careful efforts by others, including the case manager, to negotiate shared symbolic meanings with the client through their relationship can increase the client's motivation to reconnect with the social world.

Despite developments in public awareness of biological factors in mental illness, many persons still view it as a personal shortcoming (Gerhart, 1990) and therefore deviant. The deviance label may be mitigated if the individual cooperates with treatment in accordance with accepted medical models of practice, which include medication and other clinical treatments (Anderson, 1994). While these are often helpful for the client's improved coping and adaptation, they may be limiting if they deny the client's need to maintain a view of reality which, however distorted, represents his or her personal experiences. In other words, interventions that run counter to the client's view of the world detract from the potential for case managers and others to deal constructively with his or her essential concerns.

SYMBOLIC INTERACTIONISM
IN CLINICAL PRACTICE

Symbolic interactionism is not a practice theory, but it emphasizes attention to social role-taking to enhance a case manager's sensitivity to the dynamics of interactions with clients, and thus develop positive working relationships. Helping a client improve his or her ability to bond facilitates social adaptation if the client can learn to generalize that ability. Further, the case manager's modeling of appropriate interaction may teach the client a new way of problem solving, to learn by example (Balancio, 1994).

Symbolic interactionism suggests that case managers face routine challenges interacting with all new clients. Social interaction proceeds on the basis of each person's definition of his or her situation. The way a case manager begins work with a new client is based on his or her experiences of beginnings with clients. The worker expects, or hopes for, full disclosure of problems or feelings. This may or may not match the expectations of the client, who is new to the setting and perhaps has had different experiences with helping professionals. The client might think the situation requires acquiescence and avoidance of disclosing any negative attitudes and feelings. The appropriateness of one's definition is either confirmed or refuted as the situation unfolds and the parties react to one another. The case manager's encouragement of the client's disclosure, in an atmosphere of trust, may convince the client to redefine the situation and decide to share his or her honest thoughts and feelings.

When persons in a situation possess different amounts of social power, the role-taking behavior of the person with lesser power will be constrained. The case manager's definition of the situation when meeting a new client may be more influential than that of the client in determining how the relationship unfolds, because the worker is sanctioned as a professional expert who controls the client's access to resources. Case managers exert a kind of power over their clients that may have negative consequences as they use diagnostic labels, most of which imply deficits, in assessing client behavior. The concept of empowerment has become important in recent years in response to this problem, as case managers strive to promote practice principles that foster partnerships with clients. Framing a client's problems in ways that are not stigmatizing— that is, referring to diagnostic labels as little as possible—promotes the client's desire to form a partnership for problem-solving.

Symbolic interactionism has not yet been widely applied to case management or other mental health practice modalities because it does not include clear prescriptions for intervention beyond relationship development and maintenance. Still, some authors have noted its relevance for practice. Hollis (1964) uses role concepts to describe how the client's assumptions about the extent of the professional's role in the relationship can influence intervention either positively or negatively. Others note that the lack of congruence between the client's and worker's understanding of mutual roles is a significant factor in premature termination of treatment (Maluccio, 1979). Fischer (1978) demonstrates that positive clinical outcomes are enhanced when initial client/worker contacts are focused on clearly structuring their mutual expectations. The importance of "role induction" procedures has prompted some authors to recommend integrating educational activities about intervention in the engagement stage (Germain & Gitterman, 1996). Law (1984) notes that the worker's concepts of health and illness are strongly connected to prevailing social symbols of deviance and disease. He advocates that practitioners take a contextual (social) rather than medical approach to problems as a means of facilitating trust in the worker–client relationship.

Several authors from sociology have used symbolic interactionism to understand the challenges faced by persons with mental illness as they try to become re-integrated into "normal" society. These perspectives dramatize the importance of the worker's relationship management. Goffman (1961) describes the unintentional client devaluation by staff in the mental hospital. When hospitalized, clients become labeled as deviant because mental illness and incarceration are both negative concepts. They subsequently experience restrictions on self-determination and autonomy, along with loss of important roles, reinforcing negative aspects of the client role. Goffman (1963) also writes that all deviant persons, including clients who live in the community, experience stigmatization that is both demoralizing and difficult to overcome. The value of Goffman's work is its demonstration of how stigma negatively affects many clients' willingness to participate in clinical interventions. The case manager wanting to oppose stigma must realize that his or her employing agency may include polices and procedures that perpetuate this problem, perhaps in subtle ways.

Scheff (1984) also writes extensively about mental illness from the deviance perspective. He states that symptoms of mental illness can be understood as violations of social norms and that their meaning to others might be a factor in determining the outcomes of professional assessment. Clinical workers are trained to fit client behaviors into socially constructed diagnostic categories of mental illness based in part on empirical knowledge but also influenced by social values (as with the classification of homosexuality as a mental disorder until 1980). Once labeled, clients may become frustrated in their attempts to return to conventional social roles, as others in society (friends, family, and employers, and even case managers) may be reluctant to give up their negative classifications.

Strategies exist for addressing these problems in clinical intervention. Discharge from a psychiatric hospital (or by extension, a crisis unit or supervised living facility) should be understood by the case manager as a transitional crisis when a client's relationships to others, and sense of self, are disrupted. In managing this transition, the worker can attend to the client's loss of meanings (based on confinement or restricted social interaction) and help develop new purposes and goals through a series of guided interactions which strengthen the sense of self (Ramon, 1989–90). As a preventive measure the case manager can help the client understand the changing role expectations of others so that he or she will be prepared to meet and perhaps exceed them. As another strategy for clients in transition, workers can incorporate "status elevation" ceremonies through social reintegration activities (Rouse, 1996). The case manager can organize celebrations of the client's rites of passage, framed in positive terms, as a means of preparing him or her for new social positions.

A FRAMEWORK FOR DIRECT PRACTICE

This section consists of guidelines for relationship development with clients having serious mental illness. I reintroduce three major concepts from symbolic interactionism with direct implications for the engagement and early intervention processes.

Definition of the Situation

Definitions of situations include a negotiated awareness of the expected roles of oneself and others. Persons with mental illness and those they encounter in everyday life, including family, friends, and employers, often hold different definitions of their shared situations. For example, a symptomatic client who begins a job may define the situation primarily as one in which he or she must manage the anxiety associated with hostile, intrusive hallucinatory voices believed to come from co-workers, rather than one where certain levels of productivity through cooperation with co-workers must be maintained. If these differences are not mediated in some way, that job opportunity will fail.

Relationship development consists not only of the beginning stage of interaction, but also of a series of situations requiring ongoing negotiation of meaning from start to finish. The case manager should never assume that the client perceives the nature, purpose, and role-related behaviors of the situation as the worker does. "Starting where the client is at" is a familiar phrase in the human services literature, implying that the worker needs to appreciate the perspective of the client in beginning the problem-solving process. From a symbolic interactionist perspective, the appropriate phrase might be "start where the worker and client are, and negotiate adjustments continuously."

Case managers strive to promote self-determination and to honor the dignity of their clients. However, workers and clients have unequal power in the relationship. Case managers possess resources that clients want but cannot access on their own. In an effort to receive resources such as medication, public subsidies, housing, and clubhouse programs, clients might define the clinical situation as one in which they need to be cooperative and somewhat ingratiating rather than completely honest. The client might behave in ways that he or she feels is expected or, in other words, adopt the case manager's definition of the situation and play an appropriate role in that context. The client might accept the worker's diagnostic labels and conceptualization of problems and goals whether or not he or she agrees with them. Without addressing power imbalances, talking about worker and agency expectations, or encouraging the client's assertive participation in the treatment process, the case manager may never learn what is most central to the client's life at a given moment. The worker must actively address the nature of the worker/client relationship and the range of appropriate roles for each person to have an unconstrained relationship with the client. The worker and client will be more likely to come to a mutual understanding of roles, which will need to be reviewed continuously as situations and the relationship changes.

Case Illustration: Sarah   Sarah, who was quoted at the beginning of this chapter, defined the relationship with her doctor as including discussions about symptoms and general life experiences, not merely deciding on appropriate medications. She thought the doctor would be interested in learning how she was affected by her inner experiences. The physician's perception was different; she wanted to focus only on eradicating symptoms. Over time, Sarah adjusted her definition of the situation to mesh with the physician's, because she perceived the physician as being the more powerful figure and as having something that Sarah wanted (medication). Sarah eventually stopped talking about her self-esteem and her reactions to her hallucinations. Her definition of the situation narrowed to include medication negotiations only. As a result of the physician's failing to monitor the relationship more openly and to recognize the joint role they played in developing its parameters, Sarah withdrew from active participation in their meetings. She received appropriate medications, but the process might have had a partially negative outcome for her, not only with this physician but also with subsequent treaters, whom Sarah might also assume to be uninterested in her emotional experiences.

Case Illustration: Laura   Though Laura had been released from a psychiatric hospital 45 days into her 90-day probation, she was legally required to comply with treatment at the community mental health facility until her probation ended. She was a 40-year-old single, Mexican-American woman with a degree in law and had a diagnosis of paranoid disorder. Laura's probation was the result of her becoming delusional and hypomanic, which severely disrupted her ability to work. She needed to be forcibly taken to the hospital after a series of confrontations with neighbors and police officers. Laura, clearly a reluctant client, was outraged that she was expected to take medications. She was convinced of the reality of her perceptions and felt that others were her intellectual inferiors or even unwitting actors in government conspiracies against her. She made it clear that she came to the agency only because of the legal mandate. Further, she warned agency staff to do nothing that might become the basis for a later lawsuit.

Laura's definition of the situation included forced compliance with an unjust legal mandate. In that context she need only show up at her scheduled meetings and accept the injectable medication for the remaining 45 days. She expected her case manager to try to convince her of the need for treatment, as others at the hospital had done. She also expected to be underwhelmed by his range of concerns for her. Clearly, for her, the issue of unequal power was a major constraint to the development of a cooperative relationship. It required that she subject herself to the will of the worker and agency and prevented her from acting as she felt inclined.

Nevertheless, within a month Laura and her case manager developed a shared definition of their relationship. Understanding Laura's attitude about the agency, the worker initiated biweekly home visits to put himself on her "turf" and expand her control of the situation. He avoided participating in her medication appointments so as not to become involved in those power issues (Laura and the physician initially had strong differences of opinion about medication options). He let her know that she needn't do anything at all for him but that as long as they were together she might consider talking with him about some of her frustrations. The case manager set out to learn about her career and travels. He listened attentively to her descriptions of persecution by others, neither agreeing nor disagreeing about their truth. He learned of her family relationships and how she planned to look for work after the probation. Laura began to feel that the case manager sincerely wanted to understand her and that he had no intentions of applying his power for coercive interventions, such as the referrals for vocational counseling that others had made. Laura, who had few friends, came to view the case manager as one. He told her that when her probationary period ended he would report her compliance with the mandates to the authorities.

In his role, the case manager became a trusted confidant without being deceitful, and he tried with some success to expand Laura's range of interactions with him. The client altered her definition of the situation based on his behaviors and decided to stay involved with the agency beyond her probationary period. While still paranoid, Laura was able to function well within a limited social and occupational range. She used the case manager as a sounding board for feedback when considering major life decisions, and continued to take medications, which she perceived as being prescribed to help her rest at night.

Symbols

Symbols are by definition abstract, thus presenting problems for the case manager in relationship development with clients. Every relationship exists within a symbolic frame of reference, including shared concepts, words, and behaviors that make private experiences mutually understandable. Persons with cognitive impairments cannot engage in abstract thinking or manipulate conventional symbols as consistently as they could before the illness. Clients tend to replace conventional symptoms with private ones, so coming to know how clients use everyday words and concepts may become a challenge for the case manager. Generally, the worker should relate to the client with a concrete vocabulary and a minimum of abstract ideas. The worker needs to figure out the client's personal symbol system and, rather than dismiss it as bizarre, respect it as representative of the client's reality.

Case Illustration: Rachel   Rachel was a 35-year-old single female living alone with a long-standing diagnosis of schizophrenia. She was tormented by auditory hallucinations in which persons from her family, as well as strangers, screamed at and degraded her for being worthless. She heard the voices of angels each night, assuring her that she would survive all of her suffering and that she should not despair. Rachel also believed that she was the spiritual caretaker for her elderly parents, who lived in another state, and by concentrating on their well-being she maintained a purpose in life. Finally, she took pride in her Jewish culture and ancestry, believing that she was a direct descendant of the biblical Rachel. Clearly, the client was religiously preoccupied and, in fact, had extensive knowledge of Jewish and Christian religious studies.

Rachel's delusions and hallucinations were infused with a private symbolism. Her interpersonal anxieties were so intense that she could not sustain ongoing social interaction, but she strove in these other ways to maintain connections with her family. Through her delusions she was making efforts to find personal meaning, reassurance that hers was a worthy life. Most mental health workers categorized her perceptions as merely symptoms and discouraged her from talking about them. They reasoned that only her "rational" thinking should be positively reinforced. This approach was demeaning to the client and prevented her from entrusting to others the feelings she experienced along with her perceptions.

Rachel and her case manager met every two weeks. She initially tested him by describing some of her experiences and gauging his reactions. When he did not judge her but expressed interest and asked for more details, she shared her inner world more thoroughly. She asked about the case manager's own spiritual views, which he shared cautiously and only after he became convinced that she would not incorporate these into her delusional system. When Rachel talked about her perceptions, he focused on the feelings associated with them, again neither agreeing nor disagreeing that they were real. He understood, of course, that she would function much better in society if she had more conventional perceptions of the external world, but he also affirmed the positive intent (though not the reality) of her efforts to care for others through thought projection. Over the next several years he worked to eliminate her symptoms and anxieties with medication monitoring and gradually introducing several social rehabilitation activities. At the same time he preserved an interpersonal climate in which her issues about connection, isolation, and securing purpose could be discussed. These were growth issues for Rachel, and she and the case manager did come to share a symbol system, or shared understanding, regarding them.

Development of the Self

The case manager can have impact on a client's sense of self even if the client has other acquaintances (family and friends) with lasting significance in his or her life. The worker can become a significant other and, by guidance and example, help the client become involved in a community of supportive individuals who might further strengthen the self-concept. The client might perceive the case manager's positive feedback and role expectations as reflecting his or her potential for growth. The worker can show the client that he or she is valued in spite of his or her shortcomings, and can demonstrate faith in the client's capacity to achieve goals. This might raise the client's self-esteem and motivation to change. The case manager's modeling might help the client learn how to fulfill certain social roles that might bolster the client's social identity. The client's sense of being competent in specific situations might become stronger, and a sense of his or her role as a member of a group can also be enhanced through positive **mirroring** (reflecting strengths and competence) by the case manager. Symbolic interactionism suggests that though personality patterns do persist, the self can change more readily than some theories, such as **object relations,** tend to assume (Goldstein, 1995).

Case Illustration: Roger   Roger was a 30-year-old single white male living in a small house with his aging parents. They were a highly enmeshed trio; none had regular contact with any other people. Roger was diagnosed with a schizotypal personality disorder. He was grossly overweight, socially anxious, and suspicious of others; he had bizarre ideas, including *magical thinking.* He did not experience overt psychotic symptoms and did not take medication.

Roger's sense of self derived from his constricted family environment, where he received much negative feedback. He accurately perceived that he was intelligent, but otherwise he had low self-esteem. He was his mother's sole close companion. His father resented him for this and also for never measuring up to expectations of being a good student or athlete. Roger spent his time watching television, playing the guitar, cooking dinner with his mother, and listening to music. His significant others included his parents and various media personalities with whom he identified through television. He had no contact with peers who might give additional input into his self-concept and esteem.

Roger came to counseling because it was time away from home in an otherwise monotonous day. His earlier clinical workers generally wanted him to set rather ambitious goals, such as schooling, jobs, and social risk-taking, which Roger was afraid to pursue. His lack of motivation in these areas was based on a severe sense of inadequacy. Roger maintained the facade of an interested, cooperative client but in the end did not follow though with many of the short-term objectives leading to his ambivalently formulated goals. Sometimes this resulted in his dismissal from mental health treatment programs, further reinforcing his negative self-concept.

Fortunately, Roger and his case manager shared many interests in music and entertainment. They talked a great deal about those topics, even though they had little to do with personal change on Roger's part and might be considered superficial to some clinicians. The worker was nondirective, affirming, and sincerely encouraged Roger's interests. He did introduce behavioral goals, but these were quite modest (including, for example, walking to his sessions instead of his mother's driving him). After three months, the case manager became a significant other in Roger's life—a major influence, in fact, considering the limited range of his other interactions. Roger noticed that the case manager enjoyed his off-beat observations about society, his sense of humor, and his intelligence. Roger came to view himself more as the worker viewed him, as a man with qualities who could achieve some life satisfaction if he made gradual movements into the world beyond his household. The case manager reframed Roger's self concept from that of an enmeshed son to a person with strengths on whom his parents were highly reliant. Roger could remain with his family but also pursue interests outside the house, if he chose to do so. The worker affirmed Roger's distinct personality apart from the relationship with his parents. Roger made no drastic changes in his life but eventually got out of the house more often for solitary activities such as movies and shopping. His only regular social activity was participation in a "classic movies" club, through which he attended special screenings of motion pictures and participated in discussions about them.

OBJECTIVE MEASURES OF THE
WORKER-CLIENT RELATIONSHIP

There are a variety of instruments that attempt to measure worker-client relationships, but I do not generally recommend any of them to clinical case managers. They have not been developed and tested with clients having serious mental illness, and these clients may experience use of such instruments as intrusive and threatening, particularly in the early stages of work. I will, however, describe several instruments to highlight aspects of the relationship that they identify as most important.

The *Client Attachment to Therapist Scale* (Mallinckrodt, Gantt, & Coble, 1995) includes 36 items for client response on a 6-point Likert scale. It determines the extent of clients' sense of security, and realistic assumptions about the boundaries of the relationship; it also indicates any client concerns about the worker as potentially disapproving or rejecting. Horvath's (1994a) *Working Alliance Inventory* includes 36 items scored on a 7-point scale. Clients and workers fill it in at various intervals, and it provides comparison data on each person's perceptions of their bonding, goal-orientation, and task focus. The *Therapeutic Alliance Rating System* (Marmar, Horowitz, Weiss, & Marzialli, 1986) is a 42-item scale that focuses globally on the affective and attitudinal aspects of the worker-client relationship. It yields four subscores on the client's and worker's positive and negative contributions to the status of the relationship. The *Structured Analysis of Social Behavior* (Benjamin, Foster, Roberto, & Estroff, 1986), though quite elaborate in requiring observations and ratings of interactions by judges, assesses both the client's and worker's focus on the self (as hostile vs. friendly and with assertive vs. compliant behavior) and on the other (as hostile vs. friendly and with freeing vs. controlling attitudes). Within these domains 16 relationship styles can be articulated.

THEORIES FOR PRACTICE

I have argued in this chapter that symbolic interactionism can provide the case manager with guidelines for establishing productive relationships with clients. The clinical partnership is therapeutic in itself, but it must develop in order for other interventions to occur effectively. Other theoretical frameworks are necessary to help the case manager organize a full range of task-focused interventions with clients over time. The two highlighted in this and the remaining chapters of this book are ego psychology and cognitive/behavioral theory.

Ego Psychology

The **ego** can be understood as the part of personality, present from birth, that negotiates between our internal needs and the outside world. It is the source of our attention, concentration, learning, memory, will, and perception. Ego psychology focuses attention on ego development and adaptation throughout the life cycle. It attends to the influence of one's past and present transactions with the environment on the quality of present functioning. Ego psychology acknowledges the influence of unconscious thought processes on behavior, but the autonomy of the ego, and thus conscious thought processes, receives greater emphasis (Goldstein, 1995). Interventions based on this theory are strengths-based, as all people are assumed to possess a basic drive to mastery and competence. The case manager's ego assessment attends to the possibility of conflicts within the client or conflicts between the client and external world. Stress may result from excess environmental demands (an external focus), inadequate ego functioning (an internal focus), or reactions to normal life transitions (for example, age transitions, work transitions, parenthood, separation from significant others, and reactions to health problems). Ego psychology maintains a balanced perspective on the influences of thought and emotion on social functioning.

From this theoretical perspective the case manager assesses all of a client's ego functions including reality testing, mastery and competence, control of drives, appropriate use of defenses, and the quality of one's judgment in decision making. Change is manifested in the client's ability to achieve greater mastery of challenges, crises, and life transitions. The goal of intervention is to improve the fit between environmental conditions and the client's capabilities for coping and adaptation. The client is helped to learn new problem-solving and coping skills, to manage conflicts more effectively, and to achieve insight. In the context of mental illness, insight means that the client understands that changes in symptoms indicate he or she is under stress and reacting to it. Logical, purposeful action should follow from insight. The case manager/client relationship is founded on the worker's provision of empathy, support, and action-oriented techniques to repair problems and build strengths. Ego psychology also encourages the case manager and client to reflect on their reactions to each other, as their relationship is a basis for understanding the client's management of other significant relationships.

Cognitive/Behavioral Theory

Cognitive theory considers conscious thinking to be the basis for most of our behavior and emotions (Granvold, 1994). Though some mental processes might be categorized as unconscious, they can be brought to the surface with reflection or probing. Cognitive theory postulates that we develop mental **schema,** or general information-processing rules that develop as enduring concepts from past experiences. These form the basis for our screening, discriminating, and coding of stimuli, our categorizing and evaluating experiences, and our judgment. We are "rational" to the extent that we base our perceptions on available environmental evidence rather than relying solely on our preconceived notions of the external world. *Emotions* are defined as the physiological responses which follow our cognitive evaluations of input. That is, thoughts produce emotions.

As our schema assesses new situations by applying previously internalized knowledge, we develop habits of thinking. So long as our cognitive style helps us to achieve our goals, our thinking is considered healthy. However, our thinking patterns can feature distortions based on our beliefs, values, and prior experiences, which may prompt us to dismiss relevant environmental information. These "cognitive errors" may lead to our experience of psychological distress. Distorted thinking patterns include absolutist thinking (the tendency to view experiences as all good or all bad), overgeneralization (deficiencies in one area of life necessarily imply deficiencies in other areas), selective abstraction (focusing only on the negative aspects of a situation), arbitrary inference (reaching negative conclusions about a situation with insufficient evidence), personalization (accepting blame for negative events without sufficient evidence), and the magnification or minimization of problems.

Cognitive theory assumes that some of our beliefs are distorted, but it also assumes that the human potential to correct these beliefs in light of contradictory evidence is great. In clinical assessment, the case manager must assess the client's schema, identify any faulty thinking patterns, and consider the evidence supporting a client's beliefs in judging their validity. Change is promoted through cognitive restructuring, problem solving, self-instruction training, and stress prevention activities. The clinical case manager promotes the client's modification of thinking habits to achieve better pursuit and attainment of goals, and helps the client build problem-solving skills through rehearsal and application in the client's social environment. The worker helps the client adjust his or her expectations of negative outcomes in important life situations and modify thought patterns through which attitudes and feelings are formed. If the process is successful, the client will also experience more positive emotions. Mental illness is characterized in part by biologically-based cognitive and mood deficits, but any client's habits of thinking can be adjusted to enhance coping capacity (Bellack, 1992).

In **behavior theory** our thoughts and emotions are conceptualized as behaviors subject to positive or negative reinforcements (Gambrill, 1994). The most essential intervention is the development of new and desirable client behaviors by rearranging reinforcers; then the worker evaluates the scope of that change by concrete measurement of behavioral responses. The worker facilitates the client's achievement of goals through such interventions as relaxation training, assertiveness training, self-control of reactions to challenging stimuli, behavioral rehearsal, gradual exposure to feared situations, and systematic desensitization of negative reactions to feared situations. These modalities lend themselves to ongoing evaluation because of their emphasis on concrete behavioral outcomes.

The theoretical approaches outlined above can be used in conjunction with one another. Ego psychology can assist the worker in a process of holistic assessment and in understanding the dynamics of the client's relationship patterns.

Actual interventions derived from this assessment may incorporate cognitive-behavioral approaches. Concepts from cognitive theory are action-oriented and highly compatible with the theory of symbolic interactionism. Throughout this book, interventions for the clinical case manager will derive from these three theoretical perspectives.

SUMMARY

Symbolic interactionism, a theory of human behavior rooted in sociology, views relationships as processes in which social symbols are developed and shared, and in which each person's sense of self is affected by the role expectations of others. A client's behavior can never be considered "irrational" in an objective sense because it is always consistent with what the client understands about him or herself and the environment at that time. Through their relationship, the case manager can help the cognitively impaired client comprehend the environment from a perspective that is shared by others. This theory does not suggest specific techniques for intervention, but it provides a basis for applying a range of interventions. By attending to mutual definitions of clinical situations, use of a shared vocabulary and set of symbols, and the impact of interactions on the always-developing sense of self, case managers can help clients make connections with others and work to achieve their most personal goals. The ego psychology and cognitive/behavioral practice theories provide perspectives from which case managers can develop specific task-focused interventions for goal attainment.

4

Social Support Theory
and the Community
Context of Practice

The previous three chapters review the roles and activities of the case manager, the policy context of case management with its implications for the creative use of community resources, and the theory of symbolic interactionism, which demonstrates how people acquire and reshape their identities through social interaction. All of this material places great emphasis on the *social* nature of case management practice. But, we have not yet adequately considered the concepts of **social support** and **community.** In this chapter I provide an overview of social support theory and the types of supports persons with mental illness tend to acquire. I discuss the concept of community, highlighting four perspectives on community that client populations might internalize to reflect their sense of relationship to others. I will propose that case managers can best help their clients acquire appropriate social supports with an appreciation of these community perspectives, which predict the extent to which clients are willing to interact with community members. Finally, based on the results of a study I conducted, I provide a method for clinical case managers to assess the support experiences of their clients.

SOCIAL SUPPORT THEORY

An issue of primary significance in the public mental health field is the extent to which interventions are effective in enhancing the community adjustment of persons with mental illness. A fundamental goal of case management is the integration of clients into the larger community by providing them with a range of resources for increased independent functioning. Thus, a key goal of case managers should be to develop natural social support resources for clients as part of formal rehabilitation. Natural supports are important to client stability because the scope and availability of formal services is limited, and these services are vulnerable to shifts in political support and funding. Most important, natural supports promote normalcy in clients' lives.

Though community-based programs are preferred for working with clients, their potential for developing natural support resources has not been adequately examined. The National Institute of Mental Health (1991) asserts that "studies of the origin, nature, constitution, and evaluation of informal social networks should be pursued to determine what factors promote their development" (p. 27). It is difficult to predict which informal support networks of this or any population are desirable because, while supports are of acknowledged importance, data adequately describing their ideal characteristics have not been rigorously compiled. A goal of this chapter is to describe the range of specific social support incidents that clients identify as important and to describe a method for assessing these social support patterns.

Defining Social Support

Social support has been defined in many ways, but it can be understood as the interpersonal *interactions* and *relationships* that provide individuals with *actual assistance* or *feelings of attachment* to other persons perceived as caring (Hobfoll, Freedy, Lane, & Geller, 1990). The literature agrees that adequate social supports, which are by definition external to the individual, promote improved physical health, mental health, stress-coping capability, and community living satisfaction for a variety of populations of concern to health service providers (Bloom, 1990). Social support components have been delineated in many ways; four are offered here to illustrate their variety. Vaux (1988) suggests that social support includes social networks, reports of supportive behaviors, and perceptions of support adequacy. Sarason, Sarason, and Pierce (1990) consider it to be primarily a cognitive, or psychological, characteristic of individuals, epitomized by their beliefs about support. Veiel and Baumann (1992) organize social support into the four domains of subjective beliefs, everyday support, potential crisis support, and actual crisis support. Richman, Rosenfeld, and Hardy (1993) specify eight types of support including listening, task appreciation, task challenge, emotional support, emotional challenge, reality confirmation, tangible assistance, and personal assistance. Later in this chapter we divide social support into three categories: material, emotional, and instrumental.

A few definitions of terms are needed here. The **social network** is an individual's patterns of interaction that emerge as a result of exchanging resources with others to a sufficient degree that a mutual commitment to the relationship develops (Specht, 1986). Network relationships can occur in a variety of **clusters**, or relatively distinct social units, such as family, school, occupational, and recreational groups. Network relationships may be negative as well as positive, but the scope of one's network does tend to be an indicator of potential social support (Vaux, 1990). Accounts of **supportive behavior** include the actual episodes in which the client has experienced support. **Support appraisals** are not based on events, but on the client's perceptions of which persons provide him or her with positive supports.

How Social Support Works

During the 1970s, two schools of thought emerged around the question of how social support produces beneficial effects (Cohen & Wills, 1985). The **main effect model** holds that our awareness of support instills in us a sense of well-being. Our social network provides us with regular positive experiences and a set of stable social roles that enable us to maintain a stable mood, predictability in life situations, and external affirmation of self-worth. The "supported" person might not even experience stress in many difficult situations, because a sense of competence results from the awareness of having support. The **buffering model,** on the other hand, asserts that support is a factor intervening between the occurrence of a stressful event and our reaction, either by diminishing the stress appraisal response or mobilizing a problem-solving process. That is, support resource availability redefines the potential for harm or reduces the stress reaction. We experience stress, but to a lesser extent and perhaps for a shorter period of time because of our ability to mobilize support.

Most research on social support has focused on its buffering effects, in part because these are more measurable. Social support as a main effect is difficult to isolate because it is influenced by, and may even be an outcome of, our psychological development and ability to form personal attachments. Most data-gathering instruments are based on assessments of buffering factors. In this chapter, I focus on the buffering effects of support, as persons with mental illness generally possess fewer psychological resources than general populations for maintaining a sense of self-worth.

The person-in-environment perspective of clinical case management can explain *why* social support works. Caplan's (1990, 1989) work on treatment and prevention for mental health practitioners is relevant here. In his framework, our experience of stress creates emotional arousal, manifested in our neuroendocrine systems by an erosion of cognitive and goal-oriented functioning; disorders of attention, scanning, and information retrieval; a lack of ready access to relevant memories which bring meaning to our perceptions and judgment; and an impaired capacity to evaluate personal or environmental feedback. Memory impairments also reduce our capacity to evaluate **identity,** which, as noted in Chapter 3, provides us with a basis for reflecting and focusing our behavior. From an ego psychology perspective, social support acts as an "auxiliary ego" to reduce levels of emotional upset. Supportive others serve to compensate for our perceptual deficits, reminding us of our identity and monitoring our overall social functioning. While Caplan wrote specifically about the topics of personal loss, bereavement, and crisis, his ten characteristics of effective support are applicable to our concept of social support. They include

1. Nurturance and the promotion of an ordered world view
2. The promotion of hope
3. The healthy promotion of timely withdrawal *and* initiative
4. The provision of guidance
5. A communication channel with the social world
6. A reminder of our personal identity
7. The provision of material help
8. The containment of distress through reassurance and affirmation
9. An insurance of adequate rest and physical self-care
10. The mobilization of other support from relatives, friends, and professionals

Social Supports for Persons with Mental Illness

For purposes of this book, social supports for persons with mental illness can be classified into the three categories of material, emotional, and instrumental support. I limit the number of categories for two reasons. First, with such variety in the literature about support categories, simplification may promote greater conceptual clarity and a potential for comparisons between studies. Second, and more important, such limitation is practical for a case manager's assessment. With a small number of categories to assess and monitor, the case manager can more reliably intervene with and evaluate a client's social support utilization. Clients with mental illness often have concrete thought processes and thus are not always able to make fine distinctions between larger numbers of categories (Toomey, First, Rife, & Belcher, 1989). These three categories of support can be defined as follows:

1. **Material support** includes assistance with acquiring items we need to function in daily life. Examples include food, money, household items, clothing, furniture, transportation, and entertainment resources.

2. **Emotional support** includes useful information, advice with personal problems, time spent with friends, visitors, and other companions, welcome phone calls, kind words, good listening, and religious help. Emotional supports provide us with a sense of positive social attachment. Both types of support defined above can come from friends, family members, companions, neighbors, co-workers, people one knows from agencies and programs, church members, and others.

3. **Instrumental support** includes any action that serves as a means to some end which is of relatively minor significance and that is usually delivered by a person whom we do not know well, if at all. Examples may include the delivery of our newspapers and mail, getting directions from someone on the street, having our groceries checked out for us, and getting our hair cut. Instrumental support does not often evoke a strong affective response toward the supporter, nor does it typically involve the giving of essential material goods.

Most social support research has been done with general populations. There has not been a clear appreciation of the fact that social supports are structured, perceived, and received differently in sub-populations. Persons with mental illness, for example, have a lesser capacity to develop support resources than many other client populations due to their cognitive deficits, unstable moods, and tendencies toward interpersonal conflict and social isolation (Atkinson, 1986; Cutler, Tatum, & Shore, 1987). In the general population, people frequently report an availability of 25–30 supportive others, located in five or six clusters. In my own research, 125 persons with mental illness identified an average of 14 social network members in five clusters (Walsh, 1994b). Still, those same persons indicated that significant social support was provided by an average of only nine persons, representing three clusters.

Smaller network sizes are partly the result of social skills deficits, but they also reflect a protective distancing for persons with mental illness, many of whom function comfortably with comparatively low levels of stimulation (Crotty & Kulys, 1985). Cutler and Tatum (1983) characterized these clients as living in small networks and having high levels of ambivalence about relationships with relatives, but having few long-term relationships with persons other than relatives. Beels (1981) noted that they have smaller numbers of people to rely on for support since they are less involved in occupational and recreational pursuits. Hammer (1981) suggests that persons with serious mental illness may function best in the community with some distant social connections, as these persons can provide feedback about behavior in a manner that is not emotionally charged. Dozier, Harris, and Bergman (1987) found that moderate levels of network density were associated with fewer days in the hospital.

Social support theory suggests, however, that all persons benefit from supportive others in more, rather than fewer, clusters because this insures more sources of potential support. That is, if a person has supportive relationships at home, in the neighborhood, at school, at work, in community organizations, and among other friends, he or she will have more places to look for assistance to cover a variety of circumstances. Further, clients with mental illness tend to benefit from structure and predictability, because this provides a basis for organizing their mental processes and maintaining moderate levels of stimulation.

Many clients benefit greatly from the social support they receive from psychosocial rehabilitation and, more recently, drop-in centers (Boyd, 1997). Psychosocial clubhouses are formal organizations where clients can go to find companionship and acceptance and also to acquire vocational and recreational skills. Their programs include such work training units as kitchen, transitional employment, and clerical crews. Professional staff are highly involved in clubhouse operations. Drop-in centers are less formal places, usually governed by clients, where persons with mental illness can go for friendship and a sense of belonging. These may include vocational components but are much less "treatment" oriented. While both types of programs are extremely important, case managers should also work to integrate their clients into varieties of natural support systems as much as possible.

Clients can be helped to expand their social support systems. In my own research, two case management teams, one with a group-oriented focus and the other with primarily individual treatment, were compared with regard to natural social support resource outcomes (Walsh, 1994a). I found that participants in the group-based case management program had developed larger support networks. The group-treatment sample also reported larger network clusters with regard to recreational activities, associations, and work. This finding provides evidence that the provision of group interventions does result in support network expansion outside the treatment setting. Following a discussion of community, where social support development takes place, I present a specific procedure for assessing the supports of clients with mental illness.

THE CONCEPT OF COMMUNITY

In the 1990s there has been an expansion of the concept of **community** in the social sciences (Hardcastle, Wenocur, & Powers, 1997). Community is a more elusive concept than is sometimes acknowledged, and for that reason it deserves to be discussed in some detail. Most of us have our own notions about the concept of community, probably related to the geographic communities where we grew up. A person's view of community might be that of a neigh-borhood or small town, populated by a fairly constant group of people from a similar social class who know each other and interact cooperatively for the bet-terment of the larger group. This traditional concept of community, however, has given way to broader perspectives since the permanency and relevance of geographic settings have become less consistent in people's lives. Case managers need to understand that clients may not perceive their own communities as stable, supportive areas where many personal needs can be met.

Defining Community

The work of Hutchison (1999) is useful in considering the impact of a client's community perspective on his or her orientation to social support availability. She defines community as people bound together by *geography* or *network links,* sharing *common ties* and *interacting* with one another. Further, the *sense* of com-munity is the feeling that members *matter* to one another and to the group, and a *shared faith* that their needs will be met through a *commitment* to be to-gether. The four essential elements of the sense of community, then, include membership, the possibility of influence, the integration and fulfillment of needs, and a shared emotional connection. For persons with mental illness, the sense of community might be more difficult to develop positively than their sense of being physically tied to a geographic area.

A client's community might be *territorial,* based on geographic characteris-tics, or *relational,* based on interactions which might take place outside a geo-graphic context. These two facets of community may, of course, coexist. A major change in community life over the past three decades has been the rise in relational communities, and the subsequent decline in personal reliance on geographic communities. Consider, for example, that a person may attend school, belong to discussion groups and clubs, and have long-term personal re-lationships without physically moving beyond the 5' by 5' area of a computer terminal. That same person may live in a densely populated suburban neigh-borhood and have few interactions with neighbors. Still, some types of persons must rely primarily on traditional territorial communities. These include chil-dren and their caregivers, persons who are elderly, persons living in poverty, and persons with a variety of disabilities. Members of these groups are geo-graphically bound because of their special circumstances. None of the groups listed, for example, is highly mobile. Among the people with disabilities who rely on geographically bounded communities are those with mental illness.

Here it is important to identify two practice implications for the case man-ager. First, in developing social supports, the worker should consider that the client functions in a community of *reciprocal obligation,* and not primarily as a recipient of assistance. We saw in the last chapter how our sense of self emerges from the role expectations of others. This emergence can be enhanced by our acceptance as a contributing member of a community system. Because suc-cessful integration into a community involves giving as well as receiving, the client should be helped to develop relationships in which he or she can also be an active contributor. Second, it may be difficult at times to link clients with supports in a range of clusters. Persons with mental illness tend to rely on supports within a bounded territory, but many others who reside in that area, because they are more mobile, may cultivate a majority of their important relationships outside those boundaries.

Four Perspectives on Community

Thus far we have considered the concept of community rather generally. Now we consider four specific perspectives which clients might hold about their communities. The client's positive or negative views of their community, and their roles within it, have obvious relevance to the case manager's intervention plans. The worker needs to understand how the client is motivated to develop and maintain supports within his or her community prior to encouraging any linkages.

Community as Spatial Relations   A client might view community primarily as a set of *spatial arrangements*. This reflects my earlier point about the territorial perspective, but with the additional consideration of the physical arrangement of that territory. In assessing spatial arrangements on behalf of a client, the case manager should first consider the location of the client within the neighborhood relative to necessary resources. It is important to insure that all basic needs can be met. The assessment must then go beyond the mere availability of material, emotional, and instrumental supports to include accessibility. For example, is public transportation available? Are buildings accessible to clients with handicaps? For long-range planning the case manager should also consider population growth patterns in the neighborhood and surrounding areas, land use and zoning patterns, and relationships between the central city and surrounding suburbs. Urban areas can change so quickly that issues of resource availability and access cannot be assumed to be long-term.

An example can serve to illustrate this perspective. In one mid-size city there was an inner-city homeless shelter that served many persons with mental illness. Because of changes in zoning laws, the shelter had to move. A controversy arose between the shelter board of directors and city officials about where to relocate the shelter, which all parties agreed was an essential city resource. Some decision-makers wanted the shelter moved several miles from downtown, so that inner-city private business revitalization efforts could proceed. This was opposed by many client advocates, who argued that the majority of social services necessary for shelter residents (such as employment programs, health and mental health agencies, housing agencies, the social security administration, and others) were located downtown. If the shelter moved, it was argued, clients would no longer have access to these resources. Shelter staff argued that clients would not be able to make the two-mile trip into town for these support services. Many clients would drop out of the shelter program altogether and resume living on the streets. In the end, the shelter remained where it was. All parties eventually acknowledged that the proposed move would disrupt the spatial relationships of support services within the city so drastically that many clients might not survive. Still, the issue of shelter location would probably arise again because of business development.

Community as Contest   The community may also be viewed as a *contest*. This negative view of community characterizes people not as working together but as competing interest groups, all of which desire to protect and expand their privileges without concern for the fate of others. The client who holds this perspective views the community as a place where, as a relatively powerless person, he or she cannot trust that others will act in his or her best interest. We can all understand, at least at times, how this view of community develops. All case managers, for example, have experienced frustrations in linkage and resource development caused by human service organizations that do not seem equally responsive to all client groups. This perspective might also be found among clients who are paranoid, as well as among families of clients who have had frustrating experiences with unresponsive human service professionals.

For example, several years ago a case manager organized the first-ever family support group in his city of residence. He invited the family members of all clients with mental illness from his agency to attend, including those he did not know personally. One parent refused to consider attending, and she even berated the case manager during their phone conversation. She had become so angry with professionals who, in her view, kept crucial information about her son's mental status from her because of confidentiality rules and stigmatized her as sustaining her son's illness, that she no longer had any faith that they cared about helping clients. She believed that the support group represented the worker's insincere effort to give the appearance of reaching out to families while continuing to minimize their concerns. The woman eventually joined the family group and had a positive experience, but the leader came to understand that her earlier anger had been based on real experiences of rejection.

Case managers can regard the contest perspective as the result of client and family experiences with organizations and community actors who appeared to discount the client's welfare. If the case manager works in partnership with the client and family and is seen as advocating for the client rather than passively accepting that resources must be limited, then the client with a "contest" perspective may come to see that his or her interests can be sincerely represented and addressed even in an imperfect community system.

Community as Social System   Community might also be viewed as a *social system*. This most closely approximates the traditional notion of a predictable community structure of roles, interactions, and activities with permanent networks of organizations having clear relationships to one another. Equally important, this view assumes the existence of a uniform community culture in which members have a generally shared set of goals, values, and sense of the common good. The client who holds the social system perspective views the community as a positive entity and expects that his or her needs may be fulfilled through the processes of reciprocal obligation described earlier. This is probably the perspective most consistent with the clinical case management philosophy of community-based service.

Two examples can serve as illustrations. A supervised apartment program, including two-person units scattered throughout a larger apartment complex, was developed by a mental health center for persons with mental illness. For the 24 clients who lived there, the complex represented a small social system, including structured, client-organized task activities (such as laundry, shopping, and cooking), shared recreational activity planning, and organized problem-solving and support groups. All of these activities encouraged regular interactions and relationship development with peers. One member of this community, Jason, emerged as a "social chairman." He loved having friends over to his apartment for playing cards and listening to music almost every evening. He was less capable as a budgeter of money and allowed others to take the lead in organizing shopping trips and recreational outings.

A second example is the organization of a support and education group in one urban area for the adult children and siblings of persons with mental illness. A local mental health organization decided through a needs assessment that such a resource would bring together these persons, who had similar problems and needs but would otherwise not chance to meet, from a broad geographic territory. This group, which was led by a clinical case manager, ran for one year. Its success signifies the potential for members of a community system to develop mutual aid resources. The community's interactive tradition meant that various needs of the residents could be identified and addressed. Again, maintaining and acting on this perspective represents a positive view of community life.

Community as Social Bond   The final community perspective, though related to the social system model, goes further in identifying community as a *social bond*. This is probably the least shared perspective on community in the United States. It assumes that the collective good might take precedence over individual interests, which opposes the strong ethic of individualism in this country. The community as a social bonding experience assumes that people are inherently connected with each other and that they should always prioritize active cooperation in pursuing ends, motivated by traits of common human nature and universal dignity. This perspective incorporates the symbolic interactionist assumption that our sense of self is intimately tied to interactions with significant others. However, as stated by Bellah, Madsen, Sullivan, Swindler, and Tipton (1985), we have in the United States a "first language" of individualism, with a relative inability to conceive of the primacy of the common good. The view of community as a social bond assumes that the primary good is achieved in contributing to the group, with individual needs remaining secondary. The case manager should be alert to opportunities for clients to participate in activities that lead to these kinds of fulfilling experiences.

We probably all experience the social bond perspective at least occasionally. Few examples are so moving as those involving communities which come together in a united effort to recover after the occurrence of a natural disaster such as a flood or hurricane. It is not unusual to hear people describe how the experience has changed them forever, not because of material losses, but because of their renewed sense of fellowship. As another example, step programs represent a social bond for some people. In Alcoholics Anonymous, for example, each member must concede his or her powerlessness over the disease and must rely on other group members and a higher power to maintain sobriety. A third, more negative, example involves gang membership as a social bond experience. Young men and women who perceive no other strong interpersonal connections or transcendent values become attracted to the gang as the only place where they are viewed as having significance and a clear role. Gang members are often expected to subjugate their personal needs to those of the gang, which helps explain why members will risk their lives in activities intended to promote the gang's survival and influence.

The case manager must keep in mind that, beyond adaptation to community life, many clients will immeasurably benefit from these kinds of experiences and will come to develop an unusually strong sense of belonging to their community. Larry, a young man with schizophrenia, was determined to make a contribution to his community. Even though he had frequent episodes of active psychosis, he also had great leadership skills and helped organize a "Schizophrenics Anonymous" self-help group in his city of residence, based on a structured program first developed by the Mental Health Association of Michigan (Walsh, 1994c). He worked with the local association and several professionals in the development process and ultimately assumed leadership of three group chapters, all of which met weekly. Larry led the groups for years and gained a reputation among clients and professionals alike for his selfless work on behalf of persons with mental illness.

In the chapters that follow, I present much more about the development of social supports for clients in various kinds of community settings. But here I present a process for assessing a client's existing supports, which is always a first step in case management intervention.

ASSESSING SOCIAL SUPPORTS

Few social support measures have been developed specifically for use with psychiatrically impaired populations, and little research has been done on clients' reports of their own support experiences. A majority of instruments measure clients' perceptions of support (Cohen & Hoberman, 1983; Holahan & Moos, 1983; Procidano & Heller, 1983). In order to systematically determine social support acquisition trends among persons with mental illness, I conducted a study of 30 clients from two agencies in one large city. Clients agreed to keep diaries of their experiences in receiving support over a one-month period. This technique for determining the range of support episodes significant to this client population had not been previously implemented. For the study I designed an assessment form that can be used in any case management setting (see Appendix). For each incident of social support, participants were asked to write the first name of the person who provided support, the person's relationship to the participant, and the specific action or behavior. Participants were instructed to complete seven daily log sheets over a four-week period, with every calendar day of the week represented.

Participants were selected from two community-based mental health agencies, one suburban and one from the inner-city, in a major metropolitan area of Virginia. Together the agencies served a culturally diverse group of clients. Primary diagnoses of the participants included schizophrenia, bipolar disorder, schizoaffective disorder, and major depression. All participants were receiving case management and formal support services from their agencies. The final random sample consisted of 18 men (60%) and 12 women (40%), with 19 participants identified as Caucasian (63%) and 11 as African American (27%). Respondents ranged in age from 25 to 61, with an average age of 39.3 years.

Results

A total of 693 support incidents were recorded, and I categorized them as either material, emotional, or instrumental support in accordance with the typology described earlier. Then I categorized the clients' relationships with support providers into the social network clusters listed in Table 1. These were not delineated in advance of the study but emerged during data analysis with input from six of my colleagues. Eight clusters emerged as defined below, in order of their frequency of citation:

1. *Friends* – acquaintances identified as sharing an ongoing personal relationship characterized by intimacy.
2. *Family of origin* – biological, blood, and legal relatives, including mothers, fathers, brothers, sisters, adoptive and step-siblings, and parents.
3. *Informal community relations* – persons who occupy specific and narrow roles encountered in activities of daily living, but whom one does not generally know outside of those roles. Examples include waitresses, postal workers, lifeguards, police officers, pharmacists, and store clerks.
4. *Work* – coworkers, supervisors, and customers. Some respondents identified coworkers as friends, and they were not included in this category.
5. *Acquired family* – married and divorced spouses, as well as children (including sons and daughters-in-law) and grandchildren.
6. *Extended family* – the variety of other family relationships, including aunts, uncles, cousins, and grandparents.
7. *Neighbors* – persons with whom one lives in close enough geographical proximity that they are routinely seen and encountered in daily life.
8. *Church* – the clergy and their families, church members, and church workers.

The following list contains frequently cited examples of supportive behaviors.

1. *Material*: Loaned or gave me some money, paid me for doing a chore, provided me with a meal, let me stay in their home, bought food items for me, let me have a purchase for half price, sold me a car, helped me buy a snack, offered me cigarettes, I borrowed milk from her, she supplied me with clothes.

2. *Emotional*: Called to see how I was doing, helped me solve a personal problem, we got together for a visit, treated me with respect, asked my name, said I'm doing a good job, helped me solve a work problem, took a break with me, talked to me, went on a social activity with me, we played cards together, gave me a gift, talked about what was happening with her that day, we had a pleasant conversation, hugged me, said he would pray for me.

3. *Instrumental*: Helped me clean the house, helped me with my medication, helped me with some paperwork, got my prescription from the drug store, gave my child a ride to her class, delivered the mail, gave me information about a product, helped me with a part of my job, helped me get more work hours, performed household chores for me, gave me a ride to the store, we talked about a problem with my car, we shared the use of her phone, brought my trash cans in from the street, talked with me about weekend classes.

Discussion

Many of the cluster findings are consistent with what might be expected regarding the relative frequencies of emotional, material, and instrumental support, but there were some surprises. Persons classified as *informal community relations* are typically not considered as providing emotional support, but the proportion of this support type received in the present study (26.1%) suggests that they are more significant to persons with serious mental illness than to general populations. Case managers should not overlook the support potential of persons in these community roles. Also, a surprising amount of emotional support (74.5%) is provided by work associates. Many persons with mental illness are highly challenged by the demands of work (Danley, 1994); as a result, they seem to look to their peers for emotional support in that setting. One might expect that *neighbors* would provide proportionately more material and instrumental support than was noted, particularly since they are not intimate enough with the respondents to be placed in the *friends* cluster. Finally, the *church* category seems to offer a positive source of both emotional and material support, but few respondents appear to use this potential resource.

It was surprising that emotional support was so predominantly cited by the respondents, and that material support barely surpassed instrumental support in frequency. I was particularly intrigued by the relative infrequency of reported material support, given the fact that almost 50% of the respondent population was living in poverty. Perhaps respondents were simply not as attentive to the material manifestations of support, or took them for granted. Persons with mental illness may be more sensitive to emotionally supportive behaviors. Because of their isolation from mainstream social life, that type of support may best meet their unfulfilled needs for social affirmation. Thus, case managers should be aware that their clients may be in particular need of emotional support, despite their range of other assessed needs.

SUMMARY

Informal social support development is a major function for case managers. Rather than relying on professionals for assistance with tasks of everyday living, clients function best, and enjoy more normal lifestyles, with a workable set of informal supports. However, it is difficult to acquire supports. The case manager needs to understand the client's perspective on his or her community, and from that point assess the client's support needs and work collaboratively to develop them. The assessment tool introduced in this chapter provides one practical way of assessing and monitoring the client's support experiences. It does not reveal the client's perspective on community, but that can only be determined through the worker/client relationship. The client who sees the community as a threatening, conflicted environment may have little motivation to pursue any new supports unless his or her community perspective changes.

I recommend that case managers assess their clients' social support episodes as often as quarterly because trends in support episodes may change over time. Each assessment should be done over a course of several weeks to ascertain the full range of a client's experiences. Additionally, the case manager may want to target a particular *type* of support for assessment. For example, to understand how a client attends to his or her material needs, the worker can discuss the concept of material support with the client, articulate what constitutes the client's specific material needs, and then ask the client to document over time those persons who help provide for those needs.

Appendix: A Social Support Assessment Form

Participant Code: _____

| | (Age) | (Gender - M or F) | (Race - B, W,O) |

Date: _____

(Day of Week)   (Month)   (Day of Month)

Person Providing Support (First Name)	His or Her Relationship to You	What the Person Did That Was Supportive
1._____	1._____	1._____
2._____	2._____	2._____
3._____	3._____	3._____
4._____	4._____	4._____
5._____	5._____	5._____
6._____	6._____	6._____
7._____	7._____	7._____
8._____	8._____	8._____
9._____	9._____	9._____
10._____	10._____	10._____

Table 1   Frequency and Type of Supportive Behaviors by Source

Source	Emotional N	Emotional %	Material N	Material %	Instrumental N	Instrumental %	Total N	Total %
Friends	269	38.8%	173	64.3%	52	19.3%	44	16.4%
Family of Origin	119	17.2	58	48.8	48	40.3	13	10.9
Informal Community Relations	69	10.0	18	26.1	16	23.2	35	50.7
Extended Family	59	8.5	48	81.4	5	8.5	6	10.1
Family of Procreation	58	8.4	37	63.8	7	12.1	14	24.1
Work	55	7.9	41	74.5	3	5.5	11	20.0
Neighbors	44	6.3	28	63.6	8	18.2	8	18.2
Church	20	2.9	12	60.0	5	25.0	3	15.0
Totals	693	100%	415	59.9%	144	20.8%	134	19.3%

PART III

Working with Individuals

5

The Case Manager
and Psychotropic
Medications

I. **Case Manager Roles in Medication Management**
   a. *Physician's assistant*
   b. *Consultant/Collaborator*
   c. *Monitor*
   d. *Advocator*
   e. *Educator*
   f. *Researcher*

II. **The Psychotropic Medications**
   a. *Neurotransmitters*
   b. *The four classes of psychotropic medication*

III. **Managing Psychological and Social Adverse Effects**

IV. **Clinical Relationships and Medication Management**
   a. *Maintaining a balanced perspective*
   b. *Integrating psychosocial and medication interventions*

V. **Summary**

VI. **Appendix: List of Medications Described in this Chapter**

Clinical case management practice must incorporate a biological as well as psychosocial perspective in assessment and intervention with clients. Attention to medication is a significant part of that assessment because of clients' frequent use of prescription drugs. Though medications are targeted at the biochemical level of functioning, they also have impact on psychological and social concerns of the client and his or her significant others. In this chapter I will review the major categories of psychotropic medications and consider the range of roles that case managers might have in working with clients who receive, or are considering the use of, psychotropic medications. Case managers do not prescribe medications, of course, but must assume responsibility to become knowledgeable about, and participate in, that aspect of client care.

A model that attempts to explain the interplay between biological and environmental influences on social functioning is the **stress–diathesis model** (Yank, Bentley, & Hargrove, 1993). This model asserts that though mental illness seems to be caused by genetic factors as well as by abnormalities in brain chemistry and structure, it is also caused, in part, by environmental factors. Vulnerability and stress are moderated by the presence of protective factors such as coping skills, social support, and medication. If case managers can help build protective factors, in part through participation in medication management, they can decrease clients' impairments. This model was originally developed to explain the course of schizophrenia, but it is also relevant to other mental disorders. It is useful to case managers in clarifying how they can contribute to improved psychosocial functioning in their clients.

All mental health clinical case managers work with clients who use medications as a major aspect of their treatment. But until recently, case managers have not paid much attention to medication issues. They have historically functioned merely as physician's assistants, supporting client compliance with medications according to the physician's recommendations. Still, the range of service delivery activities for some clients has expanded to the point where case managers are occasionally asked by clients and families to respond to difficult questions about psychotropic medication use. The need for immediate action by clients and families in case of a crisis does not always allow for the postponement of intervention. Case managers cannot intervene independently of a physician or other providers, but they need to be able to respond to medication concerns quickly, based on a sound knowledge of their effects. Clinical case managers do more than complement the role of the physician. They bring a unique perspective to medication issues based on a holistic view of the person-in-environment and promote a partnership model of practice, with a view of the helping relationship as active and mutual.

CASE MANAGER ROLES
IN MEDICATION MANAGEMENT

Usually several professionals are involved with clients using psychotropic drugs, and each of them should be prepared to assume certain roles in medication management. Described below are six roles for case managers, as detailed by Bentley and Walsh (1996).

Physician's Assistant

As physician's assistant, the case manager accepts the expertise of the physician in decision-making about psychotropic drugs. The case manager's role is limited to supporting client compliance with medications on the physician's recommendations. The worker is not expected to give input into decisions involving medication prescription, use, or compliance strategy, although he or she may have a role in the assessment process.

For many years, the role of physician's assistant was most common because the legal scope of case management was limited in comparison with other helping professions and because those professions carried more authority (Gerhart & Brooks, 1983). Psychiatrists and physicians have always been the primary providers of biological interventions for persons with all types of emotional problems (primary care physicians still provide most biological interventions). With deinstitutionalization and the emphasis on community-based care, however, case managers have been called upon to initiate psychosocial interventions and also to interact with clients in a variety of natural environments where they can clearly observe the effects of psychotropic medication. But in many settings, case managers are still limited to the physician's assistant role.

Consultant/Collaborator

As a consultant and collaborator, the case manager needs to be skilled in three areas (McCollum, Margolen, & Lieb, 1978). First, the worker must be able to assess clients for possible referral to physicians. This involves evaluating the client's current levels of functioning, intensity of suffering, and capacity to manage suffering. Second, the worker must prepare clients for active participation with the physician in the assessment process. The worker's responsibilities include articulating the reasons for referral to the physician, reviewing the client's attitude toward psychiatrists, and discussing the client's expectations concerning medication. Third, the worker must be concerned with the client's ability to manage the financial costs of medication, which may be quite high.

Case managers and physicians ideally should see themselves as collaborators, specifying the range of their respective roles, promoting client adherence to medication, devising procedures to evaluate the medication's effectiveness, and accurately recording data in monitoring client response. Psychiatrists can provide in-service training to other professionals on drug categories, side effects, and assessment techniques. Case managers, in turn, can educate physicians in aspects of psychosocial intervention including supportive counseling, resource linkages, job skills, general life skills, and social skills development. Of course, disagreements may arise among the physician, case manager, and client on a variety of issues, and these must be openly dealt with toward constructive resolution.

Monitor

Medication monitoring involves the case manager's observing, and helping the client observe, the positive and negative effects of medication, the appearance or persistence of symptoms, and adherence to the medication regimen. The case manager needs to evaluate the client's response to any discomfort and help the client come to terms with the impact of the discomfort on physical and social functioning. Information from the monitoring process is shared with the client, perhaps the family, and the physician. Through these activities, the case manager helps the client become a self-monitor of medication and serves as an ongoing source of information for the physician. Finally, case managers must consult families about monitoring the client 's response to medications and his or her development of self-care skills, if the client is dependent on the family.

The case manager must help the client monitor adverse physical, psychological, and social effects of medication. The case manager can become educated about adverse physical effects through self-study and collaboration with medical personnel. I will discuss adverse psychological and social effects later in this chapter.

Advocate

The case managers can represent clients and their families to those who have power to determine how medications are administered. This role is significant because the mental health care system is often neither fully responsive nor accessible. The case manager as advocate ideally has a peer relationship with the physician and participates in all phases of decision-making regarding medication prescription. This role is crucial because the emphasis on community care makes the responsible monitoring of client medication difficult for any single person. In order to function as an advocate, the worker must have a sound knowledge of mental illnesses, psychotropic medications, and laws and regulations regarding the rights of persons with mental illness. The case manager might conflict at times with the physician and other professionals with whom treatments are being coordinated.

Case managers can also function as political advocates for clients who cannot get access to medications they want, as was illustrated quite dramatically with the introduction of clozapine in 1991. The medication had beneficial effects for some persons with schizophrenia who did not respond to the traditional antipsychotic medications. However, the cost of the medication, coupled with the need to monitor blood counts on a regular basis, created a very expensive treatment regimen. Some clients and families who could not afford the drug filed suits to gain access to it, and adjustments were made in public insurance policies which helped broaden its availability (Reid, Pham, & Rago, 1993). Because issues related to the cost of medication are serious and because restrictions on the availability of medication may arise in the future, case managers may need to be advocates not only with physicians but also with agencies, funding sources, and government regulators. This activist perspective is a reminder that medication issues arise in a broader context of social policy.

Case managers need to be aware that empowerment and advocacy efforts with clients and families may lead to their decisions to refuse medication, or to negotiate more assertively with physicians about the types and dosages of medication the client is willing to take. Such situations are likely to give rise to value dilemmas for case managers. Bentley (1993) holds that case managers need to support the right of refusal of medication or any other treatment for legal, empirical, and ethical reasons while Rosenson (1993), a family advocate, states that the professional's decision to proceed with appropriate medications, even in the face of refusal, is sometimes a prerequisite for the client to gain the judgment necessary for competent future decision-making. The case manager may believe that medication compliance is desirable for a particular client's well-being and thus feel uncomfortable if a client chooses an opposite strategy as a result of the worker's own advocacy efforts.

Educator

The role of educator is crucial in the maintenance of collaborative relationships with clients, families, and physicians. A major force behind the family advocacy movement was dissatisfaction with mental health professionals' lack of perceived efforts to help clients and families understand their rationales for decisions pertaining to medication and other interventions (Hatfield, 1990). The uses and actions of medication is a complicated, confusing issue for many professionals as well as the general public, and there continues to be a need for case managers to help clarify related topics in direct service provision through educational means. The widespread development of family psychoeducational and medication education programs is a sign of progress. But case managers also need to provide basic information about medication during individual client interventions, and they should strive to educate themselves about ongoing developments in the field. In Chapters 13 and 14, I review the importance of the case manager's ability to educate clients and families about diagnosis, medications, psychosocial intervention options, roles of professionals in different settings, and opportunities for self-help and support.

Researcher

As well as being direct service providers, case managers can add to the literature about the impact of psychotropic medication and advance the knowledge base of holistic and collaborative practice. Case studies and single-subject research designs, focused on the positive and negative effects of medications, the impact of medicines on self-control and one's sense of responsibility for problem-resolution, and engaging the hard-to-reach client in a comprehensive treatment program represent three areas of study which have not been adequately addressed.

The positive effects of a combination of medication, counseling, and psychosocial rehabilitation for clients are now widely accepted (Schooler & Keith, 1993). However, the effectiveness of various case management methods have not yet been fully tested because of researchers' inability to separate out the interactions of medication effects from other interventions. Case managers, who are on the "front lines" of practice, are in an excellent position to conduct research which will help ascertain the main effects of drugs and psychosocial interventions on client outcomes, as well as the interactions of these treatments. Through these means, the relative and combined effectiveness of medication can be evaluated in ways that may support more low-dose medication treatment strategies.

THE PSYCHOTROPIC MEDICATIONS

Dozens of **psychotropic medications** are now available, with new drugs being introduced every year. These are generally helpful to clients, but they also produce a confusing range of issues to consider including indications for use, choices among drug types, adverse effects, special precautions, the use of generic versus brand-name drugs, routes of administration (oral vs. injectable), and participation in decisions of compliance or refusal. The relative benefits and risks of medication use must always be weighed by practitioners from all professional groups and by clients themselves. In this section I describe the desired actions of four classes of psychotropic medication including the antipsychotic, antidepressant, mood stabilizing, and anti-anxiety drugs. This information should be useful to case managers as an introduction to the medications they will routinely encounter. I also summarize the actions of central nervous system neurotransmitters, chemical substances that are the targets of the drugs. The primary sources used to prepare this information include Bentley and Walsh (1998, 1996), Bernstein (1995), Kaplan and Sadock (1998), and Schatzberg and Nemeroff (1995).

Neurotransmitters

All human thoughts, emotions, and behaviors are associated with the activity of nerve cells, or neurons, in the brain and spinal cord. Molecules pass through neuron membranes to enter or leave a cell through special "channels" governed by chemical activities within the cell. Impulses travel via the cell's lengthy axon, through which one cell sends signals to neighboring cells and to the numerous dendrites which receive signals sent by other neurons. The transmission of signals through the nervous system begins when a cell generates an impulse, or a momentary change in electrical charge within the membrane. The transmission of the impulse to a receiving cell is facilitated by a chemical neurotransmitter, which is released into the synapse, or space between cells, from the axon and then attaches to receptors in the dendrite of the neighboring cell. A specific receptor usually responds to only one type of neurotransmitter. Information is passed from cell to cell along a pathway, or series of connected neurons working for some coordinated purpose. Psychotropic drugs work by modifying natural events that occur in the synapses of nerve cell pathways in specified areas of the brain. They affect brain functioning by increasing or decreasing the amount of the neurotransmitter which is activated along a pathway.

More than 100 chemical neurotransmitters have been discovered thus far, but researchers have detailed knowledge about the interactions of only five of these with psychotropic drugs: acetylcholine, norepinephrine, dopamine, serotonin, and gamma aminobutyric acid (GABA). Together these account for transmissions at less than half of the brain's synapses. Though all of these substances are crucial in regions of the nervous system concerned with emotional behavior, it is likely that medications act on neurons in other ways that are not yet understood.

Much research on psychotropic medication focuses on learning more about neurotransmitters and their subtypes, about the possible role of additional neurotransmitters in producing symptoms of metal illness, and about how new medications can be specifically targeted to those neurotransmitter subtypes believed to have a role in the production of symptoms. At the present time, any of the psychotropic medications are effective, with a few exceptions, for 60–70% of clients for whom they are prescribed (Kaplan & Sadock, 1998). The case manager, therefore, in partnership with the physician, must be active in the pharmacology process to increase the chances of client improvement.

The Four Classes of Psychotropic Medication

Since the 1950s, pharmaceutical companies have marketed drugs for four major classes of mental disorders (I do not address psychostimulants, which are primarily used for children and adolescents, in this book). Chlorpromazine, the first antipsychotic medication, was introduced in the United States in 1954, followed by haloperidol in 1958. Both of these, still in use today, help to clarify thought processes through sedation and the reduction or elimination of hallucinations. Chlordiazepoxide, the first benzodiazepine, was marketed in 1957. The first anti-depressants were the monoamine oxidase (MAO) inhibitors, which became available in the late 1950s. The cyclic antidepressant imipramine appeared in 1958 and quickly became more widely prescribed than the MAO drugs because it did not require that the client observe stringent dietary restrictions as a precaution against adverse effects. The mood stabilizer lithium, effective in treating persons with bipolar disorder, was introduced in the United States in 1969.

Psychiatry had developed all four classes of medications by 1970, and the years since have been devoted to their clinical study and the development of related and (at times) more effective compounds. Four major developments since 1980 include the anticonvulsant drugs (carbamazepine and valproate), which are used as mood stabilizers and also to potentiate the effectiveness of other medications; the non-benzodiazepine anti-anxiety agents, which do not present the potential for physical addiction; new classes of antidepressant and anti-obsessive-compulsive drugs; and several new antipsychotic medications, of which clozapine, risperidone, and olanzapine are the best-known. These newer medications serve the same clinical functions as the older drugs, but they have a different chemical composition, have different routes of action, and in some cases have fewer adverse effects.

The drugs in each of the four categories described here are used to treat the same mental illnesses and symptoms, and they often share similar actions. It must be noted, however, that in recent years researchers and physicians have experimented with prescribing some medications that were originally developed for one kind of illness to treat another. That is, the formerly distinct categories of psychotropic medications are blurring. For example, some medications developed as anti-depressants can be used to treat some anxiety disorders.

Antipsychotic Medications   It is widely accepted that persons with schizophrenia have a relatively high concentration of the neurotransmitter dopamine, or a high sensitivity at its receptor sites, in pathways extending into the cortex and limbic system. Stimulating dopamine activity seems to induce psychotic symptoms, and the **antipsychotic drugs** reduce dopamine levels in the nervous system. Almost all antipsychotic medications act in large part by blocking dopamine receptors, and thus its transmission. The medications differ primarily in their potential to induce adverse effects and in the milligram amounts in an equivalent dose. The low potency drugs, or those which are prescribed in higher milligram amounts (e. g., chlorpromazine and clozaril), tend to induce sedation, dry mouth, blurred vision, and constipation, while the high potency drugs (prescribed in lower milligram amounts, such as trifluoperazine and risperidone) tend to induce muscle stiffness. Scientists once believed that there was only one type of dopamine receptor in the brain, but they have now identified five subtypes, and the therapeutic actions of the antipsychotic medications result from the blockage of two of these. Dopamine activity reduction in persons with schizophrenia is accompanied by a reduction in many of the **positive symptoms** of that disorder, or those which feature an excess or bizarre distortion of normal functions (such as delusions and hallucinations). **Negative symptoms** feature a loss or reduction of normal functions (withdrawal, poverty of speech and thought, lack of motivation). Most of the antipsychotic medications are not as effective in reducing delusional thinking or negative symptoms, although the newer drugs seems to have greater impact in this regard.

The antipsychotic medications act on all dopamine sites in the brain, but only one of these is thought to be the site of symptom-producing nerve cell activity. The other pathways occupy areas near the base of the brain that govern motor activity. A reduction in dopamine in these other areas, which are not significant for psychotic symptoms, causes muscle spasms, tremors, and stiffness, because the transmitter is needed there in normal amounts to facilitate muscle activity. Other medications, such as benztropine and trixehiphenidyl, do not have antipsychotic effects but are prescribed along with some anti-psychotic drugs to minimize these adverse effects. Unfortunately they induce their own set of adverse effects including blurred vision, dry mouth, and constipation.

The "first generation" of antipsychotic medications included more than a dozen commonly prescribed compounds, including chlorpromazine, haloperi-dal, trifluoperazine, fluphenazine, and others. Several new types of antipsy-chotic medication have been introduced into the American market during the past 10 years, and they seem to act differently than the earlier compounds. Clozapine, risperidone, and olanzapine are the best-known of these. They do not carry the same risk of adverse effects on the client's muscular system. They selectively act on only those dopamine receptors that produce psychotic symp-toms, and they also block receptors for serotonin, which raises the possibility that this neurotransmitter has a role in psychotic symptomatology for some people. The Food and Drug Administration mandates that physicians may prescribe clozapine only if the client does not first respond to typical antipsy-chotic drugs, because of its rare but potentially serious adverse effect of white blood cell depletion. Clients using clozapine must have blood counts every two weeks to monitor this possible effect.

Antidepressant Medications   In comparison with the antipsychotic drugs, there is even more uncertainty about the way antidepressant medications work. Until the early 1980s it was believed that depressions resulted from a deficiency of norepinephrine or serotonin in the limbic area of the brain. The **antide-pressants** developed in the 1950s and 1960s, still in use, were thought to work by preventing the breakdown of neurotransmitters in the synapse, thus increas-ing their prevalence and inhibiting their reuptake by the "sender" cell after use. However, the newer antidepressants are known to act differently, with addi-tional effects on receptors and perhaps other neurotransmitter systems.

The three major types of antidepressants, each with different actions, in-clude the MAO inhibitors, the "cyclics," and the selective serotonin-reuptake inhibitors (SSRIs). Despite uncertainties about their actions, we can identify some general characteristics of these drugs. All must be taken for several weeks before the client experiences beneficial effects, as their actions are initially re-sisted by cells at their sites of action. They have a low *therapeutic index*, which means there is no great difference between the amounts required for thera-peutic effect and overdose. For example, overdose can often be achieved with only a ten-day supply of the cyclic drugs, of particular concern because these drugs are often prescribed for clients with suicidal ideas.

The MAO inhibitors were the first type of antidepressant. Tranyl-cypromine (Parnate) and phenelzine (Nardil) are the best known of these. While still effective for some clients, the MAO inhibitors are not frequently prescribed because of rather extensive dietary restrictions that the consumer must follow to avoid serious adverse effects such as hypertension, and less seri-ous effects, such as gastrointestinal problems, dizziness, and dry mouth. Their antidepressant effect results from the inhibition of certain enzymes within cells that break down norepinephrine and serotonin, thus increasing the levels of those transmitters in the nervous system. The MAO inhibitors are effective with some clients who do not respond to the other antidepressant medications, and they appear to have anti-anxiety effects as well.

The cyclic drugs, so named because of the shape of their chemical structure, were the most commonly prescribed antidepressants through the 1980s. Imipramine (Tofranil) and doxepin (Sinequan) are two examples. The cyclic antidepressants are believed to work by blocking the reuptake of norepinephrine and serotonin. The drugs are highly effective, which accounts for their long popularity. Many of them, however, produce sedation, blurred vision, constipation, and mild confusion as a result of their impact on other areas of the nervous system. Their sedative action makes them particularly useful for depressed clients who experience sleep problems. Tolerance does develop to certain of the adverse effects, but not to the therapeutic effect.

A number of new antidepressants are selective for serotonin only, which adds to the uncertainty about the scope of action of antidepressant drugs on the neurotransmitters which correlate with depression. They possibly stimulate certain neurotransmitters in ways that are not well understood. These SSRI drugs, including the well-known fluoxetine (Prozac) and sertraline (Zoloft), are more potent than the cyclic drugs. Among their attractions is that they have fewer adverse effects than the other antidepressant groups (although they may cause restlessness and headache) and less overdose potential.

Mood-Stabilizing Medications   Lithium has been the primary medication for bipolar disorder in the United States since its introduction as an antimanic drug in 1969. Lithium is the lightest of the solid elements, circulating through the body as a small ion with a positive electrical charge. It is a highly effective medication, but it requires several weeks to take effect. Lithium is sometimes given, at least temporarily, with an antipsychotic drug to stabilize a manic individual. It is not clear how lithium achieves its therapeutic effect, but numerous theories have been considered. One hypothesis is that lithium passes through cell membrane channels efficiently, and, in so doing, impedes the activity of the naturally occurring impulses that contribute to mania. The result is a stabilization of electrolyte imbalances in the cell membrane. Another hypothesis differentiates the antidepressant and antimanic effects of the drug. The antidepressant effect of lithium may result from its reducing the sensitivity of receptors for serotonin and thus increasing the amount of that transmitter in the nervous system. Its antimanic effect may relate to a reduction in dopamine receptor sensitivity and an inhibition of cellular enzymes that produce that transmitter. The common and usually transitory adverse effects of lithium include mild muscle tremors, fatigue, and diarrhea.

Lithium circulates freely through the body, unlike the classes of medication already discussed. It must be taken two to three times daily, except in its time-release form, to maintain a therapeutic effect. Eventually the amount of lithium in the client's blood is equal to that in the nervous system, and thus its levels can be efficiently monitored by measuring blood levels. Monitoring is important because adverse reactions can occur at blood levels slightly higher than a client's therapeutic level.

Two anti-seizure medications, carbamazepine and valproate, are also effective **mood stabilizers**. Like lithium, the way they work is not clear. One theory holds that they control a "kindling" process in limbic system neuron tracts that contribute to manic states. In building a wood fire, kindling refers to the low-grade burning of materials which facilitates the outbreak of a full-scale blaze. It is speculated that in mania a repetitive "firing" of low-grade electrical stimuli is set in motion, eventually producing a manic episode. The drug carbamazepine, which is also a potent blocker of norepinephrine reuptake, inhibits the firing of impulses by binding to them when they are inactive. It may also function as an inhibitor of enzymes in the central nervous system that break down GABA. The GABA neurotransmitter might have antimanic properties, and thus its increased prevalence in the nervous system might enhance mood stability. Valproate, another atypical antimanic drug, also seems to increase levels of GABA. These medications, while effective, are generally not prescribed unless lithium is first ruled out, since they have adverse effects that, although similar to those of lithium, can occasionally be more serious.

Other drugs appear to have some potential as antimanic agents, generally as adjuncts to the major drugs. Several anti-anxiety medications have been tested for antimanic qualities. They may eventually provide an alternative to the adjunctive use of antipsychotic drugs in stabilizing manic persons, because the adverse effects of the latter drugs discourage some clients from adherence.

Anti-Anxiety Medications   Several types of **anti-anxiety medication** are currently available, but the most frequently prescribed are the benzodiazepines. Diazepam (Valium) and alprazolam (Xanax) are well known drugs from this class. The name derives from their chemical structure, in which a benzene ring is fused to a diazepine ring. These drugs are frequently referred to as "minor tranquilizers." There may be natural benzodiazepine chemicals in the brain, potentiated by the GABA neurotransmitter, which evolved as fear regulators. GABA is a major inhibitory neurotransmitter in the brain, and the benzodiazepine medications achieve their therapeutic effect by increasing the effectiveness of GABA in binding with its receptors. GABA receptors in various regions of the brain mediate the anti-anxiety, sedative, and anticonvulsant effects of the benzodiazepines. The medications block central nervous system stimulation and diminish activity in areas associated with emotion. They also raise one's seizure threshold. The benzodiazepine drugs bind to specific sites on GABA receptors, but it is not clear how they achieve specificity as anti-anxiety agents. They affect neurons in the limbic system, where receptors are known to decrease anxiety. As a general rule, the benzodiazepines reduce anxiety in lower doses and act as a sedative in higher doses.

Benzodiazepines are quickly absorbed in the gastrointestinal tract and thus have a rapid effect, in many cases within 30 minutes. They do not present a high risk for overdose because they have a high therapeutic index. Their major side effect is sedation, and mild mental confusion may also occur for some people. An important characteristic of the benzodiazepines is that they can be physically addictive at some dosages with continuous use; thus clients who have substance abuse histories must use them with caution. Long-term use (several months or longer) can cause production of the body's natural benzodiazepine compounds to shut down. If the drug is abruptly withdrawn, no natural production will occur in one's system for a period of time. Clients must be tapered off these medications for several weeks or months to prevent the effects of physical withdrawal. For these reasons, the benzodiazepines are designed for comparatively short-term use, even though at times they may be prescribed for a client for periods up to several years.

Another type of anti-anxiety medication, buspirone, is fundamentally different in action from the benzodiazepines in that it enhances the effectiveness of serotonin receptors. Serotonin is believed to have anti-anxiety effects in several areas of the brain. This medication must be taken regularly to be effective, like the antidepressant and mood-stabilizing drugs but unlike the benzodiazepines. It also must be taken for several weeks before its anti-anxiety effect begins. Part of its attraction for physicians is that it is not potentially addictive. Frequently, clients who have taken benzodiazepines for an extended period of time will be gradually changed over to buspirone.

Several other, smaller classes of medications are used for the control of anxiety. These include the beta-blockers, so named because they compete with norepinephrine at "beta" receptor sites in the brain and nervous system that regulate cardiac and muscular functions. These medications are effective in treating anticipatory anxiety. They lower the client's anxiety by reducing the visceral symptoms of rapid heartbeat, muscle tension, and dry mouth. Since the client does not experience these physiological indicators, his or her subjective experience of anxiety is diminished. Finally, antihistamine drugs are occasionally taken as anti-anxiety agents. These drugs block histamine receptors in the nervous system that are associated with anxiety and agitation. They are rapidly absorbed and maintain a therapeutic effect for approximately 24 hours. Antihistamines tend to be highly sedating, however, and function effectively as anti-anxiety agents for only a few months.

MANAGING PSYCHOLOGICAL
AND SOCIAL ADVERSE EFFECTS

Adverse effects are the physical, psychological, or social effects of a medication that are unintentional and unrelated to its desired therapeutic effect. Some adverse effects may be experienced as pleasant, such as the mildly sedative effect of some antianxiety and antidepressant medications. Physical adverse effects are the most readily observable to the client and others. However, adverse effects may also be psychological, if they affect the client's sense of self, and social, if they affect how he or she is viewed by others. I consider these latter effects because they are not always highlighted by professionals.

Psychological side-effects occur when medication negatively affects the client's self-concept. Ongoing use of any medication produces several dependency dilemmas for the client. First, the client must accept at some level that he or she is, at least temporarily, dependent on a chemical agent in order to function at a desired level. Case managers must be sensitive to the effect this knowledge might have on the client's identity as a self-determining agent. He or she needs to be supported in coming to terms with the need to take medications and to gradually integrate this fact into the sense of self. The case manager, in the roles of consultant/collaborator and educator, may work with clients, family members, and perhaps others in the client's environment to help them understand the normal ambivalence generated by this identity issue.

One negative outcome of reliance on medication occurs if the client comes to feel that he or she can function adequately only with the assistance of medication and that he or she is powerless to generate change in other ways. In these situations the case manager must ensure that the client maintains an awareness of personal strengths and other resources to promote healthy social functioning. Some clients develop a dependence on the physician and other treaters, including the case manager. The client may become unassertive with these persons, not disclosing the full details of medication effects and life events, if he or she fears that doing so may disrupt whatever predictable patterns of social functioning have been established with the assistance of the medications.

Another psychological side-effect may be anger over the need to take medication. Clients' anger may center on the idea that they have a disorder requiring the intervention of medications, that treatment providers are promoting the point of view that they are "ill," and that others in their social system, including family and friends, are participating in a process of stigmatization. On the other hand, clients might simply disagree that they have an illness and might never accept the need to take medication. This is an issue which the case managers can best address by developing a relationship of trust with clients, and also through collateral work with significant others in clients' lives. Appropriate roles include that of the consultant/collaborator, who raises the issue for discussion and acknowledges the normalcy of the clients' point of view.

Social adverse effects refer to the interpersonal and organizational barriers clients face as they proceed through their lives as identified consumers of psychotropic medications. Estroff (1981) has noted the paradox that while medication may help one think more clearly, its adverse physical effects may make the client appear even more disturbed to others. Auge and Herzlech (1998) have reviewed aspects of the "sick role," which also has relevance to this issue. In receiving the diagnosis of a mental illness, and accepting treatments for it, including medication, an individual acknowledges that he or she has a condition that needs the help of experts. The client may be legitimately excused from certain responsibilities as a result of being ill, but only if he or she seeks appropriate remedies. The client's identity of being socially marginal may be reinforced if he or she resists any traditional interventions.

Acknowledging an illness to others does produce a social stigma. Coming to terms with this problem may present some clients with a no-win situation.

If the client rejects the sick role entirely but is unable to maintain work, family, and other social responsibilities, he or she will be labeled as irresponsible. The client may unrealistically persist with a job and risk losing it rather than, for example, accept temporary leave with its implications of social stigma. As another example, a person may choose to list medications and illnesses on job applications, and many employers may be reluctant to hire persons with mental disorders despite the legal implications of the Americans with Disabilities Act. These social adverse effects of taking medication may be addressed by the case manager in the roles of advocate (in the case of job discrimination, for example), monitor, and educator.

CLINICAL RELATIONSHIPS AND MEDICATION MANAGEMENT

The key to achieving successful medication management is effective collaboration with clients and their families, and with other providers such as psychiatrists, nurses, and psychologists. Two themes undergird this effective collaboration. Case managers must maintain a balanced perspective on client rights with regard to medication, and they must work toward the integration of psychosocial services with psychopharmacology. All the case manager roles described above should be built on these foundations.

Maintaining a Balanced Perspective

Effective collaboration concerning medication with clients, families, and other mental health providers includes the cultivation of a balanced perspective regarding client rights. The rights of clients, families, and society must be balanced, as well as the costs and benefits of psychotropic medication use and the roles of case management with those of other provider professions. Determining the appropriate balance between these interests is difficult. Although client's rights issues gained attention in the 1970s with landmark court battles, the struggle for balance is still seen in debates around such issues as involuntary commitment, the right to refuse treatment, and parity in medical insurance. Frequently mental illness is seen as synonymous with incompetence. This perception can lead to inappropriate substituted decision-making on behalf of clients and the undermining of self-determination in medication use.

The case manager cannot ignore that medication management often causes conflicts among client, family, and societal rights. Case managers can be caught between the desire to be collaborative with families and their ethical and legal obligations to honor the decisions of clients. Several strategies for resolving such conflicts have been offered by Zipple, Langle, Spaniol, and Fisher (1990). They suggest sharing non-confidential information with families, providing them with written information when appropriate, making referrals to support and education groups in the community, respecting release of information procedures, and using mediators when necessary. Though client rights have the preeminent position, the most effective collaboration will attempt to balance the rights of all participants in the process. Certainly the power of family support and that of support groups for clients and families has been clearly demonstrated in this regard (Hatfield, 1990).

Integrating Psychosocial and Medication Interventions

Case managers need to recognize the power issues intrinsic in combined clinical interventions and appreciate the challenges that emerge in their coordination. The most powerful treatment for clients is a combination of medication and psychosocial treatments. Solid empirical research and decades of clinical experience support combining treatments in persons having a range of mental illnesses including depression, panic, agoraphobia, obsessive-compulsive disorder, generalized anxiety disorder, anorexia, schizophrenia, and borderline personality disorder (Beitman & Klerman, 1991; Farmer, Walsh, & Bentley, 1998; Test, 1998, Wallace, 1993).

One of the important barriers to combining treatments is the ideological conflict stemming from professionals' training in certain schools of thought. For example, those trained in psychoanalytic, interpersonal or behavioral techniques have historically placed less emphasis on the role of medication compared to psychosocial treatment (Klerman, 1984). Thus, some professionals conclude that medication merely covers up symptoms and avoids more fundamental clinical issues. Those trained in biological psychiatry, on the other hand, place tremendous emphasis in pharmacology. Others call for the integration of biology and psychology in mental health. Hoffman (1990) pleads with professionals to reject the "two-track" model of treating depression, where clients receive treatment as if they have two distinct disorders: one a biological depression requiring medication, and the other a psychological depression requiring psychotherapy. Since case managers cannot prescribe medication, working toward an effective interdisciplinary approach means working toward partnerships with physicians and the management of parallel treatment.

Though several issues related to the case manager's role in interdisciplinary teams were highlighted earlier, other dynamics in the management of the client-physician-case manager relationship deserve attention. These emerge when referring a client to a prescribing physician, accepting referrals from a physician for case management, and assuming co-responsibility for a client's treatment. Goldberg, Riba and Tasman (1991) studied the attitudes of psychiatrists toward prescribing medications for persons being treated by nonmedical professionals. Most medication services (75%) were initiated by the nonmedical provider. Over two thirds of the psychiatrists were satisfied with their current level of involvement, but 25% wished they did less and 8% wished they did more with the clients. One of the concerns raised most often by psychiatrists was the need for clarity regarding after-hours and emergency availability.

There is an increasing need for so-called "three-party" treatment relationships because of the expansion of the private practice marketplace and the increasing access of case managers and psychologists to insurance reimbursement (Pilette, 1988). Community mental health centers and, more recently, health maintenance organizations have relied on nonmedical professionals to provide psychosocial treatment while physicians provide psychopharmacology. The client hopefully benefits from the strengths of each clinician, but a number of problems seem inherent to this arrangement. First, who has ultimate authority and responsibility for the client's treatment? How will disagreements be handled within a team environment? Who will decide about changes in treatment? There are questions about confidentiality and how much sharing is too much. The entry route of the client is an important factor in answering these questions. That is, how did the client come to the three party relationship? Was he or she first a client of the psychiatrist, who then made a referral to a case manager? Was he or she seeing a case manager, who then made the referral to a psychiatrist for medication screening?

Kelly (1992) advises psychiatrists to work only with professionals they know and trust, and to make it clear they are not only a medication dispenser but also a consultant. The physician should consider the case manager to be a responsible professional but not a medical colleague, supervisee, or competitor. The nonmedical professional, according to Kelly, should likewise use a physician who appreciates the complexity of parallel treatment and considers him or herself to be an important source of information, but not a co-therapist or competitor. Both clinicians need to be aware of the potential influence of psychosocial treatment on medication use and vice versa. For example, while psychosocial treatments may actually enhance medication adherence, medication may in turn help clients become better prepared for psychosocial treatment. Further, medication may heighten the client's confidence in treatment, but it may also encourage magical thinking and decrease motivation for other treatments (Bradley, 1990).

In addition, both clinicians should be aware of tensions that emerge among all participants in three-party relationships (Dewan, 1992). These include the positive and negative feelings generated in each party as a result of their interactions and activities. A positive outcome occurs when the client views medication as a nurturing act, an acknowledgement of pain. Such an acknowledgement can validate each clinician's empathy for the client. On the other hand, the client may regard the addition of a second therapist, whether physician or case manager, as evidence of a more serious disorder or a lack of interest or competence on the part of the referring clinician. The case manager may make a negative impression on the client if he or she uses the referral as a distancing mechanism, a way of devaluing investment in the client's case or an indication of secondary status compared to the physician (Bradley, 1990). In making referrals to physicians, case managers must face their own discomfort about exposing their work to another, while medical doctors who take referrals have to deal with sharing power and control and avoiding competition. Likewise, physicians must be careful not to fall into the trap of letting the client idealize him or her and thus collude with the client in devaluing psychosocial treatment. Interestingly, several authors warn against the collaboration becoming too close so that role distinctions are not clear and appropriate differences in approaches get skewed (Busch & Gould, 1993).

The foundation of partnership, balance, and integration has implications for how and when case managers make referrals to physicians. The severity of the client's symptoms is a key factor in deciding the timing of the referral. It is important for the case manager to remember that any referral to a physician is for *possible* treatment with psychotropic medication. Therefore, discussions with the client should begin with a review of the pros and cons of seeking an evaluation and an overview of what to expect in the evaluation process. The client may have questions about how to respond if he or she *is* or *is not* offered a prescription. The case manager should share knowledge about the costs and benefits of medication, given the client's concerns and circumstances, including any known potential interactive or additive effects with psychosocial treatments. Case managers should help the client decide to seek adjunctive treatment with cautious optimism. After the medical evaluation, the client and case manager should continue to address the client's responses.

SUMMARY

A majority of clients with serious mental illnesses take psychotropic medication as part of their treatment, at least intermittently. To be an effective practitioner, the case manager must have a basic knowledge of the types and actions of these medications, as well as an awareness of potential case management roles within a holistic intervention framework. In this chapter I have provided an overview of four classes of psychotropic medication used in the treatment of mental illness and five professional roles for the case manager. The information presented here is not sufficient for the case manager to fill those roles effectively, but it provides an introduction on which the case manager can build through self-study. In the chapters that follow one or more of these roles will apply in every instance where the client takes medications.

Appendix: List of Medications Described in this Chapter

Generic Name	Trade Name
Antipsychotics	
Chlorpromazine	Clorazine, Promapar, Thorazine
Clozapine	Clozaril
Fluphenazine	Prolixin
Haloperidol	Haldol
Olanzapine	Zyprexa
Risperidone	Risperdal
Trifluoperazine	Stelazine
Antiparkinsonian Medications	
Benztropine	Cogentin
Trihexiphenidyl	Artane
Antidepressants	
Doxepin	Sinequan
Fluoxetine	Prozac
Imipramine	Tofranil
Phenelzine	Nardil
Sertraline	Zoloft
Tranylcypromine	Parnate
Mood Stabilizers	
Carbamazepine	Tegretol
Lithium Carbonate	Eskalith, Lithium
Valproate	Depakene, Depakote
Anti-Anxiety Drugs	
Alprazolam	Xanax
Buspirone	BuSpar
Chlordiazepoxide	Librium, Libritabs
Diazepam	Valium, Val-release, Vazepam

6

☙

Persons with Schizophrenia

Several years ago I met with a young woman with schizophrenia. The client, though only 25, had received both in- and outpatient treatment over a seven-year period for ongoing symptoms of psychosis. At one point I asked if she thought that she had a mental illness. The client seemed confused by my question. I continued, "You have been seen by a number of professionals over the years, and all of them have treated you for schizophrenia. Do you agree that you have a mental illness?"

The client seemed startled but pleased as she replied, "What an interesting question. No one has ever asked me that before."

It was my turn to be startled. I understood that the client was indeed experiencing schizophrenia. She was struggling to complete a college education while experiencing psychotic delusions and disordered thinking, a condition requiring medication, sometimes in high doses, for control. She had limited tolerance for most social activities. Still, no one had ever encouraged the client to share her feelings about the inner experiences that were distancing her from family and friends. She had not been encouraged by a professional to reflect on what the illness (if she believed that she had one) meant to her. In short, her personal experience of schizophrenia had been discounted by treaters, who were instead focused on eradicating her symptoms. This client might have felt that a major aspect of her personality was being ignored, since persons with schizophrenia often integrate the disorder into their identities.

The *counseling* of persons with schizophrenia has been increasingly de-emphasized by mental health professionals with the rise in prominence of case management and biological interventions. I oppose this trend and present in this chapter a rationale for including long-term, relationship-based clinical intervention as a major component of a comprehensive plan for clients. I present seven practice guidelines for developing the treatment relationship.

Interventions promoting long-term, relationship-based counseling have become de-emphasized for at least three reasons. First, because the etiology of schizophrenia is focused on brain chemistry, clients are not typically considered to be good candidates for counseling as a primary treatment. Most professionals accept that schizophrenia cannot be cured, but only controlled, and this is effectively achieved in many cases with medication alone. Second, the basic needs of the persons with schizophrenia usually require the most attention because clients' downward social mobility causes frequent crises with regard to housing, health care, social support, and income. Finally, current political trends call for public mental health interventions to be as inexpensive as possible because of the crisis in health care costs (Mechanic, 1993). Efforts are focused on interventions for keeping clients with schizophrenia out of hospitals. Any encouragement by policy-makers and administrators of relationship-based counseling might create additional pressure for public financing and increase the cost of rehabilitation services beyond acceptable levels.

Despite these trends, there are negative consequences for clients in abandoning relationship-based interventions. Persons with schizophrenia, who have limited social skills and few supportive relationships, may become further isolated if their interpersonal problems are not adequately addressed.

Case managers who focus on basic physical needs and psychosocial rehabilitation services may de-emphasize or even ignore clients' purpose-in-life or spiritual issues and other **quality of life** considerations, such as security and safety. The task-oriented nature of most interventions further tends to overlook the client's *ambivalence* about goals, which is a common symptom of schizophrenia. This ambivalence may be misunderstood as a lack of motivation, and it should be processed in the context of a therapeutic relationship prior to the introduction of some interventions. For example, a client might agree to participate in a job training program, in spite of great anxieties about working, to be perceived as cooperative and to continue to qualify for other support services. If the job training ends in failure, the experience will negatively affect the client's self-esteem, and the emotional concerns behind the client's ambivalence may never be addressed. Finally, as noted in Chapter 2, clinical case managers who devote their professional lives to working with these challenging clients will likely experience lower status and pay than their peers engaged in "psychotherapy" if it is assumed that a lesser degree of clinical skill is required.

Psychotherapy has many definitions, also described in Chapter 1. The counseling of clients with schizophrenia is generally supportive (vs. reconstructive), as it promotes the optimal use of the client's strengths, enhances adaptive defenses, and elaborates improved mechanisms of maintaining self-control (Wolberg, 1988). I acknowledge that most forms of intensive therapy for persons with schizophrenia are not effective and are possibly detrimental to emotional functioning, even if coordinated with medication and other supportive interventions. Still, the widely held position that persons with schizophrenia cannot benefit from relationship-based counseling seems overstated. Between 1960 and 1984, only seven systematic studies were done on the effectiveness of psychotherapy with persons having schizophrenia, and the results were inconclusive (Wasylenki, 1992).

SCHIZOPHRENIA: A DESCRIPTION

Schizophrenia is a disorder of the brain characterized by abnormal patterns of thought and perception as inferred from language and behavior (American Psychiatric Association, 1994). It is primarily a **disorder of thought,** distinguishing it from **disorders of mood**, such as bipolar disorder. Schizophrenia includes two types of symptoms. **Positive symptoms** represent exaggerations of normal behavior. These include hallucinations, delusions, disorganized thought processes, and tendencies toward agitation. The **negative symptoms** represent the diminution of what would be considered normal behavior. These include flat or blunted affect (the absence of expression), social withdrawal, non-communication, anhedonia (blandness) or passivity, and ambivalence in decision making. A predominance of positive symptoms is sometimes called Type I schizophrenia, and a predominance of negative symptoms is sometimes called Type 2 schizophrenia. It is not clear whether these are distinct types of the disorder. About 1% of the population worldwide has schizophrenia.

Hallucinations are sense perceptions of external objects which are not present. These may be auditory, visual, gustatory (the perception of taste), tactile (feeling an object), somatic (an unreal experience within the body), or olfactory (a false sense of smell). **Delusions** are false beliefs that are maintained even though contradicted by social reality. They include persecutory (people or forces are attempting to bring one harm), erotomanic (another person is in love with the individual), somatic (pertaining to body functioning), and grandiose (an exaggerated sense of one's power, knowledge, or identity) beliefs, thought broadcasting (one's thoughts are overheard by others), thought insertion or withdrawal (others are putting thoughts into, or taking thoughts out of, one's head), delusions of being controlled (thoughts, feelings, or actions are imposed by an external force), and delusions of reference (neutral events have special significance for the person).

THE EXPERIENCE OF SCHIZOPHRENIA

The person with schizophrenia experiences pronounced sensory changes (Benioff, 1995). *Visual* changes include heightened sensitivity to light and color, a loss of perspective of figures, illusionary changes in faces and objects, and distortions in size. *Auditory* changes include hallucinations, heightened sensitivity to noise, an inability to screen out background noise, the muting of sounds, and distortions of the sounds of voices. *Physical* changes include heightened sensitivity to touch, an inability to interpret internal sensations, and tactile and olfactory hallucinations. *Cognitive* changes include loose associations, the inability to filter out irrelevant information, distractibility, overstimulation of thoughts (flooding), feelings of enhanced mental efficiency, increased *or* decreased speed of thinking, fragmentation (the inability to create a whole from the parts), delusions, and idiosyncratic explanatory systems.

Persons with schizophrenia function well with a moderate amount of face-to-face interaction with significant others (Leff & Vaughn, 1985). Likewise, they manage moderate amounts of social stimulation well. They respond favorably to attitudes of acceptance, reasonable expectations, the opportunity to develop and practice social and vocational skills, and a relatively small number of social supports (but in a variety of clusters). These include contacts with family members, friends, neighbors, work peers, school peers, informal community relations, and perhaps church members. Fifty percent (50%) of persons with schizophrenia attempt suicide, and 10% eventually succeed.

Effects on the Family

Schizophrenia has profound effects on family functioning (Hatfield & Lefley, 1993). When a person has schizophrenia, all family members share a chronic emotional burden. Common emotional reactions include stress, anxiety, resentment of the impaired member, grief, and depression. Spouses tend to blame each other for family turmoil, and siblings tend to blame parents. There is little time available for family leisure activities and one adult, usually the mother, becomes the primary caretaker of the impaired member. Siblings have some reactions unique from the parents, including emotional constriction in personality development, isolation from peers, and jealousy about the attention given to the impaired member (National Alliance for the Mentally Ill, 1989). Factors influencing the family's ability to cope include the severity of the disorder (greater severity implies better coping), the preservation of time for other activities, the ability to be proactive rather than reactive in seeking assistance, and the availability of outside support.

DIAGNOSIS AND CLASSIFICATION

According to the *Diagnostic and Statistical Manual of Mental Disorders* (DSM-IV) (American Psychiatric Association, 1994), schizophrenia is characterized by at least six months of continuous symptoms. The person must display two or more active or positive symptoms (delusions, hallucinations, disorganized speech, and disorganized or catatonic behavior) for at least one month. The remainder of the six months might feature negative symptoms, and there must also be a decline in social functioning skills. Signs of the disturbance might be limited to negative symptoms during the premorbid (prior to the active phase) or residual (after stabilization from an active phase) periods.

There are five subtypes of schizophrenia, which may represent different disease processes. The **paranoid** type features a preoccupation with delusions or auditory hallucinations but a preservation of cognitive functioning and affect. **Disorganized** schizophrenia is characterized by disorganized speech, behavior, and flat or inappropriate affect. **Catatonic** schizophrenia features psychomotor disturbances of immobility or excessive mobility, mutism, odd gestures, echolalia (repeating the words of others) or echopraxia (repeating the movements of others). The **undifferentiated** type describes persons who do not meet criteria for the first three types. **Residual** schizophrenia describes the person who displays only negative symptoms after an active episode. This phase might be transient or might persist for years. The DSM-IV also provides six course specifiers for further detailing the client's experience.

The age of onset for schizophrenia is between 15 and 40 years. Men tend to develop the disorder at an earlier age than women (50% of men who develop schizophrenia do so by age 28, while 50% of women do so by age 33). The prevalence of schizophrenia is twice as high in lower as compared to higher socioeconomic classes. The "downward drift" hypothesis holds that many persons who develop schizophrenia lose occupational and social skills and fall into the lower classes, while others with premorbid personality traits never develop adequate skills to establish themselves in stable social roles.

INSTRUMENTS FOR
MONITORING SYMPTOMS

Case managers can use a range of brief scales to assess symptoms and symptom changes for persons with schizophrenia. Three are described here. The *Psychiatric Symptom Assessment Scale* (PSAS) includes 23 items, each rated on a 7-point scale, and provides an overall score as well as scores for the domains of anxiety/depression, positive behavior symptoms, positive verbal symptoms, deficit symptoms, and paranoia (Bigelow & Berthot, 1989). The PSAS can be administered during the course of a 30-minute interview. No standardized interview protocol is included with the PSAS, but all items, and each point along the rating scale, include assessment and rating guidelines. The *Scale for the Assessment of Negative Symptoms* (SANS) and *Scale for the Assessment of Positive Symptoms* (SAPS) are complimentary instruments (Andreasen, 1982; Andreasen & Olsen, 1982). The SANS includes 25 items rated along a 6-point scale with five subscales (affect, poverty of speech, apathy, anhedonia, and impairment of attention). The SAPS includes 35 items, four subscales (hallucinations, delusions, bizarreness, and positive thought disorder), and one global assessment of affect. Both are designed for use in conjunction with client interviews, clinical observations, family member observations, and reports from other professionals.

CAUSAL THEORIES

No one knows the causes of schizophrenia. Most research at present is focused in the genetic and biological areas, but psychological factors cannot be ruled out, particularly with regard to the course of the disorder. Biological theories of schizophrenia implicate the brain's limbic system, frontal cortex, and basal ganglia as primary sites of malfunction (Lieberman & Koreen, 1993). Whether symptoms result from abnormal development or deterioration of brain function is not clear. The dopamine hypothesis, established in the 1960s, asserted that schizophrenia results from an excess of that neurotransmitter in the central nervous system. More recently, possible causal roles of other neurotransmitters, including serotonin and norepinephrine, have been proposed. Brain imaging techniques have revealed enlarged ventricles in many persons with schizophrenia which may be contributing causes in the consequent reduction in total amount of brain tissue (Lewis & Higgins, 1996). Prenatal viral exposure or brain trauma from birth complications have also been postulated as causal factors.

The genetic transmission of schizophrenia is supported by higher than average risk factors among family members of persons with the disorder (Kendler & Diehl, 1993). A monozygotic (identical) twin of a person with schizophrenia has a 47% chance to develop the disorder. A dyzygotic (nonidentical) twin has only a 12% likelihood, which is the same probability as a child with one schizophrenic parent. A non-twin sibling has an 8% chance of developing the disorder. These statistics, while compelling, leave room for the role of environmental influences.

Various psychological and social factors have been postulated as significant in the development of schizophrenia. Freud (1966) placed neurosis and psychosis on a continuum as resulting from similar psychological mechanisms. He wavered, however, between a defense and a deficit theory of schizophrenia. The defense theory conceptualized symptoms as a means of adapting to internal conflict. Deficit theory implied a nonspecific organic defect resulting in one's inability to sustain attachments to others, and a tendency to become preoccupied with internal experiences.

Developmental theorists assert that mental disorders result from the inability to progress successfully through critical life stages. For example, problems with normal separation from the primary caregiver during the first few years of life may result in schizophrenia if developmental arrests produce an inability to emotionally distinguish the self from others (Mahler, Pine, & Bergman, 1975). The failure to make the transition from adolescence to young adulthood, with its challenges of forming of peer relationships, patterning sexual behavior, revising personal values, and developing independent living skills, has also been suggested as producing a regression which may result in schizophrenia (Dawson, Blum, & Bartolucci, 1983).

Family theorists have used such terms as "emotional divorce" (Bowen, 1960), "communication deviance" (Singer, Wynne, & Toohey, 1978), the "double-bind" (Bateson, Jackson, Haley, & Weakland, 1963), and family "schisms" and "skewes" (Lidz, 1975) to describe problematic parent-child interactions that may cause a child to withdraw into psychosis. These have been largely discounted as causal influences, although family relationships do influence the course of the disorder. Adolph Meyer and Harry Stack Sullivan are examples of early 20th century theorists who cited cultural influences as significant in the onset and course of schizophrenia (Faustman, 1995).

In summary, the **stress/diathesis theory** holds that schizophrenia results from a mix of constitutional factors (perhaps 70% due to heritability and biology) and environmental and stress factors (approximately 30%) (Gottesman, 1991). Those external factors, however, are not specific to schizophrenia. They may include insults to the brain, threatening physical environments, emotionally intrusive experiences, emotional deprivation, and disruptions to cognitive processes.

Though the causes of schizophrenia are uncertain, there are clues for differentiating better and worse prognosis (Booth, 1995). Clients with better prognoses demonstrate sudden onset, perceptual changes that are experienced as strange, and a predominance of positive symptoms. They exhibit normal intellectual functions, good response to medication, adaptability to social situations, and the ability to live independently. Clients with worse prognoses feature a gradual onset, psychotic activity without subjective distress, and a predominance of negative symptoms. They exhibit intellectual deterioration, a poor response to medications, and poor social and independent living skills.

THE CLINICAL RELATIONSHIP

The Client and Case Manager's Experience of One Another

A key feature of schizophrenia, with the onset of disordered thinking, is a partial breakdown in the client's "rational" capability for perception, or ability to utilize and interpret conventional social symbols. The person's thought processes become concrete, idiosyncratic, and bizarre, and the cognitive ability to understand abstract symbols prevalent in society is lost. The person loses the capacity for interpersonal connection. This process was described in detail in Chapter 3.

The person with schizophrenia enters treatment with ambivalence about goals and skepticism about the worker's potential as an ally. Because of the thought disorder, the client has great difficulty managing relationships and has correctly learned from experience that others are likely to reject or devalue him or her. The client might feel miserable with loneliness and detachment, but at the same time feel so anxious about the emotional pain associated with social activity that he or she prefers isolation. The case manager might be perceived as a threat to the client's individuality. That is, the client might see the return to "normal" social functioning as a return to an anxiety-ridden, distressed state because he or she has lost investment in the symbols which are necessary to connect with a social group. The client feels that his or her perspective on life will not be understood. The client certainly wants to be "better," but the emotional motivation for treatment may include a magical craving for improvement rather than what the worker probably defines as a cooperative striving for change (Lantz, 1987). These characteristics give rise to certain predictable **transference** patterns, or reactions to the worker.

Because the client has little faith in human relationships, there is an initial mistrust of the case manager. The client might even feel hostility toward the worker in reaction to the conflict of both needing and fearing closeness (Kanter, 1988). Anger might be masked by passivity. In some instances the client will form a dependent relationship with the worker, valuing directives because he or she fears taking initiatives. The worker might be perceived as powerful, but the client will be disappointed if the worker demonstrates any evidence of ineffectiveness (which is likely to occur at times).

The case manager will also react to the client in certain ways that must be acknowledged for intervention to be effective. **Countertransference** can include negative reactions to the client's behavior, appearance, passive personality, or dependent traits, all of which are contrary to society's values (Minkoff, 1987). The worker might also react negatively to the client's apparent satisfaction with avoiding reality and responsibility. Other worker reactions could include an interpersonal distancing and projection of ambivalence about working with the client. These are the worker's defenses against frustration with slow client progress. They might become manifest in a blaming of the client for a lack of adequate progress as defined by the worker. The clinician could also be uncomfortable with the need to assume a more active clinical posture than is customary with other types of clients. Later in treatment, if a relationship is established, the worker might become uncomfortable with the client's strong degree of attachment. This might be the client's only significant relationship, and the worker might withdraw in reaction to feeling responsibility for the client's well-being.

The Therapeutic Climate

Every relationship exists within a symbolic frame of reference, including those shared images and behaviors that make private experiences mutually understandable. With the client having schizophrenia, communication occurs largely through unconscious and nonverbal channels. The client is ineffective with verbal communication because of having lost the ability to use conventional word symbols. The case manager's reliance on verbal strategies during the early stages of intervention can thus be counterproductive. A positive therapeutic climate, which will eventually result in symbolic connection, is promoted most effectively with the non-verbal communication of acceptance by the worker. Regardless of the verbal content of the early sessions, the client will perceive an ambience of warmth as affirming. That is, the worker and client will first connect symbolically on a non-verbal level. This is a basic principle for beginning intervention from the perspective of symbolic interactionism, but it is not an easy task, as will be demonstrated in the following case examples. The client, who is sensitive to non-verbal cues, will perceive any negative feelings, conscious or otherwise, and will prevent the connection from developing.

It is generally a mistake for the case manager to respond verbally too readily to the client who is either quiet or communicates psychotic ideas. The worker might be eager to engage the client in focused conversation, be uncomfortable with silence, wish to proceed with concrete goal-setting, or be eager to decode the client's psychotic associations. The case manager does not yet know what the client is communicating but attempts to decode the idiosyncratic symbols as if they have meanings for him or her. As a result, the client might experience increased anxiety, and further efforts at verbal communication will be discouraged by the worker's unintentional negative reinforcement. The clinician's initiation of active interventions (such as elaborate goal-setting in the first few meetings) will add pressure to the client who is already dealing with disturbing levels of anxiety. Some persons with schizophrenia, of course, achieve stable mental status and are amenable to relatively rapid engagement in the treatment process. My comments are focused primarily on actively psychotic clients who are new to a clinical setting, but I also contend that many persons with schizophrenia who appear stable have problems with clinical relationships related to the residual symptoms of the thought disorder.

CASE ILLUSTRATION: ROBYN

Robyn was a 28-year-old, single, unemployed female who lived with her younger sister in a condominium owned by her father. She had a diagnosis of schizophrenia, undifferentiated type, first developing the disorder at age 19. For almost ten years she had been minimally functional, and were it not for her father's material and emotional assistance she might have spent much more time in psychiatric hospitals than her two stays of several months each at ages 19 and 27. As an adolescent, Robyn had been an outstanding student, finishing near the top of her high school class and planning a career in nursing. However she had also been socially awkward without close friendships. Further, her mother had schizophrenia. Robyn's parents divorced in her early adolescence, and from that time she had almost no contact with her natural mother. Her father had remarried, and Robyn's stepmother tended to be critical of him for devoting so much time to his disabled daughter. The stepmother had no understanding of mental illness and felt that Robyn should be able to straighten out her life through force of will.

Robyn was referred to the mental health agency after her second hospital stay. She was an unmotivated client who came for her initial appointments only with encouragement from her father. By the time of her first session she had already stopped taking the medications prescribed at the hospital and did not propose any goals. The case manager understood that she came to the agency only to avoid angering her father, who was her sole social and financial support.

Robyn was so severely impaired that she was unable to care for her basic needs. She did not bathe, wash her clothes, or eat properly. Her body odor was so unpleasant that a group of agency clerical staff demanded that she not be permitted into the building. This demand was successfully resisted by the case manager, although he did attempt to schedule her appointments at times when few other clients were present. During her sessions, Robyn rarely initiated conversation. She answered questions tersely and without elaboration. She tried at times to articulate her thoughts but was unsuccessful, seeming frustrated at not being able to put her thoughts into words. Robyn denied hearing voices, but the case manager suspected that she did. He noted that she frequently talked to herself while staring into space. When asked at these times what she was thinking about, Robyn refused to comment. The case manager assessed that there was nothing oppositional about her presentation; Robyn was simply an extremely anxious and actively psychotic client. She often said, in tears, that "life is just too hard for me." At home she did little but watch television. She went outside every few days to shop for food or to walk to the bank. Robyn received social security disability income and, as one major strength, was frugal with her money.

The case manager made efforts for several months in biweekly meetings to gather relevant personal history and set treatment goals with Robyn, but it soon became clear that this approach was not working. She demonstrated no investment in the clinical process and did not seem to understand what the worker was trying to do. She missed appointments frequently. The case manager's own primary goal was to help Robyn accept the need for medication, as this might calm her and clarify her thinking to an extent that other rehabilitative interventions could be introduced, such as social skills training and basic self-care. The worker eventually realized that he was not likely to make any progress with this strategy of prepared agendas. He changed his goal to that of making Robyn comfortable enough in the relationship to consistently attend her scheduled appointments. The case manager consulted with both his supervisor and agency physician about this plan to get their input and support, and also to seek the physician's assurance that he would arrange to see Robyn as soon as she agreed to a medication evaluation.

The case manager presented a plan to Robyn that she accepted. The initial written service plan was not substantive (see appendix), but the case manager hoped to update it regularly with more ambitious goals and interventions. For now they would continue to meet every two weeks at Robyn's condominium rather than the agency, and they would either take a walk through the neighborhood, drive to a mall or park for a walk, or go to lunch. There would be no other agenda for the meetings. In fact, they would spend time together and talk or not talk, depending on Robyn's inclinations. The worker would not attempt to convince the client to take any particular steps, such as accepting medication or attending rehabilitation programs, unless the client asked about them.

Under these conditions a relationship did develop as evidenced by the fact that Robyn continued to schedule and to be ready for their regular meetings. However, for almost six months, little substantive verbal interaction took place. Robyn was polite, always asking how the case manager was feeling that day. She seemed at times to make efforts to communicate, but usually admitted after 20 or 30 minutes, with some frustration and almost to herself, "I just don't have much to talk about." The worker maintained a sociable posture and regularly initiated conversation, but he was careful not to bring up topics that could be perceived as threatening. Robyn continued to not bathe or wash her clothes, and although she claimed to be shopping and eating well, she looked pale and thin. The worker assumed that her sister and father were providing some reinforcement of basic self-care behaviors. However, Robyn did not give permission for the worker to talk with either her sister or parents. The worker had spoken by phone with her parents during the initial referral process but had no ongoing interactions with them.

Gradually Robyn became comfortable with the worker. She could never verbalize this, and even her nonverbal behavior and personal presentation provided few indicators. In fact, the worker resisted making any assumptions about how the relationship was developing, as he understood that he could still not relate easily to this client's private world. In time, however, he noticed that Robyn began each session by asking if they could schedule the next meeting. More dramatically, she began to talk, although vaguely, about her anxieties. Over time the worker learned that Robyn was terrified of abandonment by her family; she believed that if this happened she would need to live in a hospital for the rest of her life without anyone caring about her. Further, she felt totally inadequate to handle any stress. She was paralyzed with anxiety in social situations and, as a result, was resistant to interventions from professionals who always seemed eager for her to make changes in her life. Robyn did express interest in attending church on Sundays, but did not feel that she could tolerate being present in a congregation. The worker gave no advice about this issue but encouraged Robyn to discuss it, as her religious beliefs seemed more important to her than anything else.

It must be emphasized that these issues were raised over a period of months in the context of short conversations. Robyn remained minimally articulate. The worker did successfully link Robyn with the agency physician for medication monitoring after helping her understand that that it might reduce her anxiety and that she could stop taking medicine if it did not agree with her. Robyn began using antipsychotic medication regularly, in small doses, and eventually agreed to take more as it made her feel calmer. It did not change her presentation dramatically but did eliminate what Robyn had described as occasional screaming spells which occurred at night when she felt most afraid. The physician was particularly patient with Robyn, having learned of her history over time from the case manager, and she seemed to form an attachment to him. To the case manager's surprise she agreed with the physician's suggestion, several months into their work, to increase her dose of loxapine.

Other changes took place in the client's life. Accepting the case manager as an ally, she agreed to let him talk occasionally to her father, but only to reinforce the fact that she had a limited ability to care for herself. The case manager took advantage of the opportunity to help her father understand the disabling symptoms of schizophrenia, which were perplexing to him. The father's guilt about possibly being responsible for her illness was relieved somewhat in these meetings. The case manager was also effective with Robyn in helping her shop for more nutritional foods. During these developments, the case manager was able to update Robyn's service plan to include goals that targeted more concrete behaviors (see appendix). The agency's Peer Review Committee, which regularly read agency files and made decisions about approving ongoing care, believed that the case should be continued. The total number of hours being provided to Robyn by agency staff was not great, and it seemed that she would be at a high risk of rehospitalization if she were not followed indefinitely by the case manager.

At the end of one year of work, the sum of the client's observable growth included bathing weekly, operating a washing machine (which she used sparingly), using a therapeutic level of medications that had modest positive benefits, maintaining a structure of biweekly visits with the case manager, and allowing her father to receive education about schizophrenia. She did not become appreciably more verbal with any other persons or enter into any formal rehabilitation activities. While these changes represented small gains after a great deal of sustained effort by the case manager, they were far from dramatic and resulted in minor changes in Robyn's social functioning. Still, the client remained in treatment, which she had not done with previous workers, and was never rehospitalized.

THE CLINICAL CASE MANAGER'S
INTERVENTIONS

It may seem that Robyn's worker provided little active intervention. He initially attempted to establish certain goals, but when the client resisted, he appeared to do little beyond maintaining a schedule of vaguely structured meetings. In fact, the worker did adjust his interventions appropriately to meet this difficult client's needs. In this section I will outline the steps demonstrating that the case manager was therapeutically active and helpful to Robyn's reaching some symbolic validation so she could engage in treatment.

Respecting the Client's Inner Experiences

Clients experience their hallucinations and delusions as valid symbols. These are very much a part of their identities, and to dismiss them is to devalue the person. Many case managers make the mistake of suggesting to clients early in treatment that psychotic ideas are merely symptoms; manifestations of chemical imbalance or thought disorder. It is clinically productive for the social worker to consider delusions and hallucinations as the client's bizarre but genuine efforts to construct symbolic connections with the external world. A goal of treatment is to help the client regain symbolic repertoires which will facilitate a broader social integration, but this cannot be rushed. Clients isolate themselves in part because their idiosyncratic symbols are devalued by others.

Making No Suggestion of Change

Ambivalence is a symptom of schizophrenia. The client is confused, feeling torn by opposing inclinations to connect with and to run from others. Any action by the case manager will meet one set of needs while thwarting others. Getting "well" may be perceived by the client as returning to an even more stressful state than he or she now experiences. Thus, expectations of change will give rise to the client's resistance. Robyn's resistance to the clinical relationship only diminished when her case manager made clear that he did not expect any change on her part. Robyn needed to experience a safe therapeutic climate before risking any changes. The case manager must accept the client's symbolic world rather than expect the client to be capable of re-investing in conventional symbols. Patience in these circumstances is difficult because agency administrators, policy-makers, and insurance companies frequently pressure case managers to work for quick results.

Accepting the Client's Agenda

Once the client comes to trust the case manager in an atmosphere of warmth and acceptance devoid of pressure, his or her agendas for change will emerge. These might include goals that are contrary to agency and worker values of independent living and self-reliance. The client might not want to work, finish schooling, attend psychosocial rehabilitation activities, or live on his or her own. Still, because each person has values and aspirations for certain lifestyles and interpersonal commitments, the client will eventually identify goals. Robyn wanted to feel calmer, to rid herself of suicidal thoughts, and to have several friends. She did not want to work or to be linked with any formal social activities. She had initially not wanted to take medicines, but she changed her mind about that. The worker resisted pushing Robyn to act on any goals and gave her the time she needed to make decisions. She talked to the worker about her fears of death, of being physically hurt, and of being hospitalized. She agreed to work toward her goal of making friends by practicing scripted conversations with store clerks, whom she viewed as pleasant and non-threatening (for more on the possible significance of "informal community relations," see Chapter 4).

Concrete and Formal Communication Style

Because persons with schizophrenia lose the capacity for abstract thought, the case manager must take care to communicate clearly through direct, simple, and brief verbal interactions. Robyn's worker initiated little conversation with her, preferring to respond to her comments with clear, short replies. Even at her most emotional moments, when Robyn cried about being lonely and afraid, the worker only said, "You seem sad, Robyn. You've told me that your life is hard. I want to help. What will make you feel better?" Robyn's appointments were always on the same day at approximately the same time, and they included a predictable sequence of comments and actions from the worker. As words can be confusing, so can the worker's expressions and physical movements. The worker should explain his or her nonverbal actions when they seem to confuse the client (this can make the case manager feel quite self-conscious). Increased informality may be appropriate once the relationship includes trust, but in the early stages the client will best understand the worker if he or she is consistent in both verbal and nonverbal ways. This will insure minimal use of abstract symbolic behavior that the client is not equipped to interpret and will bring more clarity to the relationship.

Affirming Strengths and the Sense of Self

The sense of self is developed through social interaction based on a shared use of symbols. The person with schizophrenia has lost much of the ability to maintain a clear sense of self, partly due to lack of external affirmation. Robyn felt that she was inadequate and worthless as a human being because she received no reinforcement of self-worth from anyone. In an atmosphere of acceptance, the worker can help the client develop a sense of social connection by affirming any appropriate efforts to function as part of the community, however small these may seem. The worker consistently reflected back to Robyn that she had abilities and personal worth. She demonstrated the strengths of politeness, punctuality, frugality, and a liking for people and animals. This feedback helped Robyn to maintain an identity, even though not a clear one.

Allowing the Maintenance of Protective Defenses

Persons with schizophrenia typically employ **schizoid** defenses even as they resume a more conventional life style. They need to control levels of external
stimulation by avoidance, limiting interpersonal contacts, and developing a certain rigidity of routine. Further, delusional thinking itself can be an adaptive
defense for the client in that it makes sense out of otherwise uncontrollable
mental activities (Anscombe, 1987). In Robyn's case, her social withdrawal was
necessary to control the overwhelming anxiety she faced with others. Her case
manager took seriously her desire to increase her supports, but Robyn did not
agree to any suggestions for organized social rehabilitation because of her fears
of overstimulation. Had he pushed harder for Robyn to enter into formal programs, he might have lost her trust in addition to failing to make a referral.

Attending to Spirituality

Spirituality can be defined as the attempt to face the facts of one's life situation
in light of ultimate values and loyalties (Boisen, 1936). It is an aspect of existence which is not typically addressed in work with persons having major mental illnesses (this topic is addressed in more detail in Chapter 11). Though it is
appropriate to avoid proselytizing, the case manager should attend to the fact
that spiritual issues are often part of one's symbolic world. They tend to become
central to one's life during times of suffering, and thus it is probable that the
person with schizophrenia is sensitive to them. They may be manifested in conventional or bizarre ways, but they are real to the client. Robyn, despite her psychosis, maintained the traditional beliefs of Catholicism and was concerned that
her inability to tolerate attending Mass might result in her damnation by God.
The case manager encouraged Robyn to talk about these feelings and, in so
doing, validated the importance of this aspect of her life. Robyn eventually began
private church visits and watched a televised Mass every Sunday morning.

Other Interventions

Once a working relationship is established and the case manager understands
the client's priorities, supportive interventions are effective in helping the
client make positive adjustments. These are based on principles of ego psychology and include education, advice, and suggestion; encouragement and
praise; and environmental interventions focused on strengthening the client's
sense of competence (Rockland, 1993). Much of the case manager's early work
with Robyn included these activities.

Behavioral interventions are also useful in goal attainment. Social skills
training addresses deficits in interpersonal relating through the development of
specific skills needed for everyday living. Interventions which employ behavioral measurement, social learning, and specific skills training activities have
been shown to improve the course and outcome of schizophrenia as measured
by symptom reduction, improved social functioning, and an improved subjective quality of life (Liberman, Kopelowicz, & Young, 1996).

Cognitive-behavioral interventions are based on the premise that the person's behaviors are largely mediated by beliefs; and those interventions might include modifying the client's assumptions about the world, improving cognitive responses to stress, and carefully relabeling psychotic experiences as not entirely based on environmental evidence. These interventions can influence hallucinations and delusions by decreasing their frequency and the distress associated with them, and by increasing the client's awareness that the voices might really be thoughts (Kuipers, Garety, & Fowler, 1996). Robyn's case manager instituted behavioral interventions when he began organizing their community outings for specific purposes. He hoped that her exposure to more everyday situations would reduce her fears of social interaction.

CASE ILLUSTRATION: BRIAN

Brian, 19, was the older of two sons from an intact nuclear family. He experienced a sudden, dramatic, psychotic break while at college. Brian became hypomanic, agitated, and delusional. He believed that he had discovered the cure for cancer, and he visited health care clinics in his home town to discuss his procedures. Though quickly hospitalized, his psychosis did not stabilize for months. He required high doses of antipsychotic medications to experience relief from his agitation, but these did nothing to reduce his delusions. Brian had a diagnosis of schizo-affective disorder, which is a type of schizophrenia featuring mood fluctuations and (in his case) occasional manic behavior. There was nothing in his personal history to suggest pending psychological problems.

Brian was referred to a halfway house for six months following a four-month hospitalization. He could learn to live independently, have additional time to recover from his psychotic episode, and make school or career plans. None of these goals unfolded as planned, because Brian became an alcohol abuser while at the program. He kept this a secret from the staff, who were aware only of his erratic progress. Brian was going through the motions of his halfway house program while engaging in behaviors that indicated poor judgment and a second psychological disorder. Brian was referred to the present case manager when he left the halfway house and moved back home to make plans for enrolling in the local college and eventually getting an apartment. He was "stable" in that he was not hallucinating and had no delusional ideas. Brian appeared to be normal (he had no evident negative symptoms), but his thinking ability was slowed by the medication and residual effects of the psychotic episode. He was not able to think as abstractly as before. The case manager noticed that Brian's family members tended to downplay the change in his thinking because they wanted him to function as he had prior to the illness.

Brian and his parents (the younger brother was now away at college) bonded quickly with the case manager. They saw him as knowledgeable, understanding, and supportive. Regular family sessions were conducted to help Brian organize his plans, and the parents participated actively in the agency's family education and support group. Relationships between the case manager and family were positive because Brian and his parents were motivated to work toward the goals of independent living. Brian was confident in his ability to manage himself (overly confident, the case manager noticed) and particularly sought the help of the case manager in repairing relationships with old friends. The case manager felt that he was empathic, available, supportive, and appropriately directive in his work with Brian. Likewise, the physician was working with him collaboratively regarding medication.

The worker became increasingly aware during those first few months, however, that Brian's concrete thinking excluded many social symbols that his family assumed he still shared with them. His parents were status and future-oriented, and tended to talk with Brian about "success" and "happiness" in terms of college degrees and job careers. Brian was not able to comprehend these abstract terms; instead he was preoccupied with managing anxiety and struggling to get his needs met in the immediate environment. This difference in perspective became a major point of conflict within the family.

Within six months two issues arose which eventually terminated the client's and case manager's ability to work together. First, after he came to trust the worker, Brian admitted to ongoing substance abuse. Initially he acknowledged occasional drinking (one or two beers several times per week) but later admitted to drinking heavily (6–12 beers) almost every day and to smoking marijuana. In an effort to resume a social life he was attending parties with old and new friends, most of whom were substance abusers. The case manager thus became aware that Brian was at imminent risk to harm himself through these dangerous behaviors. The agency physician, learning about Brian's drinking, said he would not prescribe any medications unless the client terminated all alcohol use.

Secondly, it became clear that Brian, despite a mature presentation, was unable to make long-range decisions. He (perhaps prematurely) resumed college but did not buy the required books or invest time in study. He attended job interviews without preparing or dressing appropriately. While working as a theater usher, he applied for a management job the day after being reprimanded for giving away refreshments. He told his interviewer that he ignored some policies because he was bored and needed a management position to stimulate himself. He refused to maintain participation in an outpatient substance abuse treatment program that the case manager had arranged soon after becoming aware of his problem. He became involved with, and eventually married, a woman with four dependent children and no means of caring for them. Through all of this, Brian was defiant with his parents and the case manager, and was defensive about all negative feedback.

This example is different than the others described in this chapter because the case manager had to work harder at limit-setting and confrontation than at relationship development. The relationship development phase had moved rather quickly in this case. The worker remained close to the client's parents, but they resisted his input to slow down their own schedule of Brian's recovery from the mental illness. The case manager was able to help them understand that Brian did not perceive reality quite like they did, despite the fact that he had no florid psychotic symptoms.

Brian had initially concealed his substance abuse from the case manager in his desire to be a "good" client. When he trusted the worker sufficiently to disclose this information, he was confronted and then became secretive again, impeding the case manager's ability to work collaboratively with him. The worker could not give Brian much time to change his behaviors because the client was impulsive and at times self-destructive. The case manager tried to help Brian understand that by setting behavior limits, he was keeping Brian's physical safety, and that of his new family, at the forefront, but Brian could not accept this. At one point he accused the case manager, who was ten years his senior, of being "parental" and of not understanding his needs. Brian began missing appointments with both the case manager and physician. The case manager spent more time with Brian's parents, advising them to maintain behavioral expectations and set certain limits with Brian, because they were financing his apartment and paying other expenses. This relationship itself became difficult, as the parents tended to overlook Brian's dangerous behaviors and give him money to keep him out of financial trouble. Brian's father eventually received a job promotion and moved five hundred miles away. Then Brian was on his own, living on a monthly check from his parents.

The case manager tried to maintain contact with Brian, although he was advised to terminate the case by several colleagues who saw his behavior as enabling in some ways. The case manager did refuse to work with Brian on any other goals unless he entered an inpatient substance abuse program, and the physician stopped prescribing medications. But the case manager felt that Brian needed an available advocate or limit-setter when he experienced interpersonal problems. On the positive side, Brian was never rehospitalized, although he was once admitted to an emergency room visit for an alcohol overdose. They met infrequently; the case manager's impression was that Brian sought him out when he needed an advocate— when he was having problems with an employer or his wife. At these times Brian was still reluctant to accept negative feedback. Near the end of their work, the case manager received a phone call from Brian's wife, requesting marital counseling. The case manager agreed to see the couple to evaluate the possibility of providing this service. According to his wife, Brian stated after one session, "That guy helped me out a lot when I was first out of the hospital, but he hasn't done much for me since." The couple attended two counseling sessions but then did not return. The case manager never saw Brian again.

INCORPORATING UNITS OF INTERVENTION
INTO THE SERVICE PLAN

Today's health care environment encourages short-term interventions and measurable goals and objectives. The above examples demonstrate that, in contrast, clinical case management is a process that sometimes unfolds over many months, includes goals that are sometimes lacking in behavioral specificity, and allows for fundamental changes in the client's goals over time. For example, initial goals that focus on development of the worker-client relationship are often difficult to measure. As a means of supporting the process of clinical case management with supervisors and quality assurance regulators, I offer here a service planning model that includes *four units* of intervention. These units can be articulated as stages that are not actually distinct, but they do tend to progress sequentially. When outlined and referenced in a service plan, they can indicate progress with clients who require long-term intervention and manifest only gradual changes. I recognize that these units' terminology is not consistent with symbolic interactionism, but this is because they are written from a more traditional quality-assurance perspective.

The first unit is *engagement*. The major focus of this book is on the process of engagement, which must occur for other interventions to achieve optimal effectiveness. This includes all case manager-client interactions for establishing a working relationship. This relationship is based on a shared definition of the situation and the beginnings of a shared symbolism. If this process is successful, the client will experience a reduced sense of social isolation and will demonstrate some level of commitment to participate with the case manager in mutually negotiated activities. The client may be ambivalent about the clinical relationship, but his or her participation will become consistent.

The second unit of intervention focuses on the client's *symptom stabilization*. Through the changing sense of self that emerges from the clinical relationship, as well as through reconnection with significant others, the client relinquishes idiosyncratic symbols and develops a shared symbol system. The client becomes more socially integrated and exhibits more socially acceptable behavior. Medication usually plays a key role in ameliorating the client's cognitive or affective deficits. Symptoms contributing to the client's isolation, such as hallucinations, delusions, mania, and depression, begin to remit. Clearly many health care agencies consider this remission of the observable symptoms of mental disorder to be the primary goal of intervention.

Unit three concerns the client's *psychosocial development*. In this process the worker and client focus on the client's particular goals for personal growth, which often include social and vocational skill development. The clinical case manager incorporates many of the traditional interventions from ego psychology and cognitive/behavioral theory to help the client achieve whatever goals have been articulated. The case manager provides linkage, advocacy, and monitoring activities during this unit of intervention. Careful cultivation of new significant others occurs for the client, both professional and social, to surround him or her with supports to sustain and to enhance the sense of self. This unit, like the previous one, lends itself to measurable goals and objectives. Programmers should understand, however, that with this client population the process may not be linear. There may be a need to change goals as trial and error helps the client determine ultimate priorities. The worker and client will continue to develop new definitions of situations, including their own, as the focus of intervention changes and probably includes other participants.

The fourth and final unit of intervention is *functional stabilization*. The client has achieved a level of personal growth and adaptation that he or she finds suitable, at least for the time being. Clinical contacts might taper off as the client has more significant others with whom to interact and to share his or her symbol system. The case manager might assume less active roles, such as monitor and supporter, but he or she will still help the client use good judgment to maintain contact with appropriate others from the social milieu. The case manager might continue to represent an essential source of validation to the client. The "case" will likely stay open, but worker-client contacts will be less frequent.

SUMMARY

Developing a relationship of trust with clients who have schizophrenia is a prerequisite for effective intervention by the case manager. Symbolic interactionism provides a useful theoretical framework for undertaking this challenge. The bizarre thoughts and communications of the person with schizophrenia are intentional, and they have meaning, although these are obscured by the client's adherence to a private symbol system. Through the use of case examples, I reviewed seven components of the relationship-building process, all of which contribute to a positive therapeutic climate. Still, as evidenced in the second case example, not all clients can be successfully engaged. Following relationship development the client must make a commitment to a collaborative problem-solving process. In every case, however, case managers need to maintain their commitment to the principle of empowerment. Persons with schizophrenia comprise a group that is devalued by the larger society because of their relative lack of political and economic influence. Few professions act toward them with the dignity they deserve.

Appendix: A Service Plan Form

(Page 1)

Client: ___Robyn L.___   Case Manager: ___Walsh___   Date: ___6/8/98___

Other participants in plan: __None__

Other agency staff: ___None___

Needs: __Support in living independently from supervision;__
__support in successfully managing her condominium__

Strengths: __Robyn is determined to master Independent living__
__skills and in not having to rely on agency services. She is capable__
__of budgeting her money well and tries to structure her time__

Goals	Measurable steps	Target Date	Modality	Frequency	Staff Responsible
1.: To stay out of the hospital	Shop for food weekly	8/8/98	Casemgmnt &	Biweekly	Walsh (for all)
	Nutritious meals 3X daily	8/8/98	Counseling		
	Clean one room daily	8/8/98			
	Change clothes daily	8/8/98			
	Do laundry weekly	8/8/98			
	Take walk daily	8/8/98			
	Visit with dad weekly	8/8/98			

Client comments on plan: "I agree to go along with this service plan and achieve my goal".

_____   _____   _____
Client signature   Staff signature   Supervisor
                                                            signature

Other participant signature
and relationship to client

_____   _____   _____
Date   Physician
                              signature

This plan must be updated at least every three months

Appendix: A Service Plan Form (continued)

(Page 2)

Issues related to the person's circumstances that directly affect his or her ability to achieve goals: Robyn has been hospitalized on two occasions by relatives after demonstrating psychotic behavior (delusional thinking), an inability to focus on basic needs, and poor judgment regarding her physical safety. While Robyn is again living at home and feels pleased with this arrangement she may need assistance to insure that her problem behaviors do not occur again

Describe collaboration with parent, guardian, significant other or family, if appropriate: At present Robyn does not want others to be involved in her services here, specifically her father, step-mother, sister, and the agency physician. I will continue to evaluate the possibility of including others in Robyn's service plan and hope that she will decide to allow family collaboration toward the goal of enhancing her family supports

Inter-agency coordination of services:

1. Other agency: _____

   Services provided: _____

   Provider name and title: _____

   How is this coordinated? _____

2. Other agency: _____

   Services provided: _____

   Provider name and title: _____

   How is this coordinated? _____

3. Other agency: _____

   Services provided: _____

   Provider name and title: _____

   How is this coordinated? _____

4. Other agency: _____

   Services provided: _____

   Provider name and title: _____

   How is this coordinated? _____

Appendix: A Service Plan Form (*continued*)

(Page 3)

Client: _____ Robyn L. _____   Case Manager: _____ Walsh _____   Date: _____ 9/8/98 _____

Other participants in plan: Father and step-mother

Other agency staff: Dr. Patterson

Needs: Support in living independently from supervision, to get along better with my family, to become more comfortable around other people, having a friend

Strengths: Robyn is frugal with her money, expects her family and friends to be trustworthy, is energetic, prides herself in taking responsibility for her own needs but has learned to ask others for help when she needs it, is a spiritual person

Goals	Measurable steps	Target Date	Modality	Frequency	Staff Responsible
1. To feel more calm	Take medicine as prescribed	Ongoing	Medication Case mgmnt.	Monthly Biweekly	Patterson Walsh
2. To be more at peace with myself	Attend church weekly	12/8/98	Counseling	Biweekly	Walsh
3. To feel more comfortable around people	Talk with new store clerk at the mall every week	12/8/98	Case mgmnt.	Biweekly	Walsh
4. Have a pleasant relationship with dad and step-mom	Parents will report understanding my strengths and limitations more clearly	12/8/98	Family counseling	Biweekly	Walsh
5. Be productive every day	Shop, do laundry, bathe, eat good foods every day	12/8/98	Case mgmnt.	Biweekly	Walsh

Client comments on plan: "I think I am doing well and will be able to achieve these goals".

Date	Client signature	Other participant signature and relationship to client	Staff signature	Supervisor signature	Physician signature
___	___	___	___	___	___

This plan must be updated at least every three month

7

༝

Persons with Bipolar Disorder

Bipolar disorder is a disorder of *mood* in which, over time, a person experiences one or more **manic episodes** that are usually accompanied by one or more major **depressive episodes** (American Psychiatric Association, 1994). Medication is almost always a major, and sometimes the only, intervention modality for this disorder because of its effectiveness with so many clients. Still, the "medicalization" of bipolar disorder during the past three decades has tended to obscure its uncertain etiology. Research has continued to support hypotheses that there are psychological and social, as well as biological, components to the onset and course of bipolar disorder. Comprehensive treatment requires intervention at all three levels.

Case managers who use a psychosocial perspective are well qualified to coordinate and participate in a holistic treatment plan, along with physicians and other professionals, toward long-term client stabilization. In fact, case managers often spend more time with these clients than physicians and other members of the treatment team. In this chapter I provide case managers with an overview of common psychosocial problems and six intervention strategies for helping clients with bipolar disorder. I focus on the manic phase of the disorder, leaving the discussion of depression to Chapter 8.

THE NATURE OF BIPOLAR DISORDER

Bipolar disorder is characterized by both manic and depressive episodes. A **manic episode** is a distinct period in which a person's predominant mood is either elevated, expansive, or irritable to a degree that there is serious impairment in occupational and social functioning. According to the American Psychiatric Association (1994), manic episodes may be characterized by any of the following symptoms (a diagnosis requires that at least three be present): unrealistically inflated self-esteem, a decreased need for sleep, pressured speech, racing thoughts, distractibility, an increase in trying to reach unrealistic goals, and involvement in activities having a potential for painful consequences. Onset of manic episodes is rapid, and they may persist for a few days up to several months.

A **major depressive episode** is a period of at least two weeks during which a person experiences a depressed mood or loss of interest in nearly all common life activities. Symptoms may include (five or more must be present) depressed mood, diminished interest or pleasure in most activities, significant and unintentional weight loss *or* gain, insomnia *or* hypersomnia, feelings of physical agitation *or* retardation, loss of energy, feelings of worthlessness or excessive guilt, a diminished ability to think or concentrate, and persistent thoughts of death or suicide.

A feature of bipolar disorder that can disrupt the continuity of intervention is the **hypomanic episode**. This is a client's gradual escalation from stable mood to mania; it can last from several days to several weeks. It is a mild form of mania that may be pleasurable for the client and may result in high social and occupational productivity. Its related behaviors are often socially acceptable;

consequently, the hypomanic person sometimes receives positive reinforcement from friends and employers. The person has high self-esteem, a decreased need for sleep, a high energy level, an increase in overall productivity, and more intensive involvement in pleasurable activities. All of us would benefit in some ways from being hypomanic! At these times, however, the client's decreased **insight** (the awareness of having a mental illness requiring intervention)may lead him or her to believe that the bipolar disorder has permanently remitted and that there is no need to continue with medication or other interventions. As symptoms of hypomania increase, insight decreases, and the potential for a full manic episode becomes greater.

There are two types of bipolar disorder (American Psychiatric Association, 1994). **Bipolar I disorder** is characterized by one or more manic episodes, usually accompanied by a major depressive episode. **Bipolar II disorder** is characterized by one or more major depressive episodes, accompanied by at least one hypomanic episode. Six subtypes of bipolar I disorder reflect the nature of the most recent mood episode. The mood stabilizing medications are intended to prevent the client's mood from shifting dramatically in either direction. It is important to recognize that poor insight is a prominent characteristic in the extreme phases of bipolar disorder (Ghaemi, Stoll, & Pope, 1995). This factor presents a challenge for the case manager and other members of the treatment team who wish to ensure the client's appropriate adherence to the intervention plan.

The person with bipolar disorder does not necessarily experience mania and depression with equal frequency (Brown, 1994). Fifty percent (50%) of persons with the disorder move through alternating manic and depressed cycles. A majority of persons (70–90%) return to a stable mood and level of functioning between mood episodes. Approximately 10% experience "rapid cycling," which means that over a twelve-month period they experience four or more manic or depressive cycles. Additionally, 40% have a "mixed" type of the disorder, in which a prolonged depressive episode features bursts of mania, perhaps as brief as a few hours in duration.

Onset of a manic episode typically occurs in the mid-20s, but bipolar disorder may begin at any time, from childhood through midlife (Brown, 1994). Twenty to thirty percent of adults with bipolar disorder report that they experienced their first episode before age 20. In one study of a select sample, 59% of respondents reported experiencing their first *symptoms* of bipolar disorder during childhood or adolescence (Lish, Dime-Meenan, Whybrow, Price, & Hirschfeld, 1994). In adolescence, mania may be characterized by agitation, excitability, **labile affect**, aggression, and irritability.

INSTRUMENTS FOR MONITORING SYMPTOMS

Case managers should rely on validated measures whenever possible in assessing and monitoring a client's mental status. Systematic measures increase the validity of one's observations and promote consistency in the perspectives of all members of the treatment team. The Mania Rating Scale (MRS) is an 11-item, clinician-administered instrument which can be completed during a 15- to 30-minute interview (Young, Biggs, Ziegler, & Meyer, 1978). The scoring of scale items—including mood, energy, sexual interest, sleep, irritability, speech rate and amount, language and thought disorder, speech content, disruptive and aggressive behavior, appearance, and insight —is based on both the client's report of his or her condition during the previous 48 hours *and* the case manager's observations during the interview (with an emphasis on the latter). Four scale items (irritability, speech rate and amount, speech content, and disruptive/aggressive behavior) are given greater weight to compensate for the anticipated poor reliability of highly manic clients. Each scale item includes five levels of severity, and a client receives an overall score of 0 to 60 from a summing of all item scores. The scale has demonstrated high inter-rater reliability, along with concurrent (compared with two other scales) and predictive (hospital days) validity.

Depression can also be measured with a number of instruments. I chose the Brief Depression Rating Scale (BDRS) (Kellner, 1986) to describe here because its format is similar to the MRS. Together they can be used to assess clients in each mood state. The BDRS is an eight-item scale that measures depression by clinical observation. The case manager rates the following observations on a 9-point scale from "incapacitating" to "absent": depressive mood and feelings of despair; somatic symptoms; lack of interest, initiative, and activity; sleep disturbance; anxiety, worry, and tension; appearance; depressive beliefs; and suicidal thoughts or behavior. Individual items can be summed for a total score ranging from 8 (no depression) to 72 (high depression). The BDRS has demonstrated high inter-observer reliability and concurrent validity.

CAUSATIVE FACTORS IN
BIPOLAR DISORDER

Conceptualizing Mental Disorders

The biopsychosocial approach to assessment recognizes that no single set of factors is adequate to account for the onset of bipolar disorder (Vasile et al., 1987). A strictly medical perspective has negative implications for the client's sense of having a *role* in the intervention process: the client becomes an object who merely complies with physician decisions (although medication compliance is certainly essential). The client assumes a *passive* role rather than an *active* one in the process. The client may lose the sense of mastery, fail to take responsibility for managing the disorder, and assume the sick role with its implications of helplessness (Brown & Zinberg, 1982). An integrated approach to etiology encourages the client to actively confront the disorder and strive toward goals that are mutually formulated with the case manager and others on the treatment team. Working from this broad perspective, it is useful for us to review the genetic, biochemical, and psychosocial etiological aspects of bipolar disorder.

Genetic Factors

Family history studies, including twin and adoption studies, indicate an aggregation of bipolar disorder in families. First degree relatives of persons with bipolar disorder are 8% to 18% more likely to have the disorder than relatives in control groups, and 50% of persons with bipolar disorder have a parent with a mood disorder (Kaplan & Sadock, 1998). There is also a demonstrated relationship between bipolar disorder and major depression in family transmission. Some early researchers speculated that bipolar disorder emanates from a single gene, but this theory has lost support and studies are focusing on polygenic models of transmission (Blehar, Weissman, Gershon, & Hirschfeld, 1988). While genetic research remains promising, the "core" of bipolar disorder remains elusive. The likelihood of genetic factors are complicated by indications that bipolar disorder with late-life onset (after 40 years) has no apparent association with family history (Daly, 1997).

Biological Factors

Four areas under review in the biological study of bipolar disorder include the role of neurotransmitters, the endocrine system, physical biorhythms, and physical complications (Young & Joffe, 1997). The amount and activity of norepinephrine, serotonin, gamma-aminobutyric acid (GABA), and perhaps other central nervous system nerve tract messengers are clearly abnormal in persons with bipolar disorder. Medications are effective when they either increase or decrease these brain chemicals. Still, the causes of these imbalances are unknown. One theory holds that bipolar disorder results from a "kindling" process in limbic system neuron tracts (Bernstein, 1995). This theory was described in Chapter 5. The actions of the thyroid and other endocrine glands also account for nervous system changes that contribute to manic and depressive episodes. Biorhythms, or the body's natural sleep and wake cycles, are erratic in some bipolar clients and might account for, or result from, chemical imbalances that trigger manic episodes. Finally, damage to the limbic system, basal ganglia, and hypothalamus, which are centers of emotional activity in the brain, might contribute to episodes of the disorder. Most researchers agree that these biological processes are significant in the onset and course of bipolar disorder, but unfortunately there are no brain imaging techniques (like those available in schizophrenia research) to provide detail about them.

Psychosocial Factors

Psychological theories of bipolar disorder are criticized for lacking scientific validity and thus have received less attention in the past few decades. Psychoanalytic theorists have tended to categorize all mood disorders as reactions to losses or major blows to self-esteem (Aleskandrowicz, 1980). Bipolar disorder is often associated with significant losses in early childhood. Other clinical theorists describe persons at risk for bipolar disorder as having an external locus of control orientation and a dependence on others for approval and acceptance. Dependence on one person or ideal for gratification and affirmation can trigger an intense loss when separation from that object occurs. The manic response may represent a redirection of energy to other objects following the loss. A *first* manic episode of bipolar disorder tends to be preceded by a major stress event, which supports a psychological component to its onset.

Another characteristic associated with persons who develop bipolar disorder is extensive use of the defense mechanism of denial. With an orientation toward social desirability (clients tend to be first-born or only children), these persons tend to be incapable of introspection (DeNour, 1980), although research into personality types with susceptibility to bipolar disorder is inconclusive. One study associates these common personality traits with at-risk persons: high emotional expressiveness, high achievement ambition with a resentment of the perceived obligation to achieve, sensation-seeking tendencies, a low sense of competence, and a desire to impress others (Peven, 1996).

There appears to be an association between bipolar disorder and the upper socioeconomic classes (Goodnick, 1998). The typical client's family is described as upwardly striving but socially isolated. The future client is singled out as the family's means of securing social validation. A lack of success or social conformity will result in the family's rejection by their society. The client member never feels innately worthwhile but feels valued only insofar as he or she maintains high standards of social success (Gagrat & Spiro, 1980).

COMMON PSYCHOSOCIAL PROBLEMS

Persons with bipolar disorder tend to experience serious social and occupational problems. These include withdrawal due to low self-esteem, a loss of intimate relationships, job loss, an increased dependence on others, family conflicts, and a disruption in social routines (Kahn, 1990). The person's mood swings and erratic behavior alienate others and are a source of ongoing turmoil in family, peer, and professional relationships. Manic individuals progressively test the limits of their relationships until others are exhausted, frustrated, and drained of empathy. Because the mean age of onset for both sexes is 28 to 33 years, with a higher risk of recurrence as the client ages (Goodwin & Jamison, 1990), most spouses, family, friends, and peers do not experience the client in a manic state until the relationship has already developed. Significant others become confused by perceived changes in the client's personality and often terminate the relationship.

Persons with bipolar disorder are at a high risk for divorce (DeNour, 1980). They become dependent on the spouse for support in times of crisis, but spouses tend to see the mania at least in part as a willful act. The "well" spouse's self-esteem can diminish because of being blamed for the family's problems, acting as a buffer between the client and community, and making so many concessions to the client. If the marriage continues, other problems might include the "well" spouse's guilt feelings, need to control the relationship, and at times a learned dependence on the client's pathology for the relationship to persist. Further, the client might drain the family's financial resources with spending sprees, debt accumulation, and treatment costs.

The same interpersonal patterns described above contribute to the bipolar client's occupational problems. One study indicates a stable working capacity in only 45% of clients, and 28% experienced a steady decline in job status and performance (Bebbington, 1982). Missed work, poor work quality, and conflicts with co-workers all contribute to the decline for clients who cannot maintain mood stability. Even though bipolar clients experience lengthy periods of normal moods, work performance can be irreparably damaged by behaviors during mood swings. If the disorder begins at a young age, the client may not achieve enough education and skills to qualify for a productive career.

Denial by both the client *and* family poses another problem. When manic, the client may be reluctant to accept the need for medication and other interventions. Episodes of mania and depression are usually brief in comparison to the duration of normal mood activity, but denial tends to persist in bipolar clients during stable periods. Even after numerous prior episodes, the client may decide after a period of stability that there is no longer a need for precautionary interventions. This problem is accentuated by the client's diminished ability to distinguish normal from abnormal mood states. Of course, once a manic episode begins, the client's denial becomes more pronounced. The client is more willing to accept treatment in the depressed phase, but if the case manager has no family collaboration during assessment, the disorder may be misdiagnosed as major depression, and incorrect medications may be prescribed (see the next chapter). Because of the client's tendency to minimize problems related to the disorder, he or she cannot always be trusted to provide an accurate social history.

Another area of concern is medication adherence. It is recommended that most bipolar clients take medication during the active phases of the disorder *and* during periods of remission. Lithium, carbamazepine, and valproate are the standard mood-stabilizing medications at present, and at times anti-psychotic and anti-depressant medications can be effective as adjunct therapies. But clients often decide to stop taking the drugs, despite their usefulness, without the treatment team's awareness. The client may function well without the medications for some time, but the risk for recurrence of an active episode rises.

Seven reasons why bipolar clients stop taking their medications include

1. Denial of having a mental disorder that requires the long-term use of medications

2. A desire for personal autonomy

3. The adverse effects of the medication (lethargy, weakness, weight gain)

4. A desire to experience a hypomanic state for increased self-esteem, assertiveness, and productivity

5. A desire to prompt a manic state to draw attention to *or* avoid other life problems

6. A desire to regress in order to avoid certain responsibilities associated with improved functioning

7. Social stigma

Finally, the client may experience other emotional problems requiring professional attention. Another psychotic disorder is unlikely, but common emotional problems are fearing recurrence of a manic episode and dealing with the loss of relationships and the former sense of self. The stigma associated with having bipolar disorder sometimes creates problems with self-confidence and esteem. Depression commonly results from the above concerns. Suicide attempts might be motivated by the desire not to be a burden to others, the desire to punish others, the need to communicate distress, and an actual desire to die to end one's suffering (Milkowitz, 1996). An adolescent who develops bipolar disorder may experience an arrest in psychological development, acquiring self-efficacy and dependency problems that endure into adulthood. Often persons in both manic and depressive cycles abuse drugs and alcohol in an effort to "treat" the symptoms. In fact, there is a 60% lifetime risk of substance abuse problems among clients with bipolar disorder (Goodnick, 1998). The case manager's too-specific focus on bipolar disorder may leave the client with unresolved problems that contribute to a recurrence of mood swings.

INTERVENTION STRATEGIES

Here I describe six intervention strategies for the case manager's comprehensive treatment of these problems. These strategies are targeted to *three phases* of bipolar disorder, including the **crisis, stabilization,** and **remission** phases (Milkowitz, 1996); and the *three mood levels* of **mania, hypomania,** and **euthymia** (tranquility) (Kahn, 1990). The case manager's major goals are to empower the client to gain control of the disorder and to acquire strategies to modify its risk factors.

Special Relationship Issues

Cultivating a relationship of trust may seem like an obvious recommendation, but this is crucial with bipolar clients for particular reasons. The client may receive services for years, but the frequency and intensity of the intervention will vary depending on his or her mood stability, overall quality of functioning, and stage of the disorder. The case manager must create a sense of safety, availability, and continuity with the client through these changes. A symptom-free client, (i.e., not in apparent need of clinical services) might see the case manager and physician only every few months. If the case manager, who will certainly have more demanding clients on his or her case load, allows the relationship to wane, the client may tacitly cut off communication or fail to contact the case manager if serious problems develop. Additionally, many clients in long-term treatment for disorders they feel ambivalent about might try to minimize contact with the case manager. These clients may test the limits of the relationship by missing appointments or failing to follow through with aspects of the treatment plan and then gauging the case manager's response.

Clients tend to have formal relationships with physicians, so it is imperative that the case manager maintain a more personal, but still professional, relationship. The case manager who projects empathy and warmth and who promotes the client's sense of mastery will be seen as an ally and resource even when contacts become infrequent. When manic or depressive episodes occur, the client will be more likely to seek out the case manager or to accept the need for increased contacts. As noted earlier, communication problems are common between bipolar clients and their significant others, and for this reason the case manager's example of directness will have therapeutic benefit. Occasional phone contacts during periods of stability are one way of communicating concern for the client's well-being. The client should never feel that the case manager is interested only in a crisis. Finally, as is true with any mental illness, the case manager will want the client to feel free to talk about concerns, such as how bipolar disorder affects the client's self image and the ability to manage relationships.

Establishing Collateral Contact Agreements

The case manager should secure the client's agreement to involve significant others in treatment for two reasons. First, because stabilized bipolar clients tend to minimize their problems, consultation with a spouse, parent, child, other relative, or friend will result in a more reliable social history. Second, if the client experiences a manic or depressive episode, the clinician must be able to consult with significant others to minimize the adverse interpersonal problems which will likely occur. As the client's judgment deteriorates, he or she might drop out of treatment, but the case manager can help to reverse or minimize a downward spiral by consulting with a relative or friend who retains influence with the client.

The client recovering from an acute episode of bipolar disorder is still in crisis, so others in the client's social milieu will likely be involved with the recovery process. During a stable period, then, it is relatively easy to arrange for those persons to cooperate as collateral contacts and to secure the client's agreement to sign release of information forms. The case manager can include a "reverse contract" in this process. That is, the client makes the case manager promise to take certain ameliorative actions during any future acute episodes (Kahn, 1990). Such cooperation may be more difficult to achieve if the significant others have been out of touch with the client for some time or if the manic client wishes to avoid the case manager. It is always a mistake to wait until a crisis occurs before gathering support for the client. The issue of collateral contacts should thus be openly discussed with the stabilized client at the beginning of treatment. The case manager must discuss with the client precisely how these others will participate and then must demonstrate by subsequent action that the client's trust is warranted. These plans can be discussed again when the release of information forms must be updated.

Client and Family Education

Because bipolar disorder is confusing to the client and those close to him or her in the best of circumstances, the case manager should always include education as part of the treatment program (Bauer & McBride, 1996). The more a client and significant others understand about the disorder, the more they will be able to control it. The information given earlier in this chapter, describing the etiology and life problems associated with bipolar disorder, is appropriate for sharing with the client during the stabilization and maintenance phases. Client and family education should include attention to the following topics (Milkowitz & Goldstein, 1997):

1. The nature of bipolar disorder

2. Medications and their effects (see Chapter 5)

3. The importance of establishing and maintaining social rhythms, which includes a structuring of time and monitoring of moods. Toward this end, the client may be encouraged to complete a daily *social rhythm scale* (Frank et al., 1994); by this process the client can increase self-efficacy and control by structuring life activities and becoming more aware of mood cycles.

4. Cues and risk factors related to the onset of a manic episode

5. How to maintain intimate relationships

6. The roles of all professionals involved in the intervention phases

Client or family education can be presented in individual and family counseling or in multi-family psychoeducational group settings. Topic formats are outlined in Chapters 13 and 14.

Coordination of the Physician and Case Manager Roles

When several professionals work simultaneously with a client and when their roles are different (but complimentary), the client might receive contradictory messages from each source. Service delivery *can* be well coordinated, but when communication among professionals is not consistent, misunderstandings may develop in the client's definition of the clinical situations. Four possible differences in the approaches of physicians and case managers include the following (Brown & Zinberg, 1982):

1. Physicians tend to focus on symptom reduction, while case managers are process-oriented in relationship building.

2. The medical model tends to place responsibility for the client's improvement on the physician, but the case manager urges the client to assume responsibility in that and other areas of life.

3. The physician views affect as a symptom to be modified, while the case manager processes affective states toward psychological growth.

4. Physicians tend to avoid intimacy with clients, eliciting information only about symptom concerns, but the case manager focuses on broad themes of social functioning and encourages the disclosure of personal information.

With these contrasts in professional perspective, medication and counseling can have different effects on the client's attitudes about the intervention process (Klerman & Schechter, 1982). Drugs often effectively reduce symptoms, but counseling is effective at improving overall social functioning. The reduced anxiety which the client experiences with medication, however, may reduce his or her motivation for counseling. Conversely, counseling can have a negative influence on chemotherapy at times, as the client's anxiety about personal problems may rise to a level that symptoms formerly controlled with medication recur.

A major challenge in combining chemotherapy and counseling is that the client might come to view one as more important and might withdraw from the other. A *splitting* may occur, in which the client presents him or herself differently to each professional and, at times, even promotes conflict between them. The case manager can minimize these risks by supervising the overall treatment plan, clarifying the specific targets of each professional's interventions for the client, and meeting regularly with the physician and others to review progress and to share impressions. The case manager may also attend the client's medication appointments. The comprehensive plan will need to be updated periodically, and certainly at times one professional's role may take priority over another. The case manager must ensure that the client and each provider understands and supports the plan so that splitting is avoided.

Managing Adjustments in Strategy

The cyclical nature of bipolar disorder demands *flexibility* in the case manager's planning and intervention. I stated above that intervention occurs in three phases. When the client is in *crisis* phase, frequent meetings with the case manager and physician are indicated, and hospitalization or crisis stabilization may be necessary. Much contact with the family and significant others will be needed to control the episode and activate social supports. The client who is *stabilized* still experiences some family, social, or developmental conflicts and should be seen in counseling as frequently as any other client with similar concerns. Psychoeducational interventions should be implemented soon after the crisis resolves, although these can be helpful in every stage.

In the stabilization stage, *task* interventions become appropriate for helping the client restructure a productive life and addressing social and vocational needs. Tasks for the client include understanding his or her stress management style and sensitivity to emotional states. The case manager's linkage and referral will be prominent in this phase and may continue into the next phase as well. A client in *remission* who has satisfactorily resolved recent problems in living and who is coping with the disorder may be able to work more reflectively on growth issues. At this phase, he or she may be seen regularly or only every few months for monitoring and medication review.

The case manager should expect that the service plan will change during long-term treatment and should clarify this with the client in advance, offering clear rationales for any changes. The client's input should be sought prior to any adjustments in the case manager's pattern of interaction. Such collaboration ensures that the client will not misunderstand the case manager's motives. For example, if case management activity increases, the client might fear that he or she is decompensating when this is not, in fact, true. Perhaps the case manager is making a referral to help the client improve an occupational skill. Conversely, if sessions are decreased in frequency the client might believe that termination is imminent and might become either anxious or eager. In many cases, of course, it is the client who initiates changes in the pattern of treatment, at times indirectly, and the case manager must be prepared to consider the client's motivations and needs in these circumstances.

Attention to Other Clinical Concerns

The experience of bipolar disorder affects any client's social adjustment, but an onset in adolescence might stunt psychological growth. The adolescent who must cope with severe mood swings might not learn to form strong peer relationships, to establish a value system, to develop normal patterns of sexual behavior, and to develop independent living skills, all of which represent the transition into adulthood. The client might have developed self-injurious coping mechanisms such as substance abuse. This client, who might not become linked with a comprehensive treatment program for years, might require extensive counseling to reach an adaptive level of adult functioning (McAlpin & Goodnick, 1998). The counseling should go beyond the goals of learning to cope with bipolar disorder (although they are important) into general issues of psychological development. The client may have a fragile ego, requiring interventions of support, exploration, reflection, education, and life structuring. He or she may also benefit from the skill-building approaches drawn from cognitive-behavioral theory.

In some situations attention to related emotional problems is important for adults as well. This work tends to be concentrated in the remission phase when the client can focus more intensely on broader problems. Though the range of ego-functioning issues clients might face cannot be easily summarized, they tend to reflect recurrent interpersonal, competence, and self-esteem problems. The client's sense of self might be damaged by the consequences of behaviors performed when manic or depressed and by negative feedback received from significant others. Counseling about the use of defense mechanisms and patterns of social interaction is important in this work. At the base of these problems is the client's need for developing a sense of control of the disorder, repairing damaged relationships, moving through ordinary life transitions, and accepting appropriate responsibilities. Substance abuse interventions might be focused on better means of dealing with stress, perhaps through referral to Alcoholics Anonymous or other support groups and treatment resources.

Having considered a range of intervention strategies for the clinical case management of bipolar disorder, I now present two examples of their application.

CASE ILLUSTRATIONS

Joanne

Joanne was a single, 23-year-old college student referred to the community mental health center for outpatient care following a one-month hospitalization for an initial manic episode. She had been psychotic with paranoid delusions during her mania, which was characterized by sleeplessness, hyperactivity, racing thoughts, hypersexuality, and alcohol abuse. Joanne, who had never lived away from her parents, was well-stabilized on lithium and thiothixene at the time of her agency intake. Yet she was quite anxious, frightened by what had happened, and reluctant to resume normal activities for fear of precipitating another manic episode.

The case summary sent by the hospital staff suggested several targets for intervention. Joanne was the second-oldest of six children in a family that experienced much internal tension. Her father, a successful businessman, was a chronic alcohol abuser and was physically abusive of his wife. Most of the children were attractive, socially sophisticated, and outwardly successful, but there was a shared family denial of the father's problem behaviors. Joanne, who had no life direction, was the child most dependent on her parents. She became anxious, almost panicked, whenever they were out of town; and, in fact, she experienced her manic episode while they were on a week's vacation. With only two semesters remaining in her college curriculum, Joanne had begun failing or dropping essential courses, apparently postponing graduation and, thus, the onset of adulthood. That is, these milestones, viewed by most other young people as exciting accomplishments, symbolized for Joanne an end to an adolescence beyond which she could not function. She felt personally inadequate and wished to continue living with her parents, although intellectually she could see that it might be best for her to separate. The course of her bipolar disorder seemed related to these family issues.

With this information, the case manager and Joanne together devised a treatment program: She would be seen monthly, or more often as indicated, by the agency psychiatrist for medications. The case manager always attended these sessions to ensure continuity of care. Joanne was seen weekly by the case manager for counseling. The initial treatment issues included education about her disorder and an exploration of her overall coping style, dependency issues, and the circumstances of her mood swings, which included major depressions. The case manager suggested that Joanne write a short daily narrative of her emotional experiences to help herself become aware of her cycles and stresses.

Joanne was gradually encouraged to resume her previous level of social activity, which included part-time school, part-time work, and a moderate amount of friend and family activity. The case manager initially supported a behavioral intervention approach in devising graduated tasks for Joanne to carry out in resuming her previous life style. The psychiatrist supported Joanne's counseling as her primary means to improve her school, family, and social relationships. After six months, the case manager had developed what he felt was a close relationship with Joanne, and the counseling intensified. It focused on her fears, lack of confidence, interpersonal patterns, self-image, and preadult developmental level. Intervention became less behavioral and more ego-supportive.

Despite this apparent partnership, it took the case manager a few more months to realize that Joanne defined the clinical situation differently than he did. On one level she wanted to please her parents with recovery from bipolar disorder and with success at school and work, but on another and perhaps stronger level, she hoped that her illness would recur so she could maintain dependence on them and others. The depth of her fears about being a self-determining agent was extraordinary. Her sense of self was quite fragile; she lacked the confidence ever to become a competent individual with a life apart from her family. She was reluctant to share these fears with anyone, even this case manager whom she liked and largely trusted, because she did not want to be "found out." The power of this family system was enormous. Joanne responded to symbols of family attachment more fully than any others. The case manager became aware of these issues indirectly, by watching her reactions over time to moves toward independence. He realized that he needed to slow down the speed of his interventions so that she might process her authentic agendas more openly with him.

Joanne's parents and several siblings were included in meetings occasionally to assess their potential to encourage her separation from the family. The case manager did not schedule many joint meetings with them because of the client's enmeshment; he relied primarily on phone contact with the parents to discuss their perceptions of Joanne's progress. He learned that the parents were also dependent on Joanne to keep themselves distracted from each other, and as a result they tended to sabotage her initiatives toward independence by being critical of them and of the case manager. The parents declined several invitations to join the agency Family Education and Support Group (see Chapter 14).

Joanne made progress, although it was slow and not without setbacks. Her denial of family problems faded slowly as she learned to trust the case manager. Medication that kept Joanne's mood in a stable range was continued, with periodic adjustments, throughout her agency involvement. The thiothixene was gradually eliminated, but it had to be reintroduced in small doses on several occasions. The client worked toward partial emancipation through case management referrals to Al-Anon, a psychosocial clubhouse which featured socialization and growth groups, and a supervised apartment. Each of these programs presented Joanne with new stresses, and each prompted depressions as she adjusted to them. The case manager was active at these times in providing support to Joanne and in consulting with the other professionals involved.

Still, Joanne experienced two manic episodes during a three-year period. These were both prompted by the client herself as a means of resisting changes that she interpreted as threats to her sense of self as a dependent child. The first occurred when she stopped taking her medication and prompted a regression to avoid an imminent and dreaded move into an unsupervised apartment. Fortunately she told the case manager in time so that medication adjustments could stabilize her hypomania. The case manager, still at times unable to secure full disclosure of the client's most intimate emotions, learned again how much she feared being independent and what some tasks symbolized to her. The second episode took place one year later when Joanne was beginning a new job and when her parents were out of town for several weeks. This time a short-term hospitalization was necessary to stabilize the client, as paranoid delusions were creating intolerable anxiety for her.

Joanne remained in treatment, having made gains but still unsure of her potential to function independently of the family. Her bipolar disorder, though a biological illness, was linked to her psychological and family dynamics. The medications helped stabilize her mood swings, and the clinical case management activity enhanced her self-esteem because the case manager consistently accepted her as a person of worth and displayed reluctance to criticize her for feeling ambivalent about her goals. Despite the case manager's efforts, the parents never committed themselves to supporting Joanne's moves toward independence, and this undoubtedly hampered her progress. The physician and case manager did coordinate their efforts well, however, in promoting Joanne's goals of increased self-confidence and improved social skills. Joanne eventually moved into an apartment with a sister. She never finished college but did secure a full time job.

Ken

Ken's initial referral to the clinic followed his third hospitalization for a manic episode. He was 22 years old with a four-year history of manic cycles characterized by hyperactivity, delusions of power, excessive spending, and ventures into high-risk investment projects that inevitably failed because of his poor judgment. Ken always required hospital treatment to control his mania. When stable he was engaging, gregarious, energetic, and independent in nature. His episodes of depression were relatively mild and did not impair his ability to function. Ken could acknowledge only during his stabilization phases that he had a serious problem. When manic he believed he was normal (or supernormal), and when symptom-free for six months or longer, he believed that the disorder was cured. He accepted medication, but he was only superficially agreeable to the case manager's assistance. His case of bipolar disorder was apparently unrelated to environmental precipitants.

Ken was an only child raised by middle-class parents who divorced when he was 12. He lived with his father and kept in regular contact with his mother, who lived out of state. A grandmother lived nearby, and Ken moved in with her following his high school graduation in order, he said, to increase his independence. A maternal uncle had an unspecified mental disorder. The client's initial manic episode occurred during the middle of his senior year in high school. His family, to whom Ken did not feel close, cooperated with mental health professionals during hospital discharge planning but ceased being involved when the crisis phases ended. The family appeared to share denial of Ken's bipolar disorder. Ken's second manic episode and hospitalization occurred 18 months later, again without apparent precipitants, while he was living on his own and working as a clothing salesman. Each time he became stable, Ken had to rebuild his life by paying off debts, finding a new job, making new friends, and returning to live with his father with few outside supports. Nevertheless, he always expressed optimism about putting his life back together.

Ken's initial intervention plan included monthly visits with the physician for medication, and weekly counseling with the case manager to establish a stable work, housing, and daily living routine. Ken wanted to attend a two-year community college to receive a business education. The medications effectively stabilized his mood, and within three months he was taking a prophylactic dosage of lithium. His counseling was more problematic. As he had in the past, Ken came to believe that his problem was purely a chemical imbalance, beyond his control, and that addressing anything else was irrelevant. His father and grandmother seemed disinterested in the treatment process since Ken's mood was stable, and they did not agree to participate in any meetings. The case manager believed that Ken was discouraging their involvement.

Ken's definition of the situation was consistent with that suggested by the medical model; consequently, he seemed more comfortable with the physician. The case manager felt that Ken viewed him as a kind of "parole officer", someone to check in with periodically to "prove" that he was staying out of trouble. This attitude clearly did not pave the way for a range of clinical interventions. The social symbols in which Ken invested his energies were all material; material well-being signified success to him. Ken had learned to share a desire to make personal changes but he could not really invest in goals related to relationships. The case manager tried to help Ken expand his definition of the clinical situation by pointing out his recurrent and serious interpersonal problems. He hoped that providing Ken with resources through referral and linkage—that is, attending to his material desires—would help them develop a closer working relationship. He secured Ken an apartment and vocational assistance within several months. At this time he was scheduled for biweekly sessions but began missing or canceling appointments. Ken felt that his life was back on track and that he could function well with medication alone.

The case manager and psychiatrist met monthly to coordinate their efforts to increase the client's counseling involvement. The temptation often exists to discount the need for a regular intervention schedule when the client is stable, but the case manager was uncomfortable with the strength of Ken's denial. Eventually Ken did agree to bring his father to the agency for one visit with the case manager. The father's input regarding Ken's family and social history was helpful in convincing the case manager what he already suspected —that Ken tended to be at risk for mania, not when he was under stress to resolve social, financial, and vocational problems, but after he had become stable in these areas. The logic behind this apparent paradox was that when Ken was materially well-situated, he had no firm goals and thus experienced a lack of focus, which led to increased anxiety and put him at risk for a manic process. Having his material needs met also increased Ken's anxiety as he became aware that he had few relationships of substance. Thus, the case manager needed to pay attention to the client's mental status most closely when his social functioning was most stable. It would be a clinical mistake to cut back on Ken's session frequency as he demonstrated outward improvements.

There were no clear correlations between specific environmental precipitants and the onset of Ken's mania, but both professionals refused to reduce their frequency of contact with Ken, even when he remained stable for many months. The case manager educated Ken about the course of bipolar disorder and helped him develop a daily structure with regular times for waking, eating, working, and going to bed at night. He was symptom-free for two years before, finally, he missed several consecutive sessions and, as later reported, became manic. It was not clear if his mood escalation prompted him to miss appointments or if the mania was a result of not seeing his case manager and going off the medication. In any event, Ken left town and lost his job, money, and personal supports. He drove to California to pursue an acting career and was eventually probated to a psychiatric hospital with the long-distance help of the case manager and physician.

SUMMARY

The medicalization of bipolar disorder over the past 20 years has tended to obscure the fact that these clients require psychological and case management interventions to function optimally in their lives. Comprehensive treatment of the disorder involves a biopsychosocial approach, with interventions targeted toward the client's chemical processes, personality, coping style, defense mechanisms, social activity, and interpersonal style. Treatment generally requires more than one professional, but the case manager, because of a psychosocial perspective and expertise in negotiating social systems and in identifying appropriate services, is in an ideal position to facilitate all phases of effective interventions.

The examples of Joanne and Ken highlight similarities in the clinical case management approach with bipolar clients, whether they express complex problems in their social functioning or restrict their attention to managing an occasional "chemical imbalance." The disorder represents an interaction between the individual and environment, and while specific psychological or social triggers can rarely be isolated, certain interactive themes will become evident in the client's history if it is thoroughly assessed. The client who can accept the long-term seriousness of the disorder and who is willing to deal with its consequences has a better outcome prognosis. The case manager needs to communicate to the client, to the physician, and to any other involved professionals that chemotherapy alone is not adequate treatment.

8

Persons with Major Depression

I. **Understanding Major Depression**
   a. *Types of depression*

II. **Causes of Depression**
   a. *Biological theories*
   b. *Psychological theories*
   c. *Social theories*

III. **Stress and Coping**

IV. **Social Support**

V. **Intervention Techniques**
   a. *Phase I: The major depressive episode*
   b. *Phase II: Dysthymia*

VI. **Summary**

n the last chapter we considered the clinical case management of clients with bipolar disorder and focused on the manic phase of that illness. In this chapter I discuss the disorder of depression. The case manager may provide the interventions described here either to clients with primary diagnoses of depression or to clients with bipolar disorder who are in the depressive phase of that illness. Bipolar disorder, depressed type, and major depression are not identical, and maintaining this distinction is most crucial in considering issues of medication management. The clinical interventions I present include social support development, ego support, crisis intervention, interpersonal therapy, and several cognitive-behavioral techniques. As usual, I begin with a description of clinical depression and its various causes, and then present the clinical case management intervention techniques.

UNDERSTANDING DEPRESSION

Depression is a disturbance in mood, characterized by a sadness that is out of the range of normal emotion. It may be *primary* (autonomous) or *secondary* to other physical and emotional conditions. Clinical depression is characterized by an intensity of mood that seems to permeate all aspects of the person's life. There may be no readily identifiable causes for the depression, or the emotional state may seem out of proportion to an identified precipitant.

Depression includes five classes of symptoms. *Affective* characteristics include feelings of sadness, anxiety, anger, irritability, and emotional numbness. *Behavioral* manifestations include agitation, crying, a flatness of expression, and a slowness of physical movement and speech. *Attitudes* toward the self include guilt, shame, low self-esteem, helplessness, pessimism, hopelessness, and thoughts of death and suicide. *Cognitive* impairment is evident in the person's decreased ability to think and to concentrate. Finally, *physiological* changes include an inability to experience pleasure, changes in appetite and sleep patterns, a loss of energy, feelings of fatigue, decreased sex drive, and somatic complaints. The major types of depression, as described in the *Diagnostic and Statistical Manual of Mental Disorders* (American Psychiatric Association, 1994) are outlined below.

Types of Depression

A **major depressive episode** is a period of at least two weeks during which a person experiences a depressed mood or loss of interest in nearly all life activities. (American Psychiatric Association, 1994). The lifetime risk of major depression is greater for women (10–25%) than for men (5–12%). With each episode of major depression the likelihood of subsequent episodes increases.

Dysthymic disorder refers to a general personality style having symptoms similar to, but less intense than, those of major depression. Many people with major depression experience this disorder when in remission from the major episode, but it occurs more often by itself. This diagnosis requires two years of a continuously depressed mood. It generally has an early age of onset (childhood through early adulthood), and it produces impairments in school, vocational, and social functioning.

Adjustment disorder with depressed mood features depressive symptoms, including subjective distress and problems in occupational or social functioning, which occur within three months of an identifiable stressor. The disorder probably will not persist for more than six months. Such episodes may be characterized by depressed mood, a mixture of anxiety and depression, or a mixed disturbance of emotions and conduct. Persons with dysthymia are prone to adjustment reactions because they experience many life situations as negative.

Many practical instruments are available for the case manager's use in monitoring a client's depression over time. One such tool, the Brief Depression Rating Scale (BDRS) (Kellner, 1986), was described in the previous chapter. The case manager can use it to monitor clients with depressive disorders as well as those in the depressed phase of bipolar disorder.

CAUSES OF DEPRESSION

The clinical case manager must understand the range of causes of major depression in order to complete a thorough assessment and to identify appropriate targets for intervention. Here I summarize the biological, psychological, and social factors that contribute to depression.

Biological Theories

Major depression tends to run in families, which supports a factor of genetic transmission (Kaplan & Sadock, 1998). Studies of family heritability, including twin and adoption studies, indicate that first-degree relatives (siblings and children) of persons with major depression are two to ten times more likely to develop the disorder. Genetic factors consistently account for 50% of the variance in its transmission in these studies (McMahon & DePaulo, 1996). While impressive, this figure also supports the contribution of psychosocial factors to the onset of depression. The genetic potential for depression may be transmitted as an affective temperament which makes one susceptible to a mood disorder, depending on other internal and external factors (Akiskal, 1991). No specific genetic marker that may be transmitted in major depression has been found. Late-onset depression (after age 60) is less associated with family transmission than early-onset depression (before age 20) (McMahon & DePaulo, 1996).

Many depressions are associated with deficiencies of certain neurotransmitters, or chemical substances which transmit messages along cell pathways, in the limbic area of the brain (Bentley & Walsh, 1998). These substances are naturally regulated by breaking down in synapses (spaces between cells) or through reuptake into the transmitting cell (see Chapter 5). The antidepressants developed in the 1950s and 1960s were thought to work by increasing the prevalence of nor-epinephrine in the nervous system. The newer antidepressants inhibit the re-uptake of serotonin, and it is suspected, but not yet established, that all antidepressants have effects on other neurotransmitter systems as well. At present, "interactive" hypotheses about the etiology of depressive symptoms are emerg-ing. Major depression is believed to result from combinations of the effects of norepinephrine, serotonin, and other neurotransmitters—including gama aminobutyric acid, dopamine, and the opioids—on nervous system function. Though much remains to be learned about these processes, antidepressants are effective interventions for 60–70% of persons who use them (Bentley & Walsh, 1998). This certainly supports the role of medications in the holistic treatment of depression as well as the need for teamwork among physicians, case managers, and other mental health professionals for comprehensive intervention.

Psychological Theories

Psychoanalytic theory maintains that all persons are involved in uncon-scious struggles with their desires and prohibitions and that depression results from our failure to resolve these struggles satisfactorily. Depression may also result from a real interpersonal loss, particularly during childhood. According to **attachment theory** people have an innate tendency to seek attachments to others (Becker & Schmaling, 1991). Social bonding is learned within the family during childhood, and depression may result from our inability to make and maintain affective bonds. On the other hand, excessive interpersonal de-pendency is another factor in vulnerability to depression. Depressed persons usually look for a dominant person on whom to depend. **Cognitive theory** maintains that negative thinking processes are primary in depression (Granvold, 1994). These processes, known as schema, include the screening, coding, organization, and storage of environmental information, as well as our learned habits of problem-solving. Some individuals become depressed by de-veloping negative thinking patterns about themselves, their environment, and their future. Specific stressors may activate negative schema.

There is universal agreement that life events are significant to major de-pression, but none seem to be specific to the disorder (Monroe & Depue, 1991). Life events by themselves are not predictive; it is their context and the way we interpret them which is significant. This perspective belongs to sym-bolic interactionism, with its emphasis on one's definition of situations and identification with social symbols. When depression does result from an iden-tifiable stressor (as with adjustment reactions) it is more immediately respon-sive to intervention. Particular stressful events tend to be more significant to a first episode of major depression than to subsequent episodes.

Social Theories

Learned helplessness asserts that repeated exposure to uncontrollable events results in a person's motivational (delayed voluntary response), affective (sad-ness), and cognitive (inability to perceive connections between personal action and environmental impact) deficits (Schwartz & Schwartz, 1993). Believing that one has no influence on life events produces a sense of demoralization. **Social causation** theory identifies low social status (education, occupation, income) as a cause of depression, because individuals in that condition experience more environmental stress. The **social selection** perspective adds that persons with low social status are more vulnerable to the effects of stress because of their lack of social and personal resources. Social theories of depression must also take into account that normal life transitions may produce depression in otherwise healthy individuals. For example, older adults develop depression in response to physical problems, negative life events involving losses, and the lack of a sufficient number of close relationships (Fielden,1992).

In constructing a holistic model of causal influences, it may be hypothesized that heredity and early loss experiences produce a temperament conducive to depression (Akiskal,1991). If temperamental tendencies are combined with a significant stressor, a person may experience major depression and its social consequences. Reinherz et al. (1993) conducted a 14-year longitudinal study to identify risk factors for major depression in late adolescence. For boys, risks include childhood dependency patterns, perception of themselves as unpopular, negative perceptions of their role within the family, the remarriage of a parent, early family discord, and generally high levels of anxiety during mid-adolescence. For girls, risks include having older parents and larger nuclear families, perceiving themselves as unpopular, having generally high anxiety and low self-esteem, and having negative perceptions of their role within the family during childhood. Females also report more episodes of stressful life events, including pregnancy and the death of a parent.

STRESS AND COPING

An inventory of a depressed client's stress management patterns can help the case manager identify targets for intervention. **Stress** can be understood as the body's reaction to any new situation. Its experience may be positive or negative (Lazarus & Lazarus, 1994). Stress is perceived as a challenge when it is seen as an opportunity for positive change. The challenge may be an exciting and productive experience for us, such as mastering a new skill or overcoming a limitation. Stress is perceived as threatening if we apprehend the possibility of harm, even though we might be proactive in managing the threat to avoid or minimize the harm. Negative stress (or distress) can be defined as the reaction to any event in which environmental or internal demands exceed our adaptive resources (Longress, 1995). It may be biological (a disturbance in bodily systems), psychological (cognitive and emotional factors involved in the evaluation of a threat), or social (the disruption of a social unit). **Coping** refers to the thoughts, feelings, and actions that constitute our efforts to master the demands of stress.

Seyle (1991) emphasizes biological aspects of stress and coping. A stressor calls forth the **general adaptation syndrome** including the stages of alarm (when we first becomes aware, consciously or unconsciously, of a threat), resistance (signifying the body's efforts to restore homeostasis, or a steady state), and exhaustion (the body's termination of coping efforts). In this syndrome, resistance is defined differently than is usual in clinical treatment. It is an active, positive response of the body in which endorphins and specialized cells of the immune system fight off stress and infection. The immune system is constructed for adaptation to stress, but a cumulative wear and tear can deplete the body's resources. Common outcomes of chronic stress include gastrointestinal, cardiovascular, and emotional problems.

Lazarus (1993) reviewed perspectives on psychological processes in stress management. Coping efforts may be problem or emotion-focused. The function of problem-focused coping is to change the situation by acting on the environment. This method may dominate when we view situations as controllable by action. The function of emotion-focused coping is to change either the way the stressful situation is attended to (by vigilance or avoidance) or the meaning of what is happening. When we view stressful conditions as unchangeable, emotion-focused coping might dominate. Both approaches can be combined to summarize coping as a pattern that incorporates flexibility across contexts.

SOCIAL SUPPORT

Persons with depression often isolate themselves from others when they need them the most (Vitaliano, et al., 1990). A client's depression can often be alleviated by the case manager's linkage with appropriate personal and material social supports (see a full description of this process in Chapter 4). It is important to understand that support patterns are different among social groups, and that more support is not always desirable. Caucasian older adults, for example, function best within a large social network, but for older African Americans having more network members and receiving support is associated with more depressive symptoms (Biegel, Magaziner, & Blum, 1991). Likewise, females experience greater stress with a larger social network, because they tend to assume roles as caregivers rather than support receivers (Walsh, 1994d).

INTERVENTION TECHNIQUES

The clinical case manager may work with a client having recurrent depression through periods of major depression and dysthymia. During an episode of major depression, ego support, crisis intervention, and social support development is crucial. During remission from the major episode, interpersonal and cognitive interventions are useful for adjusting any negative patterns that sustain the depression in the client's behavior and thinking. As noted earlier, intervention usually involves an interprofessional approach, including a physician who prescribes medication and monitors its effectiveness. Throughout the process, the case manager must attend to the quality of linkages with support resources and monitor their effectiveness. The case manager must also attend to the clinical relationship, because the client's attitudes about the worker are likely to change, depending on the mood state. In this chapter I focus less on relationship-building as described in previous chapters and give more attention to task interventions. The strategies described here are not intended to be specific to each type of depression, but they tend to receive greater emphasis within one type or the other.

Phase I: The Major Depressive Episode

Ego Supportive Interventions   Ego support is intended to build on client strengths and is consistent with the case manager's emphasis on both relationship development and environmental interventions. These are less task-focused than the strategies described later. Four techniques are described here (Goldstein, 1995).

1. Through *exploration, description, and ventilation,* the client is encouraged to talk freely and to vent emotions in an atmosphere of trust. Many depressed persons benefit from the opportunity to release emotions, because this enables them to think through their problems more effectively. Some clients need to vent before they can clear themselves of tension and focus on specific problem areas. The case manager must be a good listener who can encourage the client to vent about appropriate life concerns, providing some direction to the client's verbalizations while not controlling the flow of conversation.

2. The purpose of *person-situation reflection* is to help the client achieve a greater awareness of his or her patterns of problem-solving, coping, and social interaction. The worker encourages the client to engage in reflection while guiding the process onto any emerging themes of relevance to the mood disorder. The case manager always encourages the client to reflect on current, rather than past, situations and relationships, though reflection on past situations might be appropriate for long-term intervention.

3. Though the case manager promotes the value of client choice, he or she may also use *direct influence* to guide decision-making if the client is temporarily unable to exercise good judgment or if the client asks for specific input of this type. Advice-giving is not used to influence the client's long-range decision-making about such issues as jobs and relationships or even personal goals. Rather, advice must be focused on the client's needs for immediate relief—for example, how to access appropriate service resources and social supports.

4. Through *education* the case manager draws on his or her expertise to teach the client about such issues as medication and appropriate human services. The content of this education will vary, but the goal is always to help the client become better informed and empowered for better self-care.

Case Illustration: Wendy   Wendy, age 30 and divorced, experienced dysthymia, characterized by general irritability and frequent angry outbursts. She also had recurrent major depression featuring a sense of hopelessness, suicidal thoughts, and dependence on others. Wendy was particularly angry with men, having been abandoned by two husbands. This complicated her work with the present male case manager, and their meetings were characterized by her venting much sarcasm and anger for his alleged ineptitude. Wendy had difficulty focusing on her own problems and desires for change.

The case manager accepted that though Wendy seemed to benefit from antidepressant medication, she was not yet able to apply herself consistently to participate in a holistic rehabilitation plan. She needed to work through her feelings about the case manager, which in fact represented her need to be able to experience and express negative emotions. The case manager suppressed his personal reactions and eventually pointed out that her outbursts seemed to be based on her fears of rejection by him. Wendy did not at first accept the validity of this observation, but eventually, once she perceived the case manager as trustworthy, she redirected her energies to an intervention plan focused on improving her relationships with specific relatives and employers. The case manager began each meeting by asking Wendy to share her moods and attitudes about significant people in her life, including himself. He was able to point out themes in her relationships, including that of conflicts caused by her assuming, without clear evidence, that others criticized her.

Crisis Intervention   A **crisis** is an upset in one's equilibrium due to some hazardous event that is experienced as a threat, challenge, or loss (Hepworth, Rooney, & Larsen, 1997). The crisis poses an obstacle that the client cannot overcome through usual methods of problem solving. A major depressive episode always signifies a crisis in one's life. Crises include three stages. First comes a sharp increase in tension. Next, the person's failed coping efforts escalate tension and contribute to symptoms of major depression and a sense of being overwhelmed. The person may be particularly receptive to receiving help at this time. Finally the crisis episode ends, either negatively (ongoing depression) or positively (successful management of the crisis).

The case manager's two goals in crisis intervention are alleviation of the client's distress and establishment of an improved quality of life through assisting in the development of new, more effective coping strategies. Crisis assessment must address the meaning of the hazardous event to the client, its range of precipitating factors, and the client's support systems. Interventions, focused on problems in living rather than pathology, include a "here and now" orientation and the employment of tasks as primary strategies for change. These tasks are intended to enhance the client's support systems. For healthy crisis resolution the client must become able to connect the current stress with patterns of past functioning and initiate improved coping methods. The case manager must provide the client with reassurance and encouragement that the episode will pass. The worker also focuses on material support arrangements. As the crisis phase ends, the case manager must provide anticipatory guidance so that the client will be better able to prevent a recurrence of a crisis. This includes a review of the tasks accomplished and the development of new coping skills and social supports.

Assessing Suicidal Ideation   Depressed clients are often at risk for suicide attempts, and one who has attempted suicide is at an even higher risk for additional attempts. As a preventive activity, the case manager should link the depressed client with an emergency services facility so that he or she can readily access the resource if needed. The case manager may also ensure the availability of a mobile crisis team if one is available. Hawton (1989) has provided a list of assessment questions (the third item on this list is my own) for use with clients who have attempted suicide:

1. Why did the attempt occur? Investigate the nature of relationships with significant others, employment or school concerns, finances, housing, legal issues, social isolation, use of substances, physical health, social adjustment, loss, and bereavement.

2. What was the nature of the attempt? Determine whether the attempt was planned or impulsive, whether the client was alone, how likely the client was to be found, the nature of precautions to prevent or insure discovery, the nature and amount of substances taken (if any), the client's expectations of the effects of those drugs, the presence of a note, and the client's willingness to accept help afterward.

3. Does the client possess or have access to the means for another suicide attempt? Determine whether the client has guns, knives, other weapons, or potentially lethal drugs.

4. What are the person's coping resources and supports? The numbers and types of persons in the support network may be assessed as adequate or inadequate to provide the client with a safe environment.

Case Illustration: Ben   Ben was 44 years old, unemployed, twice divorced, and currently engaged. He was suffering from a major depression characterized by feelings of extreme helplessness and frequent suicidal thinking. Ben had a 25-year history of alcohol abuse, and only after he had recently stopped drinking (with the help of an inpatient program) did his depression surface. He discovered that he was a different man than he had always imagined himself to be, and he felt inadequate to care for himself. Every day he awoke with great fear, wondering if he would survive the upcoming day. He often lay in bed crying for several hours and then began calling on friends for help. He didn't want to be alone.

For several months Ben was in or near a crisis state. The case manager could not possibly respond to all of his demands for attention, so he constructed a support system for Ben, including persons from various network clusters whom he identified as receptive to his present needs for help. These included his parents, fiancée, one nephew, a neighbor, his Alcoholics Anonymous sponsor, a minister, two old friends, several members of a suicide hotline, and staff at a local emergency services unit. The worker's goal was to provide Ben with a variety of options for contact so that someone would always be available to him. The case manager approached each of these people (most by phone) to secure their agreement to participate in the plan. Ben agreed with the case manager's direction to not call these people at will, because they might tire of his demands, but to contact only three of them per day—during the morning, daytime, and evening hours. It was hoped that with such structuring of his network, Ben might feel more secure. The plan worked fairly well. Ben's suicidal inclinations often made him seek help from people more times than the case manager had recommended, but with the case manager's enforcement of limits, he eventually calmed somewhat.

Phase II: Dysthymia

Interpersonal Therapy   This perspective considers interpersonal conflicts to be a major source of depression, and the goal of the case manager is to help the client repair these (Swartz & Markowitz, 1995). During assessment, the case manager pays particular attention to the status of the client's current relationships with an "interpersonal inventory." The intervention plan focuses on significant role transitions, grief processes, and interpersonal disputes or deficits. The client and case manager devise tasks toward improvements in these areas. The client's relationship with the case manager is used as a model for making changes in other relationships. The worker's linkages often focus on social activities that will further help the client develop interpersonal skills.

Case Illustration: Jeremy   Jeremy was 30 years old, single, and unemployed with a ten-year history of recurrent major depression interspersed with periods of dysthymia. He attended a mental health center biweekly for medication and supportive counseling. Jeremy's depression appeared to be primarily biological. His father, paternal uncle, and paternal grandfather had all committed suicide in early adulthood or midlife. Jeremy himself had made two serious suicide attempts, the first at age twenty, with no clear precipitants to those attempts. The pervasiveness of depression and its effects within his family created deep conflicts among Jeremy, his mother, and two sisters. He had not seen his sisters in many years because, he said, they had always been critical and demeaning of him. Visits with his mother, which he maintained only out of a sense of duty, made Jeremy more depressed and prompted his suicidal thinking. Still, he was lonely, having no close relationships. His other interpersonal patterns were characterized by pleasant but superficial relationships from which he withdrew as his depression worsened.

The case manager explored Jeremy's interpersonal patterns, hoping to discover any external contributors to his depressions. It seemed that the client tended to terminate relationships, perhaps hastily, out of guilt after withdrawing when experiencing a major depressive episode. Jeremy eventually admitted to a desire to reconcile with his family. He felt guilty about his estrangement from his mother but even more so wanted his sisters to understand how hard his life was. The case manager arranged several conferences in which he educated the family members about major depression and Jeremy's powerlessness at times to control his moods. He helped Jeremy communicate with his sisters, as the client was verbally ineffective when under stress. The case manager supported the idea of a formal family reunification at Thanksgiving, and suggested that Jeremy take responsibility for planning the event. It was a success. The family remained emotionally distant from one another but maintained occasional contact on good terms. Jeremy felt considerable relief.

The case manager next helped Jeremy transfer his learning to other relationships where he might risk self-disclosure about his moods rather than abandon the relationship. This was also a slow but successful process with regard to a new employer. In spite of his successes, Jeremy's depressions continued. At these times the case manager made unannounced home visits (they had agreed on this strategy in advance) to encourage Jeremy to remain in contact with the case manager and the agency physician. Jeremy found his family support particularly helpful in coping with his depressive episodes, but it did not alter their frequency.

Cognitive-Behavioral Interventions   As noted earlier, depression may be characterized by patterns of thinking that produce and also might result from negative self-evaluations. The case manager's assessment of a client's thinking patterns, and efforts to promote cognitive and behavioral change, are important in dysthymia when the client is capable of sustained participation in a strategic process. Cognitive interventions are focused on the client's thinking, while the behavioral components involve activities in which the client tests new thinking patterns. While many techniques are available, here I review problem solving, cognitive restructuring, social support skills training, and exposure therapy. In applying all of these techniques, the case manager should attempt to simulate real-life situations as much as possible. Using homework, enlisting the participation of the client's significant others, and using the natural environment all contribute to that end.

Problem Solving   The goal of this technique is to help the client become a more systematic problem solver so that he or she can achieve personal goals more effectively (Hepworth, Rooney, & Larsen, 1997). It assumes that the client's inability to generate and carry out problem-solving strategies contributes to ineffectual behavior and subsequent depression. Problem solving can be a creative, collaborative process in which the number of alternatives for solving a given problem, and thus the likelihood of selecting an effective response from the pool of alternatives, is increased. The five steps in problem solving include orienting the client to the logic of the process, articulating a specific problem in concrete terms, mutually generating a list of alternative solutions, implementing a mutually selected and preferred alternative, and evaluating its outcome.

Cognitive Restructuring   The goals of cognitive restructuring are the elimination of thinking patterns that produce mood problems and an adjustment of the client's beliefs about the self and the world (Lantz, 1996). The process assumes that dysthymia results at least in part from the client's negative assumptions about the self (I am worthless), the world (it is a cruel place), and the future (nothing ever turns out the way I plan). Clients with cognitive distortions believe that certain life experiences cause undesired emotions, but the case manager educates the client about the mediating role of negative thinking in the experience of depression. The case manager and client then perform a mutual assessment of the client's environment to locate the sources of cognitive distortions, determine how these can be replaced, implement tasks toward that end, and then evaluate how well these tasks reinforce new thinking patterns.

Two examples can illustrate this process (Burbach, Borduin, & Peake, 1988). In the *triple column technique,* a sheet of paper is divided into three columns, across which the client records a specific stress event, the thoughts which follow the event, and the emotional correlates of those thoughts. The client is asked to reflect on and discuss each automatic thought. The worker's expectation is that the client will eventually see the arbitrary nature of cognitive evaluations of the stress event, and record and practice more constructive thoughts as replacements. The scheduling of reinforcing activities adds a behavioral component to this technique. The client and worker agree on activities, broken down into manageable steps, for the client to implement that may encourage a new cognitive response. The client is asked to rate the sense of mastery and pleasure experienced with each new activity in a "diary" of emotional experiences.

Many people engage in conscious self-talk in managing the challenges of everyday life. *Self-instruction training* is a form of cognitive restructuring in which the client is helped to increase control over his or her emotions by improving the quality of self-directed speech. The technique assumes that behavior is mediated by internal speech consisting of words and that self-dialogue may be dominated by negative cues. The case manager thus assesses problem behavior and its relationship to internal dialogue. The worker models adaptive behavior and demonstrates how overt self-directed speech can guide that behavior. The case manager instructs the client to rehearse new self-talk and to apply it in real life situations. The client's self-talk practices and emotional outcomes are processed in subsequent meetings.

Social Support Skills Training   Interpersonal competencies are both cognitive (knowledge about relationships, perceptual skills, decision-making skills, and cognitive assessment skills) and behavioral (self presentation, social initiatives, conversational skills, relationship maintenance, and conflict resolution). In skills training, the worker and client identify any deficits in these areas that contribute to depression, and they follow a structured plan for new skill development (Richey, 1994). As with problem-solving this includes a series of deliberate steps. The worker and client discuss the rationale for skill development and together identify a deficit. The worker breaks down that skill into its component parts. The worker models the social skill and organizes role-plays of each skill component with the client. They evaluate the role-plays to ensure the client's understanding and beginning mastery of the skill. The client then applies the social skill to real-life situations and processes successes or failures with the case manager.

Exposure Therapy This is a purely behavioral technique intended to reduce the client's depression by guiding his or her exposure to, and mastery of, situations evoking it (Thyer & Bursinger, 1994). The technique is appropriate when the target problem instills anxiety in the client. The case manager and client jointly plan a program of exposure to the dreaded situation. After the two parties isolate its anxiety-evoking elements they construct a hierarchy of tasks leading to mastery of that situation. This hierarchy may include as many as ten graduated tasks. The client is invited to choose any task in the hierarchy as a starting point to practice. Finally, the task process is initiated through real-life applications or artificial simulations. If successful, the client moves up to the next task on the list. The case manager provides the client with ongoing support and the power to terminate a task at any time. If progress is possible, it should be evident in the early trials. If the client does not experience success, the process is begun again with a "lower" ranked task from the list or perhaps a revised hierarchy. The case manager must plan with the client for a reward system when progress is made.

Case Illustration: Margaret Margaret was 65 years old and married with seven adult children. She was referred to the case manager during a hospitalization (her third in six years) for major depression. She was psychotic during this episode, believing that she had been kidnapped and placed aboard a submarine. Margaret stayed in bed most of the day. When roused by staff she sat in the lounge with her head down, noncommunicative and tearful.

Through most of her life Margaret had been an energetic and productive housewife. She was sociable and well-known in her neighborhood, actively involved in the lives of her children and participating in community activities. Most notably she was the originator and coach of a successful girl's track team. Still, there were problems in her domestic life. He husband was abusive of her, physically and emotionally, and she had been a problem drinker for many years. When she became even moderately depressed and withdrawn, her husband and a daughter became abusive in an effort to rouse her out of her lethargy. She was the "hub" of the family; others needed her to be functional at all times. Her depressions became more debilitating after age fifty. Her children were leaving home, and she and her husband were alone together more often, which exacerbated their conflicts. She became withdrawn, tired, and disinterested in the outside world. From the perspective of symbolic interactionism, her sense of self changed to that of an ineffectual person because of negative mirroring from her husband and the changing domestic situation in which her role as a parent was no longer valued.

Margaret stabilized quickly on antidepressant medications and responded well to the support of her case manager. He assessed many negative thinking patterns in Margaret, including the belief that she was incompetent as a wife, mother, and friend. Her self-image was that of a peacemaker who needed to subjugate her interests to stabilize the family, and she felt that she had no right for individual pursuits. In one family meeting she did express a desire to develop a life outside the family, which threatened her husband. Because of this, the case manager continued with family meetings in which Margaret's goals, but also those of her husband, were addressed. The couple was not able to develop intimate communication, but they did come to understand each other's needs more clearly. Her husband was helped to understand her needs for social interaction, and she was reminded of his needs for security.

Margaret's own case management focused on cognitive restructuring and improving her problem-solving skills. She wanted to socialize outside the house, become active in her church, and volunteer at a nearby home for persons with mental retardation. The case manager elicited the family's support of these activities so long as she would agree to be home at certain times of the day for meal preparation, shopping, and laundry. The case manager helped Margaret devise tasks for pursuing her three goals in ways that she could gradually experience mastery. Together they established graduated task hierarchies for all of Margaret's social goals since she tended to approach them all with high anxiety and a fear of failure. Margaret was particularly receptive to self-talk strategies, because she had always begun her days with internal "pep" talks, looking at herself in the bathroom mirror. Despite her motivation, it took many months for Margaret to adjust her thinking patterns.

SUMMARY

The causes of depression may be primarily biological, but psychological and social conditions also have an impact on the onset and course of the disorder. A primary treatment of clients with major depression is medication, and thus the role of the physician is essential. Clinical case management strategies help depressed clients make constructive cognitive, behavioral, and social adjustments in their lives, which will compliment and perhaps in some cases reduce the need for medications. I have presented in this chapter a variety of interventions intended to help clients resolve interpersonal conflicts, adjust negative thinking patterns, and develop new skills and behaviors toward a reduction of their depression. These are all appropriate strategies for clinical case management as they include elements of counseling and environmental work.

9

Persons with
Schizotypal
Personality Traits

The schizotypal personality is a relatively new category of mental disorder, having been introduced in the 1980 edition of the *Diagnostic and Statistical Manual of Mental Disorders* (DSM-III). It was developed by a task force attempting to refine the old diagnostic concept of borderline schizophrenia (Spitzer, Endicott, & Gibbon, 1979). Persons with the disorder are currently described as exhibiting a "pervasive pattern of social and interpersonal deficits marked by acute discomfort with, and reduced capacity for, close relationships as well as by cognitive or perceptual distortions and eccentricities of behavior" (American Psychiatric Association, 1994, p. 641). The disorder is said to characterize 3% of the general population, but such persons are unlikely to seek out assistance from mental health professionals and are thought to have little potential for personal growth. While similar in some ways to schizophrenia, the relationship of this personality type to schizophrenia is unclear. It may be a precursor to schizophrenia in some persons, a mild form of the disorder, or one of the schizophrenia "spectrum" disorders, along with paranoid and schizoid personality disorder (Kendler & Walsh, 1995).

Persons with schizotypal personality traits have received little attention with regard to their clinical presentation and responsiveness to intervention. Because literature on intervention is scant, the schizotypal personality might not be well understood by many case managers. In this chapter I hope to familiarize clinical case managers with the clinical presentation of the schizotypal client as it pertains to the selection of intervention strategies. A sensitivity to the special characteristics of these clients will assist the case manager in facilitating a relationship that promotes the client's personal growth or adaptability to life circumstances.

THE CONCEPT OF
PERSONALITY "DISORDER"

The DSM, which I reference frequently in this book, is the primary source for categorizing mental illnesses in the United States. Because it has included a section on personality disorders since 1980 (ten are now listed), the idea that a personality can be "disordered" has gained acceptance among many professionals. According to the DSM, **personality traits** are "enduring patterns of perceiving, relating to, and thinking about the environment and oneself that are exhibited in a wide range of social and personal contexts" (p. 630). When these traits are inflexible and maladaptive, and when they cause significant distress or functional impairment, they are said to represent **personality disorders.** This is a controversial idea, as it often promotes a negative labeling of individuals and supports a medical rather than biopsychosocial perspective of human behavior. The person-in-environment perspective on social functioning asserts that, while there is evidence of disorders of brain functioning in some mental disorders, normality or abnormality is generally found in the *interactions* of persons with their external circumstances. Even some proponents of the concept of personality disorder acknowledge that personality *patterns* may be a more valid means of thinking about this issue (Davis & Millon, 1994).

Some theorists have proposed that the DSM *categorical* system for describing problem personalities should be replaced by a *dimensional* system, in which sets of traits rather than entire personalities are classified as adaptive or maladaptive (Nigg & Goldsmith, 1994). Given that many diagnostic criteria, or traits, overlap among the ten personality disorders, the dimensional method would, in my view, represent a positive advance from the disease model. I support such an approach, and in this chapter I focus on maladaptive sets of personality traits rather than "disorders."

PERSONS WITH SCHIZOTYPAL PERSONALITY TRAITS:

A General Description

The schizotypal person exists on the fringes of society. He (most are male) is secretive, preferring privacy and maintaining few personal attachments or obligations. When involved with family or peers he tends to be withdrawn, requiring assistance with daily living. When living independently he often becomes a drifter, unable to sustain jobs or relationships. His vocational roles are peripheral to the mainstream and tend to reflect a preference for isolation. He looks and acts strangely; most people he encounters perceive him as odd. His speech combines intelligible comments with personal irrelevancies. He seems always to be ill at ease in social encounters. His creation of an illusory inner world, representing private symbolization, serves to bring cohesion to the schizotypal person's existence. Sometimes he purposely dresses or behaves strangely to draw attention to himself and, in that way, affirm his existence. He is simply not able to manage the normal responsibilities of school, work, family, or peers. He is a concrete thinker, not psychologically minded.

The schizotypal person becomes irritable and anxious when under stress. His tendency to become easily overstimulated can at times produce brief psychotic symptoms, including **depersonalization** experiences and auditory hallucinations. Still, he does not perceive himself as disturbed. The schizotypal person accepts life as it comes. He displays little expressiveness in face-to-face contact and conveys a joyless, bland orientation to the world. Being concrete and affectively shallow, he lacks the intellectual and emotional depth to experience distress as something to be resolved with sustained, self-directed effort. It follows that he does not seek counseling unless pushed to do so by others. When meeting with a case manager, he defines the situation as a source of stress from which he must distance himself for self-protection. Internally, the person experiences a fragmented sense of self with random impulses and uncoordinated patterns of self-control. He is barely able to manage anxiety, fulfill basic needs, and cope with conflicts. His coping practices are haphazardly assembled, leading to impulsive actions with few sublimations to accommodate others' perceptions of reality.

A Clinical Description

At present there are nine criteria for the diagnosis of schizotypal personality disorder, any five of which the client must possess (American Psychiatric Association, 1994). These include ideas of reference, odd beliefs or magical thinking, unusual perceptual experiences, odd thinking or speech, suspiciousness, inappropriate affect, odd behavior, a lack of close friends, and excessive social anxiety. With no *single* criterion being mandatory, a range of personality patterns may "qualify" for the diagnosis. Some theorists, uncomfortable with this lack of specificity, have outlined what they perceive to be the core features of the person with a schizotypal personality.

Two basic theoretical perspectives have emerged out of genetic, family, and clinical research on the schizotypal personality (Kendler, 1985). *Family* theorists, those who study clusters of disorders within families, assert that schizotypal personality features are characteristic of socially marginal but nonpsychotic relatives of persons with schizophrenia. These persons tend to display the *negative* traits of the personality, similar to the negative symptoms of schizophrenia (see Chapter 7) and including flat affect, a lack of close friends, suspiciousness, and a tendency toward high anxiety states. *Clinical* theorists, on the other hand, who assess clients in agencies, stress the presence of *positive* symptoms including mild thought disorder, magical thinking, ideas of reference, unusual perceptual experience, odd thinking and speech, and peculiar behavior or appearance. Others have proposed *three domains* of symptoms, including *cognitive disturbance, interpersonal problems,* and *disorganization* (odd behavior and speech) (Raine et al., 1994). Several researchers have noted gender differences in schizotypal personality. Men are diagnosed with the disorder more frequently (Kotsaftis & Neale, 1993) and tend to demonstrate the negative symptoms of the disorder (Miller & Burns, 1995; Raine, 1992), while women tend to demonstrate the positive symptoms.

Based on the DSM traits, the discussion here, and my clinical experience, I propose three essential features of the schizotypal personality type relevant to clinical case management practice. These include mild *cognitive disturbance,* pervasive *interpersonal problems* due to a poor tolerance of social stimulation, and a *restricted capacity for emotional experience.* The first two of these are well represented in the DSM. Of the nine criteria, four relate directly to issues of cognitive impairment (ideas of reference, odd beliefs or magical thinking, unusual perceptual experiences, odd speech), two others indicate interpersonal problems (social anxiety, one or no close confidants), and two suggest a mixture of both (odd behavior or appearance, suspiciousness).

Only one criterion incorporates restricted emotional range (inappropriate affect), but my clinical experience with this characteristic deserves greater weight. Schizotypal persons are usually striking in their flatness of affect. They seem to experience little emotion, with affect limited to states of anxiety or

anhedonia. Whether this feature is constitutional or environmentally produced is a matter of debate; I discuss this issue later. But, with such poverty of emotion, schizotypal individuals are incapable of deriving the satisfactions from relationships or other life experiences that most people can enjoy. Nothing much stimulates their flatness of affect. Further, social isolation contributes to their oddness of thought and behavior. They gradually lose touch with the conventions of reality and with everyday checks against irrational thinking. Attempting to fill their inner void, schizotypal persons create fantasy worlds of private symbols. Such fantasies provide them with an effective short-term alternative to social stimulation but add little substance to their lives. The pattern of idiosyncratic thinking results in further alienation, and a cycle of further distancing is generated.

The schizotypal personality has some similarities with the schizoid, avoidant, and borderline personality patterns, and with schizophrenia. The *schizoid* individual is alienated from others, but not from himself. He maintains clear thought processes and finds some satisfaction in solitary pursuits. The *avoidant* person feels detached from others, but not truly alienated. He wants to become part of a social milieu, even though he cannot easily do so because of his anxieties and fears of rejection. The avoidant person is uncomfortable with himself, although less so than the schizotypal person, and he maintains clear thought patterns. The *borderline* client, although anxious and distrustful, tends to be very much involved with people, unlike the schizotypal person. The person with borderline personality displays much affect, is a constant help-seeker, and cannot tolerate being alone.

The similarity of schizotypal personality to schizophrenia is striking. Persons with either disorder can appear detached, confused, odd, and lead marginal lives. Indeed, some adolescents with schizotypal features develop schizophrenia by early adulthood. However, there are distinctions. Persons with schizotypal features do not experience delusions, hallucinations, or loose associations except during transient psychotic episodes, which are not common to all schizotypal persons. Their social functioning tends to be impoverished but does not deteriorate over time.

The clinical case manager must recognize that these traits, which seem to indicate a poor prognosis for change, are in fact seen to varying degrees in schizotypal clients. For example, although anhedonia is invariably present, the client may have interests in certain life activities which the case manager can support. Additionally, these same features may be present to lesser extents in clients carrying other diagnoses. The intervention techniques discussed below are most appropriate for clients with schizotypal personality traits but are also applicable to clients exhibiting symptoms of schizophrenia or other conditions which feature cognitive disturbance, interpersonal anxiety, or anhedonia.

Case Illustrations

Leanora   Leanora was a 43-year-old unemployed widow fighting to retain custody of her two adolescent children. After her husband's death from cancer eight years ago, her parents-in-law accused her of being an unfit mother and successfully acquired temporary custody of the children through the county children's service bureau. Leanora wanted the children with her, and after many appeals the children's bureau was preparing to return them. At this time a casual friend suggested to Leanora that getting counseling for herself would further impress the bureau. This is why she set up her initial appointment. For unclear reasons, however, Leanora chose to keep her counseling a secret from everyone.

During her initial meetings with the case manager Leanora was suspicious, quiet, and ill at ease. She had no particular counseling agenda, except to note vaguely that she wanted to "get out to the pool," which made no sense to her case manager. Her affect was constricted, her communications were terse and obscure, and her vocabulary was primitive. Her grooming was haphazard; on some summer days she came dressed in a fur coat, mini-skirt, and hiking boots. Most sessions lasted only 15 to 20 minutes. Leanora would suddenly announce that she had to leave, sometimes to "get to work," and walk out, although she always made a point of rescheduling for the following week. Eventually she disclosed that her work involved collecting aluminum cans for recycling. Otherwise, Leanora spent her time taking long walks through her town of residence. She had a positive relationship with her mother but with no one else.

Despite her odd presentation, the case manager realized that Leanora was not psychotic. She was, in fact, a college graduate with an impressive athletic background. She had married shortly after finishing college (after becoming pregnant) but had done little since then except raise her children as best she could and tolerate a neglectful husband. Leanora actually felt relieved when he died, saying "being married never did me any good." She had functioned marginally, with no relationships outside her immediate and extended family, since leaving college. And for several months of weekly sessions, it remained unclear to the clinical case manager why Leanora was coming in and what her goals were.

Daniel   Daniel, who was 25, single, and unattached, came for counseling at the insistence of his vocational counselor as a condition of his remaining in a job training program. Daniel had a desire to work, primarily to keep himself occupied, but he had a poor work record. After no more than three months on any job, all unskilled, he became anxious, paranoid, fearful that others could read his thoughts, and disturbed by frightening ideas of references, or the belief that neutral events had special (threatening) significance for him. As the symptoms persisted, Daniel quit his job and began looking for another. Away from work he had no significant discomforts. Instead he isolated himself in rooming houses and listened to the radio, with virtually no social contacts or activities. Daniel moved to new locations every three months or so for, as he said, "a change," but aside from occasional visits with family members he had no acquaintances.

Daniel had never seen a case manager before, except that his mother had schizophrenia, and as a child he had participated in occasional family sessions. He did not feel that he had a personal problem but was agreeable to weekly sessions as an adjunct to his job training. Like Leanora, Daniel could tolerate only 20-minute interactions. He seemed to lack any sense of discomfort except for a general anxiety. He did not admit to increasing discomfort during a session but announced at a certain point that he was finished talking for the day. He could articulate no particular agenda for his involvement at the agency. Daniel was cooperative, but aloof and distant.

SCHIZOTYPAL PERSONALITY DEVELOPMENT

Accounting for the development of any personality type is a speculative process. Research suggests that personality has a hereditary basis (Millon & Davis, 1996), but its extent is unknown, and the environment is a strong factor as well. Some theorists assert that genetic influences account entirely for schizotypal traits, while others believe that its genetic base, although important, is overstated.

For many years biologically-based theorists have noted a close relationship between schizotypal personality and schizophrenia. Studies have consistently shown that the personality pattern is higher in the nonpsychotic relatives of persons with schizophrenia than in control groups (Kendler & Walsh, 1995; Maier, Lichtermann, Minges, & Heun, 1994). In 1950, Rado introduced the phrase "schizotypal" (schizophrenia + phenotype) personality organization to describe persons with a genetic predisposition to schizophrenia (Kaplan & Sadock, 1995). These persons were said to have an inherited pleasure sensory deficit (located in the thalamus). Rado asserted that a majority of schizotypal persons maintain a sense of cohesion by remaining dependent on others for care, learning to intellectualize as compensation for their lack of an affective life, developing adaptive modes of magical thinking, and having access to a few manageable pleasures.

A decade later, Meehl (1962) described *"schizotaxia"* as an inherited neural integrative defect. He wrote that persons so afflicted demonstrate mild cognitive problems, social aversion, anhedonia, and ambivalence. Schizotaxia was a necessary but insufficient condition for schizophrenia, and only a minority of persons would develop the psychotic disorder. Schizotaxic individuals could remain well-integrated if they lived in supportive interpersonal environments, had relatively low anxiety tendencies, and acquired stress management skills. More recently, Fish (1987) developed a measure of an inherited schizotypal trait, based on gross motor and visual motor skills, language development, height, weight, head circumference, and physical growth. From these measures, repeated on children over a period of years, Fish was able to predict an eventual onset of schizotypal personality, and even schizophrenia, with modest success.

Other theorists stress interpersonal influences on schizotypal personality development. Genetic factors are not discounted, but they are not given primacy as causative agents. A number of longitudinal studies have pointed to some environmental influences on the development of schizotypal personality, although it remains unclear which factors are specifically associated with it. The anxiety, negative attitudes, or psychosis of a mother with schizophrenia may produce an environment fostering schizotypal features in the child (Olin & Mednick, 1996). Goodman (1987) asserts that a poor social environment characterized by understimulation of the child creates social competence deficits associated with schizotypal personality. Weintraub (1987) states that childhood separation from parents for prolonged periods creates vulnerability to cognitive and social impairments. McNeil, Cantor-Graae, and Sjostrom (1994) add that organic damage from birth complications may account in some cases for the passivity and short attention spans in these children. Wilson and Costanzo (1996) found that a child's *anxious* attachment to parents is associated with the positive traits of schizotypal personality, while *avoidant* attachment is associated with its negative traits. Goldstein's (1987) research indicates that family communication deviance (the inability to maintain a shared focus of attention) and negative attitudes toward one another may support a reticent, eccentric cognitive and personality style in some children.

From the above discussion of schizotypal personality, I will postulate one developmental scenario. Heredity may predispose certain individuals to a constricted affective range and hypersensitivity to overstimulation. Stimulus impoverishment during infancy, whether generated by parents or genetics, may set in motion an underdeveloped biological capacity for emotion and a deficient learning of attachment behaviors. In an atmosphere of indifference the child may become socially reticent, insensitive, and uncomfortable with intimacy. Further, a fragmented, vague style of family communication may impede normal socialization. As the child grows, his affective style and obscure thought patterns make him unattractive to others, and he remains isolated. The possibility of varied experiences is reduced and the person becomes alienated, gradually escaping into a world of private symbols. This inwardness, as an effort to fend off pain, provides a temporary solution to his dilemma, but the fantasy world is not one of substance. The person becomes alienated from himself as well as others, and by late adolescence or early adulthood the schizotypal pattern becomes entrenched.

INSTRUMENTS FOR MONITORING SYMPTOMS

More than 20 observational and self-report scales are available for assessing and monitoring symptoms in persons with schizotypal personality traits (Vollema & van den Bosch, 1995). Raine (1992) has developed a particularly useful scale, the Schizotypal Personality Questionnaire (SPQ), a 74-item scale which assesses DSM characteristics and includes subscales corresponding to each of the nine traits. The scale has demonstrated high reliability and fair validity. Because the SPQ is rather lengthy and thus impractical for clinical use, Raine and Benishay (1995) constructed a brief form of the instrument. The SPQ-B is a 22-item self-report scale which can be completed in five minutes. The instrument provides a total score as well as three subscales to assess the factors of cognitive/perceptual deficits, interpersonal deficits (both negative symptoms) and disorganization (positive symptoms). All items require a yes or no response, yielding a total score of 0 to 22. Subscale scores can also be tallied. Case managers can use this tool as an ongoing part of their work with a client to measure clinical status and changes.

CLINICAL INTERVENTION

Persons with schizotypal personality are generally not thought to be promising candidates for growth, but research on this topic is slight. Their extreme discomfort with sustained human interaction suggests that a counseling relationship of any type, especially a collaborative one, would be difficult to tolerate. Further, they are reluctant to perceive themselves as having problems or to view other people as resources in problem resolution. When schizotypal persons initiate contact with service providers, it is usually because some other person or agency is acting coercively. In the case examples described earlier, one client saw agency attendance as a means of satisfying a children's service bureau, and the other was required to seek counseling as a condition of receiving vocational services. Karterud, et al. (1992) noted in one study that clients with the schizotypal personality pattern tended to drop out of treatment at high levels even after choosing voluntarily to participate in a therapeutic clubhouse community.

Still, many schizotypal clients can be helped, although not often dramatically. Their potential for growth is related to their ability to develop an attachment with the case manager. The worker needs to attend to the relationship above all else, and then include simple cognitive and behavioral approaches to improve the client's social behaviors (Kotsaftis & Neale, 1993). The case manager can assess the client's potential for collaborative work by considering three aspects of current functioning. First, if the client is a *self-referral,* or expresses even vague interest in reducing his discomfort when referred by another person, the possibility of change is greater. Second, if the client has some *personal attachments* (spouse, children, friends, relatives), however conflicted, there is a higher likelihood of growth. Finally, if *affective symptoms* (usually depression) are present, the possibility of developing a clinical relationship is enhanced (Stone, 1983). These factors all support the client's potential to form an attachment with the case manager, which is a prerequisite for any positive impact.

Due to the schizotypal client's characteristic interpersonal anxiety and tendency to feel overstimulated, individual intervention is always the treatment of choice. Some family work may be productive, but group modalities are rarely indicated. Five realistic goals with these clients include

1. Easing loneliness

2. Preventing further isolation

3. Avoiding overstimulation through stress management

4. Accentuating strengths

5. Helping the client understand feelings more clearly

These goals can rarely be achieved in the context of a short-term relationship. Still, it is not necessary for the case manager to devote many hours of face-to-face service to the client, because he or she must be able to minimize stimulation and to maintain a protective distance in the intervention process. For the same reason, while low-dose antipsychotic medications are often helpful for persons with schizotypal personality traits, not many other persons will likely be participating in the service plan. Thus, while the case manager must intervene patiently for many months if possible, this is not a costly investment for an agency insurance provider.

The case manager must bring to the setting an attitude of acceptance and concern and a personal ability to find satisfaction in helping the client make modest gains. Introspective approaches are much too threatening to schizotypal clients. Some case managers, eager to have a more dramatic impact on their clients, find schizotypal clients to be dull, unrewarding, and frustrating. Clinical case management with the schizotypal client can be divided into two stages. During the initial stage, which may last three months or more, the case manager's major goal is to create a clinical setting comfortable enough that the client will remain and develop an attachment to the clinician. Because schizotypal clients are perhaps the least relationship-oriented people found in counseling, intervention strategies are unique during this stage. The second stage of treatment, beginning at approximately three months and continuing indefinitely, features more active and directive interventions, as I describe later.

First Stage: Creating a Therapeutic Ambience

Interventions during the first stage focus on allaying the client's anxieties. Persons with schizotypal features tend to drop out of clinical programs because they cannot tolerate what they perceive to be an intense relationship. They are easily overstimulated and frequently need to withdraw. Because clients do not perceive collaborative work on personal problems to be potentially helpful, they experience more incentives to drop out than to participate. The case manager must assume a passive, non-directive, but empathetic and accepting role in order to help minimize the client's anxiety. Stone (1985) refers to a "non-verbal healing ambience" in which the client is made to feel comfortable and accepted. The clinician who is pleasant but rather quiet, helpful but unobtrusive, and willing to discuss the client's agenda exactly as presented in simple language might succeed in engaging the client.

The case manager can use several methods to facilitate a therapeutic climate. Consistency and reliability in appointment scheduling help the client manage the ego-boundary confusion that can occur when his anxiety is heightened. Weekly sessions are generally indicated, because these are frequent enough to facilitate an attachment but not so regular that the client risks losing his sense of autonomy. Session length should be left up to the client. Most schizotypal clients can tolerate only 15 to 30 minutes of interaction early in the relationship. The case manager should respect the client's termination of sessions at unpredictable times. During sessions the client should be permitted to set the pace and agenda, no matter how tangential it seems. The introduction of material by the case manager, however well-intentioned, might be perceived by the suspicious client as implied criticism or a threat. And, because schizotypal clients are obscure in their communications, the clinician needs time to learn the client's language (symbols) and to become able to relate to him on those terms. Principles from symbolic interactionism, detailed in Chapter 4, are applicable in this regard. Finally, because minimizing anxiety is a goal of this intervention stage, the case manager must not target the client's mild cognitive disturbance for change activities. The client's fantasies, for example, are not to be confronted, and the clinician must be careful not to inadvertently dismiss or ridicule them. Cognitive symptoms are dealt with in the second stage of intervention.

The case manager's task during the first stage of treatment is to promote the development of a mirror transference, which is a concept from self psychology (Flanagan, 1996). During normal development, a child first gains positive self-esteem and affirmation by receiving consistent approval from caregivers. In mirroring, the case manager assumes a similar role by reflecting back to the client, without expectations, his personal worth. In any situation that the client presents, the case manager affirms, verbally or with nonverbal expressions of interest, his uniqueness and value. Schizotypal clients have a fragile sense of self, and they require ongoing affirmation to learn that they exist on a par with others. This acceptance not only sets the stage for more active interventions at a later time, but also is therapeutic in itself because it provides the client with a greater sense of security in his generally unstable existence.

If the client freely remains in the clinical relationship for several months, the case manager can assume that an attachment has developed. Regular session attendance may be the only evidence of this attachment, since schizotypal clients display little warmth or affect. In other words, the case manager must not look for *affective* evidence of change; behavioral indicators are more reliable. Intervention may now become more active. The case manager may abandon neutrality in an effort to provide the client with directives that will enhance his social adaptation. The case manager focuses less on the client's anxiety level and more on his cognitive processes and habits of managing stress. The client's characteristic anhedonia is likely to persist but may become less pervasive if he is helped to recognize and build on some personal assets.

Second Stage: Cognitive and Behavioral Change

Because schizotypal clients function on an intellectual rather than affective level, interventions during the second stage are task-oriented, including some cognitive restructuring. As the client describes his everyday concerns, the case manager points out how he might think about, approach, and resolve them differently. Reality testing with the client is helpful as a means of modulating some of his misperceptions. The case manager should gradually become directive, as teaching, advice, and social skills training become the basis of the intervention. Stress management techniques focused on relaxation can be an important means for the client to learn about and manage internal cues of distress.

Schizotypal clients become confused by subtlety, ambiguity, and generalization, and may terminate the relationship if the case manager does not provide concrete directives and feedback. The client can only internalize specific advice provided in simple language. Relative to their concrete thinking style, it is noteworthy that schizotypal persons cannot generalize feedback from one situation to another. The case manager must repeat and review stress management and social skills techniques in different situations, despite apparent similarities between them. The worker may feel uncomfortable about giving advice, and feel in a sense that he or she is assuming responsibility for the client's behavior, but it must be emphasized that the case manager gives directives only about routine problems in day-to-day living. As noted in the discussion of ego psychology interventions in Chapter 9, advising a client whether or not to leave his family would be inappropriate, but suggesting how to manage a specific conflict with a co-worker could be helpful.

Any interpretation of client behaviors or attitudes must be "here and now" in nature. The case manager's interpretations of the client's actions should be framed in terms of the need to manage his current anxieties. Feedback of greater depth will be misunderstood, will perhaps be perceived as threatening, and in any case will seem irrelevant to the client. In all here-and-now interpretations, the client's available coping strengths need to be affirmed; his sense of self must be continuously reinforced. Confrontation, on the other hand, should be avoided. The client must be permitted to maintain his adaptive fantasies and other defenses. For example, the schizotypal client's projection of negative feelings onto the case manager, a practice common to many clients who function on an intellectual level, should be respected as valid from the client's perspective. The case manager can disagree with the client's assessment of the worker's motives but should also empathize with the client's point of view.

Successful outcomes for the schizotypal client require intervention over time. As noted earlier, growth is likely to be modest. The client may wish to remain in the relationship permanently if the case manager becomes the center of his life routine, but even so the hours of service will not be great. This long-term scenario, of course, raises negative countertransference issues. The case manager may wonder if long-term intervention in a context of modest growth is worth the effort. Perhaps the case manager will feel uncomfortable as the client's only "friend." In my view, intervention of indefinite duration with the schizotypal client is often indicated, as the quality of the client's life is markedly improved primarily through the consistency of the relationship. A planned termination should be implemented gradually.

Case Illustrations

Leanora   The case manager's interventions with Leanora were largely unfocused during the three months spent assessing her personality patterns. Even so, much of what he provided seemed helpful. Leanora began most sessions with the question "How do I get to the pool?" which the worker eventually understood to mean, "How can I plan time for myself so that having my children back home doesn't become too stressful?" But Leanora could communicate only on a primitive level. For months she and her case manager spent their 20 minutes per week discussing how Leanora could arrange a visit to a local swimming pool twice weekly. Their discussions gradually expanded to include outings to the bowling alley, basketball courts, and shopping mall. The case manager was impressed that this severely impaired woman had few social skills, an almost paranoid view of the world, an ongoing state of mild confusion, and nothing from which to draw pleasure but her solitary sports activities. Much later, Leanora disclosed that she did see men on occasion, but she was not comfortable enough with the case manager to discuss this topic at length. The case manager was surprised to discern from Leanora's consistent session attendance and increasing (but never extensive) disclosures that she enjoyed her counseling.

After six months in treatment (but only 12 hours of direct service), Leanora's level of social adaptation improved significantly. Her manner of dress became more appropriate; in fact, she seemed to model herself after the worker in this way. She began discussing her child care concerns and always tried to follow through with the case manager's directives related to them. Her efforts at child discipline were often unsuccessful, but she never blamed her case manager for this. It became apparent to him that Leanora could not generalize social skills from one situation to another. They reviewed the same basic topics repeatedly, all of them focused on increasing Leanora's sense of competence in her home, and helping relieve her anxieties by learning to take time out for herself. After one year of treatment Leanora looked and felt much better, but her changes were not radical; to her neighbors she probably remained the eccentric lady on the block who was best left alone. She continued to attend short, weekly therapy sessions. Her case manager felt that Leanora was able to benefit from treatment because of her external connections—the children for whom she felt responsible. No further complaints were filed about her parenting from her extended family or neighbors.

Daniel   Daniel's work proceeded differently. His months of regular session attendance indicated some level of attachment to the case manager, but he remained aloof and flat in his interactions. His sole focus was to get a steady job. The case manager suspected that if he succeeded at that task, Daniel would terminate the relationship. His potential for maintaining long-term attachments seemed limited. Throughout his adult life no circumstances had arisen to counter his strong tendencies to withdraw.

Daniel came weekly to the mental health center, usually excusing himself to leave after 15 to 20 minutes. He asked many questions about how he might succeed on a job and eliminate his compulsion to walk away after a few months. The case manager's efforts to teach stress management were frustrating because Daniel rarely experienced anxiety on a conscious level. Only when he became overstimulated to the point of panic did Daniel understand that something was wrong.

A turning point in intervention occurred when his vocational counselor, upset at his poor performance in a sheltered workshop, threatened to terminate his case. Daniel turned to his case manager as someone who might advocate on his behalf. The case manager contacted this vocational counselor and shared information about some of Daniel's personality dynamics relative to maintaining employment. Because he had several panic episodes at the workshop, Daniel agreed that medication might be useful in helping him tolerate the placement. He began seeing the agency physician for medication evaluations and taking a small dose of thiothixene for anxiety control. Daniel's anxiety, or panic, was of course a signal that psychotic symptoms might develop. He never experienced symptoms when away from work, but it seemed that his potential for steady work would be increased with the aid of the medication. Throughout this process, Daniel's sense of his case manager as an ally increased.

The case manager's intervention techniques with Daniel, as with Leanora, were reality-based, concrete, supportive, and non-confrontational. Daniel's goals did not change; he wanted a job but had no desire to change any other aspect of his life. Though he still rarely experienced his anxiety subjectively, he learned to accept that it existed for him and was manifested in his desires to abruptly terminate from jobs, living arrangements, and people. Daniel came to believe that the prescription of low-dose psychotropic medications could help him in work settings, but he would not agree to take medication on weekends or his days off. Daniel remained in contact with the case manager for one year (only 24 hours of face-to-face service) and left when his participation in the vocational program ended. The relationship helped Daniel with his sense of connection to someone, his awareness that he could not tolerate groups of people in any setting, and his acceptance of medications as a preventive measure when engaged in work. He probably did not "feel" as good as Leanora, however. It remained uncertain whether he could find and sustain suitable employment.

SUMMARY

Clients with schizotypal personality traits are not frequently encountered in case management settings and are considered rigid and difficult to help. Their basic personality features include mild cognitive disturbance, severe interpersonal anxiety, and a restricted capacity for emotional experience. A patient and flexible case manager can help schizotypal clients in modest but significant ways to improve their abilities to cope with interpersonal stress and anxiety. Intervention must be focused first on the clinical relationship and later on concrete, here-and-now problems in living. The case manager will not likely involve many other professionals with these clients, or pursue as many linkage activities, due to their limited ability to tolerate social interaction.

10

Persons with
Paranoid Ideation

Perhaps more than any other term in clinical practice, "paranoia" is as familiar to the lay person as to the professional. In everyday conversation it describes persons who seem overly suspicious and distrustful of others. Because the trait is so commonly observed, differentiating pathological from "normal" paranoia can be difficult for clinical case managers. In fact, its classification as an indicator of pathology has been problematic for researchers throughout this century. Many studies of persons with paranoia include individuals with other mental disorders, further confounding a clinical understanding of its essence (e. g., Refsum, Zivanovic, & Astrup, 1983).

In this chapter I consider the assessment and intervention of clients who do not have other psychotic disorders but whose paranoid ideation causes them significant problems with relationships and responsibilities. The themes I develop apply not only to clients with delusional disorders and paranoid personalities, but also to clients with paranoia as a secondary feature. I discuss the various causes and reinforcers of paranoia and provide the case manager with guidelines for clinical intervention. The biopsychosocial perspective serves as an organizing framework for these topics.

EVOLUTION OF THE CONCEPT

An element of paranoia in one's orientation to the world is adaptive. To be suspicious and mistrustful is healthy in many settings, because some persons do have the potential to cause us harm. Some authors assert that the evolution of the trait has been reinforced by our need to avoid victimization by predators (Fraser, 1983; Siegel, 1994; Strauss, 1991). In 20th century urban America there is certainly a need for vigilance, particularly among immigrants and members of ethnic and racial minority groups who endure acts of prejudice and violence every day. Meissner (1981) suggests that prejudice, or fear of the unknown in persons different than oneself, is rooted in paranoia. Pathological forms of paranoia are uniquely characterized by the person's rigidity and inflexibility in interpreting or defining social situations (Kheshgi-Genovese, 1996).

Paranoia as a mental disorder can be defined as ideation that features gradually developing and systematized delusions, without hallucinations, with the preservation of intelligence, and with emotional experience and behavior congruent with the delusions (American Psychiatric Association, 1994). A clinical description of paranoia was first articulated in 1883 by the German psychiatrist Kraepelin. He considered it to be distinct from schizophrenia, which in contrast to paranoia is characterized by the presence of hallucinations, a deterioration in social functioning, and emotions and behavior which may not be congruent with one's thoughts. Early in the 20th century, the Swiss physician Bleuler argued that paranoia was not a distinct disorder but a symptom of schizophrenia (Kaplan & Sadock, 1998). Debate about the nature of delusional disorders persists (Kendler & Tsuang, 1981). Researchers differ on whether paranoid disorders are distinct from other psychoses, and as a result, formal diagnoses of delusional disorders are rarely made. There is more agreement about the specificity of paranoid personality disorder (Millon & Davis, 1996). I acknowledge the professional debate about the labeling issues involved in classifying any personality as "disordered" (Mattaini, 1994), but I utilize the terminology here for purposes of descriptive unity with the literature.

Definitions

Earlier I defined paranoia as a feature of one's orientation to the external world. With regard to pathology, the DSM-IV (American Psychiatric Association, 1994) includes three major diagnostic categories for paranoia (other than the subtype of schizophrenia). **Delusional disorder** is defined as the presence of nonbizarre delusions that persist for at least one month. The five types of delusions include erotomanic (being the object of another's love), grandiose, jealous, persecutory (the most common), and somatic. The disorder is most common in middle and late adulthood. With an estimated lifetime morbidity risk of .05 –.1 % it is a relatively rare condition; only half as prevalent as schizophrenia. **Shared psychotic disorder** is less common than delusional disorder; it refers to a delusional state that develops in one person involved in a close relationship with another person who also has delusions. The third diagnostic category, that of **paranoid personality disorder,** is characterized by a pattern of such pervasive mistrust and suspiciousness of others that their motives are interpreted as malevolent. It is more commonly diagnosed in males, having a reported general population prevalence of .5–2.5 %. Symptoms of paranoia may also be present as secondary characteristics in other diagnostic categories, including substance abuse and organic disorders.

SOURCES OF PARANOID IDEATION

Biological Influences

No evidence has been found for genetic transmission of delusional disorders (Kendler & Davis, 1981; Millon & Davis, 1996). Still, paranoid ideation has many biological triggers, and the elements common to all of them are the production of perception or memory problems. The person must "fill in the blanks" of sensory experience. In the absence of complete information, coupled with anxiety, the individual may attribute the origins of stimuli to illogical sources.

Delusions may develop as a result of excessive activity within the limbic system (Siegel, 1994). This system is the center of emotional activity in the brain that generates feelings within us. Some persons, for a variety of physiological reasons, might experience excess activity in this region. When the person cannot readily understand the reason for such emotions as fear, anxiety, or dread, he or she must search for explanations. That is, if a person feels afraid, he or she must identify an external source of that fear. The conclusions drawn might end in paranoid thinking.

Paranoia might result from the effects of medical disorders. With respect to this fact, DSM–IV indicates that a diagnosis of delusional disorder should be made only after the psychological effects of a substance use or medical condition have been ruled out. Stoudemire and Riether (1987) summarize these conditions as including *metabolic* problems (e. g., vitamin deficiencies, liver failure, toxins, and lupus), problems of the *endocrine* system (thyroid and other glandular dysfunctions), *neurological* problems (dementia, tumors, multiple sclerosis) and *infections* (such as typhus and malaria). A variety of drugs can foster delusional ideation, including both street drugs (marijuana, amphetamines, hallucinogens, and cocaine) and prescription drugs (Block & Pristach, 1992). Sensory loss, particularly visual and hearing impairment, is associated with paranoid symptoms in elderly persons (Munro, 1981). These deficits contribute to feelings of social isolation, poor communication, and detachment from reality. The preoccupation with internal stimuli and distorted perceptions can lead to the development of paranoid ideas.

Psychological Influences

Freud (1966) believed that the defense mechanism of projection was key to the development of the paranoid perspective. In this process a person begins to experience an undesired emotion but then represses it. To protect the ego, the person unconsciously projects this negative feeling onto another person. For example, a son may have hostile feelings toward his mother, but because he does not wish to acknowledge feelings that are a threat to their relationship, he perceives instead that she is hostile toward him. The son does not subjectively experience his emotion and can also justify any negative feelings about his mother because of the hostility he perceives in her.

Other analytic thinkers have elaborated on Freud's formulation of the origins of paranoia. Meissner (1981) states that in normal development we internalize the presence of significant others in order to tolerate the threat of separation from them. The parents of the person who develops paranoia tend to act out patterns of aggressor and victim with each other, and the child internalizes both characteristics. The internalized characteristic of "victim" results in the person's assumptions that others are acting against his or her interests, and the internalization of the "aggressor" characteristic promotes the person's projection of negative impulses. Shapiro (1965) agrees that the paranoid individual has learned to assume the victim position in relationships from patterns of childhood rejection. The person also learns to play on the guilt of primary caretakers by being manipulative. Meissner adds that paranoid projections, though distortions of reality, provide the individual with a sense of purposeful involvement with others. The rigidity and detachment of the paranoid system is maintained for the individual's need to keep a cohesive sense of self. Garfield and Havens (1991) state that the paranoid person's mistrust is directed not only toward the outside world, but also toward the self. The paranoid system serves to provide the person with an externally directed organizing framework for day-to-day living.

Beyond parent–child interactions, other interpersonal factors may contribute to paranoia. Swanson, Bohnert, and Smith (1970) write that an individual may develop high anxiety and paranoid traits as a result of efforts at relationship development during childhood and adolescence if there has been an absence of emotional support from primary caregivers. Erikson (1959) acknowledges that adolescence is a particularly difficult period in personality development. Persons may become alienated from others if pressured to adopt social roles that are not reflective of the true self. The adolescent may also become isolated from others if he or she does not succeed in early efforts at intimacy. Communications theorists, such as Bateson (1991), state that a lack of clear expectations from significant others might create confusion in adolescents about the attitudes of others and subsequently might create difficulties with trust. Major life transitions can also create levels of stress that feature paranoia. Retterstol and Opjordsmoen (1991) found that, while seven percent of new mothers experience transient delusional disorders, one-third as many fathers also develop them.

Johnson (1977) developed a "paranoid-depressive" continuum where we all can be placed with regard to our orientation to the world. Depressed persons tend to internalize responsibility for their life experiences, while paranoid persons externalize responsibility for personal events. One's location at any point on the continuum is considered to represent normal functioning, except at the extremes. This conceptualization is supported by Candido and Romney (1990), who found that depressed persons tend to attribute the causes of negative personal events to the self (vs. chance or others), while paranoid persons attribute cause to others. Bentall, Kaney, and Dewey (1991) also found that paranoid persons consistently make attributions of negative events to other persons rather than themselves or to uncontrollable environmental circumstances.

Lewis (1985) considers this same continuum and addresses the question of why, in gender comparisons, men are more often paranoid and women are more often depressed. In her view, women are socialized prior to adolescence into reliance on the presence of others for general social comfort. They are more likely to experience relationship loss, predisposing them to depression. Men, on the other hand, are more at risk of becoming socially detached because of their socialization into independence and discomfort with intimate relationships. They are also socialized into aggressive roles that tend to foster paranoia in the disinclination to trust others.

Social Influences

A less commonly used theory of human behavior for conceptualizing paranoia is symbolic interactionism, which was described in Chapter 3 and which is the major theoretical framework of this book. In social action, each person develops a conceptual repertoire of possible responses to a given situation and selects from among them the alternative deemed most suitable for achieving goals at that moment. According to Magaro (1981), the paranoid person's cognitive style features symbolic thinking that is limited to several rigid conceptual categories, and perceptions must be distorted to fit into this existing schema. In one's need to be alert to threats, any element of a situation that might confirm this expectation is generalized to the entire relationship. The person is not able to tolerate unstructured relationships because they are not predictable.

Most, if not all, of the paranoid person's relationships reinforce the victimization theme. These meanings develop out of previous relationships with significant others and possibly from biological influences. Most non-paranoid people develop and continuously revise a longer list of alternative responses to situations. The paranoid person, however, lacks flexibility in assessing situations and tends to look for confirmation of preconceived ideas. The person's sense of self continues to be characterized by a lack of ability to influence the outcomes of social events. The individual is unlikely to change without assistance because he or she restricts social interactions so that the opportunity to develop alternative definitions of situations is minimized.

AN INSTRUMENT FOR
MONITORING SYMPTOMS

It is not always a good idea to measure a client's paranoia with a formal, self-administered scale. The client's being asked to complete a "test" might raise suspicions of the case manager's negative motives in working with him or her and might damage the potential for a positive relationship. But if the client seems willing to participate in such an assessment, and particularly if a relationship has already been established, the Paranoia Scale is a useful measure (Fenigstein & Vanable, 1992). This consists of twenty items for client response on a 5-point Likert scale (1 = not at all applicable to me; 5 = extremely applicable to me). Items were selected for the scale based on paranoid beliefs that people or forces are trying to control one's thinking, people are against one in various ways, others are talking about or watching a person, others' motives are to be mistrusted, and others have ill will toward a person. The client can score between 20 and 100 on the scale. Though not diagnostic, the Paranoia Scale can monitor symptoms over time. The relative brevity and non-clinical wording of this instrument make it useful for clinical settings. The scale has demonstrated very good reliability and construct validity, although primarily with non-clinical populations.

INTERVENTION

It is unlikely that paranoid clients will seek out counseling voluntarily, because they are generally not attracted to counseling as a support alternative. They tend not to take responsibility for personal problems because it is others, not themselves, who must change. The case manager may experience negative reactions to the client whose rigid, oppositional patterns are frustrating to a collaborative problem solving process.

The intervention techniques I present below are intended for use with clients having delusional disorders and paranoid personalities, but also with clients for whom paranoia is a milder, but still significant, impediment to problem solving. As an example of the latter type of client, a person recovering from heart surgery in a medical setting will, from the perspective of the treatment team, have primary needs related to the rehabilitation process. However, the client might also demonstrate paranoid ideation that makes him or her reluctant to ask others for appropriate assistance and support. The case manager might decide to intervene with regard to this client's paranoid ideation to facilitate a better medical prognosis.

The general goal of intervention with the paranoid client, from the perspective of symbolic interactionism, is to help the client become less self-centered, to expand his or her list of possible interpretations of interpersonal situations, and to acquire flexibility in deciding how to interact with others. Magaro (1980) summarizes this last goal as extending the client's range of perceptual input. Change can occur through cognitive-behavioral methods (Ritzler, 1981) but only after a relationship of trust between the worker and client is developed. In order to benefit from cognitive interventions, the client must also be able to think abstractly, not require an emotional encounter with the worker, and must have a capacity for adequate functioning in some areas (Burbach, Borduin, & Peake, 1988). If the case manager and client can develop a strong enough relationship to discuss alternative meanings of social situations, the client's sense of self in relation to others might change. Further, the development of trust in the clinical relationship might extend to others in the client's environment. Still, change for paranoid clients might be modest because of their rigidity and negative attitudes about therapy. The worker needs to be alert to changes in the client's social interactions, because these positive changes may precede observable changes in mental status.

There are four phases of intervention with paranoid persons, including the introduction, definition of the clinical situation, alternative hypothesis testing, and consolidation of gains. Each of these includes subphases of clinical activity.

Phase One: Introduction to the Setting

Consistency in worker presentation   In the beginning sessions, the case manager must attend to his or her physical presentation to the client. The paranoid person cannot tolerate unstructured relationships, and thus the worker might facilitate the establishment of trust with a formal, matter-of-fact personal style. This might include strict regularity in meeting times, use of the same office each time, and attention to clear communication. It might be therapeutic to schedule meetings less frequently than is typical for the case manager's practice to allow greater "space" for the client during this early phase of intervention. The paranoid client will be suspicious about the case manager's thoughts, particularly if the worker is overly abstract, not sufficiently verbal, or insufficiently responsive. If challenged, the worker should be open about his or her emotional responses because the client will otherwise make distorted assumptions about them. Facial expressions, body posture, and even physical movement should remain as non-intrusive as possible. The worker should retain a formal presentation at least until he or she becomes aware of a range of behaviors that are comfortable for the client.

Explanation of the clinical process   A major task for the case manager is a clear explanation to the client about the details of intervention at the worker's agency. The worker explains his or her role so the client can begin to understand what kinds of worker behavior can be expected. The client will have many questions about procedures; if appropriate, these should be answered directly. The client's curiosity about the worker's intervention plans cannot be answered in any detail, of course, because they will not yet have been formulated. It is also important for the worker to avoid sharing any personal information that the client might request. The client may be dissatisfied with the amount of information provided, particularly with its lack of detail, because no amount of explanation will satisfy his or her curiosity. But the client will begin to develop a frame of reference for eventually negotiating a shared definition of the clinical situation.

Acceptance of the client's perspective   (Fraser, 1983). The case manager should communicate, verbally and affectively, concern for problems from the perspective of the client, without offering to assist in problem solving until asked. The worker neither agrees nor disagrees with the content of the paranoid ideation. This is a very difficult posture to maintain, particularly because the client may ask directly for the worker's opinions. While not agreeing with the reality of the paranoid delusions, the worker can affirm the client's emotional tone. Pretending to agree is never appropriate, as the client will eventually realize this deception and have his or her initial mistrust confirmed. As the client describes episodes of victimization by others, the worker should state that, because he or she has not been present during these episodes, there is no basis on which to disagree with them. The worker communicates interest by encouraging the client's sharing, asking for details about situations, and acknowledging that the client's conclusions represent plausible hypotheses. The content of the delusion is not validated, but the client's emotions that result from the delusion can be affirmed.

Acknowledging that trust must be earned   The worker addresses the trust issue directly by acknowledging that it is indeed difficult to trust others. It should be pointed out that the worker should not necessarily be trusted initially, either; the client is justified in being suspicious of a new acquaintance. In this way the clinician is able to accept and reinforce a basic premise of the client, however different from the worker's perspective, and demonstrate an empathy that may become a point of engagement.

The case manager's empathy and stance of neutrality with the paranoid client is not easy. The above considerations are difficult to manage, and they create much tension for the worker during the early sessions. Thus, it is important to understand that this phase is not preliminary to, but is a central component of, intervention. The introduction of the worker and of the treatment process to the paranoid client has significant implications for relationship development and for the client's subsequent ability to engage with the case manager. If this step is successfully managed, the client will take a beginning step toward learning that not all persons are antagonists. The client can broaden his or her definitions of interpersonal situations based on the worker's acceptance. The client's self-concept might begin to incorporate the possibility of positive external regard. Still, the paranoid client might reject the worker's intentions despite these efforts (Fenigstein, 1996).

Case illustration   Ronald, a 42-year-old, unemployed, African-American male, had a delusional disorder. He lived as a guest in the homes of his ex-wife and mother, coming to the mental health agency at the insistence of his mother. If he did not get help for his "temper," as Ronald put it, she would not allow him to live with her any longer. Ronald did not reveal much to his male worker, but insisted that people throughout his neighborhood were talking about him behind his back, accusing him of being useless and weak and saying that he should either be killed or put in jail. Ronald was frightened by these perceptions and occasionally confronted a neighbor with great vehemence for making such remarks, threatening to retaliate with physical harm. These delusions put him at great risk for rejection, conflict, and legal trouble.

Ronald provides a good example of the influence of culture on the development of paranoid ideation. As a physically small member of a minority group, living in the inner-city of a major metropolitan area, he had been subjected in a real way to the kinds of attitudes that he was now experiencing as delusions. Now he was face to face with a Caucasian case manager of approximately his own age, in an agency located in a part of the city that was primarily Caucasian and middle class. There were few African Americans among the agency staff or clientele. Ronald was extremely uncomfortable, and tension was evident in his vocal tone, expression, and posture. The case manager was precisely the type of person whom Ronald would expect to think poorly of him.

Ronald was hypervigilant with the case manager's every move. The worker, while aware of Ronald's anxiety, attempted to initiate a standard intake interview process. Soon it was apparent that Ronald would not engage in this procedure. Ronald confronted the worker, first about his physical behavior. "Why are you looking at me that way?" "Why did you move your hand over to the desk just then?" "Why do you always nod when I'm talking?" Additionally, Ronald openly demonstrated his distrust of the worker's motives. "Are you going to talk to my wife about this?" "Have my neighbors been on the phone to you with their lies?" "Do you have friends on the police force whom you can call if I turn out to be trouble?"

For several months their weekly meetings returned to these themes. The worker quickly abandoned efforts to complete a standard intake, because his questions were perceived as intrusive, and as Ronald said, "I don't want information about my personal life getting out, anyway." The worker, while feeling somewhat defensive, talked about the plausibility of Ronald's concerns. He explained his own nonverbal habits (and, in fact, being forced into reflection, learned a great deal about himself in the process), including why he sat in the chair the way he did, what kind of room lighting made him comfortable, etc. He reviewed the nature of the agency's mission, its requirements regarding paperwork, legal issues around worker/client relationships, and the limits of what he could do in trying to help Ronald. Throughout this time, the worker never challenged Ronald's delusions. He voiced respect for Ronald's resilience in the face of such stress and affirmed as a strength his desire to have some friends.

Phase Two: Defining the Clinical Situation

Negotiation   By this point, the worker has facilitated the development of a setting where the client is willing to participate. Next, the worker attempts to promote a shared definition of that clinical situation; a mutual understanding of the purpose for meeting and an agreement on goals. The worker cannot be completely open with the client about their differences but can try not to directly contradict the client's perspective *nor* to reinforce the delusions. The worker wants to reduce the presence or influence of delusions in the client's daily living. The worker and client need to agree on goals that will permit a comfortable interpersonal distance for the client. A type of goal that is generally agreeable is the reduction of the client's emotional distress through an application of new coping strategies that do not require direct confrontation of others.

Speaking from the perspective of the generalized other   The worker can keep the focus off him or herself as a source of the client's suspicions when exploring or beginning to challenge delusional material by sharing concerns as they might be voiced by third parties (Weiden & Havens, 1994). For example, the worker can say, "Are you sure that your boss is bugging your car? It just doesn't seem likely" or "Some people might have a hard time accepting that your boss bugs your car. Do you worry about their reaction?" Both questions address the same issue, but the first places the worker in the role of skeptic, while the second can be interpreted as the worker joining with the client to consider how others unfamiliar with the situation might react to it. In the latter example it is unclear whether the worker agrees with the client.

Through the strategies noted above, a shared definition of the clinical situation may emerge between the worker and client, despite their disagreement on the reality of the client's situation. The worker understands the client's point of view and its impact on his or her ability to manage relationships. The client perceives the worker as an empathetic, interested outside party who wants to understand his or her perspective, and as one who is willing to assist in resolving problems. The client might still doubt that the worker's contributions will be substantive and might not wholly trust the worker's motives.

Case illustration   Shelita was a 37-year-old, single, unemployed, African-American college student, living alone in an apartment. Though she had a paranoid personality, none of her perceptions were grossly delusional; but she had an unyielding mistrust of all persons, even those within her family. In fact, she admitted racism in that she was particularly distrustful of African Americans. She came to counseling because she was concerned about failing in school (she was an art major). She once had a positive experience in adolescence with a psychologist after she was assaulted by a relative. Shelita thus saw the agency as a sanctuary, although she was skeptical that any worker could understand her life circumstances. She was not ambivalent about entering counseling but was so rigid in her projections that it was difficult for the case manager to help her identify problems for work.

The case manager had difficulty negotiating a treatment approach with her. Shelita believed that her problems would be solved only if she moved to another part of the country, because it was the cruelty of people in her present "provincial" environment that made her unhappy. Shelita's desire was for the worker to listen to updates on her life's events each week, and then to advise her on how she could more successfully avoid other people. The worker, in contrast, perceived that Shelita's negative feelings about others was the source of her interpersonal problems.

They established trust rather quickly because of the worker's consistent displays of empathy, the fact that he was Caucasian, and her prior positive experience with the mental health professional. Further, the worker did not challenge, at first, the reality of Shelita's paranoid ideation. It was difficult, however, to agree on problems for work. Soon the worker began gently to confront her paranoid thinking patterns. The success of this strategy was facilitated by his use of the third person in his communications. For example, Shelita had difficulty in her classes because of negative feelings about classmates and professors. The worker said, "You've told me what your first impressions of your classmates were, Shelita. They certainly seem unpleasant. Now, I'm not in the class, so I don't know what those people are like. Do you think that everyone else looks at their classmates the same way? Don't you suppose that at least some of the others feel more optimistic about making friends there? Have you noticed anyone getting along well with the professor? How can they do this, since he is so arrogant?" With this line of questioning the worker took the imagined perspective of a third party, or generalized other (classmates), rather than more directly saying, "I would never walk into the classroom with the expectation that people will be difficult, Shelita. I have always considered, at least at the start, that the professor has a lot to teach me."

These confrontations gradually moved the worker and client toward a consideration of other ways for Shelita to approach situations. The client began to accept that the worker would routinely challenge her interpretations of situations. Shelita never believed, or admitted, that the case manager's perspective might be legitimate. She often stated, in fact, that he was missing the point of her life events, but added that she knew he meant well. She agreed in time at least to consider some of his thoughts about approaching relationships differently. Still the only impact the worker had was in the way Shelita looked ahead to social situations. On the night before a new class, for example, she would

consider that her group might include a few decent people. Once in the classroom she regained her paranoid rigidity and was critical of others. Still, Shelita and the worker had come to understand their expectations of each other,
and Shelita was reflecting on her patterns of social interaction.

Phase Three: Alternative Hypothesis Testing

Following the development of a shared definition of the situation, the worker
can intervene more actively to modify the client's perspectives on relationships.
This can be described as "hypothesis generation testing" (Magaro, 1980). It is a
cognitive-behavioral approach in which the worker attempts to help the client
increase the number of conceptual categories, and consequently the number of
possible behavioral responses, into which perceptions can be organized. The
case manager maintains a focus on here-and-now situations and cultivates the
client's strengths in reworking his or her relationships with others.

Formulate a hierarchy of situations   Ideally, the clinician and client
should construct a list, and then a hierarchy, of situations in which the person's delusional perspective is most troublesome. The partners can choose to
work with either the least distressing situation or that which the client is most
eager to address. The worker looks for specific stressors in the client's life that
contribute to the persistence of paranoid ideation, since the client does not
typically see the connections between stressors and false beliefs.

Reframing   As the client shares his or her interpretation of specific situations, the worker offers several alternative explanations for the behavior of
others and asks the client to consider them. The worker does not necessarily
endorse an alternative, because this may come across to the client as overly
confrontational. The worker and client can role play situations, sharing their
thoughts as well as verbal interactions aloud as a means of processing them.
Given that the paranoid individual's intellect is intact except for those issues
surrounding the delusions, the worker may be able to point out logical incon-
sistencies in the client's perspective that he or she may consider.

Prescribing new behaviors   This strategy follows the reframing of the
client's perceptions. The worker suggests how the client might alter his or her
own behavior in a situation to test out the plausibility of a new definition, and
in so doing approach relationships in those settings differently. Because paranoid individuals are attuned to persons rather than environments, the worker
should identify and ask the client to investigate environmental variables which
might influence the outcome of an interaction. These strategies can be implemented as assigned tasks to be processed at subsequent sessions. The worker,
of course, needs to avoid prescribing any behavior that might be destructive to
the client's role within a setting. For example, the client should not risk losing
a job by confronting a co-worker. This practice, if successful, may generalize

beyond particular interactions as the client learns to become more thorough in evaluating situations from multiple perspectives.

Case illustration   Tracy, a 26-year-old single, Caucasian female living with her parents, came to the mental health center at the suggestion of a relative. She had a paranoid personality and delusional disorder. That is, her basic personality style featured paranoia, but when under stress she also developed delusions of persecution that persisted for up to six weeks. She tended to spend all of her time at home; she had no friends, although she would occasionally go drinking in taverns. Her appearance and level of intelligence were within a normal range.

Tracy had completed high school and a business school program. She had recently lost a job due to arguments with two co-workers, in which she confronted and filed grievances against them for conspiring to get her fired. Tracy had a number of boyfriends, but none of these relationships lasted and she concluded in every case that she had been physically or emotionally abused. Despite her symptoms there was a part of Tracy that wanted to feel close to other people. She was lonely.

Tracy was initially a difficult client for her case manager. She always kept her appointments but was suspicious of the case manager and not shy about confronting any perceived mistakes he made. She was particularly angry during a session when the worker had arrived five minutes late. The case manager felt that the client behaved aggressively as a way of demonstrating her personal worth to him. He met with Tracy weekly for several months, with no apparent progress, until finally the relationship improved. Tracy came to trust the worker's positive intentions because of his steady acceptance of her. Given that she had never really trusted anyone before, he became the most significant person in her life at this time. The worker was uncomfortable with this transference but began to work more actively with Tracy so that she might deal more flexibly with her world.

Tracy had begun working again as a secretary. The issue of job success headed her list of priorities for clinical work, followed by meeting new peers away from work and developing interests outside the household. Tracy came to the office and described what had happened at work during the previous week regarding her interactions with co-workers and supervisors. Invariably these were reported as unpleasant. She highlighted their efforts to reject her as a colleague, their criticisms of her work, and their efforts to get her fired. Tracy suspected unrealistically that the other secretaries were jealous of her because she had earned the favor of her boss.

Systematically, the worker challenged Tracy to defend these conclusions and to consider other interpretations of situations. "What exactly did the receptionist say to you?" "How did you conclude from that that she was being malicious?" "What was her body language?" "Could she have meant something else from what she said? Let me suggest what she might have meant." "Why do you think that people are so attentive to you? Don't they have plenty to worry about without focusing on you?" The worker was able to use the relationship to encourage Tracy to consider alternative messages without alienating her. This was not easy; Tracy always considered what the worker said but found it difficult to incorporate in her repertoire of possible explanations. She continued moving from job to job. The difference this time was that she kept working. She did not retreat into her household.

The worker provided in vivo interventions by making numerous site visits to Tracy's place of employment. They met there on several occasions during Tracy's breaks so that, introduced to the other staff as a "friend," the worker could become familiar with the physical environment and have a better frame of reference for addressing her concerns. Usually they met at Tracy's workplace and then went to a nearby fast food restaurant to complete their session. The worker hoped that getting Tracy into the habit of taking lunch breaks away from the office might help her meet some other working persons in the neighborhood. This turned out to be successful, as Tracy eventually became friendly with a man from a nearby small business.

Phase Four: Consolidation of Gains

By the ending phase of intervention, the client trusts the worker well enough to tolerate confrontation and direction without misinterpreting the worker's motives. The client's sense of self might incorporate an internal locus of control, or possibility of self-attribution, for the outcomes of some interpersonal events. The client has achieved some gains, and the worker focuses on generalizing them so that the relationship can end constructively. The trust the worker has elicited may be transferred to others in the client's environment. In this phase, the worker educates the client about aspects of his or her cognitive style, addressing the client's social networks, and introduces stress prevention activities.

Stress reduction activities   Everyone benefits from learning stress reduction activities, but these take on added significance with the paranoid client. The client, who is accustomed to projecting blame, must assume some responsibility for the stress associated with his or her reactions to others. The client might not feel that he or she has any responsibility for the origins of stress but might learn to influence its emotional outcomes. Various relaxation activities help the client to use foresight in managing social situations. For some clients, the worker may suggest strategies for avoiding situations likely to increase tension levels. Particular strategies will depend on the client's interpersonal style, the persons with whom he or she feels comfortable, and the initiative the client is willing to take. Even at this stage of intervention, the worker might not challenge the reality of delusions that the client holds. The worker might respect these but apply his or her awareness of the client's interpersonal patterns to help the client minimize their effects.

Social network intervention.   Networks were defined in Chapter 4 as those significant others in a client's environment who can be counted on to provide material or emotional assistance. An element of trust is involved in any supportive network relationship. The case manager has helped the client learn that there are at least some others who are trustworthy, and the client can be helped to identify those who may become ongoing supports for the client in light of the expanded repertoire of behaviors. These might include family members, neighbors, friends, co-workers, or even casual community individuals with whom the client has regular contact. Such persons might be brought into the agency for joint meetings, although in most cases they should be identified, discussed, and left to the client to seek out as desired. These persons may already have been identified in the prior stage of intervention, but they should be reviewed again during termination.

Case illustration Nancy was a 25-year-old, married, Caucasian female, unemployed and living with her husband, who had a sales position and was out of town on business several days per week. Nancy had a delusional disorder that was initially misdiagnosed as schizophrenia during a brief psychiatric hospitalization when she was 21 years old. She expressed incapacitating fears of molestation by a vaguely defined "gang." Her professional workers gradually realized that she experienced these delusions of persecution episodically, that overall her social skills were within a normal range, and that her ability to attend to many of her needs did not deteriorate. At times the delusions were comparatively mild, but they never disappeared. They became more pronounced as her anxiety level increased. She was seen by the agency physician, who initially decided to withhold medications due to her pregnancy.

When her delusions were prominent, Nancy would not leave her house or even go upstairs by herself, for fear that she might be assaulted. The delusions became most severe during her pregnancy, and it seemed that her physical changes, anxieties about motherhood or some combination of both contributed to her anxiety. At this time she came to the mental health center, accompanied by her husband. The case manager was able to engage the client in treatment rather quickly, and even initiate some resource linkages on her behalf, because of her desperation for help. Nancy was linked with prenatal services while she and her husband were seen together at the mental health agency for intervention regarding her mental status and their relationship.

The case manager looked for patterns in Nancy's delusions to see where intervention might be focused. It seemed that she was most paranoid when alone. When others were present she could relax and focus her attention away from her fears. Nancy's delusional thinking persisted through this period but, with the case manager's support, was less incapacitating. She did develop a habit of calling her case manager once or twice daily for reassurance. The worker had to set limits on this; Nancy could call only once per day at a particular time.

Five months later Nancy's daughter was born. Several weeks later the case manager referred her for another medication evaluation, and she agreed to take a low-dose antipsychotic drug to reduce her anxiety. Nancy enjoyed motherhood but persisted in her fears of being in public alone, not with concern for her baby's safety, but for her own. Nancy called her husband at work several times per day, even though he came home on his lunch breaks. When he was out of town she called and often visited with her sister and mother, who both lived in a nearby county. Despite Nancy's fears, the baby seemed to be doing well. She and her husband decided to terminate the counseling, feeling like they were getting along well and could handle the situation on their own. Still, while not actively delusional, Nancy remained anxious and fearful.

The case manager had concerns about the rescue behaviors of the family system (mother, sister, aunts, and husband) and devoted their final four sessions to discussion of these issues. Nancy's delusions were real, the worker explained to her and her husband, but they also served a purpose. She was afraid of being alone, and by acting on her fears she was able to keep her husband, sister, and mother close by. They kept her company, helped her deal with the outside world, and helped with the baby. The worker pointed out that Nancy's strengths might be best developed with her increased ability to be alone. She might enjoy the mobility and freedom from relying on the schedules of others. Further, other family members, as helpful as they were, might grow to resent spending so much time with her, away from their own jobs and friends. The worker suggested that the family work together on a plan to help Nancy increase her range of independent activity. The case manager made a list with Nancy and her husband of the most troublesome stressors (shopping and driving a car), and outlined behavioral strategies for reducing them. Reinforcers of family member presence were included in all of these. The case manager agreed to consult in person or by phone about Nancy's progress if the family wished. The family thanked the case manager for his ideas and set out to implement them with success.

SUMMARY

Paranoid ideation, manifested as symptom, delusional disorder, or personality characteristic, is seen in many clients of mental health agencies. The case manager might have difficulty helping the client with paranoia to make changes toward appropriate goal attainment because of the person's inability to accept responsibility for change. However, persons are paranoid to different degrees, and many clients can be helped to broaden their definitions and response repertoires to social situations. Conceptualizing paranoia from the perspective of symbolic interaction allows consideration of intervention techniques that compliment the influence of biological precipitants and psychology's traditional concerns with defensive functioning. The client-worker relationship is of paramount importance to beginning work with the paranoid client. Gains may be modest, but these are clients who do strive for human connection, often in bizarre ways, and can be helped to do so more effectively.

11

⚘

Incorporating Existential Themes Into Clinical Case Management

In the past ten years, interest has expanded in existentialism and spirituality as aspects of human functioning important for clinical assessment and intervention. Along with the biological, psychological, and social influences on quality of life, existentialism and spirituality are often considered to be a fourth major dimension of the holistic person. Existentialism can be defined as the search for, and adherence to, meanings, purposes, and commitments in one's life that lie outside the self (Krill, 1996). Religion is one's sense of identification with a fellowship transcending the self, and it represents an attempt to face the facts of difficult life situations in light of ultimate loyalties and values (Boisen, 1936). It gives the individual a frame of orientation and may include an object of devotion (Fromm, 1967).

In my view these two concepts overlap to such an extent that they can be discussed together. I incorporate them both as **existentialism** to maintain a sense of their breadth. In this chapter I demonstrate how purpose-in-life issues are appropriate for integration into clinical case management practice. Further, they can be incorporated into the book's theoretical frameworks of ego psychology, cognitive theory, and symbolic interactionism. Each of the theories contains propositions that are consistent with existentialism and spirituality. Thus, the case manager who addresses such issues with clients has much to draw upon for direction.

SIGNIFICANCE FOR WORK WITH CLIENTS AND FAMILIES

Existential concerns reflect one's sense of life purpose, basic values, and commitments to persons and groups. Case managers who focus *only* on a client's physical and psychosocial rehabilitation may de-emphasize or even ignore the client's most essential quality of life considerations. Case managers may focus on what clients *should* do, as a reflection of societal values, rather than what they *want* to do, which reflects personal values. Persons with mental illness, who have limited social skills and perhaps few supportive relationships, may feel more isolated if they perceive that essential parts of their being are not being adequately addressed in the clinical relationship.

Family functioning is highly disrupted when one member develops mental illness. In many cases families assume primary caregiving responsibility for the member whose capacity for independent functioning is significantly impaired. Paradoxically, as the family becomes more involved in the ill relative's life, its ability to comprehend his or her inner experiences diminishes. The person's cognitive processes become distorted, and the family becomes confused about how to relate to the ill relative. Still, while mental illness alters the client's thoughts, moods, and behaviors, it does not always alter his or her prior *value* systems. The case manager's inclusion of existential issues in family education and intervention might help a family with shared values to become more cohesive. Of course, processing the member's sense of existential purpose might also draw attention to conflicts that exist between the client and family in this regard.

AN OVERVIEW OF EXISTENTIALISM

A basic tenet of existentialism is that all of us are free to make the commitments to persons, causes, and values that are consistent with our nature. There are two contrasting perspectives on this idea (Frankl, 1988). On one hand, we may *create* what is meaningful in our lives. That is, there are no "objective" or external sources of meaning that we must observe. Meanings *emerge* within us and reflect our interests and values. An example is the person who chooses to devote her life to working with abused children, having realized that doing so fulfills a personal preference which is important to society but is unrelated to a necessary choice. The second perspective holds that at least some meanings reflect a reality that exists independently of us. It becomes our challenge to *discover* meanings that exist objectively. Some religious groups believe that there is a divine plan and a correct set of beliefs about a supreme being and codes of conduct, and that persons should live in accordance with this plan. In summary, some believe that "outer" reality is nothing other than a reflection of "inner" preferences with regard to values, while others hold that "inner" meanings are, or should be, a reflection of an "outer" reality. It is possible to hold both views simultaneously, as we may consider some purposes to be objective and others to be based on our preferences.

Existential meanings can be summarized into the following types, which may overlap (Frankl, 1988):

1. *Belief systems* may be religious or secular. One can believe in the teachings of the Baptist faith because of its divine origins, or in the golden rule (act toward others as you want them to act toward you) because of purely humanitarian commitments.

2. *Social concerns* include commitments to causes or social groups. One can demonstrate such a purpose, for example, in volunteer service of various types, commitments to bettering the quality of life for certain oppressed groups, or environmental concerns.

3. *Creative pursuits* include art, music, and literature, but may also include creative approaches to one's work— for example, the development of innovative agency programs. Also included in this category is the *experience* of creative pursuits which bring meaning to one's life. Some persons feel most alive, for example, when responding emotionally to a piece of music.

4. *Hope* includes the defiance of suffering. This comes to the forefront of existence at those times when one experiences great self-doubt or despair, but is also able to recognize that he or she values life enough to persist in overcoming the adversity, a process that might result in growth.

Existential concerns arise from, or help us manage, anxieties produced by confrontations with *death,* the possibility of *isolation* (or being alienated from others), and *freedom* (the responsibility involved in choice), as well as concerns about our place in the world (Yalom, 1980). Coming to terms with these issues is a challenge for all people. While we may not deal with these concerns on a daily basis, they influence how we organize our lives.

Some emotions provide signals that we are struggling with existential concerns (Lazarus & Lazarus, 1994). Most prominently, *anxiety* results from uncertain threats to our identity and future well-being or from life and death concerns. Anxiety is fueled by our struggle to maintain a sense of connection to others, and we often feel threatened by the fragile nature of life. If we end a relationship with a close friend through conflict, separation, or death, we may feel a partial loss of self in that our identity has been invested in maintaining that connection.

The emotion of *guilt* results from thoughts or actions which we perceive as violations of important social standards of conduct when they are observed by others. Guilt results from a perceived "moral flaw" in which we have not behaved in accordance with an important value. A religious person who sins may feel guilt, and a case manager who provides poor service to a client may feel guilt. In both cases the emotion results from the violation of a primary value regarding appropriate attention to life commitments.

The emotion of *shame* is similar to that of guilt, but refers more specifically to the failure to live up to a personal (rather than social) ideal. It may not be noticed by, and may not directly affect, another person, but it is within our own awareness. A Caucasian person who believes in equality of opportunity may feel shame when he reacts negatively to an African American family moving into his neighborhood. It is also important to emphasize that persons experience positive emotions such as *happiness* and *joy* when they behave in ways that affirm the existential self. A client who performs well as a Habitat for Humanity volunteer may experience great joy from making a contribution to the community.

Incorporating Existentialism into Practice

Existential issues are not appropriate to address with clients in all practice situations (May & Yalom, 1995). The partnership model of practice, with its value of self-determination, mandates that case managers accept problems and goals from the client's perspective. In general, existential concerns may not be appropriate to raise with clients who are absorbed in immediate problems for which they are seeking practical assistance. On the other hand, purpose-in-life issues may be appropriate for intervention when the client is troubled by anxiety, guilt, and shame or demonstrates inclinations to look beyond the self and immediate situation in understanding personal dilemmas. Existential issues should be included as part of a multidimensional assessment with *all* clients, as it is always possible that one's present problems and needs may contribute to, or result from, struggles with a broad life concern.

With regard to utilizing existential themes in clinical practice, the challenges for the case manager are fourfold:

1. To understand his or her own existential issues and their impact on practice.
2. To consider client functioning within a broad context of meaning (that is, bring consistency to the client's present and ultimate concerns).
3. To encourage client disclosure of existential concerns when appropriate.
4. To help clients identify meanings and purposes which can guide them in making growth-enhancing decisions.

Existential *interventions* can be guided by attention to the following four principles:

1. To encourage the client's active investment in life (vs. being passive).
2. To encourage the client to look externally for solutions to problems rather than to be preoccupied with internal emotions.
3. To encourage the client to care about something outside the self.
4. To remove obstacles to the client's natural inclinations to look externally for solutions.

EXISTENTIALISM AND MENTAL ILLNESS

Sixty years ago, Boisen (1936) outlined characteristics of spirituality still relevant to persons struggling with mental illness. He concluded from research done with hospitalized persons that there was a connection between religious reflection and the isolation experienced by persons with mental illness. The sense of isolation can be conceptualized as estrangement from those with whom the person seeks relationships. Boisen also noted that certain issues are common to those experiencing spiritual struggles and emotional breakdowns. In either case, persons question their identities, place in the world, and potential for growth. These observations are quite consistent with the client's loss of capacity for symbolic interaction as discussed in Chapter 3.

The symptoms of mental illness, whatever their biochemical causes, can be understood in part as indicators of internal struggles. Boisen summarizes that persons with mental illness can respond to their problems by making *no attempt* to face them, attempting to *escape or project* them, or *actively struggling* with them. The outcome of the struggle to recover from or adjust to a mental illness depends in part on the presence of a nucleus of purpose around which a new sense of self can be formed. The choice to face difficulties is, of course, a positive step.

More recent research indicates that existential concerns are central to the lives of persons with mental illness. Holford (1982), in a naturalistic study of 42 subjects divided into "religious" and "control" groups, investigated the prognostic significance of religious ideation in adults with mental illness. She found that traditional religious elements tended not to be involved in psychotic ideation. Personal prayer, found to be important to over half the respondents, was generally used in constructive ways. Sullivan (1993) conducted a qualitative research study of 40 persons with serious mental illness who were functioning with a sense of success. Forty-eight percent (48%) stated that existential or spiritual beliefs were central to this success. Only vocational activity (85%), medication (70%), and support from friends (58%) were cited more frequently. Respondents indicated that their spirituality was helpful as a problem-solving guide, a means of social support (through attendance at religious functions), and a means of making sense out of life dilemmas.

Mental health practitioners tend to feel uncomfortable or unqualified to address existential issues with clients. Sheridan, Bullis, Adcock, Berlin, and Miller (1992), in a random survey of 328 Virginia social workers, psychologists, and counselors, found that respondents valued religious or existential dimensions in their own lives. They addressed these issues to varying extents in their clinical practices, but expressed reservations about the potential abuse of doing so, particularly with regard to imposing their beliefs on clients. Further, 77% stated that these issues were rarely or never addressed during their clinical training. Sheridan and Bullis (1991) presented further data from this sample (n=159) indicating that professionals struggled with these issues with no consensus about pursuing them in practice. The same interventions were viewed by some clinicians to be appropriate and by others to be unethical.

Imbrie (1985) is one of few professionals to make recommendations for integrating existentialism into practice. He wrote that counselors should support the spiritual ideas of the client, whether conventional or bizarre, because doing otherwise would deny a part of the client's self. The person with psychosis who maintains an existential focus is demonstrating an interest in and a commitment to *something* external, and this usually implies an acceptance of responsibility for the self and others. He concludes that the practitioner must strive to know more than the client about the client's religious dogma, so that he or she can promote the ideas inherent in most faiths of belonging to a community.

The next two sections of this chapter provide a basis for the incorporation of existential themes into client assessment from the perspectives of ego psychology and cognitive theory.

THE EGO PSYCHOLOGY PERSPECTIVE

Essential ego functions include reality testing, the integration of stimuli, drive control, defensive functions, judgment, the sense of the world and self, and relationship management. The ego is a *center of initiative*, an organizer of all those activities. Ego psychology assumes the existence of basic drives, and one of these is the drive to *mastery and competence* (Goldstein, 1995). That is, all of us have an innate tendency to seek equilibrium with our environments by managing challenges and taking initiatives toward mastery. This drive evolves throughout life from our talents, successes in mastering developmental tasks, affirmative interactions with others, motivations deriving from our aspirations, and our innate relationship-seeking focus. It follows from the existence of this drive that we must strive to make sense of the environment toward our goal of finding satisfaction with, and seeking direction for, action.

In logotherapy, an existential perspective that derives from ego psychology, the **will to meaning** is conceptualized as an aspect of the drive to mastery. It is a basic, enduring tendency to obtain what satisfies our nature (Frankl, 1988). We all have this innate drive either to create or to discover meaning and purpose in life beyond our physical existence and survival. Through the will to meaning, Frankl introduces several propositions that may add to the case manager's understanding of how people struggle with meaning. As stated earlier, many people do not often reflect upon their existential purposes. This is because recognizing purposes beyond the self includes an awareness of vulnerability, responsibility, and the potential for loss. A person's experiences with suffering, guilt, and death can result in a suppression of the will.

Ego psychology asserts that we use a variety of defense mechanisms to minimize the direct impact of anxiety. The drive toward mastery and competence is subject to the same defensive activities as other impulses. The will to meaning may be relegated to the unconscious with the result that we remain unaware of its influence and instead remain consciously occupied with less threatening ideas. This is not a satisfactory resolution of the problem of anxiety, however, as we then experience indirect symptoms of distress.

The case manager who uses an ego psychology intervention approach might select from numerous strategies including exploration and ventilation, education, direct advice, life structuring, and reflection (Woods & Hollis, 1990). When appropriate, the clinician should help the client become aware of existential impulses that have been defended out of awareness. Though growth-enhancing, this might unfold as a painful process for the client. The case manager must always be aware that attention to existential concerns cannot be managed comfortably. The worker cannot shield the client from the risks involved in making and sustaining commitments. For that reason, as stated earlier, existential reflection should not always be a part of intervention.

THE COGNITIVE THEORY PERSPECTIVE

Cognitive theory is fundamentally different from ego psychology in several ways. As described in Chapter 3, this theory considers conscious thinking to be the basis for almost all behavior and emotions (Granvold, 1994). Principles of existentialism fit within cognitive theory's assumption that people are active participants in constructing their realities. Cognitive theory is a motor theory; the mind does not passively receive and process external stimuli, but is active in constructing the reality it seeks to apprehend. Cognitive structures tend to be rigid, but internal propositions change as one's knowledge of the world influences how he or she assesses new situations. Operations, or habits of thought, also evolve as one either accommodates (makes internal adjustments to) or assimilates (comfortably incorporates) new situations. As thinkers, the sense of self evolves as persons actively participate in the processing of stimuli and define their realities in accordance with it.

Specific concepts of cognitive theory that relate to the theme of existentialism include *motivational direction* and *justification for action*. People develop life meanings and purposes through the process of reciprocal influence described above. They strive to make sense out of their internal and external experiences, and thinking represents the effort to create or maintain meaning and significance from experience. Persons develop interests, focus their attention on stimuli which have meaning for them, and develop preferences, or values. They are drawn to stimuli that pertain to their meanings, and they find satisfaction when they fulfill those meanings.

Existential struggles can be understood as developing from cognitive errors, or habits of thought that lead to the distortion of input from the environment and the experience of psychological distress. These errors result from certain biased processing patterns based on internalized beliefs, values, and experiences. Some habits of thought that may have been functional in prior situations produce distortions in new situations. Some symptoms of mental illness, particularly delusions, reflect the person's effort to make sense out of a distorted reality.

In assessment, the case manager must assess the client's (or family's) schema with regard to how a problem is perceived, and identify any faulty thinking patterns which may be contributing to the problem by considering the evidence supporting the client's beliefs. The case manager must come to understand the client's ultimate values and life purposes as reflected in motivations for behavior. Through this process of focusing, the worker helps the client consider long-term as well as immediate goals because they are relevant to understanding presenting problems. During intervention the case manager, through a variety of here-and-now interventions that promote new ways of understanding and acting on challenges, can help the client adjust cognitive processes in ways that will better facilitate goal attainment or develop new personal goals.

CASE ILLUSTRATIONS

To illustrate how clients frequently maintain their earlier existential or religious orientations following the onset of mental illness, I present the stories of eight clients. All of them were participating in a service milieu that included medication and clinical case management, and all agreed to discuss their purpose in life issues. The clients were asked the following two questions:

1. What thoughts do you have now about your purpose in life, and how are these affected by your religious beliefs, if you have any?
2. What religious beliefs did you have, if any, when you were growing up?

I followed up the clients' responses with other questions for clarification. What follows are summaries of those conversations.

Brad

Brad is 35 years old, single, unemployed, and living alone. He has a college degree but has been disabled from work for ten years because of hallucinatory experiences, which he describes as "mental interference" from others. Brad believes that, via thought insertion, businessmen from around the country are stealing his ideas as they negotiate with him for corporate jobs. Brad spends most of his time isolated in his room, tormented by the voices in his head. He was raised in the Roman Catholic church, to which his parents, whom he sees regularly, still belong.

Brad says now, "A purpose to life? I don't know. I've never really thought about it. I'm not sure if God exists. He probably does. But I'm not sure because he wouldn't let innocent people suffer and die." When asked about an afterlife, Brad replied, "I'm not sure. Well, I guess there must be one, because my grandfather still speaks to me. I don't know where he is, but he's somewhere. I think people's spirits or souls live on, but I have no idea where they are, or in what form. There could be a heaven, but hell is less likely. I have no idea where they might be. But I guess the point is, we're supposed to be here to get some things done. What I have to contribute must be important because so many people are trying to keep me from doing it, or even figuring out what it is. But it will come to me. Once I figure it out it will help my parents, too, I imagine."

Robyn

Robyn, 28, is a severely impaired, single, white female with schizophrenia who lives with her younger sister and is supported by her parents. She rarely bathes, washes her clothes, eats a balanced meal, or has contact with anyone outside her family. She is paralyzed by anxiety and hears voices which are critical of her. Like Brad, Robyn was raised a Catholic, and her Italian family is highly involved in that religious culture. Though Robyn does not attend Mass, she watches it on television every Sunday.

"I'm Catholic," she says first. "I used to go to church but I can't anymore. But I'll go to heaven for sure. I'm afraid that I won't live very long. Life is just so hard for me. But I'm a good person. I'm no good for anyone else, but I'll go to heaven." She states that she would go to church with her father if he asked. "I don't think there's any point for my living. But I never hurt anybody so that must count for something. I think if you never hurt anybody, that actually counts for something, because you're letting them do what they want to do. And whenever you respect somebody you are helping them succeed."

Kitty

Kitty, aged 25, has schizophrenia but is more functional than the above two clients. She lives at home, attends college (with marginal success), and participates in dance classes, but still experiences bizarre somatic delusions. She was raised in a traditional Catholic background, and in spite of her distortions about people in this world, maintains those beliefs.

"My purpose in life is to develop my talents, serve God, and be the best person that I can be." She attends Mass weekly, one activity that she has continued with her parents. This provides the family with an element of shared purpose despite their general estrangement from one another. "I believe in heaven and purgatory, but not hell." When the case manager commented on the fervency of her beliefs, Kitty commented, "I don't really think about these things very often. I do question things at times, why I have certain problems, or why my parents hate me. But I'm still young and I'll eventually decide what I can do with my talents to be useful to other people, or maybe just raise kids."

Phil

Phil, 46, has experienced confused thinking for almost 20 years. He is extremely solitary, inactive, and passive, and lives alone on disability funds. His routine is limited to watching sports on television, taking occasional walks, and visiting with his sister and mother once per month. Phil was raised in the Lutheran faith, but he became an atheist in his early 20s.

"There's no God. No question about it. There's no meaning to anything." Despite Phil's isolation, he does have a conventional sense of ethics. "People still have to lead moral lives. They need to do good, and get along with others. You know, the golden rule idea." Phil was asked how he contributes to the common good. "I'm patient. I try to get along, and don't cause problems for anyone." Phil's family, all of whom belong to a church, obviously cannot use their religion as a basis for relating to him, but they share a similar value system. "I get along with my family pretty well. I think they know that I'm smart and they understand me better than most. I have a mental illness and everybody thinks I'm crazy, but I'm not much different since I got this way, and only my family seems to know that."

Ronald

Ronald is 42, African American, and paranoid. He feels harassed, always tormented by the auditory hallucinations that he perceives as others expressing negative judgments about him. Routinely, Ronald is barred from public places after confronting innocent people whom he suspects of verbally abusing him. He also approaches other persons in the agency aggressively at times, including his case manager, for expressing their dislike of him in non-verbal ways. Ronald had a Baptist upbringing but has no formal church affiliation at present. His religious beliefs in the context of his mental status are surprising.

"I think about religion almost every day. I do believe in God and heaven and purgatory. But not hell. There is something good about everyone. Sometimes I get angry at God because I have had to deal with mental illness, but not always. If the Lord loves me, he'll show me a rainbow. Still, I don't go to church, but that doesn't matter, because most people who do are hypocrites." Ronald's family is actively religious, but they refuse to participate in his mental health programs and have not yet established a format for resolving their problems with him. Ronald was asked if they ever discuss religious matters. "No, because I just get upset when they try to tell me what to do. They should listen to me about this stuff, though. I think I know more about how to lead a charitable life than they do."

Sarah

Sarah, 33, is perhaps the most overtly religious and existential of all the clients described here. She is plagued by auditory hallucinations, thought blocking, and periods of high anxiety that limit her capacity to tolerate being with others. She lives alone, hundreds of miles from her parents and siblings, although they keep in touch with her regularly. Sarah is bright, having almost earned a master's degree in English literature prior to her psychiatric decompensation. She is Jewish and has maintained a deep involvement in that faith and culture since becoming ill. Sarah is philosophical about religion in a broad sense. She hears the voices of her parents, picking up on their everyday conversations as if they were present in the same house.

"My purpose in life now is to take care of my father. I watch over him constantly because he has always been so kind to me, more than anyone else. And my mother is not considerate of how hard life is for him. Doing this keeps me very busy. People think I don't do much, but I'm watching over him. I do have other interests, for example in astrology and books in general. I think about Jesus Christ, too, whom I've become interested in even though I'm Jewish. God always tells me that things will work out for me in the end." Some of Sarah's ideas are more reflective of her psychosis. "The biblical Sarahs all were able to remove people from this life and place them in an afterlife. I am the fourth Sarah. I'm pretty sure that I lived in Nazi Germany and was persecuted. Reincarnation happens to all of us, though."

Sarah is most interested in caring for her father, but her personal values indicate a potential for other commitments. "I like to be around people, even though they don't seem to like me much. I think I'm a good caregiver. I could take good care of people if they would let me. Or even animals."

David

David is 31, single, and living alone. He has schizophrenia but supports himself and functions with a degree of independence by managing a paper route. He has almost daily contact, at least by phone, with his mother, who lives nearby. David is pleasant even as he maintains a solitary existence. He tries to make friends but without much success, because he shares his psychotic ideas with them and has a limited tolerance for stimulation. He grew up as a member of a Protestant denomination and went to church on occasion, but without a strong attachment. Now, however, David maintains an elaborate system of religious delusions. He believes that he is the son of Satan, and that as a positive force in the world he mediates a struggle between humanity and God, whom he characterizes in negative terms.

"God hypnotizes people through music and they lose their free will. He should be working to make them free, not hypnotize them and keep them captive." David has written a 300-page manuscript that attempts to educate people about the war going on between God and the son of Satan. "As far as I know, I'm the only one working to help humankind with this problem. I don't know why it's just me. I'm not sure how it will all work out, if people will understand what God is doing to them." David believes in heaven and hell. He experiences visual hallucinations of religious figures whom he believes watch over him. David does not discuss these thoughts with anyone other than his case manager. "Most people don't seem to be interested in religion, or at least this important side of religion. For most of them, they've been hypnotized not to think about it. And I don't bring it up much. I've tried to tell my mom about it, but she wants me to be quiet. I know that some people think you're nuts when you tell them these things." Despite David's psychotic ideas, he and his mother have enhanced their relationship with a task formulated around his values, which will be described later in this chapter.

Carla

Carla, 39, is a single, unemployed, white female living with a male friend. Prior to becoming disabled by mental illness she had a lengthy work history in computer programming. Hers is a mechanical mind, and the religious beliefs that evolved after her psychotic decompensation reflect this. "The human mind is an energy information pattern that borrows the brain to function. Our brains transmit their content telepathically, and this content can be stored in the unused portions of other brains up to a radius of three miles away. When we die, our souls, or selves, are linked among other brains, and so we can reawaken as spirits. Spirits, you see, live within the unused brain material of people. They travel by moving their patterns to brains in new locations. They can tap into a human psychic receiver and send a voice so that you can hear them." Carla states that she became aware of the spirit world when, during a psychotic break, her mind was accidentally rewired to perceive spirit messages. She believes that God exists as some type of ultimate spirit, perhaps the cumulation of all spirits. "There is no heaven or hell because there is really no end to life."

Carla's stated purpose in living is to understand more about telepathic behavior. She views herself as a scientist. Her male friend, who also has a psychotic disorder, encourages her interests, and they maintain a stable relationship. "I have a major contribution to make and have written several articles outlining my ideas. People need to learn that there is really no end to life because this will make them relax more about getting older."

In each of the stories presented above, the client expresses clear attention to existential or spiritual issues. Some clients think about them frequently, while others do so rarely. Some of their concerns are characterized by delusional ideas, but others have practical concerns about their futures and their place in the world. In *every* case the case manager might use this information to construct interventions for channeling the clients' interests into areas that could help them feel more fulfilled. What follows are examples of how this was, in fact, accomplished with two clients.

APPLYING EXISTENTIAL THEMES
TO FAMILY INTERVENTION

Case managers, like other mental health professionals, have made advances during the past twenty years in developing collaborative relationships with clients and their families (I will address this trend in detail in the next chapter). They no longer blame parents for causing pathology in their children, and they are more likely to educate and support families while providing rehabilitative services to the relative with mental illness. The onset of mental illness changes much in a family's relationships, but case managers must also help families realize what does *not* change as a result of the illness. I have attempted in this chapter to highlight one aspect of the relative's personality that might not change during the illness, the existential or religious orientation. If case managers can incorporate this theme into family interventions, the family may be helped to maintain cohesion through the many difficulties that ensue. To illustrate a framework for family intervention based on this theme, I will describe how existential themes were processed in work with two families. One case involved a client who maintained her religious beliefs; the other concerns a client who assumed new and bizarre existential ideas with the onset of mental illness.

In family intervention, members need to take risks in exploring their experience of each other. The worker attempts to facilitate problem resolution in part by searching within the family for a common set of loyalties and values from which members can communicate their needs. Shared existential purposes can provide symbols reflecting a common value system, and interactions based on these purposes can unite a family that has been disrupted by mental illness. In fact, as a person with mental illness moves along the continuum of increasing isolation, family rituals may provide a way for members to share experiences without the threats implicit in more intensive interventions.

Kitty

Kitty's Roman Catholic orientation was unchanged from her premorbid mental status. It was consistent with that of her parents, with whom she lived (an older brother had recently moved away). Still, during the family stresses relating to her mental illness, the issue of religion was overlooked. Like many families in this situation, her parents became frightened and confused because Kitty was not the same person she had been as a younger adult. Her parents looked to doctors, psychologists, and case managers for solutions to her illness. Because these discussions were focused on symptom control, little attention was devoted to practical matters for enhancing family cohesion. Kitty's parents had conversations with their pastor that were helpful in dealing with their own struggles, but not for helping them understand their daughter's increasing inaccessibility.

The case manager coordinated a range of interventions for Kitty and her family. Kitty received medication and supportive counseling; she also attended a clubhouse program while continuing to attend college classes. The case manager met with the family regularly for collateral counseling, support, and education. The parents had different opinions about Kitty's desire to increase her independence by moving out of the house. Her mother, who was frustrated with Kitty's erratic behavior, seemed to want her to leave, while her more protective father had reservations about Kitty's potential to care for herself. Many arguments developed among the three persons about conflicting family goals. Counseling sessions were rarely peaceful when all family members were present.

As one way of building a sense of cooperation, the case manager suggested that the family participate as a unit in some type of charitable activity. He assumed, correctly, that they would base this within their church organization. They indeed did so, becoming members of a committee that raised funds for other church members experiencing financial crises. As part of this activity they attended a weekly discussion group on related Biblical literature. In the context of the church this activity reminded the family of the common value base that they shared but had not been observing outside of Sunday church attendance. Kitty was able to participate appropriately. This intervention was productive in softening the conflicts that continued to erupt around issues of emancipation, self-care, and personal responsibility. Kitty expressed satisfaction that she was performing a useful function for other people, which she saw as part of her purpose in living.

David

David's family consisted of his mother, father, half-sister, and several extended family members. His primary caregiver was his mother, who was divorced from his father and lived near his apartment. David saw or spoke with her daily. She was very involved in his life and concerned about his well-being, but he was also a support to her because she had a limited social network. Though she supported David's independent living by reinforcing his daily activity structure, she was frightened by his religious delusions. Nothing upset her more than hearing about his spiritual preoccupations, even though he led a quiet life and did not impinge on others in any way.

David received counseling, medication, and case management services, as well as family interventions. The case manager had regular consultative phone contact with his mother and occasional joint sessions with her and David; he also arranged for her participation in his multi-family education and support group. He described David's religious preoccupations to this mother (not in his presence) as certainly far removed from his Lutheran upbringing, but with ethical similarities. David was trying to live a purposeful life and provide service to others, in other words, to give of himself. However, the thought disorder made it impossible for David to maintain conventional symbols of good and evil. While it was impossible precisely to understand where his ideas originated, it was clear that he was not hurting anyone and that he was trying to make a contribution to the world even as he felt cut off from it.

The case manager suggested that his mother talk to David about applying his ideas on a small scale, in addition to his "grand" one, in ways that might demonstrate in concrete terms his caring for others. After much discussion and working through David's ambivalence about the idea, the client volunteered to take over responsibility for the "garbage detail" in his apartment building, which was primarily populated with older adults. Each week he collected and carried the garbage of three dozen elderly residents to the curb and then washed their containers. This did not make David's mother feel any better about his grandiose ideas, but it did help her to accept that his actions could be positive, that he could interact with people in a manner that was socially acceptable and useful. Given the severe nature of David's social isolation, this task, which occupied eight hours per week of his time, represented a substantial investment.

SUMMARY

Existential concerns, which include ultimate values, life meanings, and purposes for living, are central to lives of all people but are not frequently included as part of the holistic process of case management assessment and intervention. The clinical practitioner should realize that attention to these concerns does not require a new theoretical orientation but that it can be incorporated into the ego, cognitive, and symbolic interactionism theories. The concepts of the drive to mastery and competence, motivational direction, and shared meaning are central to this understanding. When it is appropriate to address purpose-in-life issues with a client, these theories can provide frameworks for intervention.

Case managers must be cautious about projecting their own purpose-in-life orientations onto clients and families. But because of their relevance to all persons, existential concerns are always appropriate for case management assessment. Further, in families experiencing the fragmentation that occurs with mental illness, cultivating these themes can provide a basis for family healing. In this chapter I have reviewed several theoretical frameworks for intervention along with examples of their application. This is a relatively untapped area of clinical work, however, and practice research on a larger scale is needed to provide case managers with more information about the impact of mental illness on existential and religious beliefs and with additional ways of addressing the topic in case management.

PART IV

Working with Families

12

♋

Engaging the
Family of the Person
with Mental Illness

In the past 25 years, the nature of relationships between mental health professionals and families of persons with mental illness has changed dramatically (Lefley, 1994). Through the 1960s (and beyond), a majority of professionals believed that families bore primary responsibility for causing the mental illness of a client relative and, as a result, often treated families with critical condescension. Clients were encouraged to become independent from families, in part to escape their negative influence. Families felt stigmatized and did not perceive that professionals wanted to offer them practical assistance in their interactions with the client relative. This tension became particularly acute during the era of deinstitutionalization (1955–1980), when family members became the primary caretakers for persons with mental illness living in the community.

Since then, and largely due to the organized advocacy of family members through the National Mental Health Association, the National Alliance for the Mentally Ill, and other organizations, a sense of mutual respect and collaboration has begun to emerge between the two groups. Still, remaining among many families and professionals are attitudes of distrust that can result in negative outcomes for the ill relative. For this reason the clinical case manager must always assume an attitude of partnership in working with families and must resist any reactions of defensiveness if family distrust is evident. In the next three chapters I present strategies for working collaboratively with families toward the goals of client and family growth. In this chapter I focus on the case manager's initial engagement of the family. In Chapter 13 the case manager's role as family educator is highlighted, and in Chapter 14, I discuss working with families in group settings.

RELATIONSHIPS BETWEEN
PROFESSIONALS AND FAMILIES

As described in Chapter 3, schizophrenia, the major affective disorders, and other long-term mental illnesses have always had distressing effects on the families of clients with mental illness. Over 75 % of all families indicate a significant negative impact (Lefley, 1996). Unfortunately, theories proposing family dysfunction as the major contributing cause of the client's illness were dominant in the United States through the 1960s, precluding the potential for treatment alliances between professionals and family members (Howells & Guirguis, 1985). Family concepts such as "emotional divorce," "communication deviance," the "double-bind," and family "schisms" were commonly used to describe problematic parent–child interactions that caused a child to withdraw into psychosis. Such theories added to the family's sense of guilt and stigmatization.

During the era of deinstitutionalization, families became the primary caregivers of their client relatives, as more than 50% of clients in the community were living with relatives (Fellin, 1996). In a national sample of 140 members of the National Alliance for the Mentally Ill (NAMI) it was found that these families were generally not knowledgeable about, and were even distrustful of, standard clinical treatment (Spaniol, Jung, Zipple, & Fitzgerald, 1987). They wanted supportive, practical advice on the management of their impaired family member.

At this same time, research clarified that long-term mental disorders are not caused primarily by childhood upbringing and family interactions, but by strong biological components. The medical aspects of mental illness were legitimized, freeing families from the socially isolating impact of blame. This, along with the family advocacy movement described below, established a new basis for positive working alliances between professionals and families. Case managers could help families achieve greater objectivity about mental illness, modulate their levels of emotional involvement, learn to set limits on the client's maladaptive behaviors, and promote more effective personal and social functioning. Additionally, families could be helped to deal with the burdens of hopelessness, social isolation, and threats to their sense of well-being.

Family Self-Help

The self-help phenomenon was pioneered by groups with special problems such as alcoholics and the parents of handicapped children. Implicit in self-help groups is the perception that their needs are not fully understood by professionals (Katz, 1993). Most groups tend to be nonbureaucratic and based on experience and common sense. Families of persons with mental illness became active in self-help in the late 1970s (Vine, 1982). The Parents of Adult Schizophrenics, founded in California in 1974, began as a group of ten family members interested in advocating on behalf of their loved ones and quickly grew into a statewide group. Threshold, founded in Maryland in 1978, began with 35 members, but within five years it was an official consultant to county governments on all mental health issues.

Unfortunately, these developments reflected family member antagonism toward the mental health professions. This was borne out by Hatfield's (1978) early study of 89 members of one self-help group for families of persons with schizophrenia in Washington, DC. More than half the membership reported a low level of satisfaction with all forms of therapy, and a majority noted resentment of their stigmatization by society *and* the mental health professions. Professionals were perceived to be blaming families for causing family members' disorders. The consumer movement was in part intended to hold mental health professionals accountable for the services they provided (Lamb, 1982).

The National Alliance for the Mentally Ill (NAMI) was formed in Wisconsin in 1979. Today it is a major national organization including over 150,000 families in 1100 local and state affiliate groups. While not representative of all families dealing with mental illness, NAMI has effectively articulated the needs of families to its own members, mental health professionals, and policy makers. It has established mutual support services as well as legislation that has resulted in increased resources for this client group and their caregivers. In response to family advocacy, mental health professionals have become more involved in working with families within a partnership model.

Independence from professional involvement has often been cited as a hall-mark of the family consumer movement, but in fact families have long expressed a willingness to accept professional expertise offered in an atmosphere of support (Gartner & Reissman, 1982).

THE IMPACT OF MENTAL ILLNESS
ON THE FAMILY

Fortunately, much research has been done on the specific challenges and needs faced by families with a client member. Hatfield (1978) focused on the psychological costs of schizophrenia to families with a child or adolescent client member. She found that

1. All family members in the household suffer emotionally.
2. Siblings tend to blame parents for the client's behavior.
3. The client's siblings tend to be rejected by their friends.
4. Spouses tend to blame each other for the problem.
5. One individual, usually the mother, tends to assume primary responsibility for the client's care.
6. All family members lose time and energy for leisure activities.

Lefley (1996) performed an extensive literature review to identify both the objective and subjective burdens experienced by families, which adds detail to the above list. *Objective* burdens include

1. Economic dependency
2. Frequent disruption of life routines
3. A high investment of time and energy in caregiving, including time devoted to interactions with service providers
4. Financial costs of treatments
5. Little time for social activity
6. Few social relationships with persons outside the family
7. Stress related to securing appropriate residential placements

Family *subjective* burdens include

1. Grief and mourning for the relative's personality prior to the illness
2. A lower quality of mental and physical health
3. Stigma
4. Disappointment related to changing personal goals
5. Worries related to aging and who else might assume care of the ill relative

Siblings are a neglected family sub-group in the literature. Lefley (1996), however, summarized their unique stresses as

1. Anger about the loss of parental attention
2. Guilt about the sibling's disability
3. An inability to tolerate intimacy with persons outside the family
4. A sense of growing up too fast within the family
5. Premature marriage to escape the home
6. Distress related to the family's social withdrawal (including the family's moving)

Older siblings (females in particular) tend to assume client caregiving roles more frequently than younger and male siblings (Greenberg, Kim, & Greenley, 1997). Their subjective burden, however, is related more to observations of the ill relative's symptoms than to caregiving demands. Siblings also tend to experience a lesser sense of burden when they perceive the ill relative's behavior as out of his or her control; thus sibling education about the nature of mental illness is useful.

Much less research has been done on the impact of mental illness within minority families. Research over the past ten years, including a recent study of 180 minority families around New York City, consistently shows that African-American families with an ill relative tend to experience less depression and subjective burden than Caucasian or Hispanic families (Stueve, Vine, & Struening, 1997). This may be due to the availability of outside social and religious supports as well as a resilience acquired through coping with socioeconomic stressors. African-American families are also less "clinical" in how they assess a client member's problems and mental status, which implies that they may be less eager to participate with professionals in standard interventions. The case manager may have more difficulty characterizing mental illness as a biological disorder with some minority families.

Terkelson (1987) writes that the negative effects within a family are qualitatively different depending on the level of each member's involvement with the client. Through interviews conducted with a convenience sample he outlines three "tiers" of involvement which have implications for how and to whom family education and intervention should be focused:

First Tier. One adult within the family becomes the primary caregiver and becomes consumed with that role. This is usually a female (mother, sister, or daughter).

Second Tier. More than one adult functions in a major caregiving role, and for this reason all family members are able to reserve some time for outside activities, even though the impact of mental illness is a major disruption for them all.

Third Tier. Family members outside the home assist in the care of the client relative. Responsibility is distributed throughout the family to the extended family, which has a positive effect of minimizing stress on particular members.

Lefley's (1996) literature review notes four stages of adjustment which families experience when a member develops mental illness. These include *denial,* a *recognition* of mental illness, the *search for causes and treatments*, and *active attempts to adapt* to the chronic problem. Clearly, the case manager needs to assess and respect whatever stage a family is in and to help members work though their emotional reactions toward acceptance of the illness and proactive problem solving.

Spaniol and Jung (1987) identify themes of *positive* family coping in the literature. These include *acceptance of the reality* of the disorder, a healthy degree of *emotional distancing*, learning to *set limits* on the client's behaviors, the ability to actively *seek advice*, and the ability to *take care of one's own physical and emotional needs.*

Despite the burdens experienced by families with an ill relative, it is important to emphasize that positive experiences may occur in the face of this adversity. In a national study of 131 members of NAMI, Marsh et al. (1997) found evidence of family resilience in their strengthened interpersonal bonds, shared commitments, sense of competence, growth experiences, sense of mutual support, and gratifications from activities provided on behalf of the ill relative. The ill relative also expressed feelings of pride in some personal qualities and in their contributions made to family members, other consumers, and the mental health system. Mannion (1997) found similar evidence of resilience in spouses.

It was also found in a large-scale comparison of families which *did* and *did not* include a relative with mental illness that the degree to which *all* parents perceive relationships with adult children as positive depends not on the presence of disability, but on perceptions of caregiving burden and episodes of gratifying interactions (Pickett, Cook, Cohler, & Solomon, 1997). Thus, helping families relieve some of their caregiving burden through education is likely to produce an atmosphere conducive to more positive interaction. Case managers need to appreciate that positive family developments can accompany the negative effects of mental illness.

DESIRED CHARACTERISTICS
OF CASE MANAGERS

Authors with experience in working with families often recommend the type of professional best suited to function as a family service provider. Not surprisingly, these characteristics do not reflect a particular professional affiliation, but rather one's general knowledge and values. These characteristics are consistent with themes outlined in Part 1 of this book, but they merit repeating because, sadly, they are still not widely shared by clinical case managers. Bernheim (1994) states that the family worker should be active, warm, a good negotiator (or mediator, in our terminology), and a good teacher. Communication skills are essential, because the worker needs to be able to stimulate discussion and provide useful feedback. Anderson, Reiss, and Hogarty (1986) add that the family worker should be experienced in working with clients having mental illnesses.

Hatfield (1990) more specifically suggests that the new professional should re-ceive very early career exposure to families, as well as knowledge of mental ill-ness. She recommends that they be non-judgmental, non-blaming, empathetic, have the ability to "take heat" (similar to my own principle of accepting criti-cism without defensiveness), and maintain a healthy skepticism about *any* theo-ries of mental illness. Marsh (1992) eloquently proposes a "competence paradigm" for family intervention in which the worker moves the emphasis away from family pathology to focus on family strengths.

It is no doubt true that mental health professionals as a group have not been, and are still not always, sensitive to the needs of families. There are, however, some serious barriers to family collaboration. Many well-meaning case managers face constraints in working with clients, with the issue of confidentiality perhaps being the most common. Clients who do not want their families involved in treatment can prevent this by reserving their legal right to confidentiality. In such cases family members may resent the case manager's perceived unwillingness to share any clinical information. Restrictive agency policies for case management practice may also discourage workers' efforts to meet with family members.

Case managers may also have honest disagreements with family members about the appropriate family role in the intervention process. A client's goals of increased independent functioning does not mandate that the family be ig-nored, but it can move the focus of treatment away from the family unit. These issues are complex, and often families blame professionals for insensitivity when the intended outcome does require change in the family's patterns of interaction. Through preparatory guidance, case managers can prepare family members for their normal resistance to constructive changes and thus preempt many potential conflicts.

WHETHER AND WHEN
TO ENGAGE THE FAMILY

The process by which persons with mental illness and their families become clients in out-patient or hospital settings is often different from that of less se-verely impaired clients. At the time of intake the family may be at or near cri-sis. The stress levels of all members are likely to be high, characterized by much conflict. Further, not all members of the family are likely to enter treat-ment at the same time or with the same level of interest, if they participate at all. The clinical case manager must give special consideration to these and other issues if he or she hopes to intervene effectively with the family unit. In the remainder of this chapter I show how the case manager can assist the client and family to come together in a setting where constructive intervention can take place. Much has been written about how to intervene with families, and these strategies are presented in detail in the next two chapters; but less atten-tion has been devoted to facilitating the entry of a family into an agency, which is often a more challenging task.

Just as not all clients with less debilitating emotional problems are treated with family interventions, neither should these be implemented for all clients with mental illness. When any individual client enters counseling, the case manager, through a multidimensional assessment, must first determine the most appropriate unit for intervention. This may include the individual, group, family, organizational, and community levels. Intervention should begin at the point of "maximum reverberation," or that level where significant change is most likely to occur (Compton & Galaway, 1994).

Family treatment may *not* be appropriate if the client has little or no contact with the family and desires none, however marginal his or her functional level might be. Family work may be useful on only a limited basis if the client is realistically working toward goals of emancipation. Finally, family work may be impossible, regardless of how useful it might be, if the family declines to participate or the client refuses contact on the principle of confidentiality. If the case manager believes that the client's goals could be more fully realized with family participation, he or she can offer this perspective to the resistant client over time in hopes that they can agree on a compromise strategy.

Nuclear family (parents, siblings, spouses, children) or extended family (aunts, grandparents, etc.) intervention is indicated if the client lives with or close to these persons and if he or she is dependent on them emotionally or financially so that regular contact is maintained. Still, it is only on a case-by-case basis that the worker can determine to what extent, and what type of, family intervention will be productive for all involved. In some instances the family sees the client as dependent, but the client, and perhaps the case manager, have a contrary perspective. Even in these cases some joint resolution of these perspectives is desirable which may involve family contact.

Case Illustrations

Beth   Beth, age 46, had a 20- year history of schizophrenia, characterized by acute psychotic episodes interspersed with long periods of marginal but self-reliant functioning. She was divorced, but her ex-husband and two adult sons lived in the same metropolitan area. Beth took medication, saw her case manager every two weeks, and worked as a part-time dishwasher. She lived alone in a small apartment and had no social life. Although she called on her husband at times to borrow small sums of money and saw her sons occasionally for short visits or to request transportation, she had no desire to alter her family relationships. Neither did her ex-husband or sons (by her report) wish to change their somewhat formal relationships with her. It seemed that the four of them had achieved a balance in their family system that they did not want to disrupt. The case manager offered to provide consultation to the family, believing that with some education about mental illness and its consequences they might be more accepting of Beth's behavior and have a more clear understanding of their roles in her life. Beth, however, had no inclination to address family issues in her treatment, and thus family intervention was not initiated. Beth's intervention continued to focus on her own quality of social functioning and coping with schizophrenia. Her family interactions remained predictable and cordial.

Taylor   Taylor, age 20, suffered an acute manic episode during his first year in college. This was his first move away from home (150 miles) and, despite some recent personality changes indicating impatience and agitation, he had never before exhibited psychotic symptoms. Returning home to his parents, he was diagnosed with schizophrenia, and he spent the next three months in a psychiatric hospital. Gradually his symptoms subsided with the help of medications and the hospital's therapeutic milieu, and he returned home again. Now, this intelligent and once-productive young man could tolerate only a part-time clerical job. He spent most of his free time isolating himself at home, where his confused, still-frightened parents tended to dote on him excessively. At the mental health center where he was referred for outpatient care, Taylor was assigned to a physician for medication monitoring and to a case manager for counseling and psychosocial rehabilitation services. The case manager recognized that family interventions might be indicated in this case because each member needed to come to terms with the mental illness and its implications for their future. Along with weekly individual counseling sessions, he initiated biweekly family visits to help the parents set some limits in their support of Taylor and to gradually foster his greater independence. The parents were also enrolled in the agency's nine-week family psychoeducational program (see Chapter 15).

Ideally, the case manager always maintains an appreciation of each family's diverse circumstances. Only after a full assessment of family membership, patterns of interaction, and quality of relationships should *mutual* decisions about the scope of intervention be made.

STRENGTHS AND LIMITATIONS
OF THE CASE MANAGER

In any intervention, the case manager is a part of the system he or she is observing. While assessing a client or family through some theoretical frame of reference (ego-psychological, cognitive, behavioral, etc.), the reflective case manager should concentrate with equal emphasis on his or her own feelings about the participants, such as fear, attraction, amusement, disgust, etc. These **countertransference** issues (personal reactions to clients and families) are as important as attention to the intervention plan, because they influence decisions about strategy in ways the case manager might not always be aware of (Kanter, 1985b). Unfortunately, the topic of countertransference currently receives little attention in many health care settings because of the increasing emphasis on short-term, action-oriented therapies (Austin & McClelland, 1996).

Many case managers (none more than I) love working with clients and families who are struggling with severe mental illness. Others, however, are prone to negative personal reactions about working with these clients on a regular basis (Minkoff, 1987). This is not necessarily because these case managers lack empathy, but it might be for any of the following reasons:

1. Their own needs for gratification not being met when the potential for client change is perceived as minimal
2. Frustrating aspects of the client's chronic dependency
3. A desire to provide "growth" rather than "maintenance" services
4. Uncomfortable social class discrepancies between themselves and their clients
5. The apparent lack of value for this type of work among agency administrators (as evidenced, for example, by lower pay scales, limited supervisory opportunities, and limited staff development opportunities)

Families coping with mental illness are often in crisis or conflict, and this can make extended intervention with them difficult for the worker. The case manager's personal values cannot be kept out of professional practice (Kanter, 1995). Acknowledging and working through both positive (case managers can also do *too much* for their clients) and negative personal reactions with supervisors and coworkers, as well as pausing for self-reflection, can result in the case manager's greater enjoyment of family intervention. The denial of these reactions can result in his or her inability to work diligently with certain clients and families.

Case managers might not have choices about the particular clients they are assigned to work with, but there are always choices to make regarding intervention strategy. A reluctant case manager may consciously or unconsciously allow an unmotivated, ambivalent client or a chaotic family to drop out of treatment by performing less outreach than is typical, or by choosing to see them irregularly. Such choices may be clinically appropriate, but in the best interests of the client those decisions should not be made based on the case manager's own ambivalence or negative reactions to the client. Decision-making about family intervention should be grounded as much as possible in sound clinical judgment (although this will *always* be influenced by the case manager's attitudes).

In summary, the personality, values, and clinical biases of the case manager regarding work with clients and their families serve either as assets or liabilities during the beginning phase of treatment. I believe that case managers should assume that *any* negative feelings they hold about treating certain clients *will* be communicated verbally or nonverbally in the relationship, even if they try to hide them, and will limit the potential for client and family engagement.

Case Illustration

Terri Terri, age 31, had schizophrenia along with histrionic personality features. She was well-known throughout the county mental health system because of her frequent hospitalizations and referrals to numerous agencies and crisis centers. She had a reputation for being oppositional, loud, and unrealistic in her demands for service, nor did she follow through on her goals. The case manager assigned to work with her at the present agency was aware of her reputation. He assumed that she would be difficult and would probably not make any significant changes in her lifestyle. At their first meeting he learned that Terri was living on social security benefits in a rented trailer with her three-year-old son. Terri had recently joined, but then dropped out of, two vocational and social rehabilitation programs, and now she expressed no interest in any programs beyond medication maintenance and supportive counseling. The case manager readily agreed to her request, believing that other interventions would likely fail. It soon became evident to him that Terri was not responding to the rather general emotional support he was providing her.

After three months of this routine, the case manager learned that Terri had been rehospitalized with a severe psychotic episode and that her son had been placed in the custody of the county children's services agency. The case manager was shocked to learn from the hospital staff that Terri had been visiting her parents several days per week during the past year, demanding money for food. Her parents had become quite angry with Terri for this perceived exploitation. They arranged for her eviction from her trailer so she would need to return home permanently and help with the housework as a debt repayment. The stress of this ongoing family conflict had taken a severe toll on Terri's mental status.

The case manager further learned that her parents had complained to the hospital staff about the inaccessibility of Terri's agency case manager. He had not been aware that Terri was having any contact with her family or that her family even lived in town. She had denied any involvement with them, but in retrospect the case manager could not recall exploring Terri's nuclear family issues very persistently. He had allowed his preconceptions about Terri and her lack of potential for improvement to get in the way of a thorough assessment and what might have been a more effective intervention strategy involving her family. The case manager was particularly embarrassed because he normally prided himself on having a family outreach orientation.

APPROACHING THE CLIENT

Persons with mental illness are generally referred to hospitals or agencies by an outside source. The family might initiate treatment, thus straining those relationships, or some other party might be involved such as an employer, friend, or the police. Clients might be involuntarily placed in hospitals, or they might "voluntarily" enter under a threat of probation and then be referred to an outpatient agency by hospital staff. One characteristic of mental illness is that the client does not always seek treatment on his or her own, and thus admission to an agency usually occurs at a time of personal and family crisis. Feelings between the client and family or significant others are likely to be strained. Sometimes crisis can bring a family closer together, but more often a psychotic episode (or the withdrawal associated with some illnesses) causes serious disruption in the client's interpersonal milieu.

Given these circumstances the case manager must be careful about the timing of implementing a family intervention plan. The client might be reluctant to participate with service providers at all and might be suspicious of a treatment plan which seems elaborate. The case manager must allow sufficient time to help the client first feel at ease, so that the client will eventually take an active role in the treatment planning process. A prerequisite for effective intervention is a relationship in which the case manager is intimately informed about the client's inner world, reactions to environments, and responses to various service resources (Kanter, 1989). This process has been elaborated in previous chapters of this book, but it applies to planning for family intervention as well. If the client is the primary service recipient at this stage, he or she must agree that a proposal for family intervention makes sense before the case manager approaches the family. Thus, before suggesting family intervention the case manager must establish a trusting relationship with the client. The following vignette demonstrates how the task of engaging the client in a strategy for family engagement can take much time.

Case Illustration

David   David, age 32, was referred to the mental health center from the state psychiatric hospital. His records indicated a history of poor compliance with outpatient care. His paranoid delusions rendered him incapable of engaging with any persons, let alone professionals. David would typically keep a few appointments at a new agency but then would become non-compliant with medications and other interventions. He was rehospitalized time and time again following predictable decompensations characterized by violent threats against neighbors. Because he lived with his parents, the case manager felt that their participation with David's treatment might help break his "revolving door" pattern.

The physician and the case manager at the current agency noticed how easily David became agitated and decided to take a low-key, client-directed approach with him. The case manager asked to see him every two weeks but developed no formal treatment plan beyond encouraging David to take his medications and to talk about whatever interested him. David tentatively agreed to this plan, but only after six months began to see it as non-threatening and somewhat supportive. He stopped taking his medications but continued to see the physician monthly, allowing him to perform a mental status exam. The physician was not satisfied with this level of contact but at least felt good that he had the opportunity to assess David for any signs of functional deterioration.

After one year of treatment (but only 18 hours of direct contact, again indicating that long-range intervention need not be time-intensive) David became willing to spend a full hour in his meetings with the case manager. He had not returned to the hospital, and he was beginning to pursue an interest in auto repair work. David also became open to the case manager's suggestion of inviting his mother to their meetings for the purpose of "calming" their relationship. His mother accompanied him to sessions once per month to discuss how she could be helpful in keeping David out of the hospital.

APPROACHING THE FAMILY

Following the relationship-building phase of treatment, the case manager and client may decide that family participation will be helpful in the achievement of goals for all members. The case manager should not be surprised when encountering reluctance from a family invited to participate in an intervention. Such reluctance, when it exists, may be justified for the reasons cited earlier in this chapter. Accordino and Herbert (1997), in their training of case managers to work with clients and families, have outlined nine distinct relationship-building skills which can serve as guidelines for family outreach and the early stages of family intervention:

1. Empathic responding
2. Promoting expressiveness
3. Facilitating discussion and negotiation
4. Problem solving mediation
5. Positive promotion of *self* change
6. Positive promotion of change in *other* family members
7. Generalizing particular solutions to other situations
8. Facilitating family activity
9. Affirming family system maintenance

A basic principle of engagement is that the case manager invites family members to define what their concerns are and accepts these *without reframing* as issues for intervention. The case manager's own rationale for pursuing family involvement is important and should be included in the treatment plan, but not so as to preempt the perspectives of others. Case managers historically have not been trained to assess problems from the family's perspective; this accounts in part for their distancing from families (Biegel, Li-yu, & Milligan, 1995). Case managers also have difficulty at times conducting unbiased evaluations of family satisfaction with treatment, as evidenced by research showing discrepancies between professional and family impressions of family treatment outcomes (Solomon, 1994). Family engagement most often occurs when the perspectives of the family, client, and case manager receive equal emphasis, when identified needs and goals are complementary.

Case Illustrations

Trent   Trent, age 37, had a long history of treatment for schizophrenia, paranoid type, prior to being seen at his new agency. His recent crisis had been severe, and even in partial remission he was experiencing troublesome auditory hallucinations. Trent perceived these as "mental telepathy" being broadcast by his enemies and intended to make him miserable. Only frequent withdrawal from others and minimal environmental stimulation helped him calm down. But Trent was married with two adolescent children, and his family expected him to function as a husband, father, and financial provider.

Trent was able to engage quickly with his case manager, who determined that Trent needed to withdraw for long periods each day as a means of coping with overstimulation. The case manager invited the family into the office to learn of their concerns for Trent and themselves. His wife maintained that Trent could benefit only from the healing effects of productive work and family interaction. The children simply wanted him to be more visible in the household. The case manager agreed that Trent did have responsibilities to his family and that their goals were reasonable. He added that these goals needed to be approached in a way that Trent could manage them— that is, gradually and with Trent's being permitted adequate time for rest.

Trent's family enrolled in a psychoeducational program so they could learn more about the effects of Trent's disorder on his functioning, and the case manager saw them in family sessions monthly. These sessions were intended to help the family balance Trent's needs with their own. The case manager saw Trent individually on a weekly basis. Within four months, Trent entered a vocational rehabilitation program where he received supervised job training. His family was able to support and praise his positive movement and, though concerned about his health and the family's finances, not to push him to move too quickly into competitive employment. The case manager, client, and family continued to agree on the goals of Trent's improved mental health and regular but restricted participation in the family milieu. All interventions were focused around this central theme.

Along with inviting the family to describe their concerns about the ill relative, the case manager should solicit their reactions to any past experiences with mental health treatment providers. Of the many families who have had prior experience with the "system," some will describe generally positive outcomes, but others will describe negative experiences. It is essential that the case manager understand why the family was disappointed. The details of the family's experiences will help the case manager organize his work to avoid producing those same disappointments. The case manager will learn about the family's attitudes toward mental illness, their expectations of treatment providers, their anticipation of change, and their own motivations and goals for treatment involvement. The clinician can avoid repeating strategic errors made by past professionals and can construct an intervention more likely to connect with the family.

Carrie   Carrie, though only 16, had a one-year history of schizophrenia with severe psychotic symptoms. She had already been hospitalized three times with only a partial stabilization of her delusions and hallucinations. Hospital staff told the new mental health agency case manager that Carrie's mother had participated in only one planning session. She didn't seem actively interested in Carrie's outpatient care. Perhaps because she was a single parent with many financial stresses of her own, she had difficulty sustaining interest in Carrie's condition except during a crisis. But because Carrie was a minor living with her mother, her case manager felt that family intervention was necessary to enhance this client and family's well being.

When the mother declined an initial invitation over the telephone for a joint session, the case manager politely asked why. The mother indicated that Carrie was more verbally articulate than she and that their being seen together would give the impression to the case manager that she was a bad mother. Carrie's mother believed that she would probably not present herself well and that the case manager would assume she was the cause of Carrie's problems. The mother stated that a psychologist at the hospital had already suggested this.

Carrie's case manager assured her mother that he was not implying blame by inviting her to the agency, but rather that he wanted to provide her with assistance in her coping with a difficult home situation. The case manager asked her to come in by herself, if she wished, for an information-sharing visit, and the mother agreed. During that meeting the case manager listened to the mother's story and affirmed her efforts to manage the household in light of Carrie's tragic and confusing situation. The case manager was aware that there might be additional family management strategies and external supports that the mother might draw upon to promote her daughter's recovery, and that the mother seemed to lack reasonable assertion skills. But during this first visit he was intent on affirming her strengths and earning her confidence.

Encouraging families to express their frustrations with the mental health system or with the client relative can be constructive in many ways. The process has been likened to grief work (Atwood, 1983). Family members can free up their energies from further channeling into client interactions, enable the treatment focus to shift toward problem areas that can be changed, and develop a truer sense of objectivity about their relationship patterns. It is essential during this process, which may continue for weeks, that the case manager accept these feelings without defensiveness. Families have a right to their feelings, and any past frustrations directed at the case manager must not be taken personally. If the case manager does become defensive, he or she risks being perceived by the family as not sincerely encouraging free expression, and as similar to professionals they have resented in the past.

During the first family contacts—which may take place in the office, over the telephone, or at the home—the case manager can further promote a working alliance by supporting the family's difficult position as caregivers. Living with or near a relative with mental illness is severely disruptive to family life, and it is impossible for all involved not to experience a range of powerful emotions such as anger, guilt, and helplessness. Family members might be reluctant to express these feelings to case managers, however, for fear that they will be perceived as hostile, unreasonable, or the cause of the client's problems. Presenting research findings on the "expressed emotion" concept, in which correlations have been drawn between the extent of family members' face-to-face contact with the ill relative and rehospitalization rates (McFarlane & Lukens,

1994), is useful at times as a basis for defusing some negative interactional patterns. In general, however, it is not possible for members to maintain an attitude of benign detachment in these family systems. The case manager who understands the inevitability of these mixed emotions can promote a supportive discussion of them early in treatment and assure all family members that their feelings are normal. Family members, feeling understood, will more likely risk disclosure and will view professional intervention as a constructive activity rather than a process in which they will be negatively judged.

Martin Martin, age 30, lived alone but was in continuous contact with his parents for material sustenance. They were his legal guardians because he had a disabling psychosis that prevented his budgeting money responsibly. During their seven years of trying to support Martin's use of medication, of his staying in treatment, and their promoting his working toward some vocational goal (Martin was intelligent and had attended college), the parents had felt repeatedly disappointed and frustrated with their son and his counselors. Martin's current case manager found them to be cooperative people but intimidated by the psychotic behavior of their son, who seemed to make new decisions about where to live and what activities to pursue every few months.

Martin's parents accompanied him to family sessions every few weeks. They were prompt, polite, and usually quiet. They rarely initiated any discussions, seeming reserved in the company of their son. After several of these visits, Martin's father called the case manager to request a session for him and his wife alone. Martin gave his permission for this, and in the meeting his father made a revealing statement. "You seem to understand the difficulty of our position," he said, "but we're not sure you know our feelings in detail." The parents described their initial apprehensions that the case manager was judging them as weak, or somehow unable to follow through with setting limits for Martin. Their impression had gradually changed; they had begun to see the case manager as more sympathetic toward their difficulties. Martin's parents wanted the worker to understand how hard they had tried to make sense out of their son's illness. They were aware that they tended to be passive, but in fact they were worn out after years of little progress with Martin.

With this turning point in their relationship, a more open communication developed between Martin's parents and the case manager, which persisted throughout Martin's treatment. The case manager wished that he could have been more actively supportive of them sooner, because the family work might have had earlier impact.

It is often helpful for the case manager to meet the family without the client present for one or several sessions. In this way the possibility of one family member's becoming a scapegoat during the ventilation process is precluded, and those present may feel freer to discuss their primary concerns. The case manager can demonstrate empathy for the family's position by acknowledging their constructive roles as "unofficial case managers" and not intruding on the existing system unless invited to do so. Most families are relieved when the case manager points out that he or she will continue in that role. The case manager should also discuss the importance of the family's use of outside supports. Any changes which take place as a result of the family's implementation of new home management interventions will give rise to new stresses for all concerned. Each family member must be prepared for some negative consequences of these, even though they may signify progress for the ill relative. If the engagement process between the case manager, client, and family proceeds well, the case manager will become a significant member of the family's support system.

SUMMARY

A client's family can best be engaged in a treatment program if the case manager gives early consideration to the family atmosphere and its relationship patterns. These need to be addressed prior to any specific intervention strategies utilized by the case manager. Both the client and family must come to feel that the case manager has empathy for their respective life situations, has understanding for their concerns, will accept problem formulations from all points of view, and can offer practical assistance toward the resolution of those problems. Of equal importance is the case manager's need to understand him or herself as one who will have subjective and emotional reactions to the client and family system. Overall effectiveness in enhancing the client system's quality of life depends in large part on the case manager's ability to manage these reactions and maintain objectivity as much as possible regarding the client system's needs.

13

**Case Managers
as Family Educators
about Mental Illness**

Mental illness commonly isolates the client from others in a community. In Chapter 12 we saw that often family assumes much responsibility for providing emotional and material support to the client in the absence of outside contacts. We also considered the effects of mental illness on family members and the challenges of engaging families in an intervention plan that might help them, as well as the client relative, adjust to the facts and implications of mental illness. In this chapter, I discuss the case manager's important role as a family educator about mental illness. I begin with an overview of the research on what families want from case managers and proceed to discuss ways case managers can address the most pressing needs of families.

WHAT FAMILIES WANT FROM
MENTAL HEALTH PROFESSIONALS

Studies investigating the kinds of help families want from mental health professionals yield consistent results. Hatfield (1983) surveyed 138 consumers from nine states. The most frequent responses included help with

1. Understanding the illness
2. Understanding medications
3. Learning to motivate the client member to change
4. Learning realistic expectations for client member change
5. Resolving crisis situations
6. Reducing their own anxieties

Families reported no relationship between what they wanted and what they received from professionals. Families rated treatment providers high in their capacity for listening, their respect for family expertise, and their appreciation of the family's difficulties. Treatment providers were rated low, however, in their desire to educate the family about the mental illness and in their capacity to produce positive behavioral outcomes for the client. Friends and relatives were rated higher than professionals in their support value to family caregivers.

Garson (1986) surveyed 199 California members of the National Alliance for the Mentally Ill (NAMI) on the same question. Families reported that they wanted

1. Encouragement to play an active role in the client relative's treatment
2. Support
3. Respect
4. Not to be blamed for causing the mental illness
5. Information about mental illness
6. Crisis service availability
7. Ethical behavior from service providers

This survey was done early in the consumer movement, but mental health clinics were reported as helpful by only 6% of respondents. Families listed housing and vocational rehabilitation services as their greatest needs. The issue of the client member's lack of productive activity was also highlighted, and in another study of 1400 NAMI members 45% of families reported that their ill relative engaged in nothing productive (Lefley, 1994).

Mermier (1993) asked 268 families in Michigan what they wanted to know about mental illness. Responses included information about the following:

1. The signs and symptoms of mental illness
2. How to get into treatment
3. Facilitating hospitalization
4. Arranging for outpatient treatment
5. The pros and cons of the ill relative's living at home
6. Choices for the relative's living outside the family home
7. Dealing with aggressive behavior
8. Dealing with substance abuse
9. Preventing suicidal behavior
10. Managing stigma
11. Maintaining positive family relationships
12. Managing money
13. Procuring self-help

In summary, Hatfield (1990) states that families need education, support, consultation, psychoeducation, and family collaboration. In her view, any family educational program should include these topics:

1. Understanding mental illness
2. The personal side of mental illness, including accounts of the ways mental illness can impact on the day-to-day functioning of family members
3. Available interventions
4. Creating supportive environments
5. Coping with crisis situations
6. Long-range planning for the client relative

FAMILY EDUCATIONAL INTERVENTIONS

Families have clearly stated that they want to better understand the disabling mental disorders as well as to learn strategies for their own coping and management of the ill relative. As part of a comprehensive treatment plan, educational interventions can help families enhance their objectivity, develop reasonable expectations for client change, and take better care of their own needs. Bernheim (1994) states that work with families should be guided by two overall goals: *reducing family distress* and *supporting adaptive competence*.

Case managers and other professionals rightly feel that they have special knowledge about mental illness and that they can make significant contributions to help struggling families. Psychiatrists traditionally have been viewed as expert in areas of biology and medication; but in community mental health settings, case managers' levels of involvement in psychosocial rehabilitation give them the experience and knowledge to work with families on the practical aspects of living with or near an ill relative. They have much first-hand data for assessing family situations through home visits and observations of the client in other natural settings. Their multifaceted roles provide them with an excellent basis for responding to the range of family concerns noted above.

Family educational interventions can be carried out effectively in psychoeducational groups, single-family sessions, or both. Groups can provide each family with an opportunity to learn from the experiences of others. Single-family work, however, ensures that educational material will address that family's situation. I propose five areas for inclusion in any family educational intervention plan based on the foregoing discussion of family needs: diagnosis, medication, community resources, professional roles and intervention strategies, and managing the unmotivated client relative. If families can be helped to understand these issues, they will have a greater likelihood of promoting a positive adjustment for the ill relative while taking adequate care of their own needs.

Diagnosis

Many families are aware of a relative's psychiatric diagnosis, but fewer understand what is meant or implied by it. The case manager's providing information about how a diagnosis of mental illness is made can help families to understand how professionals decide on interventions and to have reasonable expectations for client change.

Material from the *Diagnostic and Statistical Manual of Mental Disorders* (American Psychiatric Association, 1994), this country's most widely used classification system, provides a useful basis for case manager-family discussion. The criteria for each disorder contain no biases toward particular causes, so the case manager can deal with that issue separately. Further, the *behavioral nature* of the criteria make the process of diagnosis fairly comprehensible and amenable to discussion *if* the case manager simplifies the technical jargon.

The case manager should not share the criteria exactly as written in the DSM but should provide less technical summaries. Using schizophrenia as an example, I offer one simplification of the DSM diagnostic criteria that can be developed into a handout for a family.

In educating families about diagnosis, case managers should emphasize the following three points:

How professionals decide to apply one diagnosis rather than another. Diagnosis should be based solely on observable behaviors, not on speculations about

Table 13-1 Characteristics of Schizophrenia (A Handout for Family Members)

Schizophrenia

There is no single definition, and no one knows exactly what it is, but schizophrenia can be understood as

A disorder of brain functioning,

Characterized by abnormal patterns of *thought* and *perception*,

As inferred from *language* and *behavior*.

A *diagnosis* of schizophrenia requires that *two of the following five* symptoms must be observed during the same one month period:

1. *Delusions,* or strange beliefs which no one else shares

2. Hallucinations, or perceptions of activities which are not real. These are most often voices but can also be visions, smells, tastes, or touches

3. *Speech which is difficult to follow*, does not make sense, or moves from topic to topic without apparent logic

4. *Behavior which is strikingly different*, and less organized, than what has been usual; or behavior which indicate a mental or physical "slowing down"

5. *Changes in emotional expression* which feature less energy, motivation, and responsiveness to the environment

Because of the above changes, the person's general effectiveness at school, on the job, with friends, and in self care reflects a deterioration. This deterioration *must be evident for at least six months.*

Schizophrenia includes the five subtypes listed below. Each of these includes the symptoms described above, but they are differentially pronounced.

1. *Paranoid* type—the person is preoccupied with certain delusions or auditory hallucinations, but does not display serious impairments in speech, disorganized behavior, or emotional expressiveness.

2. *Disorganized* type—the person's illness is characterized primarily by impairments in speech, behavior, and a lack of emotional expressiveness.

3. *Catatonic* type—symptoms feature bizarre difficulties with movement. These may include peculiar and excessive body postures that seem to lack a purpose, a state of motionlessness or stupor, or a purposeless repetition of words or phrases spoken by others.

4. *Undifferentiated* type—This is a "catch-all" category that includes persons with schizophrenia who do not display prominent features from one of the other categories.

5. *Residual* type—The person has experienced the positive symptoms of schizophrenia, but these have diminished, and more evident now are the negative symptoms of withdrawal, flat affect, and passivity.

---

inner processes. The case manager should note that criteria overlap from many diagnostic categories, such as schizophrenia and bipolar disorder, manic type. Behavioral patterns are more accurately observed *over time*, which implies that a client's earlier diagnosis may be less precise than a later one (if it has been changed). The family should be assured that a diagnostic change does not imply that earlier treatments have been inappropriate. Diagnosis does have implications for medication, but other interventions should always be individualized and based on the client's particular biopsychosocial characteristics.

Families should be reminded that the causes of mental disorders are uncertain, although it is accepted that they are primarily biological rather than environmental. Contrary to a case manager's fears, families usually appreciate learning that professionals are uncertain at times in assessing mental illness early in a client's history. Diagnosis is a process rather than an episodic act, and this makes the family's input important in making precise judgments.

Distinguishing the positive and negative symptoms of the disorder as listed in the diagnostic criteria. These two types of symptoms are usually associated with schizophrenia, although all disorders include some symptoms that are overt and bizarre, and others that indicate a decrease in movement, activity, and motivation. The importance of understanding both types of symptoms cannot be overemphasized. Few family members question the presence of a mental disorder when witnessing such positive symptoms as delusions, hallucinations, mania, and agitation. However, when only the negative symptoms are present, including withdrawal, flat affect, impaired concentration, and lack of motivation, an observer may assume laziness or malingering. Such a misunderstanding can create significant conflict within the family, because criticisms of the client relative are most often directed at the negative symptoms (Leff, 1996). Family members who understand that mental illness can be characterized by both types of symptoms may be better able to maintain objectivity about the client's level of impairment.

Review the issue of prognosis with single families, rather than citing general findings in group settings. In group settings many families tend to compare their client relatives with those of other participants and to become discouraged when hearing another family's story of a chronically low-functioning client. With all serious mental illnesses, the prognosis for a complete return to normal functioning is poor, but each case is unique. In fact, the case manager can help families define recovery as the client's ability to realize his or her personal aspirations, rather than as a complete and permanent remission of all symptoms (Hatfield & Lefley, 1993). Case managers need to be realistic with families, who often long for a complete recovery. It is devastating, however, for a family to conclude that there is little hope of a relative's return to the premorbid level of functioning, a perspective that some professionals are too quick to communicate.

Chronicity is not merely a function of the central deficit of mental illness, shared by all who have that disorder. It is related to the interplay over time of personal adjustment, psychological development factors, and community attitudes toward persons with mental illness. In short, case managers should help families appreciate that, although diagnostic criteria have become more standardized, no standard prognosis can apply to any client, and no reason exists to assume that clients cannot improve in many areas of social functioning.

Medications

The topic of medications was covered in detail in Chapter 5. The case manager's need to perform mental status assessments requires that he or she understand the role and actions of medications and be able to communicate with clients and families about them. Additionally, case managers must have current knowledge of the effects of the new medications (each year several are introduced into the market) and be able to talk with families about their availability. Families should always be referred to a physician for medical information, but the kinds of practical questions family members typically ask about medications are within the informed case manager's expertise. In my experience, the concerns of families are represented by one or more of the following commonly asked questions:

1. Why are *these* medications being prescribed, and what are they supposed to do?
2. Will the medication *cure* my family member's mental illness?
3. *How long* will my relative need to take them?
4. Do the medications have to be taken *exactly as prescribed?*
5. Can there be any harm in *stopping* the medications all at once?
6. What *side effects* should we look for, and what should we do about them?
7. Are any dangerous *long-term adverse effects* possible?
8. Can *mixing* the medications with other drugs or alcohol cause problems?

Rather than waiting for families to ask these questions, the case manager should organize medication information into a systematic presentation with handouts. In family education, case managers should be prepared to discuss all four categories of psychotropic medications, including the antipsychotic and anticholinergic medications, antidepressants, mood stabilizing medications, and antianxiety drugs. Because families want to understand how these drugs affect the client relative's behaviors, case managers will rarely need to address the drug's intricate biochemical actions. It is the case manager's responsibility to be informed about medications, not only because families need to be educated but also because he or she must be able to help with medication management as a go-between for the client, the family, and the physician.

Case managers should prepare a brief handout that lists for families the most commonly prescribed medications in each category of their interest (see Table 2 for one example). Family members are almost always confused by the varieties of medication and the differences in their potency, and the simple process of categorizing and comparing dosages serves to clarify this subject. Medication information sheets, now widely used by physicians for distribution to clients, are a useful supplement to such a list. As a means of simplifying the therapeutic effects of these medications, case managers should emphasize the *anxiety-reducing properties* of the antipsychotic and antianxiety medications, which contribute to the client's greater sense of control and focus, and the *mood-stabilizing properties* of the antidepressant and anti–manic drugs, which facilitate more stable, consistent social functioning. For example, talking about the medication's differential effects on the positive and negative symptoms of mental illness, and their differential impact on delusions and hallucinations, can sometimes overwhelm a family member's desire to understand. Maintaining a

Table 13-2 Mood-Stabilizing Medications

Drug	Trade Name	Preparation*	Usual Daily Dosage
Lithium	Lithium carbonate	C, I	900–2100 mg., and 8mEq (milligram equivalents per 5 ml.)
	Lithonate	C	900–2100 mg.
	Eskalith	C, T (includes slow release)	900–2100 mg.
	Lithobid	T (slow release)	900–2100 mg.
	Lithotabs, Lithane	T	900–2100 mg.
	Lithium Citrate, Cibalith-S	I	8 mEq
Valproate	Depakene, Depakote	C	1200–1500 mg.
Carbamazepine	Tegretol	T, I	400–1600 mg.

* T = tablets, C = capsules, I = injectable

focus on the basic properties of the drugs and the eight questions above can help families resolve most of their concerns.

Many families are less informed about the adverse effects of medications than about their positive impact. Case managers should especially emphasize side effects and show how these can be minimized. Medication noncompliance often results from the client's frustration with side effects, and family sensitivity to the issue can enable them to empathize with the ill relative's concerns, to be alert to these effects and their severity, and to promote compliance by encouraging communication with the case manager and physician. If the family and client are forewarned, common side effects such as sedation, tremor, stiffness, dry mouth, blurred vision, and weight gain can be anticipated. The family can report these to the case manager without becoming overly alarmed, and the physician can quickly initiate corrective measures. Psychotropic medication represents a primary intervention with mental illnesses, but the drugs have limitations that must be acknowledged. Families deserve to know both risks and benefits so they will be able to help in monitor drug effectiveness.

Community Resources

Case managers are probably the most knowledgeable mental health professionals about social services resources and agency networks. They routinely do planning, linking, monitoring, advocacy, resource monitoring, resource development, and resource evaluation with their clients. Case managers should educate families about the range of services potentially useful to them, both formal and informal, and include written information for family reference. Most families will be familiar with some, but not all, such resources. Formal community resources include mental health counseling centers, clubhouses, drop-in centers, emergency services providers, halfway houses, supervised apartments, group homes, vocational rehabilitation agencies, medical care clinics, alcohol and drug-treatment centers, telephone hotlines, welfare and social security departments, and transportation services. Natural resources are variable among communities but include all organizations that provide interested persons with social and recreational experiences.

Linking clients with relevant supports is largely a creative process in that it may take a case manager years to fully comprehend a community's resources and the best method of integration for a client's welfare. It is thus understandable that families rarely possess sophisticated knowledge of social services. When families are well informed, however, they can provide effective linkages themselves on behalf of their client relatives, and perhaps attend to their own needs through family support services.

It is equally important that case managers elicit and process the family's feelings about the service providers they have encountered. Families frequently become angry at some staff and agencies following an initial negative experience and then generalize this attitude to other agencies. Just as family members sometimes need an opportunity to vent frustrations about their ill relative as a step toward more constructive interactions, so do they need to process negative encounters with agency providers. For example, one parent became frustrated with a pharmacist who seemed reluctant to provide her with information about discounts on medications. That parent never pursued the issue with other pharmacists and thus missed out on a drug subsidy resource for her son that was available elsewhere in the neighborhood. This type of incident is so common that the case manager should always encourage families to continue with assertive resource investigation, and perhaps provide the family with strategies for self-advocacy. Working with mental health service bureaucracies is a frustrating activity for all of us, but these agencies may in the end be very beneficial to clients and families. The family should be dissuaded from discounting potential resources on the basis of a single negative encounter.

Professional Roles and Intervention Strategies

A family's understandings of mental health professionals' roles and responsibilities derive from its experiences with particular agencies and service providers. But philosophies of care and staff responsibilities often differ among agencies. Clients and their families tend to encounter providers in many settings over the years (such as hospitals, mental health centers, health clinics, etc.), and they often become confused by the different and sometimes contradictory responsibilities held by persons with the same professional titles, as well as their different methods of intervention.

Thus, families need to be educated about the overall system of mental health care. This knowledge can help them make informed choices about *what* services to seek from *which* agencies, how to collaborate more appropriately and effectively with staff from the various professional groups, and how to understand the rationales behind treatment changes that occur after a client member's transfer from one agency to another. In this educational process the case manager should include information about the roles of mental health professionals in agency settings, the basic philosophies of intervention used by these professionals, and the roles the family may provide at different stages of the client's illness and recovery.

The types of professionals working in the mental health field include social workers, psychiatrists, psychologists, nurses, activity therapists, and mental health technicians, among others. Case managers should explain to family members the differences in education and role (both legal and traditional) among these professionals and the expertise each brings to a treatment team. Families also need to understand how professional roles can differ in various settings. For example, a social worker might function as a client's primary treatment provider in a community mental health agency, but in a hospital the social worker might only assist with family assessment and discharge planning. Likewise, in the hospital the psychiatrist might occupy the primary treatment role, but in a mental health center this professional might only monitor medication. If family members do not understand these differences, they will become confused about why, for example, the agency physician is not more involved in the client's overall intervention plan.

Models of Intervention   Talking with families about intervention models presents the case manager with an even greater challenge. For example, Turner (1996) lists more than 20 theories which might guide intervention activities for case managers and other therapists. Family understanding of intervention alternatives will *not* be enhanced by an introduction to such a vast array of theories. Because education is supposed to provide families with comprehensible, useful information, an outline of only three broad models of intervention—medical, developmental, and psychosocial — is more practical (Dawson, Blum, & Bartolucci, 1983). As I describe below, these tend to change in emphasis during the course of a client's recovery from a crisis episode.

The *medical model* assumes that mental illness is caused by an underlying biological disturbance. Mental illness is conceptualized as a brain disease that results from neurotransmitter imbalances. The mental health professional bases a diagnosis on clusters of symptoms, and the diagnosis suggests specific treatments, usually with medication, for controlling the illness. The primary relationship is between the physician and client. Psychiatrists, physicians, and nurses are most often associated with this role.

Developmental models emphasize that human personality develops through transitions from birth to death. Each new stage builds on previous stages, and the individual who confronts a difficult transition might make a positive adjustment or take an alternative path to mental disorder. Erikson's (1968) eight stages of development are useful for this educational purpose because they address the entire life span and focus both on interpersonal and environmental challenges.

An example of a development significant to mental illness is the transition between adolescence and young adulthood. In Erikson's framework, in this stage the person either develops a capacity for interpersonal intimacy or retreats into social isolation. Challenges at this stage include forming peer relationships, revising personal values, patterning sexual behavior, and becoming independent. If the person cannot master these challenges, he or she might develop defense mechanisms or avoidance strategies that in extreme cases, might produce the symptoms of mental illness. The members of many professional disciplines use developmental models of stress and coping, although psychologists are most often associated with this perspective. Developmental models include a strong emphasis on counseling for confronting transitional challenges.

Psychosocial models integrate the inner life of the person with the individual's relationships with society. There is a dual focus on the psychological and social sides of people, and the concept of an internal disease is de-emphasized. The practice theories of ego psychology and cognitive/behavioral theory fit within this perspective, as does the human behavior theory of symbolic interactionism. The person cannot be understood apart from the conditions of his or her environment, because qualities of both have significant influence on social functioning. Intervention usually emphasizes connecting the client with social supports and resources to promote a sense of competence along with social and vocational rehabilitation. Case managers are closely associated with this model of intervention.

Stages of intervention The process of recovery from a crisis episode of mental illness can be somewhat arbitrarily broken down for families into five stages: crisis, stabilization, adjustment, growth, and maintenance. In each stage, the goals of professional intervention and the primary staff involved may be different. Further, the level and type of family involvement may also vary to reflect the client's changing level of competence. This framework provides the case manager with an effective means for helping families comprehend the roles of professionals and appreciate that, while their participation is always important, family roles may change over time. Table 3 presents a summary of how the three models of intervention change in emphasis during the client recovery from a crisis.

Crisis. The first three stages describe interventions provided during the client's recovery from an active psychotic or other crisis episode. In the context of mental illness, a crisis is an onset or recurrence of symptoms of a severe mental illness *along with* the failure of the client's normal support network (this is discussed in more detail in Chapter 8). The client or family acknowledges the need for intensive professional help through crisis intervention and perhaps hospitalization. The case managers who become involved offer support to the family, help them understand the nature of the client's disorder, and obtain an initial social and developmental history from the family. Medical intervention, highlighting the physician's role, dominates with medications as a focus of treatment.

In *stabilization*, the client's more extreme symptoms of psychosis or depression subside, but the client requires careful supervision and support because he

Table 13-3 Stages of Recovery From a Psychotic or Crisis Episode

Stage	Focus of Intervention
Crisis	Medical
Stabilization	Medical Developmental—Psychosocial
Adjustment	Developmental—Psychosocial Medical
Growth	Developmental—Psychosocial Medical
Maintenance	Developmental—Psychosocial—Medical

or she is still emotionally fragile. Social functioning returns to normal but only within the limits of a protective, supportive environment. Intervention, which may shift to a new team in an outpatient setting, moves beyond the disease concept to a promotion of general mental health. Intervention includes obtaining a more detailed social history from the family and helping them understand how the home environment, if utilized, can be structured to facilitate client stabilization. Interventions should include regular family meetings for establishing a predictable, low-stress environment for all members. The crisis episode and its resolution is reviewed with the client and family so that they can integrate the experience into their ongoing family life. They must all understand that a recurrence of a crisis episode is possible and must learn to prevent the kinds of stress that might prompt it.

The medical model might still prevail as a frame of reference for monitoring signs of symptomatic recovery and for helping the client appraise what has happened. There might still be uncertainty about the client's capacity to function with smaller doses of medicine. But the psychosocial tasks of planning and implementing rehabilitation activities, and the developmental issues of the client's premorbid functioning and its possible contributions to both the crisis and recovery, will assume greater attention.

In *adjustment,* the client must adapt to an altered self-image and the new ways in which family and peers view him or her. Intervention becomes more focused on rehabilitation activities. Treatment includes providing ongoing education and support to the family, promoting the client's independence or reduced dependency, considering the client's social and vocational goals, and preventing family over-protectiveness as a natural reaction to crisis. Medical intervention is limited to monitoring the medication. Psychosocial approaches guide the client's attempts to become reestablished in a suitable social milieu. Developmental work provides a frame of reference for exploring conflicts, impasses, and possible problems of motivation. The frequency of staff meetings with the family might begin to diminish in the absence of family conflicts or concerns. The case manager maintains regular contact with the family to insure that the members are attending to their needs.

In the *growth* stage, the client moves beyond a return to normal living to new areas of personal development. Some symptomatic relapses might occur in response to new stresses and difficulty with change, but the client must be discouraged from avoiding realistic life challenges. Intervention becomes more long-term in focus and includes taking social risks, developing vocational skills, and coping with the stresses that accompany new experiences. Family involvement might become peripheral if the client is working toward independent living, or sessions might be continued to help the family promote the client's emerging sense of competence. The psychosocial and developmental models guide the tasks of this stage.

The *maintenance* stage applies only to clients for whom long-term case management is indicated and permanent limitations from the mental disorder are acknowledged. Interventions include controlling symptoms, minimizing social dysfunction, and maximizing strengths through cognitive-behavioral activities and the quality of the client-family-case manager partnership. Treatment includes staying in regular contact and a close working relationship with the client and family, linking the client with a range of support services, monitoring medications, and maintaining an emphasis on normalization. The case manager should educate the family about ongoing intervention strategies for preventing further decline.

The medical model continues to govern decisions about medication. The developmental model is useful for processing client reactions to life events and considering changes in goals, lifestyle, and relationships. The psychosocial model, however, dominates in securing and maintaining support systems for the client and guiding vocational pursuits. Family involvement in treatment might be on a regular or on an as-needed basis, but the case manager should maintain a positive relationship with the family to address their concerns in an atmosphere of cooperation and trust.

The Unmotivated Client

The difficult issue of motivating the withdrawn, resistant client to accept intervention merits special attention in consultation with family members because it is often a primary complaint. Although many clients make good adjustments to their illness and engage actively in rehabilitation, others resist individual or family interventions. The problem of engaging the unmotivated client in treatment, even for basic symptom control, is often as perplexing to professionals as it is to families. The negative symptoms of mental illness can, at least for a time, contribute to low motivation for a client to risk new relationships and challenges.

We saw in Chapter 3 that to engage an ambivalent or unmotivated client, the case manager must succeed in establishing a shared definition of the situation and a set of symbols for communicating with a client. Family observers often interpret withdrawal, ambivalence, and flat affect as laziness and have difficulty distinguishing the personality style from the illness. It is difficult for them to integrate the ill relative's impaired thinking style into their family patterns. An essential case management function is to educate the family about this frustrating aspect of mental illness so that they might manage their frustration while continuing to encourage the client member to take appropriate risks toward change. The family also deserves to understand that the client member's resistance is not due to their own lack of appropriate effort.

Negative symptoms, which are a part of mental illness, can be intensified by two other factors. First, they might represent a temporary convalescent phase after a crisis episode. The client needs time to regain psychological strength after such a major blow to the self-image. This might represent a type of depression, a grieving for the previous self. This, coupled with the family's collective grief, might be overwhelming to the client. He or she might eventually feel more capable of taking initiatives. Symptoms contributing to a lack of motivation might also be related to the adverse effects of some medications, which underscores the importance of family communication with the physician. Families need to understand that the client can overcome these deficits to varying degrees but might need time to do so.

Case managers can stress that, following a crisis, the client might be generally intolerant of high stress levels and major challenges, such as looking for work or returning to school. In the early stages of recovery the client will function best in an uncomplicated, structured, low-key environment. Expectations for a broader range of activity can be gradually increased as the person demonstrates increased coping capability, although recognizing this does not imply that the family should expect nothing of him of her. The family that appreciates these points will less likely become overwhelmed with frustration during interactions with the client member and be better able to maintain an atmosphere that facilitates positive adjustment.

Research consistently indicates an association between a family's "expressed emotion" (defined as regular and intensive face-to-face contact, critical comments, and expressions of hostility) and the likelihood of client relapse, although this is not a causal relationship (Leff, 1996). Long-term mental illness within a family naturally fosters these emotional expressions at times. Mental health professionals have tended unrealistically to assume that families should be able to control their negative emotions. The attitude of benign indifference with which professionals often encourage families is an impossible ideal, because interactions among close family members, even in the absence of mental illness, often produce tension and anger.

Families need to be reassured that client motivation cannot be forced. Still, the reluctant client must be urged forward gently, even in the face of some discomfort, or he or she may never overcome the handicaps of the disorder. The most a family or professional can do is to let the client know that progress is expected, nurture the client's interests, encourage any activity in a positive direction, and contribute to a steady environment where growth can take place. The case manager must concretely and simply convey how progress can be achieved.

SUMMARY

This chapter has highlighted five aspects of mental illness about which clinical case managers should educate families as part of a comprehensive service plan. The teaching aspects of case management can provide families with knowledge and skills that they can use to strengthen their overall growth and coping potential. Families can promote more stable housing or community environments for themselves and their ill relative with an understanding of the various mental disorders and their roles in the treatment process. Clinical case managers, as primary service providers, have a responsibility to develop the knowledge and skills necessary to provide educational materials for families in a thorough, practical manner. The case manager might involve other professionals as co-educators in this process because members of the treatment team representing other professions all have areas of special expertise. The relationships fostered by case managers with families through this educational process often facilitate open lines of communication for the duration of the client's treatment, which is essential for fostering both the client's and the family's growth.

14

ℭℨ

The Family Education and Support Group

In this chapter I continue to focus on the case manager's *education* of families of persons with mental illness. I expand this focus, however, to include *support* provision and specifically consider the potential for case manager-led groups to accomplish these goals. Though I describe a variety of group formats, I elaborate on one program that I conducted for many years, known as the Family Education and Support Group.

PSYCHOEDUCATIONAL PROGRAMS

Psychoeducational programs can be defined as time-limited, closed groups conducted by mental health professionals for the purposes of educating and providing support to a lay membership. Such groups, though similar in general purpose, may have a variety of formats depending on size, duration, session length, content, and range of membership (such as nuclear vs. extended families, siblings, and neighbors). Groups may be *open* or *closed*. Open groups attract a broad membership and provide immediate support to members, but they are also less stable, requiring more time for trust to develop and stimulating less personal disclosure. Closed groups require a longer-term commitment from members, but they are more stable, they encourage a deeper exploration of relevant issues, and they tend to be more cohesive. In all cases psychoeducational groups should function as only one part of a comprehensive intervention plan, because they cannot provide adequate treatment by themselves. Clients and perhaps family members should participate in other programs for counseling, medication, and rehabilitation services.

Several authors specify the types of education that should be included in a group program. Anderson, Hogarty, & Reiss (1986) include the following topics:

1. The experience of mental illness for the client relative
2. The causes of mental illness
3. Its psychological and biological manifestations
4. The impact of mental illness on the family
5. Medications
6. The combined effects of medication and psychosocial intervention
7. What families can do to promote the client relative's recovery

Hatfield (1990) outlines a similar listing of educational topics addressed in her groups:

1. Understanding mental illness
2. The personal impact of mental illness on families
3. Understanding professional interventions
4. Creating supportive environments

5. Coping with crisis situations

6. Long-range family planning

She adds that the group leader, in addition to being a knowledgeable professional, must possess skills in stimulating discussion and providing feedback.

A Survey of Group Types

The leaders of psychoeducational groups may emphasize either the education or support component, *or* attempt to balance both. The following eight examples of psychoeducational programs serve to illustrate their variety.

1. In an early Thresholds parents group, provided at a psychosocial rehabilitation agency of the same name in Chicago, mental health professionals provided education and client management strategies to family members (including the client relative in *one* meeting) in a weekly, open-ended and ongoing 12-session series (Dincin, Selleck, & Streicker, 1978). Outcomes included parents' reports of more positive attitudes toward their ill relative, their improved ability to manage family stresses, and a greater appreciation of their own needs.

2. In another early program single families attended six weekly sessions provided by mental health agency professionals following the client's hospital discharge. Leaders integrated skills training with educational approaches to improve family stress management (Goldstein & Kopeikin, 1981). Outcomes were measured in terms of client rehospitalization rates during a six-month follow-up period.

3. A purely supportive psychoeducational program in Europe sought to enhance families' ability to cope with the stress of caring for an ill relative without overtly attempting to change their behavior (Byalin, Jed, & Lehman, 1982). A mental health clinician met with a family in their home *only* as often as the family requested. The professional attempted to affirm that the family was not responsible for the ill relative's mental disorder and offered whatever support might be helpful to the family.

4. One research team randomly assigned clients with schizophrenia to four treatment groups, each containing some combination of family intervention, social skills training, behavior therapy, and medication (Hogarty, Anderson, Reiss, & Kornblith, 1991). The psychoeducational component of their comprehensive intervention consisted of a day-long "survival skills workshop" in which several professionals provided groups of families with information and an overview of the social skills training that would be provided to their client relatives. This eight-hour session was followed by single-family sessions every two to three weeks, for six months to one year, in which information from the workshop was applied. The program was evaluated after one year by comparing rehospitalization rates among the four groups.

5. In a "social intervention" program, a nine-month, biweekly relative's group was led by professionals, but it focused on member sharing of client

management strategies (Leff, Kuipers, & Berkowitz, 1983). Through a screening process, families who tolerated client behaviors poorly were matched with families characterized by attitudes of acceptance. Within the groups, the more accepting families were described as having a positive impact on the attitudes of the more critical members.

6. Another set of family intervention approaches is known as behavioral family therapy (Falloon, Boyd, & McGill, 1984). These can be provided through educational workshops, communications training with multiple families, problem-solving skills training, and home-based interventions. The interventions are designed to educate families about mental illness, improve family communications, instruct the family in problem-solving skills, and promote the application of problem-solving strategies to specific family concerns. Behavioral family intervention is based on the rationale that families can become attuned to the warning signs and ongoing risks of relapse with schizophrenia and can become effective, self-directed problem solvers.

    One example of this approach involved two single-family educational sessions provided by several mental health professionals in the client's home with all family members. The first session focused on the nature of the client's disorder, and the second considered issues of medication and home management. Handouts were given to family members for future reference. Follow-up studies confirmed that family members retain information presented in this format over an extended period of time. Another intervention model involves four-month weekly sessions of continuing education for family groups. Content is focused on teaching behavior modification techniques that families can use to shape the ill relative's behavior. Outcome measures for these programs have included rehospitalization rates, client compliance with intervention, and measures of family cohesion.

7. Another program included families and professionals in a 10-week group series, meeting once weekly, with guest speakers every two weeks (McLean, Greer, Scott, & Beck, 1982). The purposes of the program were to provide families with information about mental illness, to enable them to take more time for themselves, and to help them acquire behavior management techniques for their households. One finding in this program was that an informal coffee hour at the end of each meeting helped with member sharing.

8. Psychoeducational courses on a variety of mental health topics have also been conducted for the general public (Womack, Maiuro, Russo, & Vitaliano, 1983). There are indications that such courses attract persons from the community who may need professional help but who are unwilling to engage in traditional therapy programs because they fear stigma.

    It must be acknowledged that education and support groups have not always used precise measures of effectiveness. Two recent studies demonstrate the difficulty of monitoring impact. In one experimental study of 225 families in the Philadelphia area, divided into the three treatment groups of family intervention, individual consultation, and no intervention, it was found that members might not learn and retain more information about mental illness than did a control group over a six-month period (Solomon, Draine, Mannion, & Meisel, 1997). Conversely, a survey of 131 members of 14 psychoeducational groups from the Chicago area found that members identified significant educational and family relationship benefits from their participation (Heller, Roccoforte, Hsieh, Cook, & Pickett, 1997). It was also found that participants who gained the most from their group experiences had less support outside the group and actively provided support to other members. The authors note that the opportunity to *provide* education and support seems as beneficial as receiving it.

The psychoeducational approach lends itself to a variety of group formats. In the remainder of this chapter I describe in detail my own Family Education and Support Group. This group has much in common with those already described and is practical for implementation in most agency settings.

THE FAMILY EDUCATION AND SUPPORT GROUP

Purposes and Goals

The Family Education and Support Group is a nine-session, nine-week program for the adult family members of clients. The dual purposes of the group are to provide families with *education* about their ill relative's disorder and provide a setting where they can *support* and *problem-solve* with each other. It is hoped that as a result of the group experience, families will become more effective therapeutic agents in the home, develop more constructive relationships with professionals, and develop support networks for themselves. The group is designed to be led by a case manager specializing in services to this client population. With its nine-week format, it can be offered three times per year (winter, spring, and fall) to facilitate participation by new families. Summer is not a good season for such a program, because many families cannot easily make long-term commitments. It is recommended that there be very little or no cost for the course so that families will be more likely to attend. Appendix A includes details about the step-by-step organization of the group.

The five goals of the program, which should be circulated to referring staff and prospective members, stem from the dual purposes noted above and are listed below:

1. For professionals and the families of persons with serious mental illness to determine together what may be realistically achieved in the social adjustment of impaired relatives

2. To educate families about current theories of those disorders that result in mental illness, including causes, course, degree of impairment, interventions, and prognosis

3. To educate families about the purposes and actions of the various medications used in the treatment of mental illness

4. For family members to act as an ongoing mutual support system in the day-to-day management of ill relatives, with special emphasis on reducing and controlling behaviors disruptive to the family

5. To inform families of the various agencies locally available to provide services to clients and families, including vocational services, welfare agencies, housing providers, clubhouses, drop-in centers, and advocacy organizations

Other goals emerge within each particular group. Members are encouraged to take initiatives with regard to priority setting during the pre-group phone survey (see the following) as well as during the early weeks of the course. In my experience the following goals are most frequently articulated by family participants:

1. To become well educated enough about the mental health service system to advocate for quality services on behalf of the client relative

2. To reduce feelings of guilt and social isolation

3. To reduce the displacement of negative emotions onto other family members

4. To enhance the pursuit of activities in the family that do not center around the client member

Group Process

In an ideal group, members take much initiative in agenda-setting over the nine weeks. The case manager, who initially provides a structured base for developing an agenda, becomes less directive and more facilitative as the weeks pass. In this way, each course adapts to the interests of its members, whose concerns may be outside the scope of the leader's agency-focused experience.

Striking a balance between education and support and encouraging member initiative requires attention to a number of group leadership principles as follows (Atwood, 1983):

1. The group can best develop into a cohesive unit and maintain a task orientation if it is time-limited with a closed membership.

2. A facilitative style of leadership is mandatory. The case manager shares responsibility for setting goals and agenda with the members. Families may initially want the leader to take charge, but the balance should shift as the group process develops.

3. Family problems must be addressed as they are defined by the members, not as the case manager might define them. Families are the experts in dealing with family management issues. The open-minded case manager can learn much from the family perspective.

4. The case manager must be willing to provide the kinds of clinical information families desire. The leader can make educational presentations, or act as a broker in recruiting other professionals for special topics.

5. The case manager must promote ongoing support among members by gradually relinquishing dominance of leadership activities as the weeks pass.

6. The case manager must accept without defensiveness, and even promote, the expression of members' negative feelings. This principle may be difficult to uphold because some of this ventilation will be directed at the mental health profession itself. The leader must appreciate the frustrations that many families have encountered with professionals and must prepare to be a target for ventilation during the first few meetings. If the leader becomes defensive, he or she may stifle the members' potential to develop feelings of comfort, trust, and affirmation within the group.

With the educational material presented, families can develop reasonable expectations for client change. They can further help each other maintain greater objectivity about family problems. These processes begin with the predictable ventilation of negative emotion. Gradually, the case manager's presentation of educational material provides a basis for group interaction and coalescence, and members will begin to focus more on solutions than problems.

Setting the Agenda

The case manager first promotes the emphasis on member agenda setting during member recruitment. Program referrals might be taken from staff within the case manager's own agency and from other community agencies serving the same clientele. He or she might arrange for ongoing publicity about the program, or publicize each new course separately. The program dates, times, and a short summary of each session's content can be included on a one-page announcement for this purpose (see Appendix B). All sessions should be held at the case manager's agency or another suitable community site during evening hours for the convenience of members. Meetings are recommended to be 90 minutes long, with an additional 30 minutes reserved afterward for member socialization. It is a nice touch to provide light refreshments during the social time if possible.

The case manager must contact each referred family prior to its formal acceptance into the group. This is accomplished in two steps: sending each family a short letter describing the course, and following up one week later with a telephone call. During the phone conversation, the leader answers any questions the family member may have about the program. If the person decides to join, the case manager conducts a brief phone survey to solicit input into the group's content (see Appendix C). In this survey the family member is asked questions about his or her level of knowledge about the relative's mental disorder, the extent of involvement in the relative's treatment, and expectations about the outcome of the group series. This information enables the case manager to plan sessions in accordance with member needs. Finally, the case manager asks the family to make a commitment to attend at least three sessions, since securing a nine-week commitment without a trial is unrealistic.

Examples of Group Participants

No two families are alike, but here I provide descriptions of three persons with different expectations who have attended the Family Education and Support Group. Later in this chapter their thoughts about the group at termination are described.

Mary, age 40 and divorced, complained of feeling ignored during the previous five years when she tried to communicate with her son's treatment team. She had, in fact, never had an opportunity to speak with a mental health professional. Mary became angry with the case manager when he contacted her about joining the group. She accused him of providing another superficial program that would make him feel good about working with families when, in fact, nothing would change for them. She felt blamed for her son's psychosis and was concerned that in the new group this would happen again. The case manager encouraged her to talk and listened quietly. Mary became tearful and admitted feeling guilty about her son's persistent problems. She finally agreed to give the group a try, saying that she hoped to get suggestions about how to improve the relationship with her son. She had tried to do what she thought was right over the years but never felt confident that she knew how to be supportive of him.

Donald, age 60, described his difficulties with his wife of 35 years who had a history of bipolar disorder. He was frustrated with psychiatrists because over the years they had prescribed a variety of medications for his wife with mixed results. He was angry that the short- and long-term adverse effects of the medications had never been clearly explained to either of them. He had read much about his wife's disorder but was still not sure how he should respond to her mood changes. Donald hoped that the group could help him with this. He also wished to learn more about medications and the heredity factor in mental illness, because he feared his wife's disorder might be acquired by their children.

Linda, age 26, was less clear in her comments to the case manager. Her mother had a serious mental illness of some type and had always been odd and reclusive around the house. It had been Linda's job to take care of her mother and to see that she took her medicine. Linda's goal was to become educated about mental illness and medications in a general sense because she did not know much to begin with. She seemed anxious at the prospect of joining a group, afraid of what she might learn and concerned that others might look down on her for being so devoted to her mother. Linda admitted that being her mother's primary caregiver was more stressful now that she was married. She wanted to start her own family but felt guilty about abandoning her mother.

Schedule of Meetings

Week #1: Orientation and Introductions   The case manager is more verbal in this first session than any other, tending to dominate the first 45 minutes. The members do not know each other, might not know the leader, and in any case are anxious about how the course will proceed. It is the case manager's responsibility to set a positive tone for their relaxation, even though some members might not be comfortable until the second or third meeting.

The leader introduces him or herself with a detailed professional background sketch, focusing on work with persons having mental illness. The leader then reviews the purposes and goals of the group and summarizes the input given by members during the phone survey about what they want to achieve in the meetings. The leader assures members that they will be under no pressure to share personal information. They are also informed of three basic ground rules: that members must speak one at a time, that confidentiality must be maintained unless specifically waived by a member, and that members can have outside contact with each other only if they acknowledge this to the group, as a means of preserving cohesion.

Families are then asked to introduce themselves. They can say as much or as little as they wish about their backgrounds with the ill relative and their hopes for a positive group experience. Some families will be talkative, and others will say little. The case manager might take notes to record some comments expressed by family members for use in planning topic presentations and discussions.

The meeting generally ends after introductions. There is a minimum of problem-solving at this first meeting, although some members may ask for feedback. The case manager thanks members for their participation and sharing, and suggests that they begin the process of education and mutual support at the following meeting. Before ending, participants are asked to complete the Member Assessment (the pretest of the group evaluation; see Appendix D). Individuals who miss the first meeting are asked to complete the form during the short break at the second session (a person who does not attend the first two meetings will have missed too much to remain on the roster).

Week #2: Community Resources The rationale for family education about formal and informal community resources was provided in the previous chapter. This topic is scheduled for the second session because it stimulates much sharing and is not so sensitive as to intimidate member participation. The group process is significantly enhanced during this session. Most families contribute to the discussion even if they have been reticent during the first week, and the emerging group norm of interaction, if lively, will continue through the coming weeks. Members typically do an excellent job of teaching each other about the variety of resources in their communities.

The range of *formal* resources that merit highlighting includes the following:

- Mental health centers
- Clubhouses
- Emergency service providers
- Emergency food and housing providers
- Halfway houses
- Supervised apartments

- Group homes
- Vocational rehabilitation agencies
- Recreation centers
- Low-cost medical care clinics
- Alcohol and drug treatment centers
- Telephone hotlines
- Departments of social services
- Food stamp providers
- Transportation services
- Volunteer agencies

All members learn much in this session because of the breadth of their individual experiences. The case manager is responsible to inform members of other agencies that might serve their needs beyond those familiar to the group, including informal resources. As noted in the last chapter, the case manager should elicit family member feelings about service providers they have experienced. If members have had negative interactions with certain resource organizations, it is important for the worker to help them see that the agencies might at other times be more beneficial to their families.

Week #3: Presentation on Diagnosis During this session, families are familiarized with the process of diagnosing mental illness. The case manager may conduct this presentation or invite another professional expert to do so. Information about what a diagnosis means, and about how a diagnosis is reached, can help families better understand the experience of mental illness and the rationale for professionals' decisions about intervention. An emphasis on the biological basis of mental illness (though not ignoring psychological and social influences) might also relieve some family member guilt about the ill relative's situation. Families might be helped in these ways to accept the reality of the mental illness and to acquire reasonable expectations for client change.

Details about the content of a presentation based on the *Diagnostic and Statistical Manual of Mental Disorders* (American Psychiatric Association, 1994) were outlined in the previous chapter. Several additional points are important for the case manager to consider when organizing this presentation for a group. First, the case manager must collect specific diagnostic information about group members' ill relatives and focus the discussion only on those categories. These will generally include schizophrenia, schizoaffective disorder, bipolar disorder, and major depression, but might include others. Sometimes a family will report a less typical diagnosis, such as obsessive-compulsive disorder or borderline personality disorder, and the case manager must insure that the content is included in the presentation. Some family members are not aware of their ill relative's diagnosis, but by this time the case manager should have an idea of the general category from the family's description of symptoms.

The issue of uncertainty in determining causes of mental disorders must also be addressed. Many families wonder how effective treatments can be provided when exact causes are not known. This can be explained by drawing a parallel between mental illness and the physical illness of diabetes (Arieti, 1979). In diabetes, it is not known why the pancreas ceases to function adequately. The disease runs in some families, but even so not all family members are affected. It tends to occur in persons who are overweight or who consume high carbohydrate diets, but even so it afflicts only a small percentage of them. And, though most cases are treated successfully, none are cured. Such is the case with the long-term mental disorders, which appear to be the result of complex causes too difficult to isolate. Various familial and developmental patterns are evident in many, but not all, cases, and there are no clear predictive patterns in the course of the disorders. They cannot be cured, but they can be treated and controlled.

Finally, social time must be reserved at the end of this meeting for informal conversation between the presenter and families. In this context the presenter can give family members an opportunity to react to the discussion and perhaps to ask questions too personal to raise in the group.

Week #4: Group Discussion of the Previous Week's Presentation This meeting includes an open-ended discussion of issues related to having a family member with mental illness. It is the first session devoted to mutual support rather than to education, and it establishes a pattern of meetings alternately devoted to formal presentations and informal discussions. Family members must be encouraged to rely less on the case manager and to focus more on sharing their knowledge and experiences with each other.

Group participants, having had time to consider the material presented during Week #3, usually arrive at this session with many follow-up questions. They are eager to clarify their understanding of diagnostic issues, but they will also want to discuss other unrelated issues relevant to their family situations. The case manager has several responsibilities in this process. He or she should not dominate the discussions or present much new educational material but should be prepared to answer questions about diagnosis and to inform members where more information is available. Most of all, the case manager encourages members to discuss their concerns with each other. As this occurs, the leader must insure that the group focuses substantively on one member's concern before another member raises a topic. Others tend to identify with issues raised by one member and to begin applying it to their own family situation, which can draw attention away from the member who initiated the topic. Also, no participant must be permitted to dominate the discussion to the extent that others feel excluded. This is a facilitative challenge for the leader.

Common questions and comments which members bring to this session are listed here.

- "Are patients given tests to find out if there is an organic reason for mental illness?"

- "Do people with schizophrenia and bipolar disorder get better as they age? If not, what do they have to look forward to?"
- "What about difficult birth as a cause of mental illness?"
- "Does the way the family interacts have an impact on the patient, or is this a minor influence?"
- "Do drugs like PCP cause mental illness? Would it happen even without the drugs?"
- "What about alcohol? Does it contribute to psychosis?"
- "What is a 'familial pattern'?"
- "What if you expect too much and push too hard?"
- "If a person is delusional, then 'talk' therapy isn't going to help, is it?"
- "I've had good experiences with my son's counselors, but none of them has been able to tell me how to promote my son's independence."
- "Why doesn't my husband want to do more for himself? When will he get back to normal?"
- "What makes my daughter so seclusive, and what can I do about it?"
- "How do I get my son into treatment if he needs it but won't go?"
- "You try to help, but after awhile it gets you down."
- "I have no way of knowing if my expectations are reasonable or not."
- "Who is going to take care of my daughter when my husband and I aren't around?"
- "How can I arrange to talk with my son's counselor when he won't agree to this?"

Week #5: Presentation on Psychotropic Medications This session is a formal presentation by a psychiatrist, physician, pharmacist, or the case manager on the classes, types, and actions of medications used in treating mental illnesses. The credentials of the presenter are not as important as his or her knowledge base and ability to communicate effectively to family members about this difficult topic. I regularly conducted this presentation, but began doing so only after studying for several years, working with clients and their families, and listening to physicians give similar presentations to consumer and family groups.

Many clients are helped enormously by medication, but families tend to be aware of its limitations. They may have been disappointed when psychiatrists were unable to produce lasting positive results with medications, or may have wondered why physicians changed medications frequently, as if unsure of themselves. They have witnessed both major and minor adverse effects, have dealt with their ill relative's non-compliance, and have observed instances when terminating medications seemed to result in the relative's improvement. They wonder why the medications cannot cure, and they might have been frustrated with the psychiatrist's apparent unwillingness to meet with them to discuss the medication.

This presentation must be general, covering the antipsychotic, antidepressant, mood stabilizing, and anti-anxiety classes of medications. Many family members have had experience with all four categories, but others are unsure of the medications their ill relative has taken. The goal of this session is to address the following issues:

1. Why the medications are used

2. The four general classes of psychotropic medication and the types of disorders they attempt to treat

3. The specific medications in each of the four classes, their differential effects, and why they differ in dosage requirements (milligrams required for therapeutic effect)

4. How physicians, with input from others on the treatment team, make decisions about prescribing specific medications from those available in a class

5. How the medications act on the nervous system

6. Their short and long term positive and negative effects

7. How long they need to be taken

8. How family members can learn more about their ill relative's experiences with medications, and provide appropriate input to the treatment team

9. The importance of the clinical relationship in medication intervention

10. The issue of "polypharmacy," or using several medications simultaneously

11. The combined effects of medication with other substances such as caffeine, tobacco, and alcohol

Week #6: Group Discussion of the Previous Week's Presentation As in the fourth session, the case manager comes to this meeting prepared to respond to questions and comments stimulated by the presentation on medications. For assistance with this task, he or she should bring reference materials for consultation in dealing with matters of a technical nature. A variety of texts are available for this purpose, and members will prefer those which are concise and relatively non-technical.

One of the major positive outcomes of this session is that many families will become curious enough about medication to approach their ill relative's physician for additional information or input. The case manager should encourage all members to follow up on the topic in this way.

Discussion topics other than those related to medication will emerge during this session as the case manager maintains a facilitative rather than directive role. This is the second of the program's informal discussion sessions, and members become more assertive as they feel more comfortable in the group. Listed here are common questions and comments that family members voice during this session.

- "Do the antipsychotic medications treat anything other than psychosis?"
- "Why are my wife's medicines changed sometimes?"

- "Can these drugs cause birth defects in offspring?"

- "It seems like you can't be sure which medications will work until you try them."

- "Can the side-effect of blurred vision cause problems for my son's eye condition?"

- "My son had some of these side-effect problems before he became sick."

- "I get frightened when the doctor reduces my son's medications."

- "This all strikes me as a lot of guesswork."

- "Can you reach a point of permanent toxicity if you take the drugs for many years?"

- "My daughter is 26 years old. She takes risperidone and imipramine. What will these drugs do to her by the time she is 46 or 56 years old?"

- "The risk seems to be taking a chance of brain damage from long-term use or allowing my son to remain withdrawn."

- "When my daughter goes off her medicine she goes right back into schizophrenia."

- "How do you decide when to reduce the medicine?"

- "How long does it take to develop tardive dyskinesia?"

- "Is my son's constant pacing due to side effects or due to the schizophrenia?"

- "I learned last week that caffeine can have adverse effects for my son. Why hasn't the doctor told me about the dangers of caffeine?"

- "Can some people avoid all these side-effects?"

- "Can doctors provide electroshock treatment instead of giving drugs? Which is more dangerous?"

Week #7: Professional Roles and Intervention Strategies This meeting includes a presentation by the case manager on the specific roles of mental health professionals in various agency settings and the major models of intervention used. The case manager should emphasize that professionals ideally take a team approach, even when not formally organized into a team, with each discipline making special contributions to a holistic effort on the client's behalf. This material is always interesting to families, who often have incomplete or erroneous impressions of professionals' roles in the mental health service system. Members tend to have strong reactions to this material, which stimulates much productive discussion.

Topics to be included in this presentation were noted in the previous chapter. A major difference in their discussion within a group is that members can offer their own observations about professional roles and interventions, and in doing so can provide each other with a well-rounded picture of the service system. Much of what is shared by families will be critical, and though these experiences must be validated the case manager should try to leave all members with a sense that they understand the mental health system better and feel more positive about their potential participation in that system. Special emphasis should be given to the family's role in the counseling process, to the issue of confidentiality, and to how family members can increase their access to professionals working with the ill relative.

The presentation should be organized in the following manner:

1. The case manager provides an overview of the mental health disciplines and their respective function in hospitals and outpatient settings (primary professionals include psychiatrists, psychologist, nurses, social workers, mental health technicians, activities therapists, vocational rehabilitation counselors, and others with whom members are familiar).

2. Families are asked to share how they understand the roles of these professionals.

3. The case manager provides an overview of three models of interventions (medical, developmental, and psychosocial) and asks for member feedback on their observations of these different models.

4. The case manager presents the five stages of intervention and rehabilitation with clients having long-term disorders (crisis, stabilization, adaptation, growth, maintenance) and asks members to identify which stage their ill relative is in currently, and whether their relative has tended to cycle through the stages.

5. Families are invited to share their observations of how professional interventions change as the ill relative moves through the service system.

6. The case manager leads a discussion of the implications of this information for family members as participants in the intervention process.

Week #8: Group Discussion or Presentation Group members are likely to be fairly self-directive by this time, and this meeting can proceed in one of two ways. As one option, the group might have previously identified topics of mutual interest for which they request a presentation by the case manager or a guest speaker. Examples of such topics include information on vocational rehabilitation or other specialty services, information from an attorney about legal system developments that may help or hinder service acquisition for clients and their families, and information on insurance coverage for mental illness. The case manager should not plan a presentation before surveying members a few weeks prior to this session to assess their interests.

Alternatively, members may chose to devote this meeting to additional sharing and open discussion. If this is their choice, the leader conducts the meeting in the same manner as in weeks #4 and #6, with one exception. The leader must keep in mind that there is only one remaining session and must begin bringing recurring group themes to closure. In preparing for this meeting, for example, he or she should review the group's evolution and identify any topics that have generated much interest and that might require additional attention. The leader is facilitative, but also more directive at this time in moving the members toward termination.

Week #9: Termination The case manager's responsibilities in this session include facilitating member sharing, introducing a speaker from a local family organization for a short presentation on advocacy opportunities, directing a termination process, and collecting evaluation forms.

The meeting begins with the case manager's encouraging members to address any "unfinished business" from previous sessions. Following this, a short presentation (no more than 30 minutes) is made by a representative from a consumer group such as the Mental Health Association or Alliance for the Mentally Ill. The guest provides an overview of the organization's mission and activities and then highlights ways family members might participate as advocates for their family members or as service providers to other families. The case manager could provide basic information about these organizations, but a representative can do a much better job of describing the experience of participation.

In the second half of the meeting the case manager asks members to share their impressions of the group experience. A useful strategy for initiating this process is to review the entire nine-week course, including its goals, what emerged as significant themes, what information was presented, and what members shared with each other. The leader then asks members to respond to the following questions:

1. What did they learn that was important to them?
2. How comfortable did they feel about sharing personal concerns with the group?
3. How can they apply their learning to situations outside the group?
4. How can they generate support systems for themselves outside the group?
5. How do they feel about termination?

Finally, members are asked to complete and return the evaluation forms. Those who miss the final session can be phoned and asked to fill out the evaluation at home; if they will do so, the case manager can send them a copy with a stamped return envelope. The case manager should reserve 30 minutes of socialization time at the end of the meeting so that members can say goodbye to each other.

Examples of Group Participants Mary, who had been quite skeptical about the potential of the group to be useful for her, changed dramatically. She enjoyed the opportunity to ventilate and to hear from others about their situations, which were quite similar to her own. She gained assertiveness with her son and his treatment providers and made more sustained efforts to provide them with information about her son's condition. Along with four other members, Mary participated in a professional conference along with the case manager about the utility of the group experience. Donald also had positive experiences with the group, although his were less dramatic. He was still not sure how to interact with his wife when she experienced mood changes, and this remained a major frustration for him. He did benefit from increased knowledge about medications and diagnosis that he thought would help him monitor his wife's response to interventions. Linda, however, had a negative experience with the group. She seemed to become increasingly upset the more she learned about mental illness and its impact on families. This awareness seemed to increase her fears, and she began to feel overwhelmed with her own family situation. The case manager, sensing this, spent time with Linda outside the group setting to be supportive of her concerns. Still, Linda dropped out of the group after five weeks, saying that she wasn't ready for an experience of such intensity.

GROUP EVALUATION

One basic question is used to evaluate the Family Education and Support Group: Do families have more involvement with supportive individuals and groups outside the nuclear family, and less involvement with their ill relative's daily life, immediately after completing the program? Increased involvement with support resources, including the relative's treatment providers, indicates improved coping skills and increased participation in the client's rehabilitation. Less involvement with the ill relative suggests reduced dependence of the client on the family. I developed the Member Assessment form as a pre- and post-group survey to help case managers answer the above question.

The independent variables for evaluation are the ill relative's *level of independent living skills* (ILS), and the family member's *level of social support* (SS). My definition of "independent living skills" is the ability of the relative to manage a budget, maintain physical health, keep his or her surroundings clean, maintain supportive relationships with family and friends, engage in regular community activity, and participate in mental health treatment programs. My definition of "social supports" is all resources outside the nuclear family, including extended family, friends, neighbors, co-workers, peer groups, service organizations, and mental health professionals, which provide the family with opportunities to speak freely about the stresses of living with or near a relative with mental illness, and which promote the family member's relaxation, coping skills, and physical health.

The Member Assessment evaluation form is included as Appendix D of this chapter. Respondents receives two scores for each administration. The ILS variable, with 14 items and a 0–3 range in scoring (negative to positive) contains a range of 0–42. The SS scale, with 10 items, has a range of 0–30. The pre- and post-group scores can be compared with one another as an indicator of program impact. The narrative comments included with each item can be summarized for additional feedback. Content validity for the scales was established with the assistance of a panel of eight experts consisting of professionals, family members, and clients. Reliability was established by having 15 families complete test/retest administrations of the survey one week apart.

SUMMARY

Many persons with mental illnesses are emotionally and materially dependent on their families. Though these relationships may be generally satisfying for all members, they include occasional or frequent tensions related to the chronicity of mental illness and its negative impact on family functioning. My goal in Chapters 13 and 14 has been to provide case managers with a variety of strategies for facilitating a more cohesive family system and enhancing the family's sense of competence and control through the organized provision of education and support services. Whether the case manager works with families individually or within groups, the benefits to family members from this process may be considerable.

The Family Education and Support Group is designed to cover a range of topics that should meet the most pressing needs of family members. Participants gain knowledge of mental health diagnostic, medication, and counseling techniques, as well as a better understanding of the mental health system. They learn how other families have addressed the problems they all share in living with or near a relative who has mental illness. They can experience support and empathy, come to know that they are not alone in their situation, and gain new ideas on how to promote adaptive functioning in their client relatives. Members also acquire a better grasp of how to approach mental health professionals when advocating for improved services. The experience of mental illness can in these ways be de-mystified for families, resulting in their improved ability to manage the challenges of having an ill relative.

APPENDIX A: GROUP PLANNING AND ORGANIZING TASKS

1. Compile a group information packet including a statement of purpose, list of goals, and course outline.

2. Secure administrative support and approval for the program.

3. Distribute program information packets to all case managers and other professionals who are invited to make referrals to the group. This information should include the projected starting date and should be distributed two months prior to that date.

4. Survey professionals two weeks later for a list of possible referrals. Note the family members' relationships to the client (parent, spouse, sibling, etc.) and the client's diagnosis.

5. Send letters of invitation to family members one month prior to the start date.

6. Phone each family one week later to discuss the program and to learn whether or not they plan to join the group. Complete the *Phone Survey for New Group Members* for all families who decide to attend.

7. Secure verbal commitments from any guest speakers. Distribute program information packets to them.

8. Inform all referring professionals of their clients' family members who will be attending the group.

9. Send reminder letters to group members one week prior to the start date.

10. Prepare a meeting schedule sheet to be distributed to members at the first group session.

APPENDIX B: SAMPLE COURSE OUTLINE

Family Education and Support Group

Schedule of Meetings

Note: All meetings will take place on Monday evenings, from 6:00—7:30 PM in the Bridge Counseling Center Annex, located behind the main building.

March 5:   Orientation and introductions.

March 12:   Group discussion on the range of services available in the county for persons with mental illness and the feelings of family members about the quality of the service agencies they have dealt with.

March 19:   A guest speaker, Dr. James Himelick of North Area Mental Health Services, will present current theories about the causes, course, and treatment of the severe mental illnesses.

March 26:   Follow-up group discussion on Dr. Himelick's presentation.

April 2:   A guest speaker, Dr. Michael Wollan of this agency, will speak on the uses and limitations of medications in the treatment of mental illness.

April 9:   Follow-up group discussion on Dr. Wollan's presentation.

April 16:   Group discussion about the various intervention modalities commonly used in mental health agencies, and how families can best involve themselves in that process. A film presentation on types of counseling will follow.

April 23:   A guest speaker, Charlene Barker of the Mental Health Association of Franklin County, will talk about family advocacy for quality services from mental health professionals on behalf of their client relatives.

April 30:   Wind-up discussion on any matters of interest to family members. Evaluation forms will be distributed for completion and then discussed. Group members can decide whether they wish to continue meeting, with or without the group leader, beyond the nine-week course.

APPENDIX C: PHONE SURVEY
FOR NEW GROUP MEMBERS

Opening Remarks: In order to be most helpful to you, I am interested in learning how much you understand about your family member's mental disorder, and what kinds of help you are seeking. I would appreciate your taking a few minutes to answer some questions. All of your responses will be confidential. The answers that you and other new group members provide will enable me to prepare subject matter most relevant to your needs.

Name: _____   Relationship to Client _____

1. How long has your family member been in treatment at this and other mental health agencies?

   _____ years   _____ months

2. How long has your family member been living with or close by you?

   _____ years   _____ months

3. Clients of mental health agencies are given a diagnosis, which is a professional term used to describe their problem. Are you aware of the diagnosis that your family member has been given?

   _____ yes   _____ no

   If so, what is it? _____

4. Have you ever been invited by your family member's case manager, physician, or other providers to participate in joint meetings?

   _____ yes   _____ no

   If so, please explain the nature of your participation. _____

   _____

5. Is your family member taking any medications as part of the treatment program?

   _____ yes   _____ no

   If so, what kind? _____

   Can you describe what the medication is supposed to do? _____

   _____

6. Is your family member involved with any other social service agencies to get help with his or her problems?

   _____ yes   _____ no

   If so, which ones? _____

   _____

7. Have you heard of any other social service agencies which you would like to learn more about?

_____ yes _____ no

If so, which ones? _____

_____

8. What are some of the main challenges you experience in living with or near your client relative?

a. _____

b. _____

c. _____

d. _____

e. _____

9. In what ways do you hope that the Family Education and Support Group can be of help to you?

a. _____

b. _____

c. _____

d. _____

e. _____

10. Do you have any other questions or comments about the group, the agency, or myself?

_____

_____

_____

_____

_____

_____

_____

_____

_____

_____

APPENDIX D: EVALUATION FORM

The Family Education and Support Group

Member Assessment

Name: _____ Date: _____

In this first series of statements, please assess the independent living skills of your family member with mental illness. Please remember that these can be possessed in degrees and do not necessarily indicate that your family member is living on his or her own at the present time. As you consider each item, use the past month as a time frame in deciding on your response. Circle the response which most closely matches your assessment of each statement as demonstrated by the example.

Example: My family member is a friendly person.

Very Rarely   Rarely   (Occasionally)   Frequently

This respondent feels that the family member is sometimes friendly, but not as friendly as he or she might be. Now, please proceed to complete the scale below, and elaborate on each of your responses in the space beneath each item. My family member with mental illness:

1. Uses money to pay his/her personal expenses in a reasonable way.

    Very Rarely   Rarely   Occasionally   Frequently

    Explain: _____

    _____

    _____

2. Takes care of housekeeping tasks without being reminded.

    Very Rarely   Rarely   Occasionally   Frequently

    Explain: _____

    _____

    _____

3. Maintains an adequately balanced diet.

    Very Rarely   Rarely   Occasionally   Frequently

    Explain: _____

    _____

    _____

4. Arranges for transportation promptly when needed.

   Very Rarely   Rarely   Occasionally   Frequently

   Explain: _____

   _____

   _____

5. Spends time with friends outside the home.

   Very Rarely   Rarely   Occasionally   Frequently

   Explain: _____

   _____

   _____

6. Engages in recreational activity outside the home.

   Very Rarely   Rarely   Occasionally   Frequently

   Explain: _____

   _____

   _____

7. Makes an effort to secure income from a source outside the family.

   Very Rarely   Rarely   Occasionally   Frequently

   Explain: _____

   _____

   _____

8. Keeps his/her clothing clean.

   Very Rarely   Rarely   Occasionally   Frequently

   Explain: _____

   _____

   _____

9. Maintains reasonable expectations of the family for companionship.

   Very Rarely   Rarely   Occasionally   Frequently

   Explain: _____

   _____

   _____

10. Takes the initiative to achieve or maintain a job.

   Very Rarely   Rarely   Occasionally   Frequently

   Explain: _____

   _____

   _____

11. Takes medication as prescribed.

   Very Rarely   Rarely   Occasionally   Frequently

   Explain: _____

   _____

   _____

12. Has a physician whom he/she visits when physically ill.

   Very Rarely   Rarely   Occasionally   Frequently

   Explain: _____

   _____

   _____

13. Purchases his/her own clothing and household supplies.

   Very Rarely   Rarely   Occasionally   Frequently

   Explain: _____

   _____

   _____

14. Meets at least monthly with a mental health counselor or case manager.

   Very Rarely   Rarely   Occasionally   Frequently

   Explain: _____

   _____

   _____

Please turn to the next page

Next, rather than thinking about your family member, please consider your own situation. Listed below is a series of statements reflecting various types of personal relationships and activities. These refer to different ways in which persons may cope with the stresses associated with mental illness in the family. There are no right and wrong answers to these items, since all people cope with stress differently. Next to the statements below, please circle the response which best describes your level of participation. Again, you may elaborate on your responses in the space below each item.

Example: I exercise to work off tension.

(Very Rarely)   Rarely   Occasionally   Frequently

This respondent hardly ever gets exercise, if at all. Please go on now to complete the scale items below.

1. I engage in personal hobbies outside the home.

   Very Rarely   Rarely   Occasionally   Frequently

   Explain: _____

   _____

   _____

2. I participate in at least one community social group.

   Very Rarely   Rarely   Occasionally   Frequently

   Explain: _____

   _____

   _____

3. I have contact with my family member's mental health service provider.

   Very Rarely   Rarely   Occasionally   Frequently

   Explain: _____

   _____

   _____

4. I spend time with my friends for purposes unrelated to my family problems.

   Very Rarely   Rarely   Occasionally   Frequently

   Explain: _____

   _____

   _____

5. I can devote uninterrupted time to my job *or* my own routine daily activities (if unemployed outside the home).

Very Rarely   Rarely   Occasionally   Frequently

Explain: _____

_____

_____

6. I visit a mental health professional for help with my own problems.

Very Rarely   Rarely   Occasionally   Frequently

Explain: _____

_____

_____

I confide in the following people about my family problems:

7. Neighbors

Very Rarely   Rarely   Occasionally   Frequently

Explain: _____

_____

_____

8. Extended family members (aunts, cousins, grandparents, etc.)

Very Rarely   Rarely   Occasionally   Frequently

Explain: _____

_____

_____

9. My physician

Very Rarely   Rarely   Occasionally   Frequently

Explain: _____

_____

_____

10. My pastor

Very Rarely   Rarely   Occasionally   Frequently

Explain: _____

_____

My family member with mental illness is a

_____ Son   _____ Brother

_____ Daughter   _____ Sister

_____ Mother   _____ Spouse

_____ Father   _____ Other (please specify:)

                                       _____

He/she lives in:

_____ My house or apartment

_____ A group home for persons with mental illnesses

_____ An agency-managed or supervised apartment

_____ His or her own house or apartment

_____ Other (please specify:) _____

He/she is now _____ years old and has received services at this and other
mental health agencies or psychiatric hospitals for approximately _____ years.

Other comments? _____

_____

_____

_____

_____

Thank you very much for your cooperation!

15

🌹

The Role of the Facilitator in Support Group Development

As noted in the last chapter, support groups for the families of persons with mental illness have become common in the past twenty years. Serious mental illness affects one in four families (Mermier, 1993), and thus the potential target population for these groups includes perhaps millions of family members. Still, while many persons do participate in support groups, other interested families do not choose to join even after learning of groups being available. Family members are often reluctant to join a support group, and little has been written about the process of leaders effectively *recruiting* members for family groups. In this short chapter I consider, based on one co-leadership experience with two other professionals, what actions by the case manager/leader might encourage family members to join a group. I also expose the reader to another type of family support group. I describe our methods for developing a Siblings and Adult Children (SAC) support group in Richmond, Virginia on behalf of the Virginia Alliance for the Mentally Ill (VAMI). I highlight the role of the facilitator, who was responsible for publicizing the group and recruiting members. That person's series of contacts and supportive relationships with prospective members was crucial in the formation and maintenance of the group.

FAMILY MEMBER RELUCTANCE
TO JOIN SUPPORT GROUPS

Terkelson (1990) describes three historical tensions that make the recruitment of families into professionally-sponsored groups difficult. These include the country's reliance on hospitals as the locus of treatment for mental illness up to the 1970s, the influence of psychoanalytic thought and its blaming of parents for emotional disorders in children, and the policies of deinstitutionalization, in which professionals forced caregiver roles onto families without providing adequate assistance and resources to them.

Though the family advocacy movement has made professionals more sensitive to the needs of families, many families who are not active members of advocacy and self-help organizations remain out of the support mainstream. Newton, Wandersman, and Goldman (1993), for example, compared members and non-members of an AMI group on measures of support group benefit. They found that non-members perceived higher personal risks to group participation and less benefit from the group than AMI members. Also, AMI members with higher levels of organizational affiliation received greater benefits from the group than members with lower levels of such affiliation. Schulze (1994), in a German study of self-help groups for families of persons with schizophrenia, found that degree of family stress was positively associated with the desire to join a support group, but not with ongoing involvement. Further, Hailey, Hewitt, and Staton (1995) compared family members who attended support groups with those who did not, and found that the latter group more often exhibited symptoms of depression. These studies imply that persons who are not affiliated with family organizations are less likely to join or benefit from a support group, and that many families with appropriate needs for education and support are not participating in these groups.

THE SIBLINGS AND
ADULT CHILDREN GROUP

Our group was based in large part on program recommendations from the national SAC network (Dickens 1989a, 1989b). This network, affiliated with NAMI, focuses on the needs of siblings and adult children of clients and on providing support, education, and resources that can enhance their lives. Siblings and adult children tend not to attend general family support groups, which are parent-dominated (Carlisle, 1984). Their needs overlap but are not the same. The unique experiences of these persons include anger, personality development that features a constricted emotional range, guilt about their comparative well-being, grief about lost family solidarity, resentment and jealousy about the attention given the ill relative by others, and social isolation as a result of the family's diminished social network (Bank & Kahn, 1982; Woolis, 1992). They need assistance to deal constructively with these issues, and their needs are sometimes overlooked in general family groups (Carlisle). Our rationale for providing this group was the absence of any other resources in our metropolitan area for the target population.

The Richmond SAC group was a professionally-sponsored endeavor of six months duration, co-led by two graduate-level social work students and me. All of us had experience as case managers in mental health settings. The primary program goal was intentionally general: to offer members support and education for coping with mental illness in the family. We hoped to give family members, many of whom were primary or secondary caregivers of the ill relative, a forum where they felt safe to share feelings and reactions to the relative's symptoms, treatment, and changes in social functioning.

The group philosophy incorporated a partnership model of problem-solving. Family members could identify and sympathize with one another's shared experiences, and as professionals we could offer practical information about specific illnesses and resource information. We routinely shared information about various disorders, treatments, research on the causes of and treatments for mental illness, community resources, and methods for coping with stress. Still, these activities were secondary to the program component of member discussion.

Meetings were held twice monthly for 90 minutes in the early evening at a "neutral" site (one not associated with a mental health treatment facility). We considered this to be important in minimizing any sense of stigma members might feel. The group remained small throughout its duration, with an average attendance of four to six members. After two months a core membership evolved of four persons who attended meetings regularly. One or two new participants attended each session. The setting consisted of a comfortable room with a circle of chairs and light refreshments. Brochures and books about mental illness from the family perspective were displayed at each meeting. We occasionally distributed copies of materials about mental health topics that had been requested by members during a prior meeting. The facilitator (who was chosen for this role because of her access to resources) *heavily* advertised the group by means of newspaper announcements, radio and television interviews for the co-leaders, and flyers to targeted mental health agencies and organizations.

Each meeting began with the introduction of any new members and a review of the group's purpose. Discussion topics were *not* prepared in advance, because members were invited to take, and willingly took, responsibility for initiating topics of immediate concern to themselves. We were initially concerned that participants might feel intimidated by the small group size and the high ratio of leaders to members, but this did not become an issue. New participants almost always talked openly and at great length, expressing their appreciation at experiencing support from others. New members usually began by describing and processing their feelings about their family situations, and then asking more specifically for information about mental illness and treatment resources. As leaders we were most challenged by our responsibility to balance the needs of new members, which primarily centered on support, with those of older members, which gradually became more education-focused. The meetings tended to be *extremely* intense emotionally; members frequently became quite tearful and distressed during a conversation. To us, this was evidence of the need for this group, as the siblings and adult children all reported having few other outlets for their frustrations. If a group member appeared to be in a personal crisis, we made sure that he or she was aware of appropriate counseling services.

THE ROLE OF THE FACILITATOR

Though the SAC group process was interesting in itself, we will focus for the remainder of this chapter on the unique facilitator role, which developed in ways that were unexpected. The co-leader who volunteered to act as the facilitator was in a student field placement at the VAMI agency. She initially assumed responsibility for advertising the group and recruiting members as one of her learning objectives. Prospective members were invited in the program literature to call that office for more information about the group. If they did so, their names and phone numbers were passed on by a receptionist to the facilitator for follow-up. The facilitator then called the prospective members back for a screening contact (only to verify that they were a sibling or adult child of a person with mental illness) and to provide additional information about the group. During these phone exchanges the facilitator noticed that callers were very eager to talk about their problems, and by taking the time to allow conversation, she began building relationships with them. Some of these calls were made from the facilitator's field placement site, but most originated from her home. Most respondents were at work or otherwise unable to talk freely during the day, and the facilitator accommodated their needs with early evening calls.

The process followed a typical pattern. During the first phone contact, the facilitator welcomed the caller and oriented him or her to the format of the group, including its time, date, place, purpose, and number of persons attending. Usually, the caller actively sought this information but was also openly ambivalent about attending the group. In every case the family member admitted feeling stigmatized and never having reached out for help before. Many persons reported not feeling comfortable in making a commitment to any group program. They also used this opportunity to research the background and qualifications of the co-leaders, which was helpful in their eventual decisions about participation. The facilitator asked if the ambivalent caller would mind being kept abreast of the group's development while he or she took more time to think about coming. The caller always accepted this invitation and expressed appreciation for the facilitator's willingness to extend herself. These phone conversations ended with the facilitator asking if she could call again prior to the next meeting.

Thus, as a matter of biweekly routine, the facilitator called each prospective member to remind him or her about the upcoming meeting, to describe how the group was developing in membership and subject matter, and to ask about the caller's problems. The person always responded positively to this opportunity to discuss his or her emotional stresses. The facilitator's personal style of interaction was to say little during the conversation, but she encouraged the caller's venting and provided gentle support. In other words, she engaged in patient, active listening.

These phone conversations were not counseling sessions, as the facilitator was intent only on encouraging the person to process his or her feelings about family problems and the anxieties associated with joining the SAC group. The calls were rather lengthy, however, sometimes lasting thirty minutes. We decided that if the caller was still sincere about possibly joining the group after the second contact, and if he or she seemed to be in a precarious family situation, the facilitator should invite the person to call the VAMI office for referral information if a family crisis developed. No prospective member ever did so, but the gesture was always much appreciated. If a potential group member did call the VAMI office in crisis, he or she would have been referred immediately to an appropriate treatment facility. We wanted the facilitator to make this offer because we found that these siblings and adult children were not adequately, if at all, acquainted with the mental health service system. The facilitator's goal was to maintain a link between the family members and the mental health service system.

Within the framework of symbolic interactionism, prospective group members seemed to need time to develop a definition of the situation that would make their group participation consistent with their perceptions of themselves and their needs. The siblings and adult children needed to come to terms with the *idea* of attending a support group prior to being present in one and then needed to formulate a definition of that situation. Through interacting with the facilitator, they seemed to get a beginning sense of themselves in relation to the other members and co-leaders. It might be an indication of the extent of their social isolation that siblings and adult children required such a lengthy process before deciding that the group situation would help rather than provide additional pain.

A majority of these potential members did eventually join the SAC group. By the time the person actually attended a meeting, the facilitator might have talked with him or her three or four times; she had also provided the other co-leaders with information about the new member's situation and needs. When the person attended a first meeting, the facilitator, who was well-known to the member by that time, greeted him or her and made introductions to the other co-leaders and members. Without fail, the new members showed delight at meeting the facilitator face-to-face for the first time. They felt reassured that they already knew one person in the group. It seemed that they maintained a special relationship with the facilitator from that point on, even though the facilitator was, as a matter of personal style, less verbal in the meetings than the other co-leaders. She was, however, always present to offer resource information and support.

Illustration: Bonnie

Bonnie was an ambivalent caller who eventually became a member of the SAC group. When she first called the VAMI office she was responding not to group publicity, but to the encouragement of her sister, who had sought support from the AMI organization in another state and had recommended that Bonnie do the same. Bonnie first spoke briefly to the VAMI secretary, who wrote down her name and phone number. The facilitator called her within a few days during early evening hours, the time of day when Bonnie had said she had more freedom to talk. She learned that Bonnie was having a difficult time coping with her mother's persistent mental illness. Bonnie was distracted from all of her own occupational and family responsibilities (she was married, had two children, and worked full-time) as she attempted to intervene in her mother's erratic behaviors in another state. The facilitator listened with a supportive ear and offered Bonnie two suggestions. Bonnie could seek out resources for her mother in her mother's home town, and she could also attend the SAC group to see if it might meet her own needs. Bonnie was given basic information about the group, including the time, date, place, and directions, and also a review of topics that seemed most important to the group members at the time. Bonnie said that the idea of a support group was not a comforting one at the moment, as she was so busy, but that she would stay in touch.

Bonnie did call back several times. During the next month she called the VAMI office twice and talked with the facilitator about her mother's recent behaviors that were keeping Bonnie in a state of distress. The facilitator again mentioned joining the support group and told her that the group was processing many of the same situations and feelings that Bonnie seemed to be experiencing. Bonnie said that she was not as uncomfortable now with the idea of attending the group, but that it conflicted with an important weekly social activity. The facilitator called her back one more time to provide a group update. Later that month, Bonnie called to say that she had been thinking about the group and had decided that she could skip at least one of her other activity meetings to attend the next session. That same week, Bonnie attended the SAC group for the first time, and she was extremely active in the discussions. She became quite emotional as she talked, but she also noted repeatedly how good it felt to meet people like herself. Bonnie soon became a "core" member of the group.

SUMMARY

Had it not been for the actions of the facilitator and the evolution of her role, the SAC group would not have survived, because overall response to the advertisements was modest. The process of recruiting members who are uncomfortable with the mental health service system, even with continuous and extensive advertising, is difficult. The evolution of the facilitator's relationships with prospective members was unexpected, but it has important implications for case managers who aspire to conduct groups for family members of persons with mental illness. My primary recommendation is that the leaders of any family education and support group designate a person who carries primary responsibility for *ongoing* outreach to prospective members and also participates in the meetings as a co-leader. More specifically, the facilitator should attend to the following activities:

1. Manage all advertising tasks, serve as the contact person for interested respondents on an ongoing basis, and reserve specific times to call potential members back. This must include evening hours, because many persons can freely talk only then because of job and family responsibilities.

2. Present him or herself as an empathic, patient, supportive individual who is willing to allow prospective members to make decisions at their own pace about joining the group. The example of Bonnie is not unusual. In fact, every person who attended the SAC group did so only after an information-gathering phone call to the facilitator, and only one member ever came to the group after a single call.

   Kathy, another member who needed time to work through her ambivalence, spoke to the facilitator several times, asking for reports on the most recent SAC group discussions as a means of deciding whether her own concerns would be appropriate for it. Andrew, another member, welcomed the facilitator's calls over a one month period. He always updated her on the family's efforts to get his son into treatment, and her affirmation helped him gain confidence that the group participants would not see him as neglectful of his son's needs.

This recommendation that the facilitator be empathic and patient may seem obvious, but it must be emphasized that prospective SAC group members felt vulnerable in reaching out and seemed to feel supported by a co-leader who gave them time, encouraged them to vent, and provided information when asked, but also did not intrude on their ambivalence by taking on a directive role. These listening skills must be developed with practice.

3. Keep a list of all prospective members that includes some basic information about their family situations. These details should include names and addresses, of course, but also information about the caller's primary concerns, the treatment and mental status of the family member with mental illness, the general effects of mental illness on the family, and the most recent events in the family of concern to the caller. The facilitator should compile brief notes in these areas so that he or she will not need to ask the caller, who is often in distress, to repeat information from week to week that has already been given. This information becomes useful to the other co-leaders prior to meeting the participant in the group setting for the first time. The facilitator should always ask the prospective member if such information can be shared with the co-leaders. This request was never denied in our SAC group.

4. Talk regularly with the group leaders, in person and by phone, about how the recruitment process is coming along, and inform them of any new members who may be attending the next meeting.

5. Be knowledgeable about the mental health system in order to make appropriate referrals for callers when necessary. This, of course, is always a primary component of good clinical case management.

Our experience demonstrated that once family members attended the SAC group, they were relieved to meet other persons, often for the first time, who understood their situation and could offer them assistance, support, stress management strategies, and suggestions for adjusting caregiving patterns. The greatest challenge for SAC group leaders might be the facilitation of each member's process of deciding to join the group. Once a member does attend, he or she seems ready to participate in the process without needing nearly as much assistance from the co-leaders.

PART V

Working with Persons Having Mental Illness in Groups

16

❧

Effective Leadership in Treatment Groups

G roup interventions for persons with mental illnesses, such as schizophrenia, bipolar disorder, and major depression, have existed in various formats for many years. These groups tend to address practical issues in
relationships, day-to-day challenges in social functioning, and problems in
coping with symptoms. Treatment groups are often effective in achieving
member goals but, despite frequent discussion in the literature of group formats and outcomes, little attention is paid to the leader *skills* required to facilitate member growth. In this chapter I consider key leadership tasks case
managers face in managing the common challenges of member *heterogeneity,*
relationships between *core* and *new* members, use of *confrontation,* encouragement of member *risk-taking,* and the relative emphasis on *long-term vs. short-
term* member concerns.

Treatment groups for persons with mental illness can be categorized in
several ways. Kahn and Kahn (1992) identify four models:

1. Groups of convenience (for the maintenance of current mental status)

2. Topic-specific groups (designed with specific subject matter, such as medication education)

3. Phase-orientated groups (for clients who face common psychosocial development issues, such as community adjustment following hospital discharge)

4. Eclectic groups (integrating broad themes of human behavior in the promotion of coping and growth over a long term)

Another typology offered by Bond and DeGraaf-Kaser (1990) differentiates groups as follows:

1. Unstructured (open-ended, including broad subject matter)

2. Structured (with education and skill development formats)

3. Experiential in-vivo (self-help and drop-in groups)

4. Structured in-vivo groups (such as supported employment)

Kanas (1986) most succinctly presents a two-group typology:

1. Interaction-oriented groups, which include goals of improving members'
abilities to relate effectively with others, and cope with demands of everyday living, through a focus on interpersonal skill-building and concrete
problem-solving

2. Insight-oriented groups, which consider present behaviors as the result of
interpersonal patterns developed earlier in life, and promote member self-
awareness and growth though reflection on crucial life stages

In this chapter I focus on those groups that are unstructured, eclectic, and
interaction-oriented with respect to the above typologies. These may be open
or closed groups, ongoing or time-limited, and within or outside of residential and hospital settings. They are characterized by a process of verbal interaction facilitated by one or two clinical case managers toward the achievement
of social adaptation goals.

A treatment group, which I co-led and which I will use as a source of illustrations throughout this chapter, was known as the SOS group. The
acronym originally stood for Survivors of Schizophrenia, but in fact the group
was attended by persons with a variety of serious mental disorders. Many participants also had problematic personality traits, substance abuse problems, and
medical problems, matching Kurek-Ovshinsky's (1991) characterization of the
"urban psychiatric population." The SOS group, which met for 18 months,
included two co-leaders, both of us clinical case managers. It was a weekly,
ongoing, open-ended group of one hour duration, held at an urban shelter
and drop-in center for homeless and other low-income adults. Five to ten
persons, with an average age of approximately 40 years, attended the meetings
each week. SOS was developed as an interaction-oriented group with the following member goals:

1. Understanding mental illness

2. Improving the capacity to cope with symptoms

3. Relationship skill building

4. Enhancing self-esteem

5. Mutual support

Members had free choice about participation, and they were given responsibility for setting the discussion agenda. Many members attended the group
regularly for months, tending to terminate only when they left the agency.

RESEARCH ON TREATMENT GROUPS

Though group effectiveness with this population is reported in the literature,
empirical research is somewhat limited. Group therapies tend to be effective in
the rehabilitation of persons with mental illness if they are fairly homogeneous
(comprised of members with similar symptoms or disorders) and if they focus
on a limited range of topics. Scott and Griffith (1982) noted that outcomes
from 10 experimental studies from in- and outpatient settings demonstrated
modest client improvements in social adaptation. Kanas (1986) reviewed 43
studies of in- and outpatient groups dating from the 1950s and found consistent evidence of positive behavioral outcomes. He concluded that interaction-
oriented groups were more effective than insight-oriented groups for persons
with mental illness. Kahn and Kahn (1992) reviewed the group treatment literature more recently and concluded that they were effective as long as leaders
recruited members who shared types of symptoms, level of recovery from the
mental illness, and the ability to process information. Most authors report
groups of 60 minutes duration, with a range of 45 to 90 minutes (Maxmen,
1984; Walker & McLeod, 1982). Less time is said to impede engagement
among thought-disordered members, while longer meetings become draining
for members who have difficulty with sustained social interactions.

Descriptions of effective group goals are consistent. Scott and Griffith (1982) place the interaction-oriented groups on the "concrete" end of their "concrete to abstract" continuum of group therapies. Kanas (1991) summarizes the goals of these groups as improved coping with symptoms and the development of social skills and relationships. Maxmen (1984) highlights the need for leaders to conceptualize mental illness as medical illness in an educational model of intervention. Wilson, Diamond, and Factor (1990) emphasize the importance of a practical orientation to insure that members can apply what they have learned outside the group.

White (1988) suggests that leader goals for members should include reduced social isolation, the acquisition of information about mental illness, ego support, guilt reduction related to perceived deficiencies, and education regarding appropriate expressions of feelings. Walsh (1994c) specifies members' learning to interact assertively with mental health professionals as another important goal. Bond and DeGraaf-Kaser (1990) add the goals of modulating emotionally charged environments and normalizing life experiences. The latter goal involves the leader's promotion of universality or affirming the sense of belonging to a community that is important to all persons (Scott & Griffith, 1982). Some authors speculate that improved medication compliance may be a realistic goal, but this issue is infrequently addressed (Kahn, 1984). Related to interpersonal skill development is the possibility for pairing, or finding within the group a friend with whom one associates outside the group (Bond & DeGraaf-Kaser, 1990; Walsh, 1994c). Noordsy and Fox (1991) use relaxation exercises to assist members in learning to diminish anxiety.

With inpatient facilities rarely used anymore as long-term treatment sites, characteristics of the client population in outpatient groups have changed. Persons with mental illness now more often exhibit substance abuse and physical health problems, and have fewer material support resources. Ely (1985) reports that these multi-challenged clients are frequently manipulative and deceitful, traits that are acquired as coping mechanisms but that alienate many service providers and peers. The dependency needs, despair, and anger of these clients can become difficult countertransference issues for leaders. Kurek-Ovshinsky (1991) adds that "adaptive narcissism"; or the development of a grandiose idea of self to correct one's wounded self-esteem, is also a common client trait. She adds that leaders must resist the temptation to confront this defense too quickly.

Two authors have done content analyses of topics that group members tend to discuss over time. Walsh (1994c) lists these, in order of frequency:

1. Coping with the symptoms of mental illness
2. Coping with secondary depression
3. The use and impact of medications
4. Family relationships
5. Employment
6. Social relationships
7. Managing conflicts with mental health professionals (see Chapter 17 for details)

Kanas, DiLella, and Jones (1984) note, also in order of frequency:

1. The mutual encouragement of contact with others
2. Reality testing
3. Appropriate expressions of emotion
4. Mutual advice-giving

Appropriate roles and activities of leaders are also addressed in the literature. Barr (1986) highlights leader responsibility for providing a sense of safety, stability, and commitment within the group, because these are difficult to establish among members. She adds that leaders must discourage group processing of "mystical," or overly-abstract, explorations of stress and coping issues, because these have limited use in problem-solving. Kanas (1991) lists leader responsibilities for being active, directive, task-oriented, and prepared to give advice and initiate topics. He emphasizes moving gradually from "general" topics to "specific" applications in discussions to minimize the possibility of anxiety-producing intrusiveness with members. Kurek-Ovshinsky (1991) agrees that leaders must respect client reluctance to participate actively, and confront its persistence only if members feel supported within the group. The leader must support all positive member contributions, affirm the members' interests, and promote the sense of universality, individuality, and reality orientation.

Wilson, Diamond, and Factor (1990) state that the leader should be perceived by members as a "three-dimensional figure" for modeling relationships. That is, the worker should be seen as "fallible" but at the same time, as demonstrating positive problem-solving skills. Toward this end a high level of activity and modest amount of self-disclosure may be useful. Bond and DeGraaf-Kaser (1990) emphasize the importance of non–authoritarian leadership. Using co-leaders of each gender is good for balancing issues pertaining to men and women (Walker & McLeod, 1982), and is also helpful in processing members' transference issues (Kahn, 1984).

Treatment groups are often conceptualized as moving through predictable stages as members become cohesive over time. Hepworth, Rooney, and Larsen (1997) identify the stages of pre-affiliation (approach and avoidance), power and control (norm-setting and the establishment of roles), intimacy (an appropriate depth of interaction), differentiation (application of group issues to individual needs), and separation (the termination process). Such process stages have limited applicability for groups with mentally ill members, however. Kurek-Ovshinsky (1991) points out that all groups tend to settle into a stage that parallels the developmental level of the members.

Persons with mental illness in groups often sustain themselves at a pre-affiliation level because of their tenuous attitudes about relationships and their inability to form strong attachments. Leaders should not view group progression as an essential outcome indicator but should tolerate and value a continuous pre-affiliation stage. White (1988) agrees that though some groups might enter into phases of intimacy and differentiation, most will persist at a formative stage. Isbell, Thorne, and Lawler (1992), in a content analysis of a group that met for over two years, noted that growth was very slow. The sense of cohesion and of member independence increased, and the perceived risk of expressing anger decreased. Kanas, DiLella, and Jones (1984) reported increased cohesion and reduced conflict over time, but also noted a persistence of member avoidance, which might represent a protective distancing. Malm (1982), in an experimental study, found modest but significant evidence of increases in member verbal behavior and emotional expression, and a decrease in feeling "unreal" or psychologically detached from others. Walker and McLeod (1982) indicate that groups for persons with mental illness go through only two stages. The first is member testing of the leaders by absences, tardiness, and displays of apparent indifference. Later, if trust develops, members come to identify with the leaders through modeling, demonstrating less preoccupation with symptoms of mental illness, and applying group experiences to community situations.

Beeber (1991) conceptualizes groups as systems, and in his framework members pass through the four stages of focusing on "we-they" boundaries external to the group (displacing conflict and other tensions), internal boundaries (differentiating themselves from leaders), subgroup boundaries (creating alliances among themselves), and, when termination approaches, external boundaries again (taking a sense of shared experience to the outside world). Scapegoating is common as a projective defense; sometimes higher functioning members blame lower functioning persons for retarding their progress. The more fragile members may act out in deviant ways (that is, with active or passive disruption) in response to this. Johnson, Geller, Gordon, and Wexler (1986) emphasize the process of member pairing, which is done in an effort to secure support and protection against anxiety. Such pairing may be functional *or* problematic for the group, depending on its effect on the overall process. Pairing among members tends to occur at all crucial transitional periods, including at the beginning, at times of member conflict with the leader, at the loss of a leader, and at termination.

LEADER SKILLS AND ACTIVITIES

Groups for persons with mental illness can be difficult to lead, but certain skills can help. Such groups typically remain at a pre-affiliation stage for long periods, sometimes permanently. Case managers as leaders will be good treatment partners for members if they can accept the possible inability of the group to cohere, if they are comfortable with ambivalence, and if they can accept some clients as having limited abilities to progress interpersonally.

Groups like SOS that serve clients with cognitive and social skills deficits must incorporate flexibility in content and leadership style to attract and retain participants. Leader roles must range from the non-authoritarian to the highly directive; they can be summarized as *pairs* of qualities along the following continuum:

1. Being nurturing while remaining firm about limits

2. Respecting resistance while encouraging positive member contributions

3. Being able to move from the general to the specific in content

4. Maintaining a safe place for clients to reveal difficulties and request help while challenging them to take risks

5. Injecting humor to offset frequently high levels of member tension

Co-Leadership

Two case managers who can work as complementary partners provide good role models for clients. Modeling the "give and take" of facilitating the group provides a positive learning experience for clients with relationship problems. Co-leaders work best after they have some experience working together, because they must know each other's interpersonal styles and must have sufficient mutual trust to risk sharing their reactions, not only to the group but also to each other. Transference and countertransference issues can become significant impediments to productive intervention in groups, as in any other clinical setting. Co-leader processing sessions of at least twenty minutes, immediately following each meeting, are essential for case managers to process their reactions and devise strategies for addressing them in future meetings. In this way leaders can translate their initially unconscious feelings into ideas for future intervention. The post-group processing time is also valuable for charting topics and themes raised by members from week to week.

Following is the first of several examples drawn from the SOS group described earlier. All of them refer to the experiences of my co-leader and me in that group.

Case Illustration: Barbara

Barbara touched off different reactions in each of us. She was a long-time client, so familiar with procedures that she was a kind of mentor for new clients. She brought this reputation with her to the SOS group and immediately assumed a parental role with other members. I reacted negatively to her behavior, finding her abrasive and being concerned that she would impede others from becoming active in the group. I was also sensitive to the fact that my co-leader and I, new to our roles, needed to develop a style of interaction, and Barbara was disrupting that process by her controlling behaviors. My co-leader, however, knew Barbara from her earlier work at the agency, and felt more positive about her potential to promote the group among clients and to help orient them to it. Each of us helped the other perceive Barbara from a different perspective, and thus we were able to plan for sessions in a way that took advantage of Barbara's strengths as a core member, though we were also aware of her potential to dominate the group. In fact, Barbara was the most consistently present core group member for a full year, and was responsible for much of the group's recruitment and orientation of members. During meetings, however, we confronted her tendencies to parent and sometimes to unduly criticize others. Further, once we became more comfortable with each other as co-leaders we were better able to appreciate Barbara's own needs rather than to see her as a potential threat to our leadership roles.

THE MYTH OF HOMOGENEITY

The literature indicates that groups function best with a homogeneous membership. Still, no two people with the same diagnosis of mental illness are alike, nor do they have the same needs. Case managers must appreciate different manifestations of mental illness among clients in groups and, in fact, must assume that groups will be quite heterogeneous with respect to behaviors and goals. We found that each meeting presented us with a mixture of clients whose personalities, strengths, and deficits were quite different. For example, some clients demonstrated prominent substance abuse as well as mental health concerns, and they intimidated some other members when focusing too much on addiction from a 12-step perspective. We also found that clients with prominent manic symptoms and those with co-existing problematic personality traits were sometimes threatening to clients with schizophrenia who displayed symptoms of withdrawal and apathy. Our efforts to enforce limits with clients who were overly active, verbal or intrusive, and, simultaneously, to nurture the more withdrawn clients' participation, were essential in creating a supportive atmosphere.

Case Illustration: Alyssa

Alyssa was a relatively new member with a complex history of substance abuse and mood disorder. She dominated the proceedings each week, encouraged by the fact that at the time most other members were not talkative. Alyssa also cajoled ambivalent clients into attending the group, and when they came she developed a pattern of speaking for them. She seemed to perceive herself as a group spokesperson, and with her controlling nature she tried to organize the agenda each week, even suggesting tasks for the leaders. This behavior was not symptomatic of her mood disorder, but was rather reflective of her aggressive personality style. We became concerned that she would alienate other members and perhaps drive them away from the group. We found it necessary to confront her intrusiveness, as her behavior seemed otherwise uncontrollable at that time. Eventually Alyssa responded to our direction, which we fortunately never expressed with inappropriate anger (we both struggled with our negative reactions to her). That is, we confronted her quickly rather than waiting until our frustration levels became high. Alyssa was eventually able to concede, to a moderate extent, that she had an important informal leadership role in the group as long as she respected the feelings of other members and the leaders.

RELATIONSHIPS BETWEEN
CORE AND NEW MEMBERS

The open membership policies of groups like SOS have many inherently positive aspects:

1. The assurance of group survival through the influx of new members
2. Persistent norms that are carried forth by core members
3. Informal leadership role availability to all members
4. Member participation in group ownership through the orientation of new members
5. Regular injection of "fresh" discussion content from new members' sharing of concerns

In open groups members and leaders must collaborate to incorporate new members into the group. New members often feel peripheral to the group process, and they might be threatened by its established culture. Core members must adapt to newcomers and take the lead in communicating policies and norms. Groups are characterized by two types of leadership, including task (structuring, directing, controlling, and processing) and expressive leadership (caring, socializing, responding) (Anderson, 1997), and members may assume either type of role.

Leaders are responsible for ensuring that the group responds empathetically to newcomers' situations. If threatened by new members, the core group may display entitlement patterns based on their seniority. The case manager can best manage member transitions by being especially attentive to new members' comments, expressing concern for their problems, and affirming their acceptance. This was a major challenge for us in SOS, as we needed to balance the needs of the core members with the newcomer's need for sufficient time to become oriented to the group. We had to be quite directive at times. In modeling a respect of differences among people, we tried to demonstrate that patience and acceptance are necessary for developing any relationships.

When orienting new members, we asked how they came to the agency, how long they had been coming, where they were from, and how they heard about the group. We elicited core member assistance in drawing new members into this conversation, largely by modeling how to welcome and integrate someone into a group. We also offered concrete suggestions for how to meet new people and suggested that all members practice this skill outside the group. It was important to recognize core members' attempts to help with the orientation process, whether successful or not, through positive feedback. This helped enhance their self-confidence while offering them leadership opportunities.

Case Illustration: Calvin

Calvin, who tended to embark on lengthy monologues about topics that were not usually interesting (or comprehensible) to the group, was present one day when Kris, a female struggling with self-esteem issues, attended for the second time. Calvin began his usual presentation on what had been happening with him and his new job prospects during the previous week. After indulging Calvin's need to be heard and sincerely inquiring about his progress on the job front, we asked him to offer others a chance to speak. Kris was encouraged by another female member (Barbara) to share her concerns with the group. With much trepidation and negative commentary about herself, Kris shared her perception that no one at the agency liked her, and that she wanted to leave. She added that this made her sad and angry. Because Calvin's need to share his own feelings had been met and because he had been reminded of the "give and take" of a group session, he was able to acknowledge Kris's need to be heard and also to support her by asking what would make her happiest in life. Calvin's attention and sincerity gave the mutual aid process a boost, offered him a chance to mentor a new member, and allowed Kris to feel joined with the group.

Subgrouping, which includes pairing, is a natural group process in which two or more members form an alliance as a means of enhancing their sense of safety and support. It can have positive and negative outcomes. The leader's ability to restructure pairs and to rely on "positive pairs" to assist with leadership enhances the group process and challenges members to consider the benefits and drawbacks of pairing. When rigid, counterproductive subgrouping occurs, leaders must pay attention to any sense of entitlement or defensiveness by core members, and defuse this without alienating them. A positive outcome of subgrouping is that members are offered opportunities to have their behavioral styles challenged within a supportive setting. Members can expand their social skills and coping strategies while leaders instruct them in adaptive responses to stressful interpersonal situations, such as meeting new people, adjusting to relationship changes, and tolerating anxiety.

Case Illustration: Jane

Jane, a vocal, occasionally disruptive female, had a tendency to pair with Lenny, a male with similar personality traits. When Kris, a new female with self-esteem problems joined the group, Jane and Lenny paired to challenge Kris about her lack of assertion and motivation. Kris presented herself to the group as disliked by most agency members. After Jane and Lenny failed to convince Kris that she had to look to herself for acceptance before feeling accepted by others, they became frustrated with her. They began ridiculing her and pointing out her inadequacies to the other members. We were unable to enlist another core member to buffer this attack on Kris, since Jane and Lenny were the only core members present that day. We tried to re-pair Jane with the female co-leader to defuse the attack on Kris and to model for the group how positive pairing is more productive than aggression. That is, the female co-leader enlisted Kris in a discussion of how it felt to be the target of aggression. The re-pairing was not successful, due to Kris's transference conflicts with women (she was suspicious of their motives with her). The male co-leader (me) picked up on this dynamic, and he began empathizing with Kris about the difficulty of feeling comfortable in a new environment. Eventually Kris and I connected well enough to demonstrate to the group, including the "negative pair," that aggression was not an appropriate means of dealing with member concerns and that it should not be tolerated.

CONFRONTATION

The fluidity of open-ended membership creates an inherent problem with the frequent occurrence of emotional boundary crossing, or intrusiveness. Persons with mental illness often need protective boundaries to avoid overstimulation. When gentle prods to honor others' needs for boundaries are not recognized, leaders might need to use confrontation. Otherwise, these episodes make members feel vulnerable and reinforce behaviors that have caused some of them to become alienated from peers in the first place. Some consistency in member attendance is desirable so that leaders can establish rapport and assess client personality dynamics before using confrontation. We could not always directly confront potentially damaging interactions among members until they seemed able to tolerate it.

When our nonverbal cues (such as directing eye contact away from the person who was talking excessively or about something inappropriate) failed to reduce a member's intrusive comments, we interrupted with suggestions about how to participate in social groups more constructively. We used examples of how the same issue may have arisen in earlier sessions to highlight that it is common (i. e., universalizing the experience). Our confrontations in fact often involved a universal statement, such as "When people interrupt others repeatedly, they are likely to lose friends," instead of directly attributing a social skill deficit to one member—"Stop interrupting again, Ashley. You do this every week." Comments framed in this way were taken less personally. Universal statements are generally effective in making sensitive issues safer for discussion.

Case Illustration: Ashley

Sometimes confrontation can be done with humor. One day, Ashley repeatedly responded to questions that were directed to one of the men. My co-leader responded, "There's something funny going on here. I'm asking questions to a man, and I keep hearing a woman's voice in response." Ashley, who tended to be abrasive and sensitive to perceived slights, laughed at the comment, apologized for her behavior, and stopped speaking for the other member.

Members can be asked to generate ideas about how the group can communicate in a more supportive, less threatening way. These brainstorming sessions often produce rich discussions that are safe, since each person can learn from the example without being singled out for negative behavior.

SAFETY AND RISK-TAKING

When group members perceive the setting to be safe, as evidenced by the verbal participation of all members and the supportive nature of most interactions, leaders can promote two other themes. The first of these is the importance of addressing one another directly. Members frequently speak to each other through the leaders to protect themselves from the possibility of negative, hurtful responses. Many members have had painful experiences with rejection by family and friends prior to reaching the group. Also, many of the clients at our agency were or had been homeless, and fears of interpersonal closeness, along with the prospect of additional professional relationships, was daunting. Our approach was subtle at first in directing members to speak to one another ("Will you say that to John now?"). After several prompting requests, we directed members more firmly to speak to the person with whom they wished to communicate ("Don't talk to me when your message is for John. He's right next to you."). Leaders must not take for granted the trepidation members feel when they are first asked to communicate directly. Explicit verbal praise is essential to building member esteem and confidence to take that risk.

The second theme involves members' practicing skills from the group in the real world. Helping members make the group process transcend the group itself is an important task for leaders. We found that routinely reinforcing member contributions, affirming member strengths among their peers, and encouraging members to use relationships outside the group to practice what we had discussed facilitated their abilities to cope with some activities of daily living. The group setting was structured to be a safe place where members could confront skill deficits that impeded their social relationships, could accept the need to improve their ability to function socially, and could acquire skills for taking on or maintaining social roles (e.g., spouse or partner, co-worker, consumer of services, or friend). Practicing new skills in a group can be daunting for persons who suffer from cognitive and social deficits, and employing them in society can be even more intimidating. Often, members do not make the connection that the group experience is a rehearsal for work to be carried out alone in the social world. This transfer of skills might be prescribed as "homework" by the leaders and might be raised as an item for review at subsequent group meetings.

Case Illustration: Abigail

Abigail experienced recurrent psychotic symptoms, and additionally she had a passive personality. She was quick to anger when feeling slighted but rarely asserted herself. Abigail had been homeless for much of the previous seven years but had recently gotten an efficiency apartment through the city's housing authority. She was concerned that her landlord was not attending to basic apartment upkeep, but rather than approach him about this she vented her anger, with much emotion, in the SOS group. Other members, partly because they identified closely with her in this situation, strongly encouraged Abigail to bring her concerns to the landlord's attention rather than to abruptly break the lease, which she was considering. The co-leaders devised role plays in which Abigail practiced confronting the landlord. Abigail appeared to learn new social skills in this process, but she still could not follow though with her stated plan. We had to be careful not to push Abigail or to let other members be critical of her inactivity, as this would deflate her self-esteem and perhaps drive her from the group. We hoped that she would eventually learn to express her needs more clearly to others (not only to the landlord). We began to point out to Abigail instances in which group members behaved directly but respectfully with each other. Almost five months later, Abigail sought out her landlord to express her need for a more efficient water heater.

TASK VERSUS LONGER-TERM ISSUES

Short-term therapeutic tasks, like problem solving and esteem building, were more often the focus of our group agenda than were longer-term, insight-oriented work. We considered integrating more content on such topics as the meanings clients ascribe to mental illness in their lives, but shifts in membership and frequent crises precluded sufficient time for addressing sensitive issues. It is difficult in a short period of time (because many members came and went within several weeks) to address adequately the cognitive and emotional assets clients have for integrating this kind of material. Some members were able to share intimate details about how their illness affected their self-concept, social functioning, and motivation for change, but these topics intimidated others who were not ready to delve into the emotional content of their illness. Encouraging member disclosure did foster some instances when they risked sharing feelings about medication compliance, their diminished capacity to function in social roles, and the chronicity of their illness. We tried to gauge members' readiness to receive information from us about chronic mental illness and the correct timing for eliciting their sharing of emotional experiences related to it. But again, the needs of the members kept us focused more squarely on concrete problem solving, reinforcing the appropriateness of interaction vs. insight-oriented groups.

Case Illustration: Billy

Billy, a male who attended group one day with Amy, a female friend from the agency, acted as if it was the last place on earth he wanted to be. He said he had come only to keep his friend company. Amy was very vocal, reacting with annoyance to most members' comments. She took informal control of the group agenda, alienating others into silence. Billy sat by and did not seem to mind her dominating the group (or him).

A long-time core member, Zack, was encouraged to talk with Amy about his experience with medication because she was lecturing the group about how she was forced to take medications in the hospital and how they were bad for you, and used primarily for control. Zack, in his typical calm and straight-forward manner, told Amy how he had taken injections for many years, because previously he had refused to stay on oral medications and as a result was repeatedly hospitalized. Amy was not patient with Zack's account, and she began attacking him while repeating her negative beliefs about medications. Zack was not deterred by Amy's negative reactions, and he continued to say that he was glad he had gotten on the injection schedule so he could stay well. Billy chimed in at this point, surprising us all (including Amy), and eloquently explained that he, too, took injections because he had been noncompliant with his medications in the past. He said that he came to hate the revolving door of the hospital and being so out of control. He could remember how bad off he had been without the medications, and that he had come to a decision to stay well. He shared his amazement that it had taken him so long to understand the now-obvious point that he was better off with medication. Zack shook his head in quiet agreement and then said, "You're right, man."

Zack's ability to educate the group and his willingness to participate in this role were essential to this interaction. And our ability to assess Amy's tolerance for receiving emotional content facilitated a positive sharing experience for her, for Zack, for the rest of the group, and for ourselves. Billy's quietly powerful contribution was an added pleasure.

SUMMARY

Treatment groups for persons with mental illness, focusing on symptom management, social skill building, and education, can serve as excellent components of a clinical case management plan. They can enhance the treatment by providing regular interpersonal experiences for members who might otherwise lead isolated lives. Case managers who lead such groups and who can draw from a continuum of leadership skills might be excellent treatment partners for this population who benefit from learning and rehearsing social skills that might be generalized to a variety of interpersonal situations. Honoring the maxim of "starting where the client is," even if that means tolerating a continuous pre-affiliation stage of the group, might inspire member trust and confidence and might ultimately promote at least modest growth.

17

Cℒ

Facilitating Self-Help Groups

In the previous chapter we considered clinical case manager skills for leading education, therapy, and support groups. In this chapter we look at another possible case manager role in groups, that of facilitator. Clients sometimes pursue self-help strategies in groups that have the same purposes, goals, and organization as those described in Chapter 16. In such groups one or several clients assume primary leadership, and the case manager might participate in a supportive role. He or she might attend all or most meetings and contribute skills that complement those of the client leaders. The case manager's supportive roles might include helping with the physical organization of the group (securing a room, resources, supplies, etc.), orienting new members, bringing educational material (handouts, videos, etc.), monitoring the group process to insure that all members feel included, and helping to diffuse some tensions that may arise.

Facilitation is an increasingly important role for case managers in self-help groups. In recent years, clients have taken more initiatives through advocacy organizations, and they are being encouraged by agencies that promote empowerment to organize and lead groups that address their particular needs. In fact, clients in some cases have moved beyond group leadership to manage a variety of self-help services including small businesses, mutual support services, and drop-in centers (Boyd, 1997). Still, mental health professionals often have important skills, developed through practice, to contribute to these groups. No one knows better than clients themselves about their own needs, but the case manager may have organizational skills and community contacts that are helpful in group development and sustenance. In this chapter, I describe a process for case manager facilitation through an example of a successful self-help group in which I participated. I describe the types of issues that arose in this group and how my activities contributed to the process.

FACTORS CONTRIBUTING
TO THE SUCCESS OF SELF-HELP GROUPS

Wilson (1989) has compiled a list of factors that usually characterize successful *and* unsuccessful self-help groups. Some of these relate to the role of the professional supporter.

Characteristics of Successful New Groups

1. A *serious* problem is the basis for the group.
2. "Veterans" with the problem are motivated to help people newer to the problem.
3. There is a committed "core" membership.
4. At least one originating member is a charismatic individual but does *not* dominate the group.

5. Immediate opportunities exist for members to be helpers.

6. Sensitive professional group support is available.

7. Practical resources (written information, videos, speakers) are available that are relevant to group themes.

8. The meeting room is comfortable and accessible.

9. Meetings are regularly scheduled.

10. The group is affiliated with a local or national organization.

11. Printed material about the group is made available for distribution.

Characteristics of Unsuccessful New Groups

1. The key initiators are *too close* to their problem—that is, they cannot maintain objectivity about the concerns of others.

2. The group development plan is overly-ambitious.

3. Key organizing members are unsympathetic toward other members or are dominating.

4. The group initiators function erratically.

5. There is no nucleus of committed members.

6. The group begins with a small number of members.

7. There is a lack of awareness of the need to involve all members immediately.

8. Group meetings lack structure.

9. The size, location, and accessibility of the meeting facility is unsuitable.

10. Professionals have too much control.

11. There is a lack of publicity or printed materials about the group.

Desired Characteristics of a Professional Facilitator

1. Substantial time is allocated to the group for organization and planning (several hours per week).

2. He or she has a warm, outgoing personality.

3. The facilitator is capable of being informal.

4. He or she is willing to let the group develop on its own.

5. The facilitator genuinely desires to be a supporter rather than a leader.

6. The facilitator is committed to being permanently linked with the group.

7. He or she has experience in working with persons who have the problem.

8. The facilitator can locate and use (as needed) material resources within his or her own place of employment for the group.

9. The facilitator recognizes the leadership potential in lay persons.

Having reviewed these characteristics, we can now consider how they played out in one self-help group, and in the process we can become familiar with another program in which case managers might like to participate.

SCHIZOPHRENICS ANONYMOUS: AN INTRODUCTION

Schizophrenics Anonymous (SA) is a self-help group for persons who have schizophrenia or a related illness. It was founded in the Detroit area in 1985 by a woman with schizophrenia in conjunction with the Mental Health Association in Michigan. At present, more than 75 Schizophrenics Anonymous groups are operating in the United States and four other countries, and all are led by persons with a schizophrenia-related illness. The official SA statement of purpose is as follows (Mental Health Association of Michigan, 1992):

1. To help restore dignity and sense of purpose for persons who are working for recovery from schizophrenia or related disorders
2. To offer fellowship, positive support, and companionship in order to achieve good mental health
3. To improve our attitudes about our lives and our illness
4. To provide members with the latest information regarding schizophrenia
5. To encourage members to take positive steps leading to recovery from the illness

Schizophrenics Anonymous is a recovery-oriented group with six steps. The group that I facilitated deleted the sixth step because it referred to "God" and some members were uncomfortable with the reference to religion. The five remaining steps are as follows:

1. I Surrender ... I admit I need help. I can't do it alone.
2. I Choose ... I choose to be well. I take full responsibility for my choices and realize that the choices I make directly influence the quality of my days.
3. I Believe ... I now come to believe that I have great inner resources and I will try to use these resources to help myself and others.
4. I Forgive ... I forgive myself for all the mistakes I have made. I also forgive and release everyone who has injured or harmed me in any way.
5. I Understand ... I now realize that erroneous, self-defeating thinking contributes to my problems, unhappiness, failures, and fears. I am ready to have my belief system altered so my life can be transformed.

The SA group described in this chapter covered a 20-month period when I served as facilitator. Katz (1993) describes features common to all "step" programs but admits that his schema represents an ideal type with much potential variability. SA is similar to other step programs in its non-political nature and promotion of lifelong membership. Unlike some groups it maintained a non-ideological status with regard to spirituality. Nor did it promote a norm of helplessness, but encouraged members' development of strength through mutual support and learning.

GROUP ORGANIZATION

This Schizophrenics Anonymous group was developed in Franklin County, Ohio, through the efforts of the Mental Health Association (MHA). The director received written information about SA from the Michigan association and, in the spring of 1991 decided to assess the need for a local group. The MHA program coordinator met with staff and client representatives from the county's community mental health centers and determined that there was sufficient interest among these actors to develop such a program. Nothing similar to SA was in operation at the time. The Mental Health Association, it should be stressed, had a history of working with the comprehensive centers in joint sponsorship of consumer groups. During this needs assessment, the MHA program coordinator learned of my background in working with persons with serious mental illness and their families and invited my participation.

The issue of mental health professionals' involvement in consumer-oriented groups is controversial. Katz (1993) recognizes a philosophical difference between consumers and professionals, noting that professionals have tended to downplay the need for *community* in the lives of consumers. Kaufman, Freund, and Witson (1989) write that professionals sometimes are suspicious of self-help groups as encouraging non-compliance with formal treatment systems. Further, group members tend to assign leadership roles to professionals participating in groups and to direct the bulk of their attention to them. Some authors express more optimism about client/professional collaboration and see a new type of "human services specialist" emerging from the partnership (Mowrer, 1984).

The Mental Health Association, while aware of the potential problems with such arrangements, had already involved professionals in its "Families in Touch" support groups for the following four reasons:

1. Agency and professional staff participation gave an important sense of credibility to the groups, both to referral sources (many of whom were staff working in the agencies) and participants, who at least initially expressed a sense of security from staff presence.

2. The professional facilitator always took responsibility for securing meeting space at no cost to the Mental Health Association.

3. Professionals provided expertise in promoting positive group interaction.

4. Professionals accessed educational resources as requested for distribution to group participants.

The MHA did attempt to limit the role of the professionals, who were in fact adjunctive to the designated group leaders, through careful orientation and quarterly facilitator meetings.

The MHA recruited an SA group leader at the same time the facilitator was chosen. The association employed volunteers with mental illness, and one employee suggested a male friend with schizophrenia, Larry, to the program director. He already led a recovery group, which provided support to persons with a broader range of mental health concerns (Low, 1978), and he had appeared on a radio show with the MHA board president about schizophrenia. After initial reluctance, based on his suspicion that the self-help program might be stigmatizing and professionally controlled, Larry studied the program materials, saw the group philosophy as worthwhile, and agreed to serve as leader.

The Mental Health Association staff conducted several planning meetings with the group leader and facilitator, and a start date was set. The facilitator secured meeting space for the SA group at a church located on a major street and bus line. The MHA preferred the use of "neutral" sites (having no association with mental health treatment facilities) for its groups to help participants avoid feeling stigmatized. Obtaining space at no cost was not an easy task, because many associations, even churches, charged fees for the use of space. The organizers agreed that weekly meetings would make the program readily available to interested persons and would help in developing a group identity among regular participants. It was decided that the group would meet from 5:30 – 7:00 P.M. on Mondays so that persons with daytime commitments could attend SA and still finish early enough to secure safe public transportation home. The ninety-minute meeting length was selected based on the previous group experiences of both the leader and facilitator. It seemed to represent an appropriate time frame for persons with serious mental illness who are limited in their tolerance of structured interactions and in their ability to concentrate. The organizers agreed that the meeting length could be adjusted in the future depending on its suitability. No fees or preregistration were required. The Mental Health Association took responsibility for group publicity. Interested persons were directed to call the professional facilitator or MHA program coordinator for details. The group leader's name and phone number were not included in publications because of the risk of prank phone calls and loss of privacy. Unfortunately, such incidents had happened in his role as leader of the recovery group; this seems to be a problem for persons who self-identify as having mental illness.

FORMAT OF MEETINGS

The *Schizophrenics Anonymous Group Leader's Manual* (Mental Health Association in Michigan, 1991) included a recommended meeting format that was followed closely, but not precisely, by the leader of our program. Group participants gathered in the designated church meeting room and sat on folding chairs in a circle around two or three tables. The leader promptly called the meeting to order, conducted a one-minute moment of silence, and then read a one-page inspirational narrative from the book *Daily Affirmations* (Lerner, 1985), originally written for Adult Children of Alcoholics. The affirmation was not always chosen for the specific date of the meeting, but for its relevance to the group or to a particular member on that day. Any references to alcohol or God as a specific being were omitted from the reading. Next, the leader asked participants to introduce themselves by first name and diagnosis. Once this was done, he asked if there were any announcements. I usually contributed these as the professional facilitator. I distributed educational resource handouts to members, informed them of any upcoming MHA or related community activities, and updated the group about any temporary changes planned in the meeting schedule (I was in regular contact with the church administrators to make sure that the meeting arrangements were secure). Some participants also shared information about upcoming consumer events being sponsored in their treatment centers or neighborhoods.

Finally, to end this formal portion of the meeting, the leader selected several readings from the SA program manual, including stories of founding group members who had benefited from program participation. Each member read one paragraph from a selection and then passed the manual to the person sitting next to him or her. No one was required to read if he or she did not wish to (and this was common). The readings always concluded with the SA *Steps for Recovery* and *Guiding Principles.* This portion of the meeting lasted approximately twenty minutes, and the remainder of the meeting was reserved for member sharing. Though the beginning portion sometimes seemed tedious and repetitious to me, group members consistently stated that it helped them prepare for the sharing process which followed. Shared discussion was the essence of this group, as Wetzel (1991) also found in a support group for persons with bipolar disorder. The meeting concluded with the Serenity Prayer recited by members standing in a circle with hands joined together.

ATTENDANCE

During the first two months, few persons attended the SA meetings, but through advertising and word of mouth attendance gradually improved. During an 18-month span, the group averaged 9 participants per week, not including me (I attended 67 of a possible 74 meetings). Approximately two-thirds of the members who stated a diagnosis reported that they had schizophrenia, and the remaining one-third experienced schizo-affective or bipolar disorder. Some participants declined to state a diagnosis or were not sure of it. Thirty participants (65%) were male, and sixteen (35%) were female. Forty-two members (91%) were Caucasian; four (9%) were African-American. There were six members (13%) who participated in at least 75% of the meetings. Eight persons (17%) attended only one group.

Schizophrenics Anonymous participants shared many reasons for attending the self-help program, and it was not intended that the group become a permanent part of each person's life. For the core members it may have been such, but for many persons SA seems to be an important source of support for a limited time span. Ten persons (22%) attended at least 50% of the meetings, with time intervals ranging from 12 to 56 weeks. That is, they were regular participants for limited time periods, eventually terminating their involvement for a variety of reasons. Other persons, of course, had limited involvement for reasons not made clear to the leader or facilitator.

A final pertinent note about attendance regards the group policy on "visitors." This issue was not addressed until I received the first of many requests from students and professionals to attend meetings as observers, generally for purposes of completing school assignments or getting exposure to a group process. The members unanimously decided to oppose anyone attending the group who did not have a mental illness. One evening, a nursing student appeared without notice and was very sternly asked to leave by several members of the group. Clearly, the SA members considered that the group was theirs alone and tolerated no violations of this source of support and privacy. The group did host two visitors from another county who were preparing to start an SA group of their own. Still, the members made clear that no professionals from that location should attend the meeting.

MEMBER-SHARING PRACTICES

The leader began the member-sharing part of the meeting by outlining a few rules of procedure. "Now we have come to the part of the meeting where each of us can share with the group how our week has gone, what is on our minds today, how we are dealing with our symptoms, and what step we are working on. Everyone will get a chance to share, and please remember not to interrupt anyone who is speaking. When it is your turn, please make clear whether you want feedback from the group or just want a chance to talk. Also keep in mind that anything is permissible to talk about except sex, politics, or specific religious issues. Who would like to begin?"

Two important characteristics of the SA group are revealed from the content of the leader's introduction. First, while SA was considered to be a "step" program, it was so in a "looser" sense than, for example, Alcoholics Anonymous. There was no expectation that members work through the steps systematically or that they be addressed at all. Instead, the steps served as an organizing framework for members when sharing their personal material. For example, one member stated, "I'm working on Step Four (I Forgive) this week because I've been too critical of myself for not concentrating better at my volunteer job." That same member worked on Step Two (I Choose) the following week, stating, "I've been thinking about how I can try harder to be calm with my family instead of relying on the medication to take care of my nerves."

That member focused on Step One the next week because it applied most directly to her life at the time. Members were not expected to progress through the steps in order, or to spend a particular amount of time on a single step. In fact, participants referred to the steps only about half the time during member-sharing. Many members shared their concerns without framing them in the context of a step.

Second, discussions about religion, except in a broad sense of spirituality, were discouraged and even terminated by the leader or facilitator when they occurred. Sometimes persons with strong religious preoccupations based all of their sharing on these ideas and attempted to dominate discussions by preaching their religious beliefs to others. This was rarely appreciated by the larger group and was cited on several occasions as reasons why a member stopped attending the meetings. Typically one or more group members reacted negatively if a member persisted in presenting specific religious themes. Participants were encouraged to recognize their spirituality as it pertains to finding or creating meaning, or a "higher purpose" in their lives, that went beyond a preoccupation with the self. In many cases these commitments involved religious attachments (see Chapter 11). But there was a diversity of spiritual orientation among members, ranging from secularism to mystical religious fanaticism, and the leader found that group cohesion was best maintained when dogmatism of any type was prohibited.

There was, in fact, opposition to reading Step Six, which refers to "God, as I understand Him" during the meetings. Several members wanted to avoid the concept of God altogether, and others objected to God being referred to as a masculine being. As noted earlier, this step was deleted from the meetings following the facilitator's suggestion. Others chose not to recite the first line of the Serenity Prayer, which also includes a reference to God. The group leader was consistent in handling this relatively minor but persistent controversy within the group. He maintained that no one need accept the original religious framework of SA.

The member-sharing portion of the meeting was constant over the 20 months. One by one, in random order, members volunteered to talk about their recent challenges. Because the SA group was 90 minutes long and consisted of 9–11 people on average, each person shared material for approximately 5–10 minutes. If a member was experiencing a particularly difficult time, he or she might share and receive feedback for up to 15 minutes. The group leader ensured that each member was given a chance to talk, and it became my role as facilitator to set limits if a member monopolized the time to present information or give feedback. Individuals were formally invited to speak only if the meeting was drawing to a close and they had not yet participated. Members generally invited feedback after sharing, but the leader made clear that if a person wished to talk without comment from others (an option frequently chosen by those who were sensitive to the impressions of others), this was permissible. Katz (1993) has also highlighted that emotional disclosure is a supportive exercise even without feedback. New members were encouraged not to share at a meeting until they first observed several others in the process, so that they could be oriented to the group's norms.

Roles of the Leader and Facilitator

Larry was very much perceived as being in charge of the group by all members. He earned their respect as a person with schizophrenia who functioned with effective leadership qualities. He shared his own problems regarding symptoms and social functioning that, while frequent, did not impede his ability to lead. Larry never missed a meeting except for occasional planned absences. He was consistently sensitive to group interaction processes and, though never dominant, was supportive or firm as required. Some key personal qualities he brought to the group were gentleness, a sense of humor, and a promotion of self-acceptance. He diffused any negative confrontations that arose, and thus the group could be characterized as orderly, calm, and positive. Because all groups take on the personalities of their leaders, this might have been a different type of group (not necessarily better or worse) with different leadership.

In contrast, I was intentionally less verbal, seeing the monitoring of group process issues as a major aspect of my role. I ensured that all members were included in discussions, that no single person dominated, and that any members in distress received sufficient attention and support. Overall, I was as talkative as the average participant. I did attempt to draw out withdrawn members and to limit the input of some domineering participants. I was most active when a member became highly distressed, which was frequent; then I attempted to bring support and stability to that person within a crisis intervention framework. I seemed to gain acceptance from the group members because of my original membership, lengthy tenure, support of the process as developed by the leader and core members, and encouragement of members to use resources from everyday life in solving problems rather than to rely on formal services.

Common Topics in Member Sharing

The group's nine primary discussion topics are listed below in order of their frequency of presentation, based on a content analysis of session summaries that I kept over a three-month period.

Coping with the symptoms of mental illness. This was *the* major group theme. Most participants struggled with the active or residual symptoms of their disorders every day. Members disclosed their difficulties in managing symptoms as they attempted to live normally, and they frequently checked out the reality of their perceptions with others. For example, one member believed that her daily activities were evaluated each evening by the local television newscasters, and she regularly asked members for their opinions as to whether this could really be happening.

Sharing about the previous week's activities. Most participants enjoyed updating the group on what they had been doing in their daily lives to maintain a healthy structure, with no request for feedback or assumption that anything was problematic. Talking about everyday activities with the group was highly affirmative for some participants, and it promoted a spirit of fellowship. Members reported on a range of activities, from success in quitting smoking to how they were raising their children. It is important to remember that SA was not merely a forum for addressing problems, but also for supporting one another.

Coping with depression. Persons with mental illness frequently become depressed (when they do not have a primary depressive illness) in response to the overwhelming difficulties in managing mental illness daily. As one member stated, "We get depressed because we cannot do so much of what other people take for granted." This depression does not indicate an additional mental disorder; in fact, it represents an existential struggle at times. It can become serious enough to produce suicidal thinking. Even members who coped well with mental illness became depressed and needed assistance in working through these episodes.

The actions and side effects of medications. Almost all members used psychotropic medications, and in sharing this characteristic they were eager to learn from each other about the relative effectiveness and side-effects of various medications. Side effects were major concerns to all persons attending SA, and occasionally members shared that they had stopped taking medications for this reason. The leader and most group members usually viewed this as an undesirable alternative and encouraged the individual to review the matter with his or her doctor and others in the support system.

Family relationships. Persons with mental illness often have conflicted relationships with some family members, and they benefit from processing those relationships. Members most frequently raised family issues when they were planning to spend time with relatives and then followed up with the group about how the visit went once it was over. Participants not only discussed tensions but also shared the positive experiences they had with their families.

Vocational concerns. Risk-taking in jobs, volunteer programs, and school programs represented a major adjustment for persons in the group. Members wondered how much they could trust new associates, how much to disclose about their limitations, and how to cope with new stress situations. SA members frequently began new jobs and school programs and updated the group on a regular basis about their relative success in those pursuits. Those with prior experience in vocational situations were particularly helpful in giving feedback.

Educational topics. Members routinely raised questions about mental disorders and their treatment. One of my primary roles as facilitator was to respond to these questions by presenting or bringing written information for distribution. My handouts included newspaper and magazine articles, Mental Health Association brochures, books, and information about upcoming conferences. Group members also contributed resources and requested that I copy and distribute them. One member shared a booklet with facts about tardive dyskinesia that proved particularly valuable to the membership. Some materials were controversial such as those about the use of mega-vitamin therapy as a primary treatment for schizophrenia. Most group members were committed to conventional treatment modalities, and they encouraged balanced discussions of these issues.

Other social relationships. As members attempted to broaden their social contacts, they came into contact with an increasing number of persons who did not have mental illness and who often felt some initial anxiety in managing those relationships. They sought support from the group in relationship building and in dealing with stigma. Persons with mental illness are very sensitive to how they are viewed by others, and they tend to pick up on both verbal and non-verbal reactions.

Dealing with mental health professionals. Even when relationships with providers were positive, members were sometimes at odds with certain intervention strategies used by their doctors or case managers. Members sought advice in how to address disagreements with professionals, whom they perceived as being more powerful in the relationship. Members did not perceive me as "representative" of professionals; and, in fact, I was not any more involved in these discussions than any others. Still, when speaking about this issue within the group, I felt a strong need to be "neutral," not appearing to defend or attack the professionals being discussed. It was a positive measure of my integration into the group that I was not seen as an outsider at these times.

This SA chapter evolved into a talk-oriented group with occasional social outings (which I did not attend) rather than an activity-oriented group. This was partly because of the nature of the program and also because of the preferences of the leader, facilitator, and core members. The program seemed most suitable to persons who had at least average verbal skills, some consistency in mental status (not necessarily at a stable level) over time, an ability to tolerate interpersonal interaction without overwhelming anxiety, and conventional views about treatments for mental illness. Types of persons who did not feel as satisfied with the SA group included those who were not verbally skilled and thus who might feel more comfortable with an activity-based group, those who became highly anxious sitting with a group of people for 90 minutes (although members routinely took individual breaks), those who experienced high and ongoing levels of symptoms that impaired their ability to concentrate, those who wanted to promote religious or political agendas, and those who were attracted to unconventional treatments for mental illness (for which little support was evident).

Group Process Themes

In addition to the topics discussed at the SA group, there were also member interaction themes that were identified in the content analysis:

Support and affirmation. This was described in the previous "topics" section.

Direct advice. When members had particular difficulty with symptoms, moods, medications, or various interpersonal issues, and when they experienced high levels of anxiety contributing to ambivalence and impaired judgment, others in the group were more apt to give direct advice than general support. Advice was generally geared toward the participants' recognition and use of their support resources. An example was the member who stated that he had stopped taking medications because of troublesome adverse effects. Other participants directed that person to consult with his doctor, family, and best friends before committing to such a risky decision. The member was not asked outright to take the medication, but was directed to seek the advice of these others in considering alternative interventions.

Provision of friendship. The members established a practice very early of visiting an ice cream parlor located one block from the meeting site for a social hour following each session. Rarely did a member decline to attend. One member hosted a well-attended Christmas party for the group. In addition, no fewer than nine members reported developing new friendships that persisted outside the group. The members did not, however, organize outings on a regular basis as an adjunct to the basic meeting schedule. One problem with the development of close relationships was that new members sometimes felt on the fringe of the group, despite the efforts of the leader and facilitator to make them comfortable.

Though accepted as a group member, I rarely attended its social outings. I could not go out for ice cream with the members because of other job responsibilities, but I would not have done so in any event. I limited my role to group facilitation, and the outings were based on friendship building. Thus I maintained some boundaries between myself and the members. I did attend the annual holiday parties and a going-away party given in my honor by the members when I had to leave the group.

MEMBER REACTIONS TO
SCHIZOPHRENICS ANONYMOUS

Near the end of my 20 months of facilitation, I surveyed twelve SA members about their experiences within the group. I asked why they attended the group, what they did or did not get from the group with respect to their needs, and how they observed others interacting in the setting. Responses varied, but they fell into the three categories listed below. This was not a systematic survey, but it does help to illustrate member experiences in their own words.

Positive Comments

"I found friends with similar problems. It helps to know I'm not the only one."
"It helps me to lay out what I go through."

"I've made two or three new friends that I see outside the group."

"It's my friends."

"I get friendship and support when I'm down. A sense of belonging to an organization that is growing and thriving."

"People get a fair hearing for their delusions."

"People can freely talk about their theories of how to deal with schizophrenia."

"They get support through their hard times, even outside of group time, with phone calls."

"I like the Step approach."

"It's easier to talk there. It's hard to talk to people outside the group who haven't experienced delusions and hallucinations."

"I receive camaraderie with the group."

"Helping others gives me satisfaction."

"I enjoy seeing other people come out of their shells."

"The book helps a lot."

"It's a good outlet for meeting people."

"I identify with people who share my problems."

Negative Comments

"I feel like certain people attack me when I'm there."

"I feel uncomfortable with Larry (the leader)."

"When somebody talks too much it makes me not want to come back."

"People there are too judgmental and don't have much empathy."

"The people don't want to confront the agencies about their inadequate services."

"I don't know......... ... I just don't like it."

Expressed Problems with
Group Organization and Philosophy

"I'd like to come, but I'm afraid that whenever I go outside my body will fall apart." (Symptoms prevented the individual from getting to the meetings.)

"Spirituality is not really promoted."

"Some people don't like to admit to having a disease." (Participants were not required to admit to having a disease, but most members did so, which established a group norm.)

"I belong to a different age group, so I don't feel comfortable," (55-year old woman; the average age of this group's members was 40–45 years old)

"I don't always come because I can't get a ride."

"Some people who are lower-functioning don't get as much out of it because it's hard for them to relate to other people." (This was a highly verbal group.)

"I've noticed some people who quit because they can't talk about politics."

"Some people don't seem to be able to sit still." (symptom management during the meetings)

SUMMARY

The Schizophrenics Anonymous self-help group was a beneficial experience for most of its participants. Using Borkman's (1984) framework, it provided a new source of social support for members and decreased their reliance on elements of the outside social network that were characterized by stigmatization and conflicted relationships. From the symbolic interactionist perspective, SA helped participants establish new identities that reflected their value as contributing members of a social group. They could define themselves in terms of *strengths,* which was often difficult to do elsewhere in their social networks. It changed members' perspectives of their overall support networks in a positive sense.

Still, SA represented only one of many types of support experiences which could provide help to persons with mental illness. Forty-six persons attended this particular group, but there were more than 4500 persons in the county with serious mental illness who received assistance each year from public mental health agencies (Franklin County ADAMH Board, 1992). These 46 persons, however, did not previously participate in any other type of self-help group. Further, this first area SA group fostered the development of two additional groups within one year. One was located in another area of the county, and the other was in a city 50 miles away. Persons with mental illness can have their needs met in many ways, and Schizophrenics Anonymous provided one useful resource for them.

Though the client leader was able to manage the group on his own, my activities as facilitator were crucial throughout. I secured space, maintained a relationship with the church administrators who hosted the group, assisted with publicity, gathered material resources almost weekly, recruited members from among the case managers in my agency and others, oriented prospective members by talking with them on the phone about the group, and mediated serious conflicts that occurred among members. Just as important, I was an active member of the group who was committed to its format and purpose. The regularity of my attendance and steady participation earned me the respect of the members.

Epilogue

One Tuesday afternoon during the time I was writing this book, I had experiences with two clients at my agency that together sum up a major theme in my clinical case management career. These sessions, which had quite different outcomes, took place sequentially at 1:00 and 2:00 P.M.

Bobbie

The first client, Bobbie, was a 34-year-old separated mother of a young son who had severe physical handicaps. When I first met Bobbie, she was distraught, tearful, lonely, and hopeless about her future. She was experiencing a recurrence of major depression, also characterized by low energy, an inability to manage basic activities of daily living, and compulsive eating. Bobbie had been prone to depressions for several years, but at this time she was in crisis, asking to be hospitalized because she was afraid of hurting herself.

Within two months, Bobbie's life had turned around markedly. Her self-esteem had risen with my mirroring of her strengths, which included a high level of motivation to change and good judgment. I had provided her with emotional support and a series of task-focused interventions. I also linked her with a variety of support services, including a parent support group for persons with handicapped children, a consumer credit counseling services bureau, an agency physician (who prescribed antidepressant medications for her), a new church with many available social activities (as she had expressed a desire to revive her spiritual life), an attorney for advice on her separation, a benevolent association that purchased a year's membership to the YMCA for her and her son, a respite service for parents of special needs children, and an Overeaters Anonymous support group. All of these referral services worked out well for Bobbie, and she felt much relief from her stresses. She never went to a hospital, and, in fact, she began looking ahead to part-time work.

At the end of our visit that day, Bobbie said, "I just want you to know that this counseling has been wonderful for me. I had a bad experience with a counselor last year and figured that this wouldn't do me much good either. I thought all counselors were too interested in the bad stuff from your personal life. But this has been great. I feel much better. I really think I'll be okay now. Thank you."

Bobbie's comments made me feel wonderful, but I just smiled, thanked her, and said I was pleased with her progress. We adjourned for the day because my next client was waiting.

Linda

Linda was a new client. Her former case manager had left the agency to take another job and had referred Linda to me. The client was looking for help in managing her moods so that she could succeed in school. She was feeling overwhelmed with stresses related to her relationships with other students, her boss (she worked part-time), and her husband.

I was fascinated with her social history. Linda was a 26-year-old married graduate student in business administration with a long history of mood instability, problems with relationships, and transient psychotic symptoms. Her diagnosis had been variously reported by previous mental health professionals as schizo-affective disorder, schizophreniform disorder, cyclothymic disorder, bipolar disorder, and borderline personality disorder. What this diagnostic confusion suggested to me was that Linda was atypical with regard to her mental illness. She would be quite a challenge to engage in a therapeutic relationship. Linda was precisely the type of client I loved to see.

I had had difficulty scheduling Linda for a first meeting and thus had talked with her several times by phone. When she came to see me she displayed a matter-of-fact attitude about our beginning but was very willing to review her history and most important needs with me. I told Linda that I would need time to get to know her before doing much active intervention. I did give her some feedback, commenting on the fact that she had personal supports (parents and several friends) that she could rely on for assistance. I reviewed my general task-focused approach with her and wondered out loud if she might want to include her husband in our work. The hour passed quickly. I was beginning to formulate some intervention strategies, including developing our relationship over a period of weeks, linking Linda with several campus groups, and perhaps offering to mediate in her occupational dilemmas.

But I was stopped short in all of this. As we were finishing, Linda said, "Is there any way I can get a different counselor?"

I was surprised, but I tried to retain my composure. "Well, we do have many people on staff here, but can I ask why you want to change?"

Linda was straightforward in her response. "I get the impression that you don't approve of me. Don't take this personally, but the way you've been talking with me today, I just don't think you respect me. You seem to think I make a lot of stupid decisions. It even comes across in the tone of your voice."

This wasn't the first time that a client had asked for a transfer from me, but I was usually surprised when it happened. I wondered: Was Linda right? Was I showing her disrespect in some way? Did my negative reactions to some of her personal accounts come across nonverbally? What *was* the tone of my voice? I said, rather awkwardly, "Linda, I can see about a transfer, but I'm not sure what staff are available right now. Can we talk about this more next week and then decide?"

But Linda seemed sure of herself. "Look, this is hard for me. I've been sitting here for 15 minutes trying to get up the nerve to ask for this. Can I please get another counselor? I'd prefer a woman, but I'll take another man if I need to."

I told Linda that, rather than schedule another appointment for her with me, I would see about a transfer and call her back. Later that day I met with my supervisor about the case. I was fortunate that my supervisor had time to process Linda's request with me so soon. We wondered if Linda's reasons for the request were just as she had said or if they were related to something else that perhaps she could not express or even comprehend. We decided to proceed with the transfer since I had seen Linda only once. I left the office that day feeling badly about the session with Linda, still wondering if and how I could have handled our first interview better.

THE CHALLENGE OF
RELATIONSHIP DEVELOPMENT

So, on that Tuesday, I went directly from one client whose life I had apparently helped change for the better, to another client who was so uncomfortable with my attitude toward her that she requested a transfer. But wasn't I the same person in both meetings?

I want to end this book by restating a point I made at the beginning. Relationship development is the basis for clinical case management, and it is always a challenge. No matter how much experience we have, we never become experts. We can (and should) read books and journals, and learn from our practice, but each time we sit down with a new client, there is uncertainty about how the experience will turn out. I have always prided myself on being able to work with almost any type of client, but I have my share of negative experiences in which, among other possible reasons, my personality simply does not mesh with that of the client. We fail to develop a shared definition of the situation that includes trust, and little benefit occurs for the client.

I believe that we should always maintain a sense of humility in our clinical case management practice. I have been helped immeasurably by the hundreds of professionals and clients with whom I have worked, but I still feel limited in some clinical situations. I have persisted in and enjoyed the clinical practice field for so long because I have more outcomes of Bobbie's type than of Linda's. But at the same time I believe it is the Lindas of the clinical world who keep me committed to my work because I am eager to learn what I could do better and what I might have missed within a client that was important.

I hope you enjoy clinical case management as much as I have.

Glossary

Adjustment disorder with depressed mood   a relatively mild and transient mood disorder characterized by subjective distress, symptoms of depression, and problems in social functioning that occurs within three months of an identifiable stressor. The disorder is not anticipated to persist for more than six months.

Adverse effects   the physical, psychological, or social effects of a medication that are unintentional, unrelated to its therapeutic effect, and unpleasant or potentially harmful to the consumer.

Anhedonia   a blandness in emotional experience and presentation.

Anti-anxiety medications   all prescription medications which have been specifically developed, or have demonstrated effectiveness, for controlling the symptoms of anxiety disorders and other disorders in which anxiety is a prominent symptom. They include the benzodiazepines and buspirone, among other drugs.

Antidepressants   all prescription medications which have been specifically developed, or have demonstrated effectiveness, for controlling the symptoms of depressive disorders. They include the monoamine oxidase inhibitors, cyclic antidepressants, and the selective serotonin reuptake inhibitors.

Antipsychotic drugs   all prescription medications which have been specifically developed, or have demonstrated effectiveness, for controlling the symptoms of psychosis and agitation in disorders such as schizophrenia, schizoaffective disorder, the manic phase of bipolar disorder, and other disorders in which such symptoms may be prominent.

Attachment theory   any of a set of theories of human development that are based on the assumption that people have an innate tendency to seek emotional attachments to others.

Behavior theory   a practice theory which asserts that all behavior, including cognitive behavior, is determined by the principles of conditioning. It avoids making inferences about internal mental processes except to assume that persons are motivated by nature to experience pleasure and avoid pain.

Bipolar disorder   a disorder of mood in which, over time, a person experiences one or more manic episodes (defined below) which are usually accompanied by one or more major depressive episodes (defined below). There are two types of bipolar disorder. *Bipolar I* disorder is characterized by one or more manic episodes, usually accompanied by a major depressive episode. *Bipolar II* disorder is characterized by one or more major depressive episodes accompanied by at least one hypomanic episode (defined below).

Buffering model (of social support) the perception of social support as a factor that intervenes between a stressful event and one's reaction. That is, a person recognizes a potential stressor, but the perception and utilization of support resources redefines the potential for harm or reduces the stress reaction.

Case management   an approach to social service delivery that attempts to ensure that clients with multiple, complex problems and disabilities receive the services they need in a timely, appropriate fashion. *Clinical case* management asserts

295

the importance of the case manager's development of a therapeutic relationship with the client as a prerequisite for maximizing positive outcomes.

Clusters   distinct categories of persons in one's social network, such as nuclear family, extended family, acquired family, friends, neighbors, informal community relations, school peers, co-workers, and other members of one's church, recreational groups, and associations.

Cognitive theory   a theory of human behavior and clinical practice which assumes that conscious thinking is the primary determinant of human behavior.

Cognitive/behavioral theory   a practice theory which incorporates principles from cognitive and behavior theories. The theory assumes that behavior is shaped by reinforcement contingencies in the environment, but it assigns special significance to the role of cognitive mediation, or the influence of thinking between the occurrence of a stimulus and one's response to the stimulus. The case manager assesses the client's thinking patterns to discover what meanings events hold for him or her and to determine if thought processes include any distortions which might be the target of restructuring activities (see below).

Cognitive restructuring   an intervention strategy that focuses on eliminating problematic thinking patterns within the client, and the adjustment of the client's beliefs about the self and world. A client with cognitive distortions believes that certain life experiences cause undesired emotions, but the case manager educates the client about the mediating role of negative thinking patterns in the experience of distress. The case manager and client asses the client's environment to locate sources of cognitive distortions, determine how these can be replaced, and implement tasks toward that end.

Community   any collective of people bound together by geography or network links, sharing common ties and interacting with one another. The *sense* of community is the feeling that members matter to one another, and a shared faith that their needs will be met through the commitment to be together. Four elements of the sense of community include membership, the possibility of influence, the integration and fulfillment of needs, and a shared emotional connection.

Coping   a person's efforts to master the demands of stress, including the thoughts, feelings, and actions that constitute those efforts. Coping may be problem-focused (the person attempts to change a stress situation by acting on the environment) or emotion-focused (the person attempts to change either the way the stressful situation is attended to, by vigilance or avoidance, or the meaning of what is happening).

Countertransference   all personal reactions of the case manager to his or her client. These can be based on the case manager's general likes and dislikes about the appearance and behavior of other people and can also be based on significant earlier relationships with people who resemble the client in certain ways. The reactions can be conscious or unconscious.

Crisis   a major upset in psychological equilibrium due to some hazardous event which is experienced as a threat or loss, and which the person cannot manage with his or her usual coping strategies.

Definition of the situation   one's perception of the role and activity expectations of all persons involved in a situation. Definitions do not arise from objective criteria, but from each participant's past experiences in similar situations.

Delusional disorder   a cognitive orientation to the external world characterized by delusions that persist for at least one month. The five types of delusions are listed below.

Delusions   false beliefs that are maintained even when contradicted by social reality. They include persecutory (people or forces are attempting to bring one harm), erotomanic (another person is in love with the individual), somatic (pertaining to body functioning), and grandiose (an exaggerated sense of one's power, knowledge, or identity) beliefs; thought broadcasting (one's thoughts are overheard by others), thought insertion or withdrawal (others are putting thoughts into, or taking thoughts out of one's head), delusions of being controlled (thoughts, feelings, or actions are imposed by an external force), and delusions of reference (neutral events have special significance for the person).

Depersonalization a sensation which is generally episodic rather than chronic, in which a person feels strange, unreal, and detached from him or herself; like an outsider or an observer of the self in a dream.

Depression a disturbance in mood, characterized by a sadness which is out of the range of normal emotion. It may be primary (autonomous) or secondary to other physical and emotional conditions. "Clinical" depression is characterized by an intensity of mood that seems to permeate all aspects of the person's life.

Disorder of mood while most mental disorders negatively impact both the cognitive and emotional aspects of a person's life, these disorders most dramatically impact one's moods. Examples include major depression and generalized anxiety disorder.

Disorder of thought though most mental disorders negatively impact both the cognitive and emotional aspects of a person's life, these disorders most dramatically impact one's cognitive functioning. Examples include schizophrenia and delusional disorders.

Dysthymic disorder a mood disorder that represents a generally depressed personality style, featuring symptoms which are similar to, but less intense than, those of major depression. The diagnosis requires two years of a continuously depressed mood (more bad days than good ones). It often has an early age of onset (childhood through early adulthood) and produces impairments in school, vocational, and social functioning.

Ego a mental structure of personality which is responsible for negotiating between internal needs of the individual and the outside world.

Ego psychology a theory of human behavior and clinical practice which views activities of the ego as the primary determinants of behavior. It considers unconscious thought as significant in human behavior, unlike the cognitive and behavioral theories.

Ego supportive interventions a set of interventions which are intended to build on a clients' existing strengths. These are often less task-focused than cognitive or behavioral strategies. They primarily include *exploration, description, and ventilation,* in which the client is encouraged to talk freely and vent emotions in an atmos-phere of trust, and *person-situation reflection,* to help the client achieve a greater awareness of his or her patterns of coping and social interaction. They may also include *direct influence* to guide decision-making in areas where the client is temporarily unable to exercise good judgment, and *education* in which the case manager helps the client become informed and empowered to develop better self-care practices.

Euthymia emotional tranquillity

Existentialism a concept that refers to a person's search for, and adherence to, meanings, purposes, and commitments in life that lie outside the self.

Exposure therapy a behavioral intervention technique intended to reduce a client's experience of depression or anxiety by systematically guiding his or her exposure to, and mastery of, situations that evoke those emotions.

General adaptation syndrome the physical process of coping with a stressor through the stages of alarm (awareness of the threat), resistance (efforts to restore physical homeostasis), and exhaustion (the termination of coping efforts because of the body's inability to sustain the state of disequilibrium).

Hallucinations sense perceptions of external objects that are not present. These can be auditory, visual, gustatory (the perception of taste), tactile (feeling an object), somatic (an unreal experience within the body), and olfactory (a false sense of smell).

Hypomanic episode, hypomania a mild form of mania that may be pleasurable for the client and result in high social and occupational productivity. Its related behaviors are often socially acceptable and consequently the hypomanic person may receive positive reinforcement from friends and employers. The person has high self-esteem, a decreased need for sleep, a high energy level, an increase in overall productivity, and more intensive involvement in pleasurable activities. Hypomania can lead into a full manic episode (see below).

Identity similar to the sense of self (see below), but more rooted in the theory of ego psychology. It refers to the extent to which a person perceives the self as having continuity and sameness, and the degree to which the boundaries of the physical and mental self are delineated from those of others.

Insight in this context, the awareness of having a mental illness requiring intervention. Insight also means that the client understands that changes or exacerbations in symptoms are indicators that he or she is under stress and reacting to it. The client is aware that he or she needs to take certain steps to reverse these changes.

Interpersonal therapy an approach to clinical intervention which considers interpersonal conflicts to be a major source of emotional distress. During assessment, the case manager attends to the status of the client's current relationships with an "interpersonal inventory". The intervention plan focuses on role transition challenges and interpersonal disputes or deficits. The client and case manager devise tasks toward improvements in these areas, and their relationship serves as a model for making changes in other relationships.

Lability, labile affect characterized by sudden and frequent changes in mood.

Learned helplessness a person's sense of being unable to control his or her environment. This is an outcome of repeated exposure to uncontrollable events which results in motivational (delayed initiation of voluntary responses), affective (decreased or sad affect), and cognitive (interference with the learning of associations between response and environmental feedback) deficits.

Main effect model (of social support) the perception of social support as related to a person's overall sense of well-being. That is, supportive others provide one with regular positive experiences and a set of stable roles which enables the person to enjoy ongoing mood stability, predictability in life situations, and feelings of self-worth.

Magical thinking primitive, illogical thinking, common in young children but symptomatic of thought disorder in older children and adults. It is characterized by superstitious thinking, beliefs in clairvoyance, beliefs in the power of thoughts to control environmental activities, and bizarre fantasies.

Major depressive episode a period of at least two weeks during which a person experiences a depressed mood or loss of interest in nearly all common life activities. Symptoms may include depressed mood, diminished interest or pleasure in most activities, significant and unintentional weight loss or gain, insomnia or hypersomnia, feelings of physical agitation

or retardation, loss of energy, feelings of worthlessness or excessive guilt, a diminished ability to think or concentrate, and persistent thoughts of death or suicide.

Manic episode, mania a period of at least two weeks in which a person's predominant mood is elevated, expansive, or irritable to a degree that there is serious impairment in social functioning. It can be characterized by unrealistically inflated self-esteem, a decreased need for sleep, pressured speech, racing thoughts, distractibility, an increase in unrealistic goal-directed activity, and involvement in activities that have a potential for painful consequences.

Mirroring an intervention technique in which the case manager reflects (mirrors) and helps the client identify his or her unique capabilities, talents, and characteristics through verbal and nonverbal positive feedback. This is particularly powerful for clients who are insecure, unfocused, and have low self-esteem.

Mood stabilizers all prescription medications which have been specifically developed, or have demonstrated effectiveness, for stabilizing the moods of persons with bipolar disorder. Lithium, carbamazepine, and valproate are the most common mood stabilizers.

Negative symptoms (of schizophrenia) those symptoms that represent a diminution of what would be considered normal behavior. These include flat or blunted affect (the absence of expression), social withdrawal, non-communication, anhedonia (blandness) or passivity, and ambivalence in decision making.

Object relations theories of human behavior that assert that a person's capacity for trust and intimacy with others is largely determined by the quality of his or her earliest relationships, most importantly those with primary caregivers. These theories are sometimes, but not always, referred to as "interpersonal" relations.

Paranoia a cognitive state which features systematized delusions of persecution and includes emotional experience and behavior congruent with those delusions. The ideas and beliefs do not include hallucinations, and the person's intelligence is unaffected.

Paranoid personality disorder an enduring personality pattern characterized by a pervasive mistrust and suspiciousness of others such that their motives are interpreted as malevolent.

Personality disorders according to the DSM-IV, a personality is disordered when traits (see below) are inflexible, maladaptive, and cause significant distress or functional impairment. The idea of a personality as disordered is controversial among some human service professionals.

Personality trait a stable personality characteristic.

Positive symptoms (of schizophrenia) those symptoms that represent exaggerations of normal behavior, including hallucinations, delusions, disorganized thought processes, and tendencies toward agitation.

Problem-solving an intervention technique that helps the client become a more systematic problem solver so that he or she can achieve goals more effectively. The five steps in problem solving include orientating the client to the logic of the process, articulating a specific problem in concrete terms, mutually generating a list of alternative solutions, implementing a mutually selected and preferred alternative, and evaluating its outcome.

Psychoanalytic theory a theory of human behavior and clinical intervention which assumes the primacy of internal drives and unconscious mental activity in determining human behavior.

Psychoeducational programs time-limited, open or closed groups conducted by mental health professionals for the purposes of educating and providing support to a lay membership about issues related to mental illness.

Quality of life a person's overall satisfaction with life, including his or her living situation, daily activities, family and social relations, financial status, occupation, safety, physical status, and mental health status.

Remission a state of cognitive, emotional, and behavioral functioning in which the symptoms of a mental illness have subsided to a significant degree. This state may be temporary or permanent.

Schema a person's internalized representation of the external world, including systematic patterns of perception, thought, problem-solving, and action.

Schizoid a personality trait or defense mechanism by which an individual purposely avoids contact or intimacy with other persons to preserve a sense of internal control and comfort. The schizoid individual tends to become overstimulated and highly anxious when in close relationships and is generally satisfied to maintain a physical or psychological distance from others.

Schizophrenia a disorder of the brain characterized by abnormal patterns of thought and perception as inferred from language and behavior. Schizophrenia is characterized by at least six months of continuous symptoms, including two or more positive symptoms (delusions, hallucinations, disorganized speech, and disorganized or catatonic behavior) for at least one month. There are five subtypes of schizophrenia. The *paranoid* type features a preoccupation with delusions or auditory hallucinations and a preservation of cognitive functioning and affect. *Disorganized* schizophrenia is characterized by disorganized speech, behavior, and flat or inappropriate affect. *Catatonic* schizophrenia features psychomotor disturbances of immobility or excessive mobility, mutism, odd gestures, echolalia (repeating the words of others) or echopraxia (repeating the movements of others). The *undifferentiated* type describes persons who do not meet criteria for the first three types. *Residual* schizophrenia describes the person who displays only negative symptoms (flat affect, withdrawal) after an active episode.

Schizotypal personality a personality style characterized by a pervasive pattern of interpersonal deficits marked by acute discomfort with close relationships, cognitive or perceptual distortions, and eccentricities of behavior.

Sense of self in symbolic interactionism, a self-definition that is fluid and is based on a person's expectations of how others think he or she should behave, think, or feel. This is a role-taking process.

Shared psychotic disorder a delusional state that develops in one person who is involved in a close relationship with another person who also has delusions.

Situation any assembly of people incorporating role expectations and joint activities.

Social causation hypothesis A hypothesis regarding the cause of depression in which lower social status (education, occupation, income) is believed to contribute to the onset and persistence of low mood, because individuals in this condition experience more environmental stress.

Social selection hypothesis A hypothesis regarding the cause of depression in which persons with lower social status (education, occupation, income) are believed to be more vulnerable to the effects of stress because of their lack of social and personal resources.

Social support the interpersonal interactions and relationships that provide persons with assistance or feelings of attachment to others they perceive as caring.

Social support skills training an intervention technique in which the worker and client identify significant deficits in social skills which contribute to the client's social or emotional difficulties and then follow a structured plan for new skill development. The worker breaks down the skill into its component parts, models the skill, and organizes role-plays of each skill component with the client. The client then applies the social skill to real-life situations and processes successes or failures with the case manager.

Social network the numbers of people with whom a person routinely interacts; the patterns of interaction which result from exchanging resources with others.

Splitting a process in which a client working with more than one human service professional presents him or herself differently to each of them, at times creating conflict between the professionals. The client may do this inadvertently, seeing each worker as having distinct and unrelated roles, or do so as a means of manipulating the activities of the workers.

Stabilization a stage in the process of recovery from an episode of mental illness in which the client's more extreme symptoms subside. Social functioning returns to normal within the limits of a protective, supportive environment, but the client requires ongoing supervision and support as he or she is still emotionally fragile.

Stress any biological, psychological, or social event in which environmental demands, internal demands, or both tax or exceed the adaptive resources of an individual.

Stress/Diathesis model or theory a perspective on the cause of mental and emotional disorders in which a disorder is considered to be the result of interactions of environmental stresses and the person's genetic or biochemical predisposition to the disorder.

Support appraisals measures of social support that are not based on events, but on a person's perceptions of having supportive persons available to him or her.

Supportive behavior measures of social support that include actual observable episodes in which a person has experienced support.

Symbolic interactionism a theory of human behavior rooted in sociology which asserts that our thoughts about the self, others, and our place in society emerges from a process of internalized interactions with others based on shared cultural symbols. Its assumptions are as follows: (a) our capacity for thought is shaped by social interaction; (b) through social interaction we learn meanings and symbols which further promote our capacity for thought; (c) shared meanings and symbols facilitate social interaction; and (d) the meanings and symbols we share are continuously modified through our changing definitions of social situations.

Symbolization the process of naming social objects and, through agreement with others, have them stand for something else.

Symbols all social objects that, through a consensus of members of a society or group, have come to stand for something else. There is a shared social meaning of the object.

Transference all personal reactions of the client to the case manager. These can be based on the client's general likes and dislikes about the appearance and behavior of others and can also be based on significant earlier relationships with people who resemble the case manager in certain ways. The reactions can be conscious or unconscious.

Will to meaning a concept from Frankl's logotherapy, defined as a basic and enduring tendency, inherent in all people, to obtain what satisfies their nature. All persons have this innate drive to either create or discover meaning and purpose in life beyond their physical survival, including commitments to other persons and values.

References

Accordino, N. P., & Herbert, J. T. (1997). Relationship enhancement as an intervention to facilitate rehabilitation of persons with serious mental illness. *Journal of Applied Rehabilitation Counseling, 28*(1), 47–52.

Ahr, P. R., & Holcomb, W. R. (1985). State mental health directors' priorities for mental health care. *Hospital and Community Psychiatry, 31*(1), 39–45.

Akiskal, H. S. (1991). An integrative perspective on recurrent mood disorders: The mediating role of personality. In J. Becker & A. Kleinman (Eds.), *Psychosocial aspects of depression* (pp. 215–235). Hillsdale, NJ: Lawrence Erlbaum.

Aleksandrowicz, D. R. (1980). Psychoanalytic studies of mania. In R. Belmaker & H. Pragg (Eds.), *Mania: An evolving concept* (pp. 309–322). New York: Spectrum.

American Psychiatric Association (1994). *Diagnostic and statistical manual of mental disorders* (4th ed.). Washington, DC: Author.

American Psychiatric Association (1980). *Diagnostic and statistical manual of mental disorders* (3rd ed). Washington, DC:Author.

Anderson, C. M, Reiss, D. J., & Hogarty, G. E. (1986). *Schizophrenia and the family*. New York: Guilford.

Anderson, J. (1997). *Social work with groups*. New York: Longman.

Anderson, T. L. (1994). Drug abuse and identity: Linking micro and macro factors. *The Sociological Quarterly, 35*(1), 159–174.

Andreasen, N. C. (1982). Negative symptoms of schizophrenia: Definition and reliability. *Archives of General Psychiatry, 39*, 784–788.

Andreasen, N. C., & Olsen, S. (1982). Negative vs. positive schizophrenia: Definition and validation. *Archives of General Psychiatry, 39*, 789–794.

Anscombe, R. (1987). The disorder of consciousness in schizophrenia. *Schizophrenia Bulletin, 13*(2), 241–260.

Arieti, S. (1979). *Understanding and helping the schizophrenic: A guide for families and friends*. New York: Simon & Schuster.

Atkinson, D. (1986). Engaging competent others: A study of the support networks of persons with mental handicap. *British Journal of Social Work, 16*, 83–101.

Atwood, N. (1983). Support group counseling for the relatives of schizophrenic patients. In W. McFarlane (Ed.), *Family therapy in schizophrenia* (pp. 189–205). New York: Guilford.

Auge, M., & Herzlech, C. (Eds.) (1998). *The meaning of illness: Anthropology, history, and sociology*. New York: Harwood.

Austin, C. D., & McClelland, R. W. (Eds.) (1996). *Perspectives on case management practice*. Milwaukee, WI: Families International.

Austin, C. (1996). Aging and long-term care. In C. D. Austin & R. W. McClelland (Eds.), *Perspectives on case management practice* (pp. 73–98). Milwaukee, WI: Families International.

Aviram, H. (1990). Community care of the severely mentally ill. *Community Mental Health Journal, 26*, 69–88.

Balancio, E. F. (1994). Clinical Case management. In R.W. Surer (Ed.), *Clinical case management: A guide to comprehensive treatment of serious mental illness* (pp. 21–41). Thousand Oaks, CA: Sage.

Bank, S. P., & Kahn, M. D. (1982). *The sibling bond*. New York: Basic Books.

Barr, M. A. (1986). Homogenous groups with acutely psychotic schizophrenics. *Group, 10*(1), 7–12.

Bateson, G. (1991). A sacred unity: Further steps to an ecology of mind. New York: HarperCollins.

Bateson, G., Jackson, D. D., Haley, J., & Weakland, J. H. (1963). A note on the double-bind–1962. *Family Process, 2*, 154–161.

Bauer, M., & McBride, L. (1996). *Structured group psychotherapy for bipolar disorder: The life goals program.* New York: Springer.

Bebbington, P. (1982). The course and prognosis of affective disorders. In J. Wing & L. Wing (Eds.), *Psychoses of uncertain etiology* (pp. 120–128). New York: Cambridge University Press.

Becker, J., & Schmaling, K. (1991). Interpersonal aspects of depression from psychodynamic and attachment perspectives. In J. Becker & A. Kleinman (Eds.), *Psychosocial aspects of depression* (pp. 131–168). Hillsdale, NJ: Lawrence Erlbaum.

Beeber, A. R. (1991). Psychotherapy with schizophrenics in team groups: A systems model. *American Journal of Psychotherapy, 45*(1), 78–86.

Beels, C. (1981). Social support and schizophrenia. *Schizophrenia Bulletin, 7,* 58–71.

Beitman, B. D., & Klerman, G. L. (Eds.) (1991). *Integrating pharmacotherapy and psychotherapy.* Washington, DC: American Psychiatric Press.

Belcher, J. A. (1994). Is community-based mental health care destined to fail? Yes. In H. J. Karger & J. Midgely (Eds.), *Controversial issues in social policy* (pp. 171–175). Boston: Allyn & Bacon.

Bellack, A. S. (1992). Cognitive rehabilitation for schizophrenia: Is it possible? Is it necessary? *Schizophrenia Bulletin, 18*(1), 43–50.

Bellah, R. N., Madsen, R., Sullivan, W. M., Swindler, A., & Tipton, S. M. (1985). *Habits of the heart: individualism and commitment in American life.* Berkeley: University of California Press.

Benioff, L. (1995). What is it like to have schizophrenia? In S. Vinogradov (Ed.), *Treating schizophrenia* (pp. 81–107). San Francisco: Jossey-Bass.

Benjamin, L. S., Foster, S. W., Roberto, L. G., & Estroff, S. E. (1986). Breaking the family code: Analysis of videotapes of family interactions by structural analysis of social behavior (SASB). In L. Greenberg & W. Pinsof (Eds.), *The psychotherapeutic process: A research handbook* (pp. 391–408). New York: Guilford.

Bentall, R. P., Kaney, S., & Dewey, M. E. (1991). Paranoia and social reasoning: An attribution theory analysis. *British Journal of Clinical Psychology, 30,* 13–23.

Bentley, K. J. (1993). The right of psychiatric patients to refuse medications: Where should social workers stand? *Social Work, 38,* 101–106.

Bentley, K. J., & Walsh, J. (1998). Advances in psychopharmacology and psychosocial aspects of medication management: A review for social workers. In J. B. W. Williams & K. Ell (Eds.), *Recent advances in mental health research: Implications for social workers* (pp. 309–342). Silver Spring, MD: National Association of Social Workers.

Bentley, K. J., & Walsh, J. (1996). *The social worker and psychotropic medication: Toward effective collaboration with mental health clients, families, and providers.* Pacific Grove, CA: Brooks/Cole.

Bernheim, K. F. (1994). Skills and strategies for working with families. In D. T. Marsh (Ed.), *New directions in the psychological treatment of serious mental illness* (pp. 166–185). Westport, CT: Praeger.

Bernstein, J. G. (1995). *Handbook of drug therapy in psychiatry* (3rd ed.) St. Louis: Mosby.

Biegel, D. E., Li-yu, S., & Milligan, S. E. (1995). A comparative analysis of family caregivers' perceived relationships with mental health professionals. *Psychiatric Services, 46,* 477–482.

Biegel, D. E., Magaziner, J., & Blum, M. (1991). Social support networks of white and black elderly people at risk for institutionalization. *Health and Social Work, 16*(4), 245–257.

Bigelow, L. B., & Berthot, B. D. (1989). The psychiatric symptom assessment scale (PSAS). *Psychopharmacology Bulletin, 25*(2), 168–179.

Blehar, M. C., Weissman, M. M., Gershon, E. S., & Hirschfeld, R. M. A. (1988). Family and genetic studies of affective disorders. *Archives of General Psychiatry, 45,* 289–292.

Block, B., & Pristach, C. A. (1992). Diagnosis and management of the paranoid patient. *American Family Physician, 45*(6), 2634–2640.

Bloom, B. L. (1984). *Community mental health: A general introduction.* Monterey, CA: Brooks/Cole.

Bloom, J. (1990). The relationship between social support and health. *Social Science and Medicine, 30,* 635–637.

Blumer, H. (1969). *Symbolic interactionism: Perspective and method.* Englewood Cliffs, NJ: Prentice-Hall.

Boisen, A. (1936). *The exploration of the inner world.* Philadelphia: University of Pennsylvania Press.

Bond, G. R., & DeGraaf-Kaser, R. (1990). Group approaches for persons with serious mental illness: A typology. *Social Work With Groups, 13*(1), 21–36.

Booth, G. K. (1995). What is the prognosis in schizophrenia? In S. Vinogradov (Ed.), *Treating schizophrenia* (pp. 125–156). San Francisco: Jossey-Bass.

Borkman, T. (1984). Mutual self-help groups: Strengthening the selectively unsupportive personal and community networks of their members. In A. Gartner & F. Riessman (Eds.), *The self-help revolution* (pp. 205–216). New York: Human Sciences Press.

Bowen, M. (1960). A family concept of schizophrenia. In D. D. Jackson (Ed.), *The etiology of schizophrenia* (pp. 346–372). New York: Basic Books.

Boyd, A. S. (1997). *The relationship between the level of personal empowerment and quality of life among psychosocial clubhouse members and consumer-operated drop-in centers.* Unpublished doctoral dissertation, Virginia Commonwealth University, Richmond.

Bradley, S. (1990). Non-physician psychotherapist-physician pharmacotherapist: A new model for concurrent treatment. *Psychiatric Clinics of North America, 13*(2), 307–322.

Brekke, J. S., & Test, M. A. (1992). A model for measuring the implementation of community support programs: Results from three sites. *Community Mental Health Journal, 28*(3), 227–247.

Brown, A. (1994). The treatment of bipolar disorder. *National Alliance for Research on Schizophrenia and Depression Newsletter,* Fall, 13–18.

Brown, H., & Zinberg, N. (1982). Difficulties in the integration of psychological and medical practices. *American Journal of Psychiatry, 139*(12), 1576–1580.

Burbach, D. J., Borduin, C. M., & Peake, T. H. (1988). Cognitive approaches to brief psychotherapy. In T. H. Peake, C. M. Borduin, & R. P. Archer (Eds.), *Brief psychotherapies: Changing frames of mind* (pp. 57–85). Newbury Park, CA: Sage.

Busch, F. N., & Gold, E. (1993). Treatment by a psychotherapist and a psychopharmacologist: Transference and countertransference issues. *Hospital and Community Psychiatry, 44,* 772–774.

Byalin, K., Jed, J., & Lehman, S. (1982). *Family intervention with treatment-refractory schizophrenics.* 20th century international congress of applied psychology, Edinburgh, Scotland.

Campbell, R. (1996). *Psychiatric dictionary* (6th ed.). New York: Oxford University Press.

Candido, C. L., & Romney, D. M. (1990). Attributional style in paranoid vs. depressed patients. *British Journal of Medical Psychology, 63,* 355–363.

Caplan, G. (1990). Loss, stress, and mental health. *Community Mental Health Journal, 26*(1), 27–48.

Caplan, G. (1989). Recent developments in crisis intervention and the promotion of support service. *Journal of Primary Prevention, 10*(1), 3–25.

Caplan, R. B. (1969). *Psychiatry and community in nineteenth-century America.* New York: Basic.

Carlisle, W. (1984). *Siblings of the mentally ill.* Saratoga, CA: R & E Publishers.

Charon, J. M. (1992). *Symbolic interactionism: An introduction, and interpretation, and integration* (3rd ed.). Englewood Cliffs, NJ: Prentice-Hall.

Clark, C. S. (1993). Mental illness. *The CQ Researcher, 3*(29), 675–691.

Clark, R. E., Drake, R. E., McHugo, G. J., & Ackerson, T. H. (1995). Incentives for community treatment: Mental illness management services. *Medical Care, 33*(7), 729–738.

Cohen, S., & Hoberman, H.M. (1983). Positive events and social supports as buffers of life change stress. *Journal of Applied Social Psychology, 12,* 99–125.

Cohen, S., & Wills, T. A. (1985). Stress, social support, and the buffering hypothesis. *Psychological Bulletin, 98*(2) 310–357.

Cole, R. E., Reed, S. K., Babigian, H. M., Brown, S. W., & Fray, J. (1994). A mental health capitation program I: Patient outcomes. *Hospital and Community Psychiatry, 45*(11), 1090–1096.

Compton, B., & Galaway, B. (1994). *Social work processes* (5th ed.). Pacific Grove, CA: Brooks/Cole.

Corsini, R. J., & Wedding, D. (Eds.) (1995). *Current psychotherapies* (5th ed.). Itasca, IL: Peacock.

Crotty, P., & Kulys, R. (1985). Social support networks: The views of schizophrenic clients and their significant others. *Social Work, 30,* 301–309.

Cutler, D., & Tatum, E. (1983). Networks and the chronic patient. In D. Cutler (Ed.), *Effective aftercare for the 1980s* (pp. 13–22). New Directions for Mental Health Services, San Francisco: Jossey-Bass.

Cutler, D., Tatum, E., & Shore, J. (1987). A comparison of schizophrenic patients in different community support treatment approaches. *Community Mental Health Journal, 23,* 103–113.

Daly, I. (1997). Mania. *The Lancet, 349*(9059), 1157–1161.

Danley, K. (Ed.) (1994). Special issue: Invited papers from experts in the field of vocational rehabilitation for people with psychiatric disabilities. *Psychosocial Rehabilitation Journal, 17*(3).

Davis, K. (1996). *Managed care and social work practice.* Virginia Commonwealth University School of Social Work.

Davis, M., Yelton, S., Katz-Leavy, J., & Lourie, I. S. (1995). Unclaimed children revisited: The status of state children's mental health services systems. *Journal of Mental Health Administration, 22*(2), 147–166.

Davis, R. D., & Millon, T. (1994). Can personalities be disordered? Yes. In S.A. Kirk, & S.D. Einbinder (Eds.), *Controversial issues in mental health* (pp. 40–47). Boston: Allyn & Bacon.

Dawson, D. F. L., Blum, H. M., & Bartolucci, G. (1983). *Schizophrenia in focus.* New York: Human Sciences Press.

DeNour, A. K. (1980). Psychosocial aspects of the management of mania. In R. Belmaker and H. Pragg (Eds.), *Mania: An evolving concept* (pp. 349–364). New York: Spectrum.

Dewan, M. J. (1992). Adding medications to ongoing psychotherapy: Indications and pitfalls. *American Journal of Psychotherapy, 46,* 102–110.

Dickens, R. (Ed.) (1989a). *Siblings and adult children's network: Group facilitator's guide.* Arlington, VA: National Alliance for the Mentally Ill/Sibling and Adult Children's Network.

Dickens, R. (Ed.) (1989b). *Siblings and adult children's network: Background information and articles booklet.* Arlington, VA: National Alliance for the Mentally Ill/Sibling and Adult Children's Network.

Dincin, J., Selleck, V., & Streicker, S. (1978). Restructuring parental attitudes - Working with parents of the adult mentally ill. *Schizophrenia Bulletin, 4,* 597–608.

Dozier, M., Harris, M., & Bergman, H. (1987). Social network density and rehospitalization among young adult patients. *Hospital and Community Psychiatry, 38,* 61–65.

Draine, J. (1997). A critical review of randomized field trials of case management for individuals with serious and persistent mental illness. *Research on Social Work Practice, 7*(1), 32–52.

Drake, R. E., & Burns, B. J. (1995). Special section on assertive community treatment: An introduction. *Hospital and Community Psychiatry, 46*(7), 667–668.

Edgar, E. (1996). Managed care basics. *NAMI Advocate, 18*(2), 6–16.

Ehrenreich, J. H. (1985). *The altruistic imagination.* Ithaca, NY: Cornell University Press.

Ely, A. R. (1985). Long-term group treatment for young male 'schizopaths.' *Social Work, 30*(1), 5–10.

Erikson, E. (1968). Identity: Youth and crisis. New York: Norton.

Erikson, E. (1959). Identity and the life cycle. *Psychological Issues, 1*(1), 50–100.

Estroff, S. E. (1981). *Making it crazy: An ethnography of psychiatric clients in an American community.* Berkeley: University of California Press.

Falloon, I. R. H., Boyd, J. L., & McGill, C. W. (1984). *Family care of schizophrenia.* New York: Guilford.

Farmer, R. L., Walsh, J., & Bentley, K. J. (1998). Schizophrenia. In B. A. Thyer & J. S. Wodarski (Eds.), *Handbook of empirical social work practice (vol. 1): Mental disorders* (pp. 245–270). New York: Wiley.

Faustman, W. O. (1995). What causes schizophrenia? In S. Vinogradov (Ed.), *Treating schizophrenia* (pp. 57–80). San Francisco: Jossey-Bass.

Fellin, P. (1996). *Mental health and mental illness: Policies, programs, and services.* Itasca, IL: Peacock.

Fenigstein, A. (1996). Paranoia. In C.G. Costello (Ed.), *Personality characteristics of the personality disordered* (pp. 242–275). New York: Wiley.

Fenigstein, A., & Vanable, P. A. (1992). Paranoia and self-consciousness. *Journal of Personality and Social Psychology, 62*(1), 129–138.

Fielden, M. A. (1992). Depression in older adults: Psychological and psychosocial approaches. *British Journal of Social Work, 32*(3), 291–307.

Fiorentine, R., & Grusky, O. (1990). When case managers manage the seriously mentally ill: A role-contingency approach. *Social Service Review, 64,* 79–93.

Fischer, J. (1978). *Effective casework practice: An eclectic approach.* New York: McGraw-Hill.

Fish, B. (1987). Infant predictors on the longitudinal course of schizophrenia. *Schizophrenia Bulletin, 13*(3), 345–409.

Flanagan, L. M. (1996). The theory of self psychology. In J. Berzoff (Ed.), *Inside out and outside in: Psychodynamic clinical theory and practice in contemporary multicultural contexts* (pp. 173–198). Northvale, NJ: Jason Aronson.

Ford, R., Beadsmoore, A., Ryan, P., Repper, J., Craig, T., & Muijen, M. (1995). Providing the safety net: Case management for people with serious mental illness. *Journal of Mental Health, 1,* 91–97.

Frank, E., Kuipfer, D. J., Ehlers, C. L., Monk, T. H., Cornes, C., Carter, S., & Frankel, D. (1994). Interpersonal and social rhythm therapy for bipolar disorder: Integrating interpersonal and behavioral approaches. *Behavior Therapist, 17,* 143–149.

Frank, J. D., & Frank, J. B. (1993). *Persuasion and healing: A comparative sotry of psychotherapy* (3rd. ed.) Baltimore: Johns Hopkins University Press.

Frank, R. G., & Gaynor, M. (1994). Fiscal decentralization of public mental health care and the Robert Wood Johnson foundation program on chronic mental illness. *The Milbank Quarterly, 72*(1), 81–104.

Frankl, V. E. (1988). *The will to meaning: Foundations and applications of logotherapy.* New York: Meridian.

Franklin County Alcohol, Drug Abuse, and Mental Health Board (1992). *FY 1993–1994 state community plan.* Columbus, OH: Author.

Fraser, J. S. (1983). Paranoia: Interactional views on evolution and intervention. *Journal of Marital and Family Therapy, 9*(4), 383–391.

Freud, S. (1966). *Introductory lectures on psychoanalysis.* New York: Norton.

Fromm, E. (1967). *Psychoanalysis and religion.* New Haven, CT: Yale University Press.

Gagrat, D. D., & Spiro, H. R. (1980). Social, cultural, and epidemiologic aspects of mania. In R. Belmaker and H. Pragg (Eds.), *Mania: An evolving concept* (pp. 291–308). New York: Spectrum.

Gambrill, E. (1994). Behavior theory. In D. K. Granvold (Ed.), *Cognitive and behavioral treatment: Methods and applications* (pp. 32–62). Pacific Grove, CA: Brooks/Cole.

Garfield, D., & Havens, L. (1991). Paranoid phenomena and pathological narcissism. American Journal of Psychotherapy, 45(2), 160–172.

Garson, S. (1986). *Out of our minds.* Buffalo, NY: Prometheus.

Gartner, A., & Reissman, F. (1982). Self-help and mental health. *Hospital and Community Psychiatry, 33,* 631–635.

Gergen, K. J. (1985). Social construction inquiry: Context and implications. In K. J. Gergen & K. E. Davis (Eds.), *The social construction of the person* (pp. 3–18). New York: Springer-Verlag.

Gerhart, U. (1990). *Caring for the chronic mentally ill.* Itasca, IL: Peacock.

Gerhart, U., & Brooks, A. (1983). The social work practitioner and anti-psychotic medication. *Social Work, 28,* 454–459.

Germain, C. B., & Gitterman, A. (1996). *The life model of social work practice: Advances in theory and practice* (2nd ed.). New York: Columbia University Press.

Ghaemi, S. N., Stoll, A. L., & Pope, H. G. (1995). Lack of insight in bipolar disorder: The acute manic episode. *Journal of Nervous and Mental Disease, 183*(7), 464–467.

Gilbert, N., & Specht, H. (1986). *Dimensions of social welfare policy* (2nd ed.). New York: Prentice-Hall.

Goffman, E. I. (1963). *Stigma: Notes on the management of spoiled identity.* New York: Touchstone.

Goffman, E. I. (1961). *Asylums.* Garden City, NY: Doubleday Anchor.

Goldberg, R. S., Riba, M., & Tasman, A. (1991). Psychiatrists' attitudes toward prescribing medication for patients treated by nonmedical psychotherapists. *Hospital and Community Psychiatry, 42,* 276–280.

Goldman, H. H., & Manderscheid, R. (1987). Epidemiology of chronic mental disorder. In W. Menninger & G. Hannah (Eds.), *The chronic mental patient/II* (pp. 41–52). Washington, DC: American Psychiatric Press.

Goldman, H. H., Morrissey, J. P., & Ridgely, M. S. (1994). Evaluating the Robert Wood Johnson Foundation program on chronic mental illness. *The Milbank Quarterly, 72*(1), 37–47.

Goldstein, E. (1995). *Ego psychology and social work practice* (2nd. ed.). New York: Free Press.

Goldstein, M. J. (1987) The UCLA high-risk project. *Schizophrenia Bulletin, 13*(3), 505–511.

Goldstein, M. J., & Kopeikin, H. S. (1981). Short and long-term effects of combining drugs and family therapy. In M. J. Goldstein (Ed.), *New developments in intervention with families of schizophrenics.* San Francisco: Jossey-Bass.

Goodman, S. (1987) Emory University project on children of disturbed parents. *Schizophrenia Bulletin, 13*(3), 411–423.

Goodnick, P. J. (Ed.) (1998). *Mania: Clinical and research perspectives.* Washington, DC: American Psychiatric Press.

Goodwin, F. K., & Jamison, K. R. (1990). *Manic-depressive illness.* New York: Oxford University Press.

Gottesman, I. I. (1991). *Schizophrenia genesis: The origins of madness.* NY: W.H. Freeman.

Granvold, D. K. (1994). Concepts and methods of cognitive treatment. In D. K. Granvold (Ed.), *Cognitive and behavioral treatment: Methods and applications* (pp. 3–31). Pacific Grove, CA: Brooks/Cole.

Greenberg, J. S., Kim, H. W., & Greenley, J. R. (1997). Factors associated with subjective burden in siblings of adults with severe mental illness. *American Journal of Orthopsychiatry, 67*(2), 231–241.

Grob, G. (1991). *From asylum to community: Mental health policy in modern America.* Princeton, NJ: Princeton University Press.

Grob, G. (1983). *Mental illness and American society: 1875–1940.* Princeton, NJ: Princeton University Press.

Hailey, D., Hewitt, H., & Staton, D. (1995). *Is there a relationship between family tier of involvement, depression, caregiver burden, and participation in psychoeducational and support groups for families of people with severe mental illness?* Unpublished manuscript, Virginia Commonwealth University, School of Social Work, Richmond.

Hammer, M. (1981). Social supports, social networks, and schizophrenia. *Schizophrenia Bulletin, 7,* 45–57.

Hardcastle, D. A., Wenocur, S., & Powers, P. R. (1997). *Community practice: Theories and skills for social workers*. New York: Oxford University Press.

Harris, M., & Bergman, H. (1987). Case management with the chronically mentally ill. *American Journal of Orthopsychiatry, 57*(2), 296–302.

Hatfield, A. B. (1990). *Family education in mental illness*. New York: Guilford.

Hatfield, A. B. (1983). What families want of family therapists. In W. McFarlane (Ed.), *Family therapy in schizophrenia* (pp. 41–65). New York: Guilford.

Hatfield, A. B. (1981). Self-help groups for families of the mentally ill. *Social Work, 26,* 408–413.

Hatfield, A. B. (1978). Psychological costs of schizophrenia to the family. *Social Work, 23,* 355–359.

Hatfield, A. R., & Lefley, H. P. (1993). *Surviving mental illness: Stress, coping, and adaptation.* New York: Guilford.

Hawton, K. (1989). Suicide and the management of suicide attempts. In K. R. Herbst & E. S. Paykel (Eds.), *Depression: An integrative approach* (pp. 197–215). Halley Court, Jordan Hill, Oxford: Heinemann.

Heller, T., Roccoforte, J. A., Hsieh, K., Cook, J. A., & Pickett, S. A. (1997). Benefits of support groups for families of adults with serious mental illness. *American Journal of Orthopsychiatry, 67*(2), 187–198.

Hepworth, D. H., Rooney, R. H., & Larsen, J. (1997). *Direct social work practice: Theory and skills* (5th ed.). Pacific Grove, CA: Brooks/Cole.

Hobfoll, S., Freedy, R., Lane, C., & Geller, P. (1990). Conservation of social resources: Social support resource theory. *Journal of Social and Personal Relationships, 7,* 465–478.

Hoffman, J. S. (1990). Integrating biologic and psychologic treatment: The need for a unitary model. *Psychiatric Clinics of North America, 13*(2), 369–372.

Hogarty, G. E., Anderson, C. M., Reiss, D. J., & Kornblith, S. J. (1991). Family psychoeducation, social skills training, and maintenance chemotherapy in the aftercare treatment of schizophrenia II: Two year effects of a controlled study on relapse and adjustment. *Archives of General Psychiatry, 48*(4), 340–347.

Holahan, C. J., & Moos, R.H. (1983). The quality of social support: Measures of family and work relationships. *British Journal of Clinical Psychology, 22,* 157–162.

Holford, N. L. (1982). Religious ideation in schizophrenia. *Dissertation Abstracts International, 43* (6-B).

Hollis, F. (1964). *Casework: A psychosocial theory.* New York: Random House.

Horvath, A. O. (1994a). Empirical validation of Bordin's pantheoretical model of the alliance: The Working Alliance Inventory perspective. In A. O. Horvath & L. S. Greenberg (Eds.), *The working alliance: Theory, research, and practice* (pp.109–128). New York: Wiley.

Horvath, A. O. (1994b). Research on the alliance, In A. O. Horvath & L. S. Greenberg (Eds.), *The working alliance: Theory, research, and practice* (pp. 259–286). New York: Wiley.

Howells, J., & Guirguis, W. (1985). *The family and schizophrenia.* New York: International Universities Press.

Hutchison, E. D. (1999). *Dimensions of human behavior: Person and Environment.* Thousand Oaks, CA: Pine Forge.

Imbrie, G. S. (1985). Untwisting the illusion. *Journal of Orthomolecular Psychiatry, 14,* 143–145.

Intagliata, J. (1992). Improving the quality of community care for the chronically mentally disabled: The role of case management. In S. M. Rose (Ed.), *Case management and social work practice* (pp. 25–55). New York: Longman.

Intagliata, J., & Baker, F. (1983). Factors affecting case management services for the chronically mentally ill. *Administration in Mental Health, 11,* 75–91.

Isbell, S. E., Thorne, A., & Lawler, M. H. (1992). An exploratory study of videotapes of long-term group psychotherapy of outpatients with major and chronic mental illness. *Group, 16*(2), 101–111.

Jerrell, J. M., & Ridgely, M. S. (1995). Comparative effectiveness of three approaches to serving people with severe mental illness and substance abuse disorders. *Journal of Nervous and Mental Disease, 183*(9), 566–576.

Johnson, B. J. (1977). The paranoid-depressive continuum. *Social Work, 22*(3), 316–317.

Johnson, D., Geller, J., Gordon, J., & Wexler, B. E. (1986). Group psychotherapy with schizophrenic patients: The pairing group. *International Journal of Group Psychotherapy, 36*(1), 75–96.

Johnson, P., & Rubin, A. (1983). Case management in mental health: A social work domain? *Social Work, 28*(1), 495.

Kahn, D. (1990). The psychotherapy of mania. *Psychiatric Clinics of North America, 13*(2), 229–239.

Kahn, E. M. (1984). Group treatment interventions for schizophrenics. *International Journal of Group Psychotherapy, 34*(1), 149–153.

Kahn, E. M., & Kahn, E. W. (1992). Group treatment assignment for outpatients with schizophrenia: Integrating recent clinical and research findings. *Community Mental Health Journal, 28*(6), 539–549.

Kanas, N. (1991). Group therapy with schizophrenic patients: A short-term, homogenous approach. *International Journal of Group Psychotherapy, 41*(1), 33–47.

Kanas, N. (1986). Group therapy with schizophrenics: A review of controlled studies. *International Journal of Group Psychotherapy, 36*(3), 339–351.

Kanas, N., DiLella, V. J., & Jones, J. (1984). Process and content in an outpatient schizophrenic group. *Group, 8*(2), 13–20.

Kanter, J. (1996a). Engaging significant others: The Tom Sawyer approach to case management. *Psychiatric Services, 47*(8), 799–801.

Kanter, J. (1996b). Case management and managed care: Investing in recovery. *Psychiatric Services, 47*(7), 699–701.

Kanter, J. (1995a). Case management with long term patients: A comprehensive approach. In S. Soreff (Ed.), *Handbook for the treatment of the seriously mentally ill.* (pp. 169–189). Seattle: Hogrefe and Humber.

Kanter, J. (Ed.) (1995b). *Clinical issues in case management.* San Francisco: Jossey-Bass.

Kanter, J. (1989). Clinical case management: Definition, principles, components. *Hospital and Community Psychiatry, 40,* 361–368.

Kanter, J. (1988). Clinical issues in the case management relationship. In M. Harris & L. Bachrach, (Eds.), *Clinical case management* (pp. 15–27). New Directions for Mental Health Services, San Francisco: Jossey-Bass.

Kanter, J. (1985a). Case management of the young adult chronic patient: A clinical perspective. In J. Kanter (Ed.), *Clinical issues in treating the chronic mentally ill. New directions for mental health services* (pp. 77–91). San Francisco: Jossey-Bass.

Kanter, J. (Ed.) (1985b). *Clinical issues in treating the chronic mentally ill.* San Francisco: Jossey-Bass.

Kaplan, H. I., & Sadock, B. J. (1998). *Synopsis of psychiatry* (8th ed.). Baltimore: Williams & Wilkins.

Kaplan, H. I., & Sadock, B. J. (1995). *Comprehensive textbook of psychiatry/VI.* Baltimore: Williams & Wilkins.

Karterud, S., Vaglum, S., Friis, S., Irion, T., Johns, S., & Vaglum, P. (1992). Day hospital therapeutic community treatment for patients with personality disorders: An empirical evaluation of the containment function. *Journal of Nervous and Mental Disease, 180*(4), 238–243.

Katz, A. (1993). *Self-help in America: A social movement perspective.* New York: Twayne.

Kaufman, C., Freund, P., & Witson, J. (1989). Self-help in the mental health system: A model for consumer-provider collaboration. *Psychosocial Rehabilitation Journal, 13,* 5–21.

Kellner, R. (1986). The brief depression rating scale. In N. Sartorius & T. A. Bans (Eds.), *Assessment of depression* (pp. 179–183). New York: Springer-Verlag.

Kelly, K. V. (1992). Parallel treatment: Therapy with one clinician and medication with another. *Hospital and Community Psychiatry, 43,* 778–780.

Kendler, K. S. (1985). Diagnostic Approaches to Schizotypal Personality Disorder: A Historical Perspective *Schizophrenia Bulletin, 11*(4), 538–553.

Kendler, K. S., & Davis, K. L. (1981). The genetics and biochemistry of paranoid schizophrenia and other paranoid psychoses. *Schizophrenia Bulletin, 7*(4), 689–709.

Kendler, K. S., & Diehl, S. R. (1993). The genetics of schizophrenia. *Schizophrenia Bulletin, 19*(2), 261–286.

Kendler, K. S., & Tsuang, M. T. (1981). The nosology of paranoid schizophrenia and other paranoid psychoses. *Schizophrenia Bulletin, 7*(4), 594–610.

Kendler, K. S., & Walsh, D. (1995). Schizotypal personality disorder in parents and the risk for schizophrenia in siblings. *Schizophrenia Bulletin, 21*(1), 47–52.

Kheshgi-Genovese, Z. (1996). The crystallization of a paranoid symptom: Three theories. *Clinical Social Work Journal, 24*(1), 49–63.

Kirkhart, K. E., & Ruffolo, M. C. (1993). Value bases of case management evaluation. *Evaluation and Program Planning, 16,* 55–65.

Klerman, G. L. (1984). Ideological conflicts in combined treatment. In B. D. Beitman & G. L. Klerman (Eds.), *Combining psychotherapy and drug therapy in clinical practice.*(pp. 17–39). Jamaica, NY: Spectrum.

Klerman, G. L., & Schecter, G. (1982). Drugs and psychotherapy. In E. Payer (Ed.), *Handbook of affective disorders.* (pp. 121–138). New York: Guilford.

Kotsaftis, A., & Neale, J. M. (1993). Schizotypal personality disorder I: The clinical syndrome. *Clinical Psychology Review, 13,* 451–472.

Krill, D. F. (1996). Existential social work. In F. J. Turner (Ed.), *Social work treatment* (4th ed.) (pp. 250–281). New York: Free Press.

Kuipers, E., Garety, P., & Fowler, D. (1996). An outcome study of cognitive-behavioural treatment for psychosis. In G. Haddock & D. Slade (Eds.). *Cognitive-Behavioural interventions with psychotic disorders.* London: Routledge.

Kurek-Ovshinsky, C. (1991). Group psychotherapy in an acute inpatient setting: Techniques that nourish self-esteem. *Issues in Mental Health Nursing, 12,* 81–88.

Lamb, H. (1982). *Treating the long-term mentally ill.* San Francisco: Jossey-Bass.

Lantz, J. (1987). Emotional motivations for family treatment. *Social Casework, 68,* 284–289.

Lantz, J., & Belcher, J. (1988). Schizophrenia and the existential vacuum. *International Forum for Logotherapy,* 16–21.

Lantz, J. E. (1996). Cognitive theory and social work practice. In F. J. Turner (Ed.), *Social work treatment* (4th ed.) (pp. 94–115). New York: Free Press.

Law, S. M. (1984). The cultural basis of health, illness, and deviance. *Health and Social Work, 9*(3), 13–23.

Lazarus, R. S. (1993). Coping theory and research: Past, present, and future. *Psychosomatic Medicine, 55,* 234–247.

Lazarus, R. S., & Lazarus, B. N. (1994). *Passion and reason: Making sense of our emotions.* New York: Oxford University Press.

Leff, J. P. (1996). Working with families of schizophrenic patients: Effects on clinical and social outcomes. In M. Massimo, A. Rupp, & N. Sartorius (Eds.), *Handbook of mental health economics and health policy, Volume 1: Schizophrenia.* (pp. 261–270). Chichester, England: Wiley.

Leff, J. P., Kuipers, L., & Berkowitz, R. (1983). Interventions in families of schizophrenics. In W. McFarlane (Ed.), *Family therapy in schizophrenia.* (pp. 173–187). New York: Guilford.

Leff, J. P., & Vaughn, C. E. (1985). *Expressed emotion in families.* New York: Guilford.

Lefley, H. P. (1996). *Family caregiving in mental illness.* Thousand Oaks, CA: Sage.

Lefley, H. P. (1994). An overview of family-professional relationships. In D. T. Marsh (Ed.), *New directions in the psychological treatment of serious mental illness.*(pp. 186–198). Westport, CT: Praeger.

Lehman, A. (1988). A quality of life interview for the chronically mentally ill. *Evaluation and Program Planning, 11,* 51–62.

Lehman, A. F., Postrado, L. T., Roth, D., McNary, S. W., & Goldman, H. H. (1994). Continuity of care and client outcomes in the Robert Wood Johnson Foundation program on chronic mental illness. *The Milbank Quarterly, 72*(1), 105–122.

Lerner, R. (1985). *Daily affirmations.* Deerfield Beach, Florida: Health Communications.

Lewis, H. B. (1985). Depression vs. paranoia: Why are there sex differences in mental illness? *Journal of Personality, 53*(2), 150–178.

Lewis, S., & Higgins, N. (1996). *Brain imaging in psychiatry.* Cambridge, MA: Blackwell.

Liberman, R. P., Kopelowicz, A., & Young, A. (1996). Biobehavioral treatment and rehabilitation of schizophrenia. *Behavior Therapy, 25*(1), 89–107.

Lidz, T. (1975). *The origin and treatment of schizophrenic disorders.* London: Hogarth.

Lieberman, J. A., & Koreen, A. R. (1993). Neurochemistry and neuroendocrinology of schizophrenia: A selective review. *Schizophrenia Bulletin, 19*(2), 197–255.

Lin, K., & Kleinman, A. (1988). Psychopathology and clinical course of schizophrenia: A cross-cultural perspective. *Schizophrenia Bulletin, 14*(4), 555–567.

Lish, J. D., Dime-Meenan, S., Whybrow, P. C., Price, R. A., & Hirschfeld, R. (1994). The National Depressive and Manic-depressive Association (DMDA) survey of bipolar members. *Journal of Affective Disorders, 31*(4), 281–294.

Longress, J. F. (1995). *Human behavior in the social environment.* (2nd ed.). Itasca, IL: Peacock.

Low, A. (1978). *Mental health through will-training.* (2nd Ed.). Glencoe, IL: Willett.

Lubove, R. (1965). *The professional altruist: The emergence of social work as a career 1880–1930.* Cambridge, MA: Harvard University Press.

Magaro, P. A. (1981). The paranoid and the schizophrenic: The case for distinctive cognitive style. *Schizophrenia Bulletin, 7*(4), 632–661.

Magaro, P. A. (1980). *Cognition in schizophrenia and paranoia: The integration of cognitive process.* Hillsdale, NJ: Lawrence Erlbaum.

Mahler, M. S., Pine, F., & Bergman, A. (1975). *The psychological birth of the human infant.* New York: Basic Books.

Maier, W., Lichtermann, J, M., & Heun, R. (1994). Personality disorders among relatives of schizophrenia patients. *Schizophrenia Bulletin, 20*(3), 481–493.

Mallinckrodt, B., Gantt, D. L, & Coble, H. M. (1995). Attachment patterns in the psychotherapy relationship: Development of the Client Attachment to Therapist Scale. *Journal of Counseling Psychology, 42*(3), 307–317.

Malm, U. (1982). The influence of group therapy on schizophrenia. *Acta Psychiatrica Scandinavica, 65*(Supplement 297).

Maluccio, A. N. (1979). *Learning from clients.* New York: Free Press.

Manderscheid, R. W., & Sonnenschein, M. A. (Eds.) (1994). *Mental health, United States, 1994.* Rockville, MD: Center for Mental Health Services.

Mannion, E. (1997). Resilience and burden in spouses of people with mental illness. *Psychiatric Rehabilitation Journal, 20*(2), 13–23.

Marcias, C., Kinney, R., Farley, O. W., Jackson, R., & Vos, B. (1994). The role of case management within a community support system: Partnership with psychosocial rehabilitation. *Community Mental Health Journal, 30*(4), 323–339.

Marmar, C. R., Horowitz, M. J., Weiss, D. S., & Marzialli, E. (1986). The development of the therapeutic alliance rating system. In L. Greenberg & W. Pinsof (Eds.), *The psychotherapeutic process: A research handbook* (pp. 367–390). New York: Guilford.

Marsh, D. T. (1992). *Families and mental illness: New directions in professional practice.* New York: Praeger.

Marsh, D. T., Lefley, H. P., Evans-Rhodes, D., Ansell, V. I., Doerzbacher, B. M., LaBarbera, L., & Paluzzi, J. E. (1997). The family experience of mental illness: Evidence for resilience. *Psychiatric Rehabilitation Journal, 20*(2), 3–12.

Mattaini, M. A. (1994). Can personalities be disordered? No! In S. A. Kirk, & S. D. Einbinder, (Eds.), *Controversial issues in mental health* (pp. 48–56). Boston: Allyn & Bacon.

Maxmen, J. S. (1984). Helping patients survive theories: The practice of an educative model. *International Journal of Group Psychotherapy, 34*(3), 355–368.

May, R., & Yalom, I. (1995). Existential psychotherapy. In R. J. Corsini & D. Wedding (Eds.), *Current psychotherapies.* (5th ed.), 262–292. Itasca, IL: Peacock.

McAlpin, C. A., & Goodnick, P. J. (1998). Psychotherapy. In P. J. Goodnick (Ed.), *Mania: Clinical and research perspectives* (pp. 363–381). Washington, DC: American Psychiatric Press.

McClelland, R. W. (1996). Managed care. In C. D. Austin & R. W. McClelland (Eds.), *Perspectives on case management practice.* (pp. 203–218). Milwaukee, WI: Families International.

McClelland, R. W., Austin, C. D., & Schneck, D. (1996). Practice dilemmas and policy implications in case management. In C. D. Austin & R. W. McClelland (Eds.), *Perspectives on case management practice.*(pp. 257–278). Milwaukee, WI: Families International.

McCollum, A., Margolen, C., & Lieb, J. (1978). Consultation on psychoactive medication. *Health and Social Work, 3*(4), 72–98.

McCrone, P., Beecham, J., & Knapp, M. (1994). Community psychiatric nurse teams: Cost-effectiveness of intensive support versus generic care. *British Journal of Psychiatry, 165*(2), 218–221.

McFarlane, W. R., & Lukens, E. (1994). Systems theory revisited: Research on family expressed emotion and communication deviance. In H. P. Lefley & M. Wasow (Eds.), *Helping families cope with mental illness* (pp. 79–103). Newark, NJ: Harwick.

McLean, C., Greer, K., Scott, J., & Beck, J. (1982). Group treatment for parents of the adult mentally ill. *Hospital and Community Psychiatry, 33,* 564–569.

McMahon, F. J., & De Paulo, J. R. (1996). Genetics and age at onset. In K. I. Shulman, M. Tohen, & S. P. Kutcher (Eds.), *Mood disorders across the life span* (pp. 35–48). New York: Wiley-Liss.

McNeil, T. F., Cantor-Graae, E., & Sjostrom, K. (1994). Obstetric complications as antecedents of schizophrenia: Empirical effects of using different obstetric complication scales. *Journal of Psychiatric Research, 28*(6), 519–530.

Mead, G. H. (1934). *Mind, self, and society.* Chicago: University of Chicago Press.

Mechanic, D. (1993). Mental health services in the context of health insurance reform. The *Milbank Quarterly, 71*(3), 349–364.

Mechanic, D. (1989). *Mental health and social policy* (3rd ed.). Englewood Cliffs, NJ: Prentice-Hall.

Mechanic, D., Schlesinger, M., & McAlpine, D. D. (1995). Management of mental health and substance abuse services: State of the art and early results. *The Milbank Quarterly, 73*(1), 19–55.

Meehl, P. (1962) Schizotaxy, schizotypy, schizophrenia. *American Psychologist, 17,* 827–838.

Meenaghan, T., & Washington, R. O. (1980). *Social policy and social welfare.* New York: Free Press.

Meissner, W. W. (1981). The schizophrenia and the paranoid process. *Schizophrenia Bulletin, 7*(4), 611–631.

Mental Health Association in Michigan (1992). *Schizophrenics anonymous: A self-help support group.* Southfield, MI: Author.

Mental Health Association in Michigan (1991). *Schizophrenics anonymous group leader's manual.* Southfield, MI: Author.

Mermier, M.B. (1993). *Coping with severe mental illness: Families speak out.* Lewiston, NY: Edwin Mellen.

Milkowitz, D. J. (1996). Psychotherapy in combination with drug treatment for bipolar disorder. *Journal of Clinical Psychopharmacology, 16*(2) Suppl., 1, 57–65.

Milkowitz, D. J., & Goldstein, M. J. (1997). *Bipolar disorder: A family-focused treatment approach.* New York: Guilford.

Miller, I. S., & Burns, S. A. (1995). Gender differences in schizotypic features in a large sample of young adults. *Journal of Nervous and Mental Disease, 183*(10), 657–661.

Millon, T., & Davis, R. D. (1996). *Disorders of personality: DSM-IV and beyond.* New York: Wiley.

Minkoff, K. (1987). Resistance of mental health professionals to working with the chronic mentally ill. In A. T. Meyerson (Ed.), *Barriers to treating the chronic mentally ill* (pp. 3–20). San Francisco: Jossey-Bass.

Monroe, S. M., & Depue, R. A. (1991). Life stress and depression. In J. Becker & A. Kleinman (Eds.), *Psychosocial aspects of depression* (pp. 101–130). Hillsdale, NJ: Lawrence Erlbaum.

Morrissey, J. P., Calloway, M., Bartko, W. T., Ridgely, M. S., Goldman, H. H., & Paulson, R. I. (1994). Local mental health authorities and service system change: Evidence from the Robert Wood Johnson program on chronic mental illness. *The Milbank Quarterly, 72*(1), 49–80.

Mortimer, J. T., & Simmons, R.G. (1978). Adult socialization. *Annual Review of Sociology, 4,* 421–454.

Mowrer, O. (1984). The mental health professions and mutual-help programs: Co-optation or collaboration? In A. Gartner & F. Riessman (Eds.), *The self-help revolution*(pp. 139–154). New York: Human Sciences Press.

Moxley, D. P. (1996). *Case management by design: Reflections on principles and practices.* Chicago: Nelson-Hall.

Munro, A. (1991). A plea for paranoia. *Canadian Journal of Psychiatry, 36,* 667–672.

National Alliance for the Mentally Ill (1989). *Siblings and adult children's network: Background information and articles booklet.* Arlington, VA: Author.

National Institute of Mental Health (1991). *Caring for people with severe mental disorders: A national plan of research to improve services.* DHHS Pub. No.(ADM) 91–1762. Washington, DC: Supt. of Docs., U.S. Government Printing Office.

Neugeboren, B. (1996). *Environmental practice in the human services: Integration of micro and macro roles, skills, and contexts.* New York: Haworth.

Newton, S., Wandersman, A., & Goldman, C.R. (1993). Perceived costs and benefits of membership in a self-help group: Comparison of members and non-members of the Alliance for the Mentally Ill. *Community Mental Health Journal, 29*(2), 143–160.

Nigg, J. T., & Goldsmith, H. H. (1994) Genetics of personality disorders: Perspectives from personality and psychopathology research. *Psychological Bulletin, 113*(3), 346–380.

Noordsy, D. L., & Fox, L. (1991). Group intervention techniques for people with dual disorders. *Psychosocial Rehabilitation Journal, 15*(2), 67–78.

Olin, S. C., & Mednick, S. A. (1996). Risk factors for psychosis: Identifying vulnerable populations premorbidly. *Schizophrenia Bulletin, 22*(2), 223–240.

Perlman, H. H. (1979). *Relationship: The heart of helping people.* Chicago: University of Chicago Press.

Peven, D. E. (1996). Individual psychology and bipolar mood disorder. In L. Sperry & J. Carlson (Eds.), *Psychopathology & psychotherapy: From DSM-IV diagnosis to treatment* (2nd ed.), (pp. 77–114). Washington, DC: Accelerated Development.

Pickett, S. A., Cook, J. A., Cohler, B. J., & Solomon, M. L. (1997). Positive parent/adult child relationships: Impact of severe mental illness and caregiving burden. *American Journal of Orthopsychiatry, 67*(2), 220–230.

Pilette, W. L. (1988). The rise of three-party treatment relationships. *Psychotherapy, 25,* 420–423.

Procidano, M., & Heller, K. (1983). Measures of perceived social support from friends and family: Three validation studies. *American Journal of Community Psychology, 11,* 1–24.

Raine, A. (1992). Sex differences in schizotypal personality in a nonclinical population. *Journal of Abnormal Psychology, 101*(2), 361–364.

Raine, A., & Benishary, D. (1995). The SPQ-B: A brief screening instrument for schizotypal personality disorder. *Journal of Personality Disorders, 9*(4), 346–355.

Raine, A., Reynolds, C., Lencz, T., Scerbo, A., Triphon, N., & Kim, D. (1994). Cognitive-perceptual, interpersonal, and disorganized features of schizotypal personality. *Schizophrenia Bulletin, 20*(1), 191–201.

Ramon, S. (1989–90). The relevance of symbolic interactionism perspectives to the conceptual and practice construction of leaving a psychiatric hospital. *Social Work and Social Sciences Review, 1*(3), 163–176.

Rapp, C. A. (1998). *The strengths model: Case management with people suffering from severe and persistent mental illness.* New York: Oxford.

Rapp, C. A., & Chamberlain, R. (1985). Case management services for the chronically mentally ill. *Social Work, 13*(5), 417–422.

Rapp, C. A., & Kirsthardt, W. (1996). Case management with people with severe and persistent mental illness. In C. D. Austin & R. W. McClelland (Eds.), *Perspectives on case management practice* (pp. 17–45). Milwaukee, WI: Families International.

Reamer, F. G. (1989). The contemporary mental health system: Facilities, services, personnel, and finances. In D. A. Rochefort (Ed.), *Handbook on mental health policy in the United States* (pp. 21–43). Westport, CT: Greenwood.

Reed, S. K., Hennessy, K. D., Mitchell, O. S., & Babigian, H. M. (1994). A mental health capitation program II: Cost-benefit analysis. *Hospital and Community Psychiatry, 45*(11), 1097–1103.

Refsum, H. E., Zivanovic, S., & Astrup, C. (1983). Paranoiac psychoses: A follow-up. *Neuropsychobiology, 10,* 75–82.

Reid, W. H., Pham, V. A., & Rago, W. (1993). Clozapine use by state programs: Public mental health systems respond to a new medication. *Hospital and Community Psychiatry, 44,* 739–743.

Reinherz, H. Z., Giaconia, R. M., Pakiz, B., Silverman, A, B., Frost, A. K., & Lefkowitz, E. S. (1993). Psychosocial risks for major depression in late adolescence: A longitudinal community study. *Journal of the American Academy of Child and Adolescent Psychiatry, 52*(6), 1155–1163.

Retterstol, N., & Opjordsmoen, S. (1991). Fatherhood, impending or newly established, precipitating delusional disorders: Long-term course and outcome. *Psychopathology, 24,* 232–237.

Rice, D. P., Kelman, S., & Miller, L. S. (1992). The economic burden of mental illness. *Hospital and Community Psychiatry, 43*(12), 1227–1232.

Richey, C. A. (1994). Social support skills training. In D. K. Granvold (Ed.), *Cognitive and behavioral treatment: Methods and applications* (pp. 299–338). Pacific Grove, CA: Brooks/Cole.

Richman, J. M., Rosenfeld, L. B., & Hardy, C. (1993). The social support survey: A validation study of a clinical measure of the social support process. *Research on Social Work Practice, 3,* 288–311.

Ritzler, B. A. (1981). Paranoia-prognosis and treatment: A review. *Schizophrenia Bulletin, 7*(4), 710–728.

Roberts-DeGennaro, M. (1987). Developing case management as a practice model. *Social Casework, 68,* 416–420.

Rochefort, D. A. (1989). Mental illness and mental health as public policy concerns. In D. A. Rochefort (Ed.), *Handbook on mental health policy in the United States* (pp. 3–18). Westport, CT: Greenwood.

Rochefort, D. A. & Logan, B. (1989). The alcohol, drug abuse, and mental health block grant: Origins, design, and impact. In D. A. Rochefort (Ed.), *Handbook on mental health policy in the United States* (pp. 143–167). Westport, CT: Greenwood.

Rockland, L. H. (1993). A review of supportive psychotherapy, 1986–1992. *Hospital and Community Psychiatry, 44*(11), 1053–1060.

Rose, S. M., & Moore, V. L. (1995). Case management. In R. L. Edwards & J. G. Hopps (Eds.), *Encyclopedia of social work* (19th ed.) (pp. 335–340). Washington, DC: National Association of Social Workers.

Rosenblatt, A., & Attkisson, C. C. (1993). Assessing outcomes for sufferers of severe mental disorder: A conceptual framework and review. *Evaluation and Program Planning, 16,* 347–363.

Rosenson, M. K. (1993). Social work and the right of psychiatric patients to refuse medications: A family advocate's response. *Social Work, 38,* 107–112.

Rothman, J. (1992). *Guidelines for case management: Putting research to professional use.* Itasca, IL: Peacock.

Rothman, J., & Sager, J. S. (1998). *Case management: Integrating individual and community practice.* Boston: Allyn & Bacon.

Rouse, T. P. (1996). Conditions for a successful status elevation ceremony. *Deviant Behavior, 17*(1), 21–42.

Rubin, A. (1992a). Case management. In S. M. Rose (Ed.), *Case management and social work practice* (pp. 5–24). New York: Longman.

Rubin, A. (1992b). Is case management effective for people with serious mental illness? A research review. *Health and Social Work, 17*(2), 138–150.

Ryan, C. S., Sherman, P. S., & Judd, C. M. (1994). Accounting for case manager effects in the evaluation of mental health services. *Journal of Counseling and Clinical Psychology, 62*(5), 965–974.

Sands, R. G., & Cnaan, R. A. (1994). Two models of case management: Assessing their impact. *Community Mental Health Journal, 30*(5), 441–457.

Sarason, B., Sarason, I., & Pierce, G. (1990). Traditional views of social support and their impact on measurement. In B. Sarason, I. Sarason, & G.Pierce (Eds.), *Social support: An interactional view* (pp. 9–25). New York: Wiley.

Schatzberg, A. F., & Nemeroff, C. B. (Eds.)(1995). *The American psychiatric press textbook of psychiatry.* Washington, DC: American Psychiatric Press.

Scheff, T. J. (1984). *Being mentally ill: A sociological theory* (2nd ed.). New York: Aldine.

Scheffler, R., Grogan, C., Cuffel, B., & Penner, S. (1993). A specialized mental health plan for persons with severe mental illness under managed competition. *Hospital and Community Psychiatry, 44*(10), 937–942.

Schooler, N. R., & Keith, S. J. (1993). The clinical research base for the treatment of schizophrenia. *Psychopharmacology Bulletin, 29*(4), 431–446.

Schulze, M. H. (1994). Self-help groups for families of schizophrenic patients: Formation, development, and therapeutic impact. *Social Psychiatry and Psychiatric Epidemiology, 29*(3), 149–154.

Schwartz, A., & Schwartz, R. M. (1993). *Depression: Theories and treatments.* New York: Columbia University Press.

Schwartz, S. R., Goldman, H. H., & Churgin, S. (1982). Case management for the chronic mentally ill: Models and dimensions. *Hospital and Community Psychiatry, 33*(12), 1006–1009.

Scott, D., & Griffith, M. (1982). The evaluation of group therapy in the treatment of schizophrenia. *Small Group Behavior, 13*(3), 415–422.

Scott, J. E., & Dixon, L. B. (1995). Assertive community treatment and case management for schizophrenia. *Schizophrenia Bulletin, 21*(4), 657–668.

Sexton, T. L., & Whiston, S. C. (1994). The status of the counseling relationship: An empirical review, theoretical implications, and research directions. *The Counseling Psychologist, 22*(1), 6–78.

Seyle, H. (1991). History and present status of the stress concept. In A. Monat & R. S. Lazarus (Eds.). *Stress & coping: An anthology* (3rd. ed.) (pp. 21–35). New York: Columbia University Press.

Shapiro, D. (1965). *Neurotic styles.* New York: Basic.

Shelton, D. A., & Frank, R. (1995). Rural mental health coverage under health care reform. *Community Mental Health Journal, 31*(6), 539–552.

Sheridan, M. J., Bullis, R. K., Adcock, C. R., Berlin, S. D., & Miller, P. C. (1992). Practitioners' personal and professional attitudes and behaviors toward religion and spirituality: Issues for education and practice. *Journal of Social Work Education, 28*, 190–203.

Sheridan, M. J., & Bullis, R. K. (1991). Practitioners' views on religion and spirituality: A qualitative study. *Spirituality and Social Work Journal, 2*, 2–10.

Sherman, P. S., & Dahlquist, B. L. (1996). Managed care viewpoint. *NAMI Advocate, 18*(1), 4–6.

Shern, D. L., Felton, C. J., Hough, R. L., Lehman, A. F., Goldfinger, S., Valencia, E., Dennis, D., Straw, R., & Wood, P. (1997). Housing outcomes for homeless adults with mental illness: Results from the second-round McKinney program. *Psychiatric Services, 48*, 239–241.

Siegel, R. K. (1994). *Whispers: The voices of paranoia.* New York: Crown.

Simpson, G., & May, P. (1982). Schizophrenic disorders. In J. Griest, J. Jefferson, & R. Spitzer (Eds.), *Treatment of mental disorders* (pp. 143–183). New York: Oxford University Press.

Singer, M. T., Wynne, L. C., & Toohey, M. L. (1978). Communication disorders and the families of schizophrenics. In L. C. Wynne, R. L. Cromwell, & S. Matthysse (Eds.), *The nature of schizophrenia* (pp. 512–516). New York: Wiley.

Solomon, P. (1994). Families' views of service delivery: An empirical assessment. In H. P. Lefley & M. Wasow (Eds.), *Helping families cope with mental illness* (pp. 259–274). Newark, NJ: Harwood.

Solomon, P. (1992). The efficacy of case management services for severely mentally disabled clients. *Community Mental Health Journal, 28*, 163–180.

Solomon, P., Draine, J., Mannion, E., & Meisel, M. (1997). Effectiveness of two models of brief family education: Retention of gains by family members of adults with serious mental illness. *American Journal of Orthopsychiatry, 67*(2), 177–186.

Spaniol, L., & Jung, H. (1987). Effective coping: A conceptual model. In A. B. Hatfield & H. P. Lefley (Eds.), *Families of the mentally ill: Coping and adaptation* (pp. 85–104). New York: Guilford.

Spaniol, L., Jung, H., Zipple, A. M., & Fitzgerald, S. (1987). Families as a resource in the rehabilitation of the severely psychiatrically disabled. In A. B. Hatfield & H. P. Lefley (Eds.) *Families of the mentally ill: Copying and adaptation* (pp. 167–190). New York: Guilford.

Specht, H. (1986). Social support, social networks, social exchange, and social work practice. *Social Service Review, 60*(2), 218–240.

Spitzer, R., Endicott, J., & Gibbon, M. (1979) Crossing the border into borderline personality and borderline schizophrenia: The development of criteria. *Archives of General Psychiatry, 36*, 17–25.

Stone, M. M. (1985) Schizotypal personality: Psychotherapeutic aspects. *Schizophrenia Bulletin, 11*(4), 576–589.

Stone, M. M. (1983) Psychotherapy with schizotypal borderline patients. *Journal of the American Academy of Psychoanalysis, 11*(1), 87–110.

Stoudemire, A., & Riether, A. M. (1987). Evaluation and treatment of paranoid syndromes in the elderly: A review. *General Hospital Psychiatry, 9*, 267–274.

Strauss, J.S. (1991). The person with delusions. *British Journal of Psychiatry, 159* (suppl. 14), 57–61.

Stueve, A., Vine, P., & Struening, E. L. (1997). Perceived burden among caregivers of adults with serious mental illness: Comparisons of black, Hispanic, and white families. *American Journal of Orthopsychiatry, 67*(2), 199–209.

Sullivan, W. P. (1993). "It helps me to be a whole person": The role of spirituality among the mentally challenged. *Psychosocial Rehabilitation Journal, 16,* 125–134.

Surber, R. W. (1994). An approach to care. In R. W. Surber (Ed.), *Clinical case management: A guide to comprehensive treatment of serious mental illness* (pp. 3–20). Thousand Oaks, CA: Sage.

Swanson, D. W., Bohnert, P. J., & Smith, J. A. (1970). *The paranoid.* New York: Little, Brown.

Swartz, H. A., & Markowitz, J. C. (1995). Interpersonal psychotherapy. In I. D. Glick (Ed.), *Treating depression* (pp. 95–121). San Francisco: Jossey-Bass.

Swenson, C. R. (1994). Clinical social work. In R. L Edwards & J. G. Hopps (Eds.), *Encyclopedia of social work* (19th ed.) (pp. 502–511). Washington, DC: National Association of Social Workers.

Taube, C. A., Goldman, H. H., & Salkever, D. (1990). Medicaid coverage for mental illness: Balancing access and costs. *Health Affairs, 9*(1), 5–18.

Taube, C., Morlock, S., Burns, B., & Santos, A. (1990). New directions in research on assertive community treatment. *Hospital and Community Psychiatry, 41,* 642–647.

Teague, G. B., Drake, R. E., & Ackerson, T. H. (1995). Evaluating use of continuous treatment teams for persons with mental illness and substance abuse. *Hospital and Community Psychiatry, 46*(7), 689–695.

Terkelson, K. G. (1990). A historical perspective on family-provider relationships. In H. P. Lefley, & D. L. Johnson, (Eds.), *Families as allies in the treatment of the mentally ill: New directions for mental health professionals* (pp. 3–21). Washington, DC: American Psychiatric Press.

Terkelson, K. G. (1987). The meaning of mental illness to the family. In A. B. Hatfield & H. P. Lefley (Eds.) (1987). *Families of the mentally ill: Coping and adaptation* (pp. 128–150). New York: Guilford.

Test, M. A. (1998). Community-based treatment models for adults with severe and persistent mental illness. In J. B. W. Williams & K. Ell (Eds.), *Recent advances in mental health research: Implications for social workers* (pp. 420–436). Silver Spring, MD: National Association of Social Workers.

Test, M. & Stein, L. (1985). *The training in community living model: A decade of experience.* New directions for mental health services. San Francisco: Jossey-Bass.

Thyer, B. A., & Bursinger, P. (1994). Treatment of client with anxiety disorders. In D. K. Granvold (Ed.), *Cognitive and behavioral treatment: Methods and applications* (pp. 272–284). Pacific Grove, CA: Brooks/Cole.

Toomey, B., First, R., Rife, J., & Belcher, J. (1989). Evaluating community care for homeless mentally ill people. *Social Work Research and Abstracts, 25,* 21–26.

Torrey, E. F. (1988a). *Nowhere to go: The tragic odyssey of the homeless mentally ill.* New York: Harper & Row.

Torrey, E. F. (1988b). *Surviving schizophrenia.* New York: Perennial.

Torrey, E. F., Stieber, J., Ezekiel, J., Wolfe, S. M., Sharfstein, J., Noble, J. H., & Flynn, L. M. (1992). *Criminalizing the seriously mentally ill: The abuse of jails as mental hospitals.* Arlington, VA: Public Citizen's Health Research Group and the National Alliance for the Mentally Ill.

Turner, F. J. (1996). *Social work treatment.* New York: Free Press.

Turner, J., & TenHoor, W. (1978). The NIMH community support program: Pilot approaches to a needed social reform. *Schizophrenia Bulletin, 4,* 319–344.

Vasile, R., Samson, J., Bemporad, J., Bloomingdale, K., Creasy, D., Fenton, B., Gudeman, J., & Schildkraut, J. (1987). A biopsychosocial approach to treating patients with affective disorders. *American Journal of Psychiatry, 144*(3), 341–344.

Vaux A. (1990). An ecological approach to understanding and facilitating social support. *Journal of Social and Personal Relationships, 7,* 507–518.

Vaux, A. (1988). *Social support: Theory, research, and intervention.* New York: Praeger.

Veiel, H. O. F., & Baumann, U. (1992). Comments on concepts and methods. In H.O.F. Veil, & U. Baumann, (Eds.), *The meaning and measurement of social support* (pp. 313–319). New York: Hemisphere.

Vine, P. (1982). *Families in pain.* New York: Pantheon.

Vitaliano, P. P., Maiuro, R. D., Russo, J., Katon, W., DeWolfe, D., & Hall, G. (1990). Coping profiles associated with psychiatric, physical health, work, and family problems. *Health Psychology, 9*(3), 348–376.

Vollema, M. G., & van den Bosch, R. J. (1995). The multidimensionality of schizotypy. *Schizophrenia Bulletin, 21*(1), 19–31.

Walker, J. I., & McLeod, G. (1982). Group therapy with schizophrenics. *Social Work, 27*(4), 364–367.

Wallace, C. J. (1993). Psychiatric rehabilitation. *Psychopharmacology Bulletin, 29*(4), 537–548.

Walsh, J. (1994a). The social networks of seriously mentally ill persons receiving case management services. *Journal of Case Management, 3,* 27–35.

Walsh, J. (1994b). Social support resource outcomes for the clients of two assertive community treatment teams. *Research in Social Work Practice, 4,* 448–463.

Walsh, J. (1994c). Schizophrenics anonymous: The Franklin County, Ohio experience. *Psychosocial Rehabilitation Journal, 18,* 61–74.

Walsh, J. (1994d). Gender differences in the support networks of persons with serious mental illness. *Affilia, 9,* 247–268.

Wasylenki, D. A. (1994). The cost of schizophrenia. *Canadian Journal of Psychiatry, 39,* Suppl. 2, 65–69.

Wasylenki, D. A. (1992). Psychotherapy of schizophrenia revisited. *Hospital and Community Psychiatry, 43,* 123–127.

Weiden, P., & Havens, L. (1994). Psychotherapeutic management techniques in the treatment of outpatients with schizophrenia. *Hospital and Community Psychiatry, 45*(6), 549–555.

Weintraub, S. (1987) Risk Factors in Schizophrenia: The Stony Brook High-Risk Project. *Schizophrenia Bulletin, 13*(3), 439–450.

Wetzel, M. (1991). Strengths and limits: Report by a bipolar/unipolar self-help group. *Psychosocial Rehabilitation Journal, 14,* 81–85.

White, E. M. (1988). The use of a medical support group on a medical/psychiatric unit. *Issues in Mental Health Nursing, 9,* 353–362.

Wilson, J. (1989). The role of self-help groups in the management of depression. In K. R. Herbst & E. S. Paykel (Eds.), *Depression: An integrative approach* (pp. 232–249). Halley Court, Jordan Hill, Oxford: Heinemann.

Wilson, J. S., & Costanzo, P. R. (1996). A preliminary study of attachment, attention, and schizotypy in early adulthood. *Journal of Social and Clinical Psychology, 15*(2), 231–260.

Wilson, W. H., Diamond, R. J., & Factor, R. M. (1990). Group treatment for individuals with schizophrenia. *Community Mental Health Journal, 26*(4), 361–372.

Wolberg, L. (1988). *The technique of psychotherapy* (4th ed.). New York: Grune and Stratton.

Wolff, N., Helminiak, T. W., & Diamond, R. J. (1995). Estimated societal costs of assertive community mental health care. *Psychiatric Services, 46*(9), 898–906.

Womack, W., Maiuro, R., Russo, J., & Vitaliano, P. (1983). Psychoeducational courses for a nonpatient clientele at a mental health center. *Hospital and Community Psychiatry, 34,* 1158–1160.

Wood, M., & Wardell, M. L. (1983). G.H. Mead's social behaviorism vs. the astructural basis of symbolic interactionism. *Symbolic Interaction, 6*(1), 85–96.

Woods, M. E., & Hollis, F. H. (1990). *Casework: A psychosocial therapy* (4th ed.). New York: McGraw-Hill.

Woolis, R. (1992). When someone you love has a mental illness. New York: Putnam.

Yalom, I. D. (1980). *Existential psychotherapy.* New York: Basic.

Yank, G. R., Bentley, K. J., & Hargrove, D. S. (1993). The vulnerability-stress model of schizophrenia: Advances in psychosocial treatment. *American Journal of Orthopsychiatry, 63*(1), 55–69.

Young, L. T., & Joffe, R. T. (Eds.) (1997). *Bipolar disorder: Biological models and their clinical application.* New York: Dekker.

Young, R. C., Biggs, J. T., Ziegler, V. E., & Meyer, D. A. (1978). A rating scale for mania: Reliability, validity, sensitivity. *British Journal of Psychiatry, 133,* 429–435.

Zipple, A. M., Langle, S., Spaniol, L., & Fisher, H. (1990). Client confidentiality and the family's need to know: Strategies for resolving the conflict. *Community Mental Health Journal, 26,* 533–545.

Author Index

Subject Index